DK EYEWITNESS

P9-AOW-797

TOP **10**
CORNWALL
AND DEVON

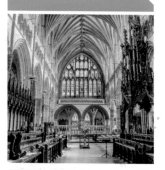

Top 10 Cornwall and Devon Highlights

The Top 10 of Everything

CONTENTS

Cornwall and Devon Area by Area

Streetsmart

Within each Top 10 list in this book, no hierarchy
of quality or popularity is implied. All 10 are, in
the editor's opinion, of roughly equal merit.

Title page, front cover and spine *Sunset
over the coast at St Agnes, Cornwall*
Back cover, clockwise from top left *The
façade of Exeter Cathedral; The idyllic
Postbridge; Trevose Head lighthouse; Coast
at St Agnes; St Michael's Mount at sunset*

The rapid rate at which the world is changing
is constantly keeping the DK Eyewitness
team on our toes. While we've worked hard
to ensure that this edition of Cornwall and
Devon is accurate and up-to-date, we know
that opening hours alter, standards shift,
prices fluctuate, places close and new ones
pop up in their stead. So, if you notice we've
got something wrong or left something out,
we want to hear about it. Please get in touch
at **travelguides@dk.com**

Welcome to
Cornwall and Devon

Rocky coves with white-sand beaches and turquoise waters. Mile-long strands where surfers skim Atlantic breakers. Bleak moorland with standing stones silhouetted against vast skies. Thatched cottages, flower gardens and cream teas. This corner of South West England has all this and more. With DK Eyewitness Top 10 Cornwall and Devon, it's yours to explore.

The counties of Cornwall and Devon are among the most popular holiday destinations in the UK. Visitors flock here for the stately homes, fishing villages, compelling towns and cities, and seaside resorts like **Torquay** and **Ilfracombe**. Wherever you go, the pleasures of rock-pooling, crabbing and building sandcastles fuse easily with more refined pursuits. Food and drink here is fantastic, with cafés, pubs and restaurants ensuring the region retains its place at the forefront of the movement towards sustainable, local produce. There are vineyards, breweries, ice-cream makers, and even a chilli plantation.

There is something magical about this far-flung peninsula, which has attracted and inspired generations of artists and writers. From Sherlock Holmes seeking diabolical hounds on **Dartmoor** and the riverside tales of *The Wind in the Willows* to Arthurian legend and the works of the **St Ives** and **Newlyn** artists, the landscapes of Cornwall and Devon have been imprinted on the world's imagination.

Whether you're visiting for a weekend or a week, our Top 10 guide brings together the best of everything that Cornwall and Devon, have to offer, from foodie mecca **Padstow** to the secluded **Isles of Scilly**. The guide has useful tips throughout, from seeking out what's free to places off the beaten track, plus seven easy-to-follow itineraries, designed to tie together a clutch of sights in a short space of time. Add inspiring photography and detailed maps, and you've got the essential pocket-sized travel companion. **Enjoy the book, and enjoy Cornwall and Devon.**

Clockwise from top: **Newquay beach**, **Eden Project**, **Dartmoor National Park**, **St Ives**, **Buckfast Abbey stained glass**, **surfboards**, **Prideaux Place**

Exploring Cornwall and Devon

Cornwall and Devon are packed with magnificent beaches, picturesque villages and historic towns, to say nothing of the area's vast moorlands, idyllic countryside and miles of coastal and rural paths. To help you make the most of your visit, here are some ideas for a two-day and seven-day break in the region. To see the Isles of Scilly when time is short, book speedboat transfers in advance.

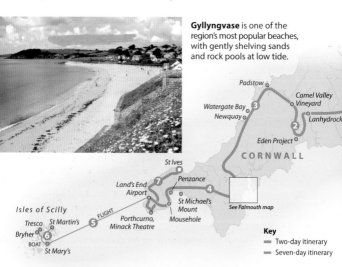

Gyllyngvase is one of the region's most popular beaches, with gently shelving sands and rock pools at low tide.

Key
— Two-day itinerary
— Seven-day itinerary

Two Days in Falmouth

Day ❶
MORNING
Start with the **National Maritime Museum** (see p19), then head up past **Pendennis Castle** (see p19) to sandy **Gyllyngvase Beach** (see p19).

AFTERNOON
Take a pleasure boat trip up the River Helford, or make the short drive to **Helford Passage** (see p104) for lunch at the **Ferry Boat Inn** (see p106). It's then just a five-minute drive to magnificent **Trebah** (see p18).

Day ❷
MORNING
Visit **Falmouth Art Gallery** (see p19), then browse the antique shops before catching a ferry to **St Mawes** (see p19) for a fish and chip lunch.

AFTERNOON
From St Mawes, follow the path along the banks of the River Fal to the sub-tropical gardens of the church of **St-Just-in-Roseland** (see p41).

Seven Days in Devon and Cornwall

Day ❶
Explore magnificent **Exeter Cathedral** (see pp24–5), with its gloriously intricate Gothic façade and breathtaking fan-vaulting, then drive to the idyllic Dartmoor village of **Widecombe-in-the-Moor** (see p16) for lunch. For some more atmospheric moorland scenery, visit the evocative Bronze Age village of **Grimspound** (see p17), then head to pretty **Dartmeet** (see p17) at the meeting point of the East and West Dart rivers.

Falmouth

St-Just-in-Roseland

River Fal

Falmouth Art Gallery

BOAT

St Mawes

National Maritime Museum

Pendennis Castle

St Michael's Mount 33 km (20 miles)

Gyllyngvase Beach

Swanpool Beach

Helford Passage

Maenporth Beach

Trebah

Ferry Boat Inn

Helford River

0 km   2

0 miles   2

Grimspound

Exeter Cathedral

Widecombe-in-the-Moor

Dartmeet

DEVON

0 kilometres   20

0 miles   20

Day ❷

Drive to Victorian **Lanhydrock** *(see pp12–13)*, for a fascinating insight into life in a country house, then move on to the **Eden Project** *(see pp14–15)*. After lunch in one of its cafés, devote the afternoon to the vast Rainforest and Mediterranean biomes.

Day ❸

Drive to the **Camel Valley Vineyard** *(see p89)*, where you can taste and buy fantastic wines. Head on to the fishing village of **Padstow** *(see pp34–35)*, Cornwall's most famous foodie destination, and perhaps treat yourself to a seafood banquet at Rick Stein's flagship Seafood Restaurant. After lunch, follow the coast road to **Newquay** *(see p90)*, with its dramatic cliffs and sweeping sands, making a stop at the surfer's haven, **Watergate Bay** *(see p50)*. Drive on to Falmouth.

Day ❹

Get a taste of **Falmouth** *(see pp18–19)* and Cornwall's seafaring past at the **National Maritime Museum** *(see p19)*, then follow the coastal route past the beaches of Gyllyngvase, Swanpool and Maenporth, stopping for lunch at a café and a swim if the weather is good. Continue inland to spend a couple of hours at the lush **Trebah** *(see p18)*. Drive to Penzance to see **St Michael's Mount** *(see pp32–3)* at sunset, then head to the idyllic fishing village of **Mousehole** *(see p33)* for dinner.

Day ❺

Take a 15-minute flight from Land's End airport to the **Isles of Scilly** *(see pp26–7)*. Transfer by speedboat to Tresco, explore the **Tresco Abbey Garden** *(see p27)*, then stop for lunch at the **New Inn** *(see p106)*. Catch a ferry to sparsely inhabited **Bryher** *(see p26)*, and follow the coast path to Hell Bay with its Atlantic breakers. Stay overnight here or return to Tresco.

Day ❻

Take a boat to **St Martin's** *(see pp26–7)* and snorkel with seals or walk the sandy beaches, then catch a boat to St Mary's for lunch with a view at **Juliet's Garden** *(see p107)*. See shipwreck finds at the **Isles of Scilly Museum** *(see p26)* before returning to Land's End.

Day ❼

Drive to the white sands of **Porthcurno** and see the **Minack Theatre** *(see pp28–9)*, an open-air amphitheatre carved into the granite cliffs. Head to **St Ives** *(see pp30–31)* to see the paintings and sculptures held at the Tate and other galleries. Dine at the **Pedn Olva** *(see p106)*, a hotel restaurant perched between the two beaches.

Minack Theatre, hewn into the cliffs, provides a stunning natural backdrop.

Top 10 Cornwall and Devon Highlights

Exeter Cathedral's magnificent rib-vaulted nave

TOP 10 Cornwall and Devon Highlights

The South West Peninsula holds some of Britain's most forbidding moorland, dramatic coastline and enticing beaches. Its history, from Celtic to Victorian times, is evident in its castles and stately homes, while a range of outdoor activities provide year-round entertainment for the whole family. Equally famed for their tranquillity and soul-stirring views, Cornwall and Devon make ideal holiday destinations.

1 Lanhydrock

This impressive 17th-century mansion, set amid gardens and parkland, is filled with Jacobean art and Victorian furnishings (see pp12–13).

2 Eden Project

Conservation is made fun at this wide-ranging exploration of the plant world, dominated by two giant greenhouses. Summer concerts, winter ice-skating and several cafés and restaurants serving great food enhance its appeal (see pp14–16).

3 Dartmoor

A range of activities is possible on this bleak expanse of moorland, which is complemented by grand houses and cosy villages sheltering thatched pubs (see pp16–17).

4 Falmouth

Falmouth is a historic port and vibrant university town magnificently located on the Fal Estuary. It is home to sandy beaches, bustling art galleries and the fascinating National Maritime Museum (see pp18–19).

Boscastle
Camelford
Bodmin Moor
Padstow
10
Wadebridge
Bodmin
CORNWALL
A30
Newquay
Lanhydrock 1
Eden Project 2 St Blazey
St Agnes
St Austell
Fowey
A390
Truro
Mevagissey
Redruth
Camborne
8 St Ives
Hayle
Penzance
9 9 A394 Helston
4 St Mawes
Falmouth
7 St Michael's Mount
Porthcurno and the Minack Theatre
St Keverne
6 Isles of Scilly 32 km (20 miles)
Lizard

5 Exeter
Rising from the River Exe, the capital of Devon has a strong historical flavour, not least in its cathedral. It also has a buzzing and vibrant contemporary cultural life *(see pp22–5)*.

Isles of Scilly 6
The islands of this windswept Atlantic archipelago are beautiful, unspoiled, and among the most remote places in Britain *(see pp26–7)*.

7 Porthcurno and the Minack Theatre
Porthcurno's outdoor attractions include a sandy beach between high cliffs and the open-air Minack Theatre, cut out of the rock *(see pp28–9)*.

8 St Ives
Home to the Tate St Ives gallery, this seaside town has a thriving arts scene, sandy beaches and excellent restaurants *(see pp30–31)*.

9 Penzance and St Michael's Mount
The region's most westerly town is home to two superb galleries and is close to St Michael's Mount, a spectacular fortified castle crowning an island *(see pp32–3)*.

10 Padstow
As well as its famous restaurants, this fishing port boasts beaches, historic houses and a popular cycle trail *(see pp34–5)*.

TOP 10 ⭐ **Lanhydrock**

This magnificent 17th-century mansion in the Fowey Valley is one of England's grandest country houses. Built by a rich merchant, Sir Richard Robartes, and reconstructed in 1881 following a disastrous fire, it remained in the same family until the National Trust took it over in 1953. Though parts of the Jacobean building survived, notably its famous Long Gallery, the dominant style is that of the High Victorian era. Some 50 visitable rooms offer a glimpse into life inside a stately home, from the huge kitchens to Lady Robartes' boudoir.

1 The Gatehouse
This pinnacled structure **(below)** was built around 1650. The main room on the upper storey was used to entertain ladies while the men hunted. It leads into the Topiary Courtyard.

Lanhydrock

2 The Gardens
The clipped yew trees and geometric flowerbeds **(above)** are striking, but it is the magnolias in the shrub garden for which the estate's gardens are most renowned.

3 St Hydroc Church
Dedicated to an Irish missionary, the church adjoining the house dates from the 15th century. A plaster panel in the north aisle displays the arms of King James I and is dated 1621.

4 Captain Tommy's Bedroom
A suitcase **(below)** kept on the cast-iron bed contains the personal items of Thomas Agar-Robartes, who died at the Battle of Loos in 1915.

⑥ The Dining Room

Decorated with stunning blue-and-gilt wallpaper designed by William Morris, the dining room **(left)** is dominated by a table set for a formal meal as it would have been in Victorian times.

⑦ The Billiard Room

This spacious room exudes the spirit of the leisured life of the gentry with its billiard table and tiger skin set against oak panelling. Old school photos and other such mementos line the walls.

⑧ The Kitchen

At the heart of the building is the main kitchen where the cook and servants worked. Its vast interior resembles a church, with soaring rafters and a gabled roof.

BELOW STAIRS

More than any other house of its period, Lanhydrock provides an intriguing insight into how a grand mansion operated. Passages lead from the main kitchen, with its elaborate ranges and gleaming copper, to sculleries, larders, a bakehouse and a dairy. At the top of the house are the nurseries and the servants' modest quarters, a stark contrast to the lavish bedrooms of the owners of the house.

⑩ The Long Gallery

Lanhydrock's pièce de résistance, occupying the entire first floor of the north wing, is its remarkable plaster ceiling which illustrates stories from the Old Testament.

⑤ The Nursery Wing

A whole suite of rooms was set aside for bringing up the younger family members. The nursery itself is crowded with a large doll's house and a rocking horse, among many other toys.

⑨ Woodland Walks

The woods and parkland of the estate are lovely to explore. You can enjoy the exuberant birdlife and, in spring, expanses of bluebells **(above)** and daffodils.

NEED TO KNOW

MAP D4 ■ Near Bodmin, Cornwall ■ 01208 265950 ■ Adm £15, child £7.50, family £37.50 ■ www. nationaltrust.org.uk

House: open Apr–Sep: 11am–5:30pm daily; Mar & Oct: 11am–5pm daily; Dec: 11am–4pm daily

Garden: open Apr–Oct: 10am–5:30pm daily; Nov–Mar: 10am–4pm daily

■ Free garden tours run from the gatehouse daily.

■ There is the Servants' Hall restaurant in the house, a café next to the car park, and a tearoom in the stables.

⭐ Eden Project

A china clay pit transformed to house two giant conservatories and extensive outdoor planting, the Eden Project is an innovative exploration of the plant world and human interaction with it. The grand spectacle of the place grabs the attention, but the Eden Project has a serious agenda, warning of the fragility of Earth's ecosystem through talks and workshops. The educational element never stifles the sense of fun. In summer, this is one of the region's best open-air concert venues, while in winter the arena becomes an ice rink.

③ Mediterranean Biome
The smaller of the two indoor biomes houses plants from South Africa, the Mediterranean and southwestern America. Exhibits include orange trees, olives and vividly coloured flowers.

⑤ The Spiral Garden
This innovative garden, designed with children in mind, explores patterns in nature. Visitors are encouraged to touch the plants, roll on the grass and clamber through tunnels.

① Rainforest Biome
Hot and steamy with a waterfall coursing through it, this luxuriant biome **(above)** re-creates a tropical climate for plants from West Africa, Amazonia and Malaysia.

② Outside Biome
In this roofless biome, plants are cultivated in Cornwall's temperate climate. Native Cornish flora is found alongside plants from Australasia and Chile.

④ The Core
The message of the Eden Project (mankind's dependence on Earth's resources) is presented with flair at the Core education centre and exhibition venue. The building's design mimics a tree, with Peter Randall-Page's granite sculpture, *Seed* **(right)**, its centrepiece.

⑥ Eden's Restaurants
The award-winning restaurants here offer globally-inspired cuisine prepared with locally sourced ingredients. There is catering for all diets as well as children's meals and Cornish cream teas. Eden's restaurants include the Med Terrace, Eden Kitchen and Eden Pasty snack bar.

The vast glass biomes of the Eden Project

⑧ Wistman's Wood

A couple of miles from the road, close to Two Bridges, this tangled wood **(left)** is a remnant from the time when the moor was completely forested. The ancient, moss-covered trunks make a fantastically atmospheric spot for a picnic.

THE HOUND OF THE BASKERVILLES

This Conan Doyle tale has various possible sources. Local legends tell of a huntsman who terrorized the Devon countryside while accompanied by a pack of red-eyed hounds. Another inspiration may be the legend of the Black Dog of Dartmoor, said to chase late-night travellers all the way to their destination.

⑩ Lydford Gorge

In this remote ravine, the River Lyd tumbles over the 30-m (100-ft) White Lady Waterfall and through dense vegetation that shelters wildlife.

NEED TO KNOW

MAP J4

Okehampton Castle:
Okehampton; 01837 52844; adm £5.90, child £3.50, family £15.30; www.english-heritage. org.uk

Castle Drogo:
Drewsteignton; 01647 433306; open Mar–Oct: 11am–5pm daily; adm £13, child £6.50, family £32.50; www.national trust.org.uk

Museum of Dartmoor Life:
3 West St, Okehampton; 01837 52295; open Apr–Nov: 10am–4pm Mon–Fri, 10am–1pm Sat; adm £5, child £3, family £13; www.dartmoorlife.org.uk

Lydford Gorge: The Stables, Lydford; 01822 820320; winter access restricted; adm £8.50, child £4.25, family £21.25; www.nationaltrust.org.uk

⑥ Grimspound

To the north of Widecombe, these circular prehistoric huts **(above)** surrounded by a thick wall are thought to have been the inspiration for the Bronze Age village where Sherlock Holmes camped in the famous novel *The Hound of the Baskervilles*.

⑦ Castle Drogo

Said to be the last castle built in England, this formidable building was constructed in the early 20th century by architect Edwin Lutyens on the whim of grocery magnate Julius Drewe. The lush grounds lead down to the River Teign.

⑨ Dartmeet

This is a renowned beauty spot **(below)** at the junction of the East and West Dart rivers. Nearby is one of Dartmoor's ancient crossing points, the famous clapper bridges.

TOP 10 ⭐ Falmouth and the Fal Estuary

A vibrant university town and port, with several sandy beaches, Falmouth owes its existence to having the world's third largest deep harbour. Artists, students, surfers, tourists and refugees from metropolitan life make this the liveliest of Cornwall's towns, with a year-round calendar of festivals. Its multihued Georgian and Victorian homes spill down hillsides, while the main street follows the river, its waters visible through many a café window.

1 Swanpool Beach and Nature Reserve

A sand and shingle beach sheltered by two headlands, Swanpool (above) is named after the brackish lagoon behind it, home to a family of swans. There is a small open-air beach café and a pleasant, short walk along the South West Coast Path to the beach of Maenporth.

2 Trebah

Trebah (below) is one of the county's finest gardens, set in a lush, subtropical, intriguingly landscaped ravine above the waters of the River Helford. Highlights here include a jungle of gunnera (giant rhubarb).

3 Flushing

This village, a short ferry ride from Falmouth, was originally called Nankersey but was renamed in the 17th century by Dutch engineers who built the piers. There are lovely riverside walks, two cosy pubs and a seafood restaurant.

Falmouth and the Fal Estuary

4 Falmouth Docks

For centuries this has been the last port of call for boats crossing the Atlantic, including solo navigators such as Ellen MacArthur. Used by naval ships, cruise liners and commercial vessels, it is best seen from a viewing point below Pendennis Castle.

6 National Maritime Museum

This museum **(left)** focuses on the maritime history of Cornwall, and on the role of small boats in cultures worldwide. Boats range from a fine19th-century canoe built for the Duke and Duchess of Bedford to international racing yachts.

FAL OYSTERS

The Fal river is the only place in Europe where wild oysters are harvested by a fleet of sailing boats. Harvesting oysters entails dragging a metal dredge along the silty seabed and scraping the oysters into a net. Oyster fishing is strictly regulated and takes place only between 1 October and 31 March.

8 Pendennis Castle

Pendennis **(below)**, dominated by its four-storey circular keep, was built by Henry VIII in 1540–42 as one of a chain of coastal fortresses designed to protect the south coast.

5 Trelissick

Set above the River Fal, and accessible by ferry from Falmouth and St Mawes (as well as by road), these colourful gardens also have a gallery showcasing Cornish art.

7 Gyllyngvase Beach

Falmouth's most popular beach is a gently shelving sandy crescent with rock pools at low tide. Gylly Beach Café and water sports add to the appeal.

NEED TO KNOW
MAP C5

National Maritime Museum: Discovery Quay, Falmouth; 01326 313388; open 10am–5pm daily; adm; www.nmmc.co.uk

Falmouth Art Gallery: The Moor; 01326 313863; open 10am–5pm Mon–Sat; www.falmouthartgallery.com

Pendennis Castle: Castle Drive, Falmouth; 01326 316594; open Apr–Oct: 10am–5pm daily; Nov–Mar: times vary; adm; www.english-heritage.org.uk

Trelissick: King Harry, Feock; 01872 862090; open 10am–5pm daily (mid-Feb–Nov: until 4:30pm); adm; www.nationaltrust.org.uk

Trebah: Mawnan Smith; 01326 252200; open 10am–4pm daily; adm; www.trebahgarden.co.uk

■ The best place for seafood and shellfish in Falmouth is The Wheel House *(see p99)*.

■ Explore the Estuary by ferries and pleasure boats operating from Falmouth.

9 Falmouth Art Gallery

This small gallery has an outstanding permanent collection, including Pre-Raphaelite paintings and engravings of Cornish landscapes by Turner to contemporary prints and children's illustrations.

10 St Mawes

Set in a sheltered corner of the Fal Estuary, and dominated by a castle, this whitewashed village has been an exclusive holiday retreat since Edwardian times.

Following pages St Michael's Mount, Mount's Bay

🔟⭐ Exeter

Rising up from the River Exe and dominated by the twin towers of its cathedral, Exeter holds more historical interest than any other city in the region. The city has a vibrant cultural life, thanks in part to its university students and the Royal Albert Memorial Museum. Its centre is walkable, while the Quay is a pleasant spot for a daytime snack. In the evening, pick from one of the city's many restaurants or visit its historic pubs.

1 The Quay

At one time a hardworking harbour, the Quay **(above)** now offers peace and quiet by day, with only a few cafés and crafts and antiques shops. In contrast, the evenings can be lively, with pubs and clubs drawing in the crowds.

2 Along the Exe

Enjoy a tranquil walk or cycle ride along the Exeter Ship Canal and the Exe Estuary, and spot a range of birdlife along the way. Bikes can be hired from the Quay.

3 Custom House

This restored 17th-century building on the quayside now houses a visitor centre with models, paintings and an audiovisual exhibition on the city's history. Regular tours of the city start here.

4 Royal Albert Memorial Museum

As well as its fine art collection, this splendid Victorian Neo-Gothic building contains a number of evocative displays featuring world cultures, local and natural history, costumes and textiles.

5 Stepcote Hill

This steeply sloped medieval lane **(below)** was once a main route. At the bottom, Tudor buildings stand alongside one of Exeter's oldest churches, St Mary Steps.

EXETER'S FESTIVALS

The Vibraphonic Festival in March brings big names from the world of jazz, funk and soul to the city, while the local gastronomy is celebrated in the Exeter Festival of South West Food and Drink (March/April), which includes chefs' demonstrations and plenty of activities for kids. Exeter Respect Festival (June) and Exeter Crafts Festival (July) both feature the work of local artists.

⑥ Exeter Cathedral

Sheltered within the harmonious Close, the 14th-century Gothic cathedral's most compelling features are its carved, honey-coloured façade **(below)** and a vaulted nave – the longest in the country.

Exeter

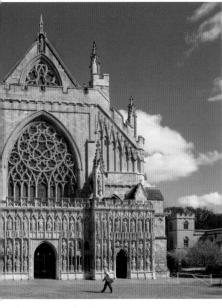

⑩ St Nicholas Priory

This Benedictine priory **(below)** survived the Dissolution of the Monasteries and today displays Tudor household items.

⑦ The Guildhall

Dating from 1330, the Guildhall still serves municipal functions but visitors can pop in to admire the portraits in the grand main chamber.

⑧ Bill Douglas Cinema Museum

Cinematic memorabilia is displayed in this centre on the university campus. Exhibits range from magic lantern slides to Charlie Chaplin posters and *E.T.* money boxes.

⑨ Underground Passages

This subterranean network was built in the 14th century to carry water into the city. Guided tours through the tunnels are fascinating.

NEED TO KNOW

Tourist Office: **MAP Q2**; Dix's Field, Paris St; 01392 665700; www.visitexeter.com

Exeter Cathedral: **MAP Q2**; Cathedral Close; 01392 285983; open 9:30am–4:30pm Mon–Sat, 11am–3pm Sun; adm £5; www.exeter-cathedral.org.uk

Underground Passages: **MAP Q2**; 2 Paris St; 01392 665887; adm £7, child (5–18 years) £4.50, family £20

St Nicholas Priory: **MAP P2**; Mint Lane; 01392 436000; open 1–4pm Sun; www.nicholaspriory.com

Royal Albert Memorial Museum: **MAP P2**; Queen St; 01392 265858; open 10am–5pm Tue–Sun; www.rammuseum.org.uk

The Guildhall: **MAP P2**; High St; 01392 665500

Bill Douglas Cinema Museum: **MAP N1**; Old Library, Prince of Wales Rd; 01392 724321; open 10am–5pm daily; www.bdcmuseum.org.uk

Exeter Cathedral

1 Gothic Façade

Apostles, prophets and soldiers jostle for space on the crowded carved West Front of the cathedral. Also look out for depictions of the kings Alfred, Athelstan, Canute, William I and Richard II.

2 Sepulchre of Hugh Courtenay

The cathedral is crammed with tombs, none more eye-catching than the 14th-century sepulchre of Hugh Courtenay, Earl of Devon, and his wife. Their tomb is carved with graceful swans and a lion.

3 Choir

Dominated by a 18-m (60-ft) bishop's throne and a massive organ case, the Choir (or "Quire") holds stalls dating from the 19th century. These feature a series of carvings, such as one that shows an elephant, dating from as far back as the 1250s.

4 Cathedral Close

The lawns surrounding the cathedral are a pleasant place to relax. They are overlooked by an array of historical buildings, including the splendid Elizabethan Mol's Coffee House, which is now a leather goods shop. The remains of a Roman bath house and a Saxon burial site lie beneath the lawns.

Impressive rib-vaulted Gothic ceiling

5 Ceiling

This is the longest unbroken Gothic ceiling in the world. It makes an immediate impression with a dense network of rib-vaulting, shafts and mouldings. One of the ceiling bosses illustrates the murder in 1170 of Thomas à Becket, Archbishop of Canterbury.

Exeter Clock

6 Exeter Clock

The clock in the cathedral's left transept dates from the late 15th century, though the minutes dial was added only in 1759. The sun and moon revolve around the Earth, in the form of a golden ball.

7 Chapter House

From the right transept, a door leads into the Chapter House, originally constructed in the 1220s but mostly rebuilt after a fire in 1413. Beneath the fine timber ceiling stands an array of sculptures from the 20th century. The Chapter House also serves as a popular venue for classical music concerts. You can pick up a leaflet for details.

Lawns at Cathedral Close

8 Plaque to R D Blackmore

Among the tombs and memorials that line the walls of the aisles, one near the door is dedicated to R D Blackmore (see p48), the 19th-century author of the rip-roaring Exmoor romance *Lorna Doone*.

9 The Towers

Dating from the 12th century, the two central towers represent the oldest part of the cathedral. They remain the most conspicuous feature of Exeter's skyline.

Carved angels, Minstrels' Gallery

10 Minstrels' Gallery

High up on the left of the nave a minstrels' gallery from 1350 depicts angels playing musical instruments.

EXETER'S HISTORY

Previously a settlement of the Celtic Dumnonii tribe, Exeter became the most westerly outpost of the Roman Empire in Britain when it was garrisoned in around AD 50–55. Saxon settlement was followed by Danish attacks, but conditions were peaceful under the Norman regime after 1068. The town's position on the River Exe allowed it to become a major outlet for wool shipments. During the Civil War, it became the western headquarters of the Royalists and sheltered Charles I's queen. In the early 20th century, bombing during World War II spared the cathedral, but devastated the historic centre. However, the founding of the University of Exeter in 1955 helped inject new energy into the city, and the Princesshay development has since reversed some of the damage done by shabby postwar reconstruction.

TOP 10 KEY EVENTS IN EXETER'S HISTORY

1 Exeter was fortified by the Romans in AD 50–55.

2 Around 878, the city was re-founded by Alfred the Great, King of Wessex.

3 In 1068, the Normans took control and expanded the wool trade.

4 The countess of Devon diverted the shipping trade to Topsham in the late 13th century.

5 The construction of Exeter Cathedral was completed in 1369.

6 In 1564–66, the Quay and the Ship Canal were constructed.

7 The city sheltered Charles I's queen in 1643, but fell to the Roundheads in 1646.

8 Trade ceased during the Napoleonic wars (1799–15), damaging the local textile industry.

9 World War II bombing flattened the city centre.

10 In 2007, the Princesshay development spearheaded a regeneration project in the historic centre.

Exeter's historic Custom House, located at the water's edge, is home to the city's visitor centre.

TOP 10 ⭐ Isles of Scilly

This archipelago of more than 140 uninhabited and five inhabited islands, scattered in the Atlantic Ocean 45 km (28 miles) off the Cornish coast, boasts some of Europe's most enchanting vistas. Reached by ferry or plane, the Isles of Scilly offer unspoiled white sandy beaches, wild moorland, idyllic harbours and subtropical gardens. Vines, pinks, narcissi and daffodils are cultivated in the mild climate, though an abundance of shipwrecks is testimony to the wild storms that can thrash the islands in the winter months.

New Grimsby, Tresco ①

Overlooking a minuscule port are the ruins of King Charles' castle **(right)**, built by Edward VI, and used as a garrison by Royalist troops during the English Civil War. It was no defence against the Roundheads, who in 1651 simply landed on the other side of the island, and used stone from the castle to build their own fortress, Cromwell's Castle, just below.

② Scilly Flowers, St Martin's

This long-established flower farm specializes in pinks and narcissi grown using traditional methods. Visitors are welcome to pop in and order flowers.

GIG ROWING

Gig racing with a crew of six rowers and a cox in broad wooden boats is a thriving sport in Cornwall and the Isles of Scilly. Historically, pilot boats would race out to guide ships to the shore through rough waters, the first to arrive winning the job. The annual World Pilot Gig championships take place in the Isles of Scilly during the last weekend of April or early May.

③ Isles of Scilly Museum

Finds from shipwrecks form the core of this museum, along with a collection of Bronze and Iron Age artifacts.

④ Sea Kayaking on St Martin's

St Martin's is ideal for sea kayaking, with many islets and islands offshore, as well as plenty of sheltered waters. Kayaks with maps and waterproof pouches are available, along with advice on where to go.

⑤ Holy Vale Vineyard

This vineyard of pinot noir, chardonnay and pinot gris vines had its first vintage in 2014. It offers tours and wine tastings with canapés.

⑥ Bryher and Hell Bay

The most dramatic feature of wild, wind-swept Bryher Island is the Atlantic-thrashed Hell Bay **(below)**, while the usually sheltered Sound between Bryher and Tresco is a pictur-esque place to swim or kayak. Wildlife and bird-watching tours are a great way to explore.

9 Snorkelling with Seals

Carefully guided snorkelling safaris enable you to swim among the colonies of Atlantic grey seals around the uninhabited Eastern Isles. The seals are so accustomed to visitors, they often come up and nibble swimmers' fins.

8 Tresco Abbey Garden

This lush landscaped garden **(above)**, with over 20,000 plants from 80 countries, was created by Augustus Smith, who took on the lease of the islands in the 1830s. Dubbed "Kew with the roof off", it was made possible by the building of huge windbreaks to protect the plants from savage Atlantic winds.

7 St Martin's Vineyard

In a former flower farm, this vineyard offers tastings of Siegerebbe Reichensteiner and Madeleine Angevine during tours.

10 Halangy Down Ancient Village

A Bronze Age tomb, Bant's Carn, tops a hill above Halangy Down **(above)** at St Mary's. It continued to be inhabited until Roman times. Excavations here have revealed 11 interconnected, stone houses with thatched roofs. Visitors can hire carts to travel around St Mary's.

Isles of Scilly

NEED TO KNOW

New Grimsby, Tresco: **MAP A4**; Tresco; www.tresco.co.uk

Scilly Flowers, St Martin's: **MAP B3**; Churchtown Farm, St Martin's; 01720 422169; www.scillyflowers.co.uk

Isles of Scilly Museum: **MAP A4**; Church St, St Mary's; 01720 422337; opening times vary, check website; adm; www.iosmuseum.org

Holy Vale Vineyard: **MAP B4**; Holy Vale, St Mary's; 01720 422333; open Apr–Sep: 12:30–4:30pm Mon–Fri (Sat & Sun by appt); www.holyvalewines.co.uk

Island Wildlife Tours: 42 Sally Port, St Mary's; 01720 422212; www.islandwildlifetours.co.uk

St Martin's Vineyard: **MAP B4**; www.stmartinsvineyard.co.uk

Tresco Abbey Garden: **MAP A4**; Tresco; 01720 424108; open 10am–4pm daily; adm; www.tresco.co.uk

Snorkelling with Seals: 01720 422848; www.scillysealsnorkelling.com

Halangy Down Ancient Village: **MAP B4**; St Mary's; open year round; www.english-heritage.org.uk

The Scilly Cart Company: St Mary's; 01720 422121; www.scillycart.co

TOP 10 ⭐ Porthcurno and the Minack Theatre

One of Cornwall's brightest gems is lovely Porthcurno Bay, cupped between cliffs on the southern coast of the Penwith Peninsula. While the village itself is low-key, there are plenty of nearby attractions. The famous open-air Minack Theatre is a unique sight, a magical place to take in some culture and entertainment. Below, the wedge of sandy beach provides amusement by day, while the coast path to either side runs through a landscape managed by the National Trust. Smaller beaches and a scattering of historical relics lie within a short clamber.

5 Porthcurno Beach

Porthcurno's beach **(left)** is among the finest on the Penwith Peninsula. Sheltered by cliffs on either side, the white sand is mixed with tiny shell fragments. Coastal paths lead to Porth Chapel and Pedn Vounder beaches.

1 Minack Theatre

On the steep cliffs above Porthcurno stands the region's famous amphitheatre, set into the rock. In summer, you can attend a variety of theatrical performances.

3 Minack Theatre Exhibition Centre

This exhibition centre tells the remarkable story of the creation of the Minack, which was the brainchild of Rowena Cade in the 1930s.

6 Treryn Dinas Iron Age Fort

This Iron Age promontory fort is set on a stunning headland. The few traces that can still be seen include four ramparts and the remains of stone houses within a ditch across the promontory.

2 The Minack's Rockeries and Garden

The rockeries and garden surrounding the theatre have become an attraction in their own right. The selection of plants – colourful succulents **(right)** and hardy shrubs – is based on plans by Rowena Cade, the Minack's founder.

4 Pedn Vounder's White Pyramid

Halfway along the path to Logan Rock, visitors will come across this peculiar structure **(left)**, placed here in the 1950s to mark the termination of a telegraph cable that once reached across the Channel to France.

THE BUILDING OF THE MINACK

Rowena Cade bought the Minack headland for £100. She built a house here and began organizing amateur theatre productions for friends in the 1920s. From this she developed the more ambitious idea of an open-air theatre, and in 1932 the first production, *The Tempest*, was staged. Rowena Cade continued to improve the site until her death in 1983.

9 The View from the Minack

In sunny weather, you could imagine yourself on Italy's Amalfi coast as you take in the inspiring view from this cliffside theatre **(left)**. The jagged headland forms a truly magnificent backdrop to performances, which run for 17 weeks of the year.

10 PK Porthcurno

In 1870, an undersea cable was laid between North America and Porthcurno. A museum exploring the history of the global telegraph system now occupies the former terminus, set within a network of underground tunnels. There are daily talks and demonstrations.

7 Minack Café

No spot is more panoramic for a snack than this lovely coffee shop, perched on a cliff edge within the complex. It is open only to visitors and playgoers.

8 Logan Rock

The 70-tonne rock **(right)** stands on an outcrop on the eastern edge of Porthcurno Bay. It was once said to rock from side to side, but has not moved since 1824.

NEED TO KNOW

MAP A6

Minack Theatre: 01736 810181; opening times vary, check website; advance booking essential; adm £7.50, child (under 16 years) £3.75; www.minack.com

Minack Box Office: 01736 810181; tickets £14, child (under 16 years) £7

PK Porthcurno: 01736 810966; open Apr–Oct: 10am–5pm daily, Nov–Mar: check website; adm £9, child £5.50, family £26; www.pkporthcurno.com

■ Visitors with specific requirements can book the viewing platform located above the auditorium.

■ Snacks are available at the Minack Coffee Shop. Alternatively, head to the Porthcurno Beach Café *(01736 811108)* for sandwiches and pasties.

■ The theatre is a real suntrap so if you are visiting in hot weather be sure to wear sunscreen and take plenty of water.

🔟 ⭐ St Ives

St Ives is like nowhere else in Britain. Its intricate maze of lanes backs onto a bustling quayside and a quartet of sandy beaches, with lovely views at every turn. As well as the region's premier art gallery, the Tate St Ives, the town has smaller galleries displaying local scenes and landscapes that attest to its role as an artists' hub. There is a dense concentration of bars and restaurants, hotels and B&Bs, many squeezed into tiny cottages.

The scenic harbour at St Ives

1 St Ives Museum

Finding this museum in the maze of back streets is like discovering a treasure chest. The quirky collection covers every aspect of local history, from geology and archaeology to mining, farming and shipwrecks.

3 Tate St Ives

Very few British galleries have such a striking setting as this, overlooking Porthmeor Beach. The design of its circular entrance **(right)** recalls the gasworks that once stood here. Inside, displays focus on the work of local artists.

2 St Ia

This 15th-century parish church **(below)** is dedicated to St Ia, the missionary after whom the town is probably named. Its features include a wagon roof and a 15th-century fort.

4 Barbara Hepworth Museum and Sculpture Garden

Sculptor Barbara Hepworth was central to the mid-20th-century arts scene in St Ives. Her studio is one of the most compelling galleries in Cornwall (see p102), showing her abstract works. Larger pieces are displayed in the garden.

5 Porthminster Beach

The largest of St Ives' beaches always has space for swimming or lounging, and is very popular with sand sculptors. Also here is the famous Porthminster Beach Café *(see p107)*.

7 St Ives Society of Artists Gallery

Housed in the former Mariners Church, this gallery is a good place in which to take in contemporary work by the Society's members. The Mariners Gallery in the former crypt also holds private exhibitions.

The Island

PORTHMEOR HILL

WEST PLACE

FORE ST

Harbour

MARKET PLACE

HIGH ST

THE STENNACK

TREGENNA HILL

THE TERRACE

10
750 metres (820 yards)

St Ives

ART IN ST IVES

In 1920, potters Bernard Leach and Shoji Hamada set up the Leach Pottery. Several artists followed, including painter Ben Nicholson and sculptor Barbara Hepworth in 1939. Along with later arrivals such as Patrick Heron and Terry Frost, they specialized in abstract work and were strongly influenced by Cornish landscapes.

9 Trewyn Subtropical Gardens

In the heart of St Ives, this quiet retreat with banana trees and other subtropical plants is a peaceful spot even in high season, and makes an ideal picnic venue.

6 St Ives September Festival

This boisterous, 15-day festival features comedy, tribute bands, local folk music and African dance. Many pubs also host music, which you can often hear for free.

8 Porthmeor Beach

Backed by cafés and the façade of the Tate, and with the promontory of the island at its eastern end, Porthmeor is the most accessible St Ives beach. Its firm sand is ideal for castle-building.

NEED TO KNOW

MAP B5

Tourist Information: The Library, Gabriel St; 01736 796297; www. stives-cornwall.co.uk

St Ives Museum: Near Smeaton's Pier; 01736 796005; adm

Tate St Ives: Porthmeor Beach; 01736 796226; www.tate.org.uk; adm

St Ia: St Andrew's St; www. stiveschurch.org.uk

Barbara Hepworth Museum and Sculpture Garden: Barnoon Hill; 01736 796226; opening times vary; adm

St Ives Society of Artists Gallery: Norway Square; 01736 795582

Leach Pottery: Higher Stennack; 01736 799703; adm for museum

■ Cars can be parked at Barnoon, above the Tate, or at the station.

10 Leach Pottery

Britain's foremost potter, Bernard Leach (1887–1979) established this pottery studio in 1920 to create his Japanese-inspired work. Today, you can see exhibitions of his pottery **(above)** and watch contemporary ceramicists at work.

TOP 10 ⭐ Penzance and St Michael's Mount

The port of Penzance sits at the northern end of Mount's Bay. Georgian buildings characterize much of the town, though the Jubilee seawater lido is pure Art Deco. The town has two galleries that continue the tradition of the colony of artists who settled in neighbouring Newlyn. Across Mount's Bay, the tiny castle-crowned island of St Michael's Mount is linked to the mainland by a causeway at low tide. It was granted to Benedictine monks from Mont-St-Michel, Normandy, by Edward the Confessor in the 11th century.

3 Market Jew Street

Penzance's main street derives its name from the Cornish "Marghas Yow", meaning Thursday Market. At its top is the domed Market House.

4 Chapel Street

Chapel Street has some of Penzance's comeliest buildings, including the Egyptian House (left) dating from 1830. Across the road is the Union Hotel, featuring a minstrels' gallery.

5 The Exchange

Behind its glass façade, the town's old telephone exchange boasts the largest single exhibition space within 300 km (180 miles).

Penzance and St Michael's Mount

1 Newlyn

Within walking distance of Penzance, Newlyn (see p104) is a busy fishing port with a thriving early-morning fish market. Attractions include the Newlyn Art Gallery, which displays contemporary art.

2 The Castle

Originally a Benedictine priory, the castle (right) was sold, along with the island, to John St Aubyn after the Civil War, and remains a stately family home. The Great Hall is known as the Chevy Chase Room after the frieze depicting hunting scenes described in the eponymous Scottish Ballad.

⑥ Mousehole
Mousehole (pronounced "mowzel") is a village (**above**) south of Newlyn, with tiers of whitewashed and granite cottages above a sheltered harbour.

⑦ The Causeway, St Michael's Mount
Set off the Marazion coast, the promontory on which St Michael's Mount stands can be reached by boat, but at low tide you can walk across a causeway.

⑨ The Chapel, St Michael's Mount
From the Blue Drawing Room, a door leads into the Priory Church (**left**) at the island's summit. Still regularly used for services, it has memorials to the St Aubyn family, who have lived in the castle since 1659.

⑧ Jubilee Pool
Located off Penzance's harbour, this lido dates back to 1935. It offers open-air, sea-water swimming for all ages during the summer and a geothermally heated pool.

⑩ Penlee House
The Newlyn school of artists, who settled in the area in the late 19th century, are well represented in this Victorian gallery and museum (*see p47*) set within a park. The exhibits reflect the town's fishing and mining heritage.

ST MICHAEL'S WAY

St Michael's Way, which runs for 20 km (12 miles) from Lelant, near St Ives, to the island, is part of a vast European network of pilgrim routes to Santiago de Compostela in Spain. It is thought to have been used by pilgrims from Ireland and Wales who felt it safer to abandon their ships and walk across the peninsula, rather than to navigate the treacherous waters around Land's End.

NEED TO KNOW

MAP B5

Tourist Information: Station Approach, Penzance; 01736 335530; www.love penzance.co.uk

Newlyn Art Gallery: **MAP A5**; New Rd, Newlyn; 01736 363715; adm £4.10; www. newlynartgallery.co.uk

St Michael's Mount: Marazion; 01736 710265; adm castle: £14, child (above 5 years) £7, family £35; adm garden: £10; child (above 5 years) £6, family £26; ferry £2.5 each way, child £1.50; www.stmichaels mount.co.uk

The Exchange: Princes St, Penzance; 01736 363715

Jubilee Pool: Promenade, Penzance; 01736 369224; adm £4.25, child £3; adm geothermal pool: £11.75, child £8.20; www. jubileepool.co.uk

Penlee House: Morrab Rd, Penzance; 01736 363625; adm £6; www. penleehouse.org.uk

🔟 ⭐ Padstow

Tucked into the Camel Estuary, Padstow is one of Cornwall's most attractive ports. Lively and smart, it is well-placed for beaches, with Daymer, Polzeath, Trevone and Constantine all within easy reach. This is mainly a fishing port whose catch is taken daily to auctions at Brixham and Newlyn, though plenty also ends up in local eateries. Foodies know the town as the domain of celebrity seafood chef Rick Stein, who has raised Padstow's profile with his luxury hotels and seafood restaurants, which are among the best in the country.

1 Prideaux Place
On a hill overlooking the town, this Elizabethan manor house **(above)** has richly furnished rooms and superlative plasterwork. Outside are formal gardens and a deer park.

2 Rick Stein's Restaurants
As well as the delightful Seafood Restaurant, Stein runs six boutique hotels, a deli, a café, a bistro, a patisserie, a fish and chip shop, a seafood bar and a cooking school in Padstow.

3 Padstow Harbour
The town's inner harbour **(above)** is where crowds gather to see the catch being brought in. On the quayside is Abbey House, Padstow's oldest building. Boat trips explore the estuary.

Padstow

4 Obby Oss
One of Cornwall's most flamboyant festivals **(left)** takes place annually on May Day, usually May 1. Processions around the town are led by the costumed figure of the Obby Oss *(see p68)*.

⑤ National Lobster Hatchery

Get close to various crustaceans at this exhibit, where tanks hold spider crabs, crayfish and sponges, and range from tiny baby lobsters to the resident giants **(right)**.

⑦ Saints Way

Crossing the peninsula to Fowey, this 45-km (28-mile) trail traces the route taken by pilgrims. It follows both ancient footpaths and country lanes from its starting point at St Petroc's Church.

⑧ St Petroc's Church

Padstow was once known as Petrocstowe, after the missionary St Petroc, who is said to have crossed the Irish Sea on a cabbage leaf. The church is famous for the Prideaux-Brune memorial and for its magnificent 15th- or 16th-century font carved from Cataleuse stone.

THE OBBY OSS TALE

The festival's origins are now lost but it includes elements of many other May Day festivities. Controlled by club-wielding "Teazers", the Obby Oss figures, in twirling hooped gowns, are probably intended to drive winter away, while the white-clothed escorts represent spring. The festivities begin the night before, when Blue Ribbon Oss leaves the Golden Lion pub.

⑩ Padstow Museum

This museum in the old station building is packed with archaeological items, nautical models, old photos and an Obby Oss costume.

⑥ Camel Trail

This is Cornwall's finest walking and cycling route, which follows a disused railway line alongside the River Camel for more than 29 km (18 miles). You can rent bikes in Padstow.

⑨ Camel Estuary

The main river on Cornwall's north coast, the Camel **(above)** is a haven for migrant wading birds that feed on the fertile mudflats. Passenger ferries cross the estuary from Padstow to Rock.

NEED TO KNOW

MAP D3

Tourist Information: South Quay; 01841 533449

Prideaux Place: 01841 532411; open Apr–Sep: 10:30am–5pm Sun–Fri, last tour 4pm; adm house: £9; adm grounds: £4; www.prideauxplace.co.uk

National Lobster Hatchery: South Quay; 01841 533877; open 10am daily; adm £7.50, child £4; www.national lobsterhatchery.co.uk

St Petroc's Church: Church St; 01841 534898

Padstow Museum: Market Place; open 10:30am–4pm daily;

adm (by donations); www.padstowmuseum.co.uk

■ Enquire at the tourist information centre about open-air brass band concerts performed in Padstow most Sundays and during some weekdays throughout the summer.

The Top 10 of Everything

Sheltered golden sands at Porthcurno Bay, Cornwall

TOP 10 Moments in History

Hingston Hill stone circle and row (Down Tor), Dartmoor

1 **2200–1700 BC: Gold Rush**
It is thought that up to 200 kg (450 lb) of gold was extracted from Cornwall and West Devon's rivers, and exported, along with tin, to Europe and Ireland. Settlements, such as Grimspound on Dartmoor, and numerous stone circles and standing stones can still be seen.

2 **AD 50–55: Roman Invasion**
The Romans established a strong garrison in Exeter and it was assumed they did not reach further west into the Celtic tribes' territory. However, the 2016 discovery of a stretch of Roman road near Newton Abbot suggests that Roman influence may have reached as far as Totnes.

3 **6th and 7th Centuries: Anglo-Saxon Villages**
During Roman withdrawal, Saxon tribes began to settle in the region, but made little headway against the Celtic tribes, whose strongholds were concentrated in Cornwall. Arthurian legends probably derive from the exploits of one of the Celtic chieftains, who resisted the Anglo-Saxons.

4 **11th to 16th Centuries: The Wool Industry**
Devon's wool industry flourished under the stability of Norman rule. Landowners of fertile inland pastures built mansions and merchants exported produce to Europe from the southern ports, which grew rich.

5 **1530s: Dissolution of the Monasteries**
The great monastic houses, which wielded huge influence and power, were suppressed by Henry VIII. Some, like the Benedictine abbey of Tavistock, were destroyed; others, such as Buckfast Abbey, became the mansions of wealthy merchants.

6 **1558–1603: The Elizabethan Era**
Devon became a strategic region during the contest against Spain. Exeter and Plymouth, in particular, were key military and naval bases. The western seaports benefited from the expansion of transatlantic trade, and the first English colonists of the New World set sail from here.

7 **1642–51: The Civil War**
Most of the region sided with the Royalists during England's Civil War, though both Exeter and

Battle in the English Civil War

Plymouth originally supported the Roundheads (Parliamentarians). King Charles I defeated the army of the Earl of Essex in 1644, but the Royalists were checked by Thomas Fairfax's army. This eventually led to the fall of Pendennis Castle and Exeter in 1646.

8 18th Century: Tin and Copper Mining

Under the Normans, Cornwall had become Europe's biggest source of tin. A series of scientific advances in the 18th century allowed the tin and copper mining industries to become highly profitable. Copper mining, concentrated around Redruth and Camborne, peaked in the 1840s.

9 1939–45: World War II

Although most of the West Country was designated safe from German attack and received evacuees from London and the Midlands, Plymouth suffered the worst bombing of any British seaport. Exeter was also targeted in the "Baedeker raids", aimed at cultural centres mentioned in Baedeker guidebooks.

Ship at Plymouth, World War II

10 21st Century

An important part of the British cuisine since the 14th century, the Cornish Pasty was awarded a protected status in 2011. Three years later, in 2014, Cornish people were officially recognized as a distinct minority group. They now have the same status as other Celtic nations.

TOP 10 ARTHURIAN SITES

Ruins of Tintagel Castle

1 Tintagel Castle
The most evocative of all Arthurian sights is the castle *(see p89)* that is believed to be his birthplace.

2 Slaughterbridge
MAP E3
This spot on Bodmin Moor is said to be the site of King Arthur's last battle, against his nephew Mordred.

3 Dozmary Pool
MAP E3
It is said that Arthur's famous sword, Excalibur, was thrown here and was received by the Lady of the Lake.

4 The Tristan Stone
MAP E4
This monument marks the grave of Drustanus, identified with Tristan (or Tristram), one of Arthur's knights.

5 Lyonnesse
MAP A6
A fabled land sunk beneath the waves, Lyonnesse is another one of the candidates for Arthur's birthplace.

6 Loe Pool
MAP B6
Like Dozmary Pool, this is a site where Excalibur was believed to have been restored to the Lady of the Lake.

7 Camelford
MAP E3
This town on Bodmin Moor is one of several places identified with Camelot.

8 Castle Dore
An Iron Age hillfort *(see p98)* said to have been King Mark of Cornwall's home.

9 Boscastle
After his last battle, Arthur's body was supposedly transported here *(see p90)*.

10 Castle an Dinas
MAP D4
This hillfort outside St Columb Major is believed to be Arthur's hunting lodge.

TOP 10 Churches, Abbeys and Cathedrals

Stained glass, St Neot's church

1 St Neot
MAP E3 ■ St Neot ■ 07342 049217 ■ saintneot.church

Located in one of Bodmin Moor's prettiest villages, this 15th-century church has stained-glass windows depicting Noah's Ark and St Neot himself. The churchyard boasts what is claimed to be Cornwall's finest ornamental cross.

2 Truro Cathedral
MAP C5 ■ St Mary's St, Truro ■ 01872 276782 ■ www.truro cathedral.org.uk

Rising over Truro, this Neo-Gothic monument was the first Anglican cathedral constructed in England after St Paul's in London.

Built between 1880 and 1910, it incorporates the 600-year-old parish church of St Mary's. Highlights of the interior include Jacobean tombs and Victorian stained glass. In St Mary's aisle, look out for the boss dedicated to Joseph Emidy (1735–1835), a formerly enslaved person who became Cornwall's top violinist and the leader of the Truro Philharmonic Orchestra.

3 St Nonna
MAP E3 ■ Altarnun ■ Open 10am–4pm daily

Known as the "cathedral of the moors", this 15th-century church on Bodmin Moor is famous for its 79 bench ends carved with saints, clowns and musicians. The Norman font with its fierce faces has been imitated in local churches, and the "vicar of Altarnun" features in Daphne du Maurier's novel *Jamaica Inn*.

4 Buckfast Abbey
This complex (see p84) was founded in the 11th century, rebuilt as a Cistercian abbey in 1134, dissolved in 1539 and rebuilt by Benedictine monks between 1907 and 1937. Today, visitors can admire its stained-glass windows and purchase specialities made by the monks, including tonic wine and beeswax.

Buckfast Abbey

Map showing locations in Cornwall and Devon, including Atlantic Ocean, English Channel, and towns such as Bude, Crediton, Exeter, Ottery St Mary, Padstow, Bodmin, Truro, and Falmouth.

5 Exeter Cathedral

Surrounded by Cathedral Close, majestic Exeter Cathedral *(see pp24–5)*, with its twin Norman Towers, was built around 1400. It is the grandest of Devon and Cornwall's churches.

6 Crediton Parish Church

The grandeur of this red sandstone structure *(see p81)* reflects the one-time importance of Crediton, which grew wealthy on wool. The church is perpendicular in style, with large windows illuminating its rich interior. The east window celebrates Crediton's most famous son, St Boniface.

7 St Mary

MAP L3 ▪ College Rd, Ottery St Mary ▪ 01404 812062 ▪ www. otterystmary.org.uk

Set on a hill in poet Samuel Taylor Coleridge's home town, stately St Mary dates from the 13th century. It was enlarged a century later by John de Grandisson, Bishop of Exeter. Noteworthy features include a 14th-century astronomical clock that still works, and the church's exquisite west window, the Apostles Window.

8 St Just-in-Roseland

MAP C5 ▪ St Just-in-Roseland ▪ 01326 270871 ▪ www.stjustand stmawes.org.uk

Situated on the Roseland peninsula, this church, on the shore of a creek, is surrounded by magnolias and palms. The church dates from 1261, but its battlement tower was added much later, in the 15th century.

9 St Enodoc

This tiny 13th-century church *(see p92)* now lies in the middle of a golf course, within sight of the Camel Estuary. The churchyard holds the grave of the poet John Betjeman, who lived for a time in the nearby village of Trebetherick.

St Enodoc and the Camel Estuary

10 St Petroc's Church

MAP D4 ▪ Bodmin ▪ 01208 77674 ▪ www.stpetrocschurch bodmin.org.uk

Built around 1470, this is the largest parish church in Cornwall and has a typical Cornish wagon roof. Look out for the superb Norman stone font carved with angels, demons and interlacing trees of life.

🔟 Houses

Opulently furnished and panelled interior of Hartland Abbey

1 Hartland Abbey
MAP G2 ■ Hartland, Bideford ■ 01237 441234 ■ House: open Apr–Sep: 2–5pm Sun–Thu; Gardens: open Apr–Sep 11am–5pm Sun–Thu ■ Adm ■ www.hartland abbey.com

Founded in 1157, this was the last English abbey to be dissolved by Henry VIII (see p38). A private home ever since, its decor and architecture are magnificent. Highlights are the vaulted Alhambra Corridor and the Regency library with Gainsborough and Reynolds portraits.

Trerice carriage clock

2 Trerice
An architectural gem with ornate fireplaces and elaborate ceilings, this small Elizabethan manor (see p92) has a good collection of English furniture, clocks and examples of needlework. The highlight is the barrel ceiling of its Great Chamber. Tudor costume days are very popular.

3 Pencarrow
MAP D3 ■ Bodmin ■ 01208 841369 ■ House: open Apr–Sep: 11am–5pm Sun–Thu (last tour at 3pm); Gardens: open until 5:30pm daily ■ Adm ■ www.pencarrow.co.uk

This elegant 18th-century mansion is noted for its porcelain and paintings, including portraits by Joshua Reynolds (see p49). The extensive formal and wooded gardens are home to England's first Victorian rock garden.

4 Lanhydrock
This 17th-century palace (see pp12–13) was rebuilt in the High Victorian style after a fire in 1881,

Atlantic Ocean

❶ Bideford
Great Torrington
❾ Tiverton
Bude Holsworthy
Okehampton
Launceston
Exeter
DEVON
Padstow ❼ Tavistock Newton Abbot
❸ Liskeard ❽ ❺
Newquay Bodmin ❹ Torquay
❷ CORNWALL Saltash
St Ives Redruth St Austell Plymouth
Penzance Truro ❿ Dartmouth
❻ Helston Kingsbridge
Falmouth
English Channel

0 km   25
0 miles   25

but the North Wing containing the Jacobean Long Gallery and the gatehouse survived. The building is filled with the accoutrements of a 19th-century mansion, including elaborate kitchens.

5 Buckland Abbey

Founded as a Cistercian abbey in 1278, Buckland (see p80) was disbanded in the Dissolution of the Monasteries, converted into a private home by the distinguished mariner Richard Grenville and subsequently acquired by Francis Drake in 1580. Drake's seafaring exploits are related here and visitors can also admire the Great Barn, which is bigger than the house itself.

6 St Michael's Mount

This rocky island was linked with Normandy's Mont-St-Michel until 1424 and later became a fortified private home. The best-preserved parts are the Chevy Chase Room, the 14th-century church and the Lady Chapel, later converted into a drawing room. The Blue Drawing Room (see p33) is embellished in Rococo style with Wedgwood Blue furnishings.

Pretty exterior of Prideaux Place

7 Prideaux Place

This fine manor house (see p34) has been occupied since 1592 by the Prideaux family. It holds numerous treasures, including loot from the Spanish Armada and the country's oldest cast-iron cannon. The expansive grounds include a classical temple, a deer park, a grotto and a 9th-century Celtic cross.

Tapestry, Cotehele House

8 Cotehele House

Hidden in the byways of the Tamar Valley, this Tudor palace (see p97) is a must for all fans of needlework, with the bedrooms adorned in heavy tapestries – the absence of electric lights has helped to preserve them. The house also has four-poster beds and finely crafted furniture. It is best to visit on a sunny day.

9 Knightshayes Court

MAP K3 ■ Bolham, Tiverton ■ 01884 254665 ■ House: open Mar–Oct: 11am–5pm daily; Nov–Feb: 11am–4pm daily (Gardens: open 10am daily) ■ Adm ■ www.nationaltrust.org.uk

The original designer of this Victorian country pile was William Burges. Later, Burges was fired, but enough of his elaborate Gothic-style interiors remain in the library, vaulted hall and the arched red drawing room.

10 Saltram

MAP H5 ■ Plympton ■ 01752 333500 ■ Open Mar–Oct: noon–4:30pm daily; Nov–Feb: opening times vary, call ahead ■ Adm ■ www.nationaltrust.org.uk

This 18th-century mansion is set in parkland, outside Plymouth. Its exterior is matched by the stately rooms inside (including the Robert Adam saloon) each decorated with a dazzling array of art.

🔟 Castles

Gatehouse of Berry Pomeroy Castle

① Berry Pomeroy Castle

MAP K5 ▪ Totnes ▪ 01803 866618 ▪ Open Apr–Sep: 10am–6pm daily; Oct: 10am–4pm daily; Nov–Mar: 10am–4pm Sat & Sun ▪ Adm ▪ www.english-heritage.org.uk

This romantic ruin on the edge of a wooded ravine is reputed to be haunted. Built by the Pomeroy family in the 15th century, the castle was abandoned 200 years later. Ever since, there have been reported sightings of the ghosts of the "White Lady" and the "Blue Lady".

② Restormel Castle

Still belonging to the Duchy of Cornwall, this perfectly circular Norman castle *(see p98)* occupies a spur overlooking the River Fowey. In medieval terms, it was a luxury residence, with unusual facilities including running water that was piped up under pressure from a natural spring. It is now a ruin, but it is still possible to walk right around the castle walls.

③ Pendennis Castle

The most westerly of the artillery forts built under Henry VIII, Pendennis *(see p19)* and its twin St Mawes were built to safeguard the port of Falmouth, the "key to Cornwall". The castle's ramparts and bastions were erected in around 1600 and the gun batteries were added during the Napoleonic wars.

④ Caerhays Castle

John Nash – architect of Buckingham Palace – designed this fantasy-Gothic structure *(see p98)* in 1810. Visitors can tour the castle, but the real showpiece is the garden, with its magnolias and rhododendrons. The adjacent curve of beach is also an excellent place to visit.

⑤ Castle Drogo

This 20th-century fortress *(see p17)* in the Teign Valley was designed to resemble a medieval stronghold by architect Edwin Lutyens, who was asked to create a replica of the castles of yore. Austere granite walls and a warren of stone corridors give the castle a spartan feel. You can play croquet here in summer.

⑥ St Mawes Castle

The most elaborately decorated of Henry VIII's coastal fortresses, this castle *(see p94)* follows a clover-leaf design, with

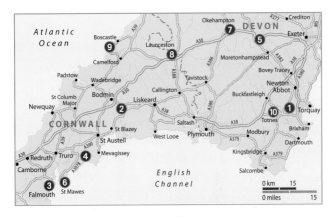

round walls that were intended to deflect enemy fire. However, the castle was never tested in war – it surrendered to Parliamentarian forces in 1646 without putting up a fight (see p39). Visitors can tour the gun rooms, governor's quarters, barracks, oubliette and kitchen.

7 Okehampton Castle

This Norman castle (see p16) on a spur above the River Okement is a dramatic sight, dominated by the remains of its keep. The fortress, once owned by the Courtenay family – later earls of Devon – was mainly used as a hunting lodge.

8 Launceston Castle

MAP F3 ■ Launceston ■ 01566 772365 ■ Open Apr–Sep: 10am–6pm daily; Oct: 10am–5pm daily ■ Adm ■ www.english-heritage.org.uk

A motte-and-bailey castle built shortly after the Norman Conquest, Launceston became the power centre from which the Earls of Cornwall

The dramatic St Mawes Castle

kept control of their vast estates. Prince Charles was proclaimed Duke of Cornwall here in 1973, receiving two greyhounds as part of his feudal dues.

Ruins of Tintagel Castle

9 Tintagel Castle

Set on a promontory above the turbulent Atlantic, the forlorn ruins of Tintagel (see p89) resemble a fairy-tale castle. It was once the residence of Cornwall's ancient kings.

10 Totnes Castle

MAP K5 ■ Totnes ■ 01803 864406 ■ Open Apr–Sep: 10am–6pm daily; Oct: 10am–5pm daily; Nov–Mar: 10am–4pm Sat & Sun ■ Adm ■ www.english-heritage.org.uk

Towering above the centre of Totnes, this classic Norman construction was erected after the Conquest to donimate the Saxon town. The stone keep was added 300 years later.

TOP 10 Museums

1 National Maritime Museum, Cornwall

This museum (see p19) displays boats from around the world, nautical equipment, interactive displays and marine art. The centrepiece is the grand Flotilla Gallery, where small craft hang from the roof.

2 Overbeck's Museum

Scientist Otto Overbeck lived in this house (see p82) until 1937. Many of his eccentric inventions, such as a "rejuvenating machine", share space with exhibits on local history. The garden offers superb views.

Exhibit at Overbeck's Museum

3 National Marine Aquarium

MAP Q6 ■ Coxside, Plymouth ■ 08448 937938 ■ Open 10am–5pm daily ■ Adm ■ www.national-aquarium.co.uk

Part traditional aquarium and part 21st-century museum, this complex presents an awe-inspiring survey of ocean life. There are more than 50 live exhibits, which together contain some 4,000 examples of marine life.

4 Royal Albert Memorial Museum

Among the displays at Exeter's largest museum (see p22) are the clocks and silverware for which the city was well-known. Sladen's study has one of the largest collections of starfish and sea urchins in the world.

5 The Museum of Witchcraft and Magic

MAP E2 ■ The Harbour, Boscastle ■ 01840 250111 ■ Open Apr–Oct: 10:30am–6pm Mon–Sat (from 11:30am Sun) ■ Adm ■ www.museumofwitchcraftandmagic.co.uk

This small museum houses everything there is to know about witchcraft and Europe's relationship with magic, including the history of local folk magic.

6 Royal Cornwall Museum

Cornwall's county museum (see p95) covers local geology and culture with collections of insects alongside Roman coins. Buddhist figures from Burma and an unwrapped Egyptian mummy are also on show.

Underwater display at the National Marine Aquarium

⑦ Museum of Barnstaple and North Devon

This museum (see p73) is the perfect place to learn about North Devon's history. Exhibits include locally minted Saxon coins, a 17th-century kiln and local pottery. Natural history is well represented as well and part of the museum is devoted to local militaria.

⑧ Museum of Dartmoor Life

Housed in a former mill, the Museum of Dartmoor Life (see p16) illustrates aspects of the moor and its inhabitants, from prehistoric hut-dwellers to the tin-mining communities.

Museum of Dartmoor Life

⑨ Fairlynch Museum

Fossils, prehistoric flints, 18th-century costumes, and a range of lace and toys help to create a picture of life in South Devon through the ages. The museum building (see p82) is fascinating in itself – a *cottage orné* – built by a local shipowner.

⑩ Helston Folk Museum

MAP B5 ▪ Market Place, Helston ▪ 01326 564027 ▪ Open 10am–4pm Mon–Sat ▪ Adm (by donation) ▪ museumofcornishlife.co.uk

This museum focuses on the social history of Helston and the Lizard Peninsula, with sections dedicated to costume, telegraphy pioneer Marconi and the locally born boxing champion Bob Fitzsimmons (1863–1917).

TOP 10 ART GALLERIES

Visitors at the Penlee House gallery

1 Penlee House
The best place (see p33) to see paintings by artists' colony the Newlyn School, with a permanent collection.

2 The Exchange
Penzance's former telephone exchange (see p32) now puts on a range of inspiring contemporary art shows.

3 Newlyn Art Gallery
Exhibitions by national and international artists, with a focus on painting and drawing (see pp32–3).

4 Burton Art Gallery and Museum
Paintings and prized local slipware are exhibited here (see p74).

5 Barbara Hepworth Museum and Sculpture Garden
View sculptures exhibited in Hepworth's former St Ives studio and in her beautiful walled garden (see p30).

6 St Ives Society of Artists Gallery
This private gallery (see p31) shows rotating exhibitions by local artists.

7 Broomhill Sculpture Gardens
This gallery and sculpture garden (see p118) showcases a fantastic collection of contemporary works.

8 Falmouth Art Gallery
A strong, eclectic collection of over 2,000 works by artists with links to Cornwall (see pp18–19).

9 Tate St Ives
This is a superb collection of works (see p30) by well-known 20th-century and contemporary artists, all with a strong connection to Cornwall.

10 Exeter Phoenix
Exeter's main arts centre (see p69) includes three galleries hosting local and contemporary art shows.

TOP **10** Writers

A portrait of D H Lawrence

4 Michael Morpurgo

The Isles of Scilly – where children's writer Michael Morpurgo has spent many holidays writing on the island of Bryher – has inspired many of his novels, including *Why the Whales Came*, *The Wreck of the Zanzibar* and *Listen to the Moon*.

5 Winston Graham

All 12 of Graham's *Poldark* novels that were written between 1945 and 2002 were set mainly around Perranporth, but also took in other parts of Cornwall, including Mousehole and Lanhydrock. The books have enjoyed great success as TV adaptations.

1 D H Lawrence

Accompanied by his wife, Frieda, D H Lawrence spent the years 1915–17 in the remote village of Zennor. He loved the "high shaggy moor hills, and big sweep of lovely sea", but was forced to leave in the face of hostility. His life in Cornwall inspired Helen Dunmore's prize-winning novel, *Zennor in Darkness* (1993).

6 R D Blackmore

Although he wrote a number of novels, Blackmore is best remembered today for his swashbuckling romance *Lorna Doone* (1869), set on Exmoor in the 17th century. Fans can visit the novel's locations, including the Valley of the Rocks outside Lynmouth.

R D Blackmore's Lorna Doone

2 Henry Williamson

The novelist and naturalist set his classic animal tale *Tarka the Otter* in the lush countryside of North Devon. The book has been the inspiration for the Tarka Trail *(see p74)*, a recreational route around the Taw and Torridge rivers.

7 Sir Arthur Conan Doyle

Dartmoor *(see p17)* inspired Conan Doyle's *The Hound of the Baskervilles*. It's based on local legends about black dogs that inhabited remote parts of the moor.

Sir Arthur Conan Doyle

3 Charles Causley

Along with John Betjeman, Causley is one of the best-known 20th-century poets associated with Cornwall. He was born and raised in Launceston, returning to live there in 1946. His work drew on hymns and ballads, and described Cornish life and local legends.

Agatha Christie at Greenway

⑧ Agatha Christie

Born in Torquay, the "Mistress of Murder" spent much of her life in South Devon, particularly at Greenway *(see p84)*, a grand mansion overlooking the River Dart. The settings of her country-house whodunnits give a strong flavour of the area. Torquay Museum has a good exhibition devoted to her.

⑨ Kenneth Grahame

Kenneth Grahame regularly took breaks in Cornwall, and began writing *The Wind in the Willows* as letters to his young son while staying at the Greenbank Hotel in Falmouth. A boat trip along the River Fowey inspired the opening scene, where Ratty and Mole make a trip along the river for a picnic.

⑩ Daphne du Maurier

Having spent many childhood holidays in Cornwall, du Maurier eventually settled outside Fowey. Drawn to Cornwall's secluded creeks and the wild romance of the moors, she set some of her famous novels here – including *Rebecca* and *Jamaica Inn*. An annual arts festival in Fowey *(see p68)* celebrates her work.

TOP 10 FILMING LOCATIONS

1 Bodmin Moor
The BBC's *Poldark* (2015–2019), has been based and filmed in the Cornwall area, notably on Bodmin Moor *(see p89)*.

2 Dartmoor
Dartmoor *(see p16)* provided the backdrop for *War Horse* (2011) and *The Hounds of Baskerville* episode of the 2012 BBC mini-series *Sherlock*.

3 Saunton Sands
This beach *(see p76)* has been the location for many films and TV series including *A Very English Scandal* (2018).

4 Teignmouth
The harbour here has been the location for a part of the film, *The Mercy* (2018), starring Colin Firth.

5 Saltram House
Plymouth's Saltram House *(see p43)* was featured in a film adaptation of Jane Austen's *Sense and Sensibility* (1995).

6 Hartland Abbey
The TV series *The Night Manager* (2016) was filmed here *(see p42)*.

7 Charlestown
This port town's harbour can be seen in *Poldark*, the *Pirates of the Caribbean* films and more.

8 Antony House
This 18th-century home was used when filming *Alice in Wonderland* (2008).

9 Caerhays Estate
Miss Peregrine's Home for Peculiar Children (2016) used this castle and estate as a backdrop setting *(see p98)*.

10 West Horsley Place
My Cousin Rachel (2017), starring Rachel Weisz, used much of this grand house and estate for filming.

A scene from *My Cousin Rachel*

🔟 Beaches

Sheltered bay at Blackpool Sands

1 Blackpool Sands
Backed by lovely woods and meadows, this family-friendly beach is an enticing sight as it swings into view on the road from Dartmouth. Its sheltered location, clear water and fine sand make it one of South Devon's best swimming spots. The renowned Venus Café provides refreshments.

2 Par Beach, Isles of Scilly
MAP B4

Majestic, bare and wild, the beaches on St Martin's are considered to be the best on the Isles of Scilly. Par Beach, on the island's southern shore, is probably the most impressive – a long, empty strand looking out onto rocks that make up the Eastern Isles. If you are planning to take a dip, be prepared for chilly water.

3 Whitesand Bay
MAP A5

This expanse of fine sand close to Land's End is a favourite with surfers and families alike. It has a good beachside café and at Sennen Cove, the more popular southern end of the beach, is the Old Success Inn (see p116). Surfing equipment can be hired and surfing courses are available.

4 Porthcurno
One of the finest bays on the Penwith Peninsula (see pp28–9), Porthcurno, with its wedge of white sand mixed with tiny shells, is squeezed between granite cliffs. The rock-hewn Minack Theatre is located to one side and there is a museum of telegraphy at the back of the beach. There are some good pubs and cafés to be found here, too.

5 Watergate Bay
MAP C4

North of Newquay, this arc of golden sand has a wild appeal. It is home to the Extreme Academy, which offers kitesurfing, landboarding and other pursuits for the adventurous. Watergate is not very sheltered, so

Watergate Bay

make sure you carry some windbreakers. During the summer months there is a drive-in cinema on the cliffs above the bay.

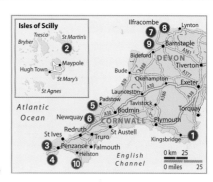

6 Fistral Bay
MAP C4

Surf enthusiasts flock to this beach for surfing competitions. A surf centre supplies equipment for hire. Most of the sand is covered by water at high tide, and strong currents mean that children especially need to be careful. Lifeguards are present throughout the summer. You can watch all the action (without getting wet) from the outdoor tables at many of the restaurants and cafés.

Surfer riding the waves at Fistral Bay

7 Woolacombe Bay

Surfers come from far and wide to Woolacombe Bay, one of the West Country's most famous surfing beaches. The beach (see p73) is popular with families and there is a warren of dunes behind for exploring. Crowds gather at the northern end, but more space can be found at the quieter southern end. The small resort of Woolacombe has shops and cafés.

8 Tunnels Beaches, Ilfracombe

MAP H1 ■ Bath Place, Ilfracombe ■ 01271 879882 ■ Open May–Sep: 10am–6pm daily; Jul–Aug: 10am–7pm daily; Oct: 10am–5pm daily ■ Adm ■ www.tunnelsbeaches.co.uk

These private beaches are named after the tunnels that have provided access to them since 1823, when the swimming was segregated. There is a tidal bathing pool and top-class rock-pooling with on-duty lifeguards. One beach is often closed for weddings.

9 Croyde Bay
MAP H1

Sandwiched between the extensive west-facing Saunton Sands and Woolacombe, this compact bay has fine sand. There are campsites nearby and the village has pubs and bars that fill up in the evenings.

10 Kynance Cove
MAP B6

This is one of the best options on the Lizard Peninsula, where beaches are few and far between. The 10-minute walk from the car park is well worth the trudge for the beach's fine white sands, rocky spires and surrounding grassy areas. Swimming is limited by the tides, but other attractions here include caves and cliffs with serpentine seams of sand.

Kynance Cove, Lizard Peninsula

🔟 Gardens

Sleeping Mud Maid in ancient woodlands, Lost Gardens of Heligan

1 Lost Gardens of Heligan

There is an air of mystery about this "lost garden". First planted in the late 18th century, the garden (see p96) was neglected to the point of decay until it was rediscovered by Tim Smit, the guiding light behind the Eden Project (see pp14–15). Smit restored the garden while preserving its wild, tangled character. The site includes walled flower gardens and a subtropical "Jungle" valley.

Trengwainton Gardens in bloom

2 Trengwainton Gardens

MAP A5 ▪ Madron, Penzance ▪ 01736 363148 ▪ Open mid-Feb–Oct: 10:30am–5pm Sun–Thu ▪ Adm ▪ www.nationaltrust.org.uk

Visitors to this diverse garden can enjoy an abundance of exotic trees, shrubs, sheltered walled gardens and a woodland area. In spring, the blooming azaleas, camellias and rhododendrons add to the colourful display. Picnic by the stream or enjoy the views from the terrace.

3 Bicton Park

This extensive estate (see p82) has formal parterres of bedding plants and a renowned collection of trees, including a giant Grecian Fir. There is an elegant Palm House, dating from the 1820s, while the Tropical House features the Bicton orchid. A woodland railway provides scenic rides through the landscaped park.

4 Trelissick Garden

Sheltered by woodlands, this Cornish garden features rhododendrons, magnolias and acers. Bordering the River Fal, the site affords views across the Carrick Roads Estuary (see p19).

5 Tresco Abbey Garden

First planted in 1834, these Isles of Scilly gardens (see p27) have been carefully nurtured by five generations of the same family. The region's climate, the mildest in the UK, has allowed the cultivation of exotic plants from around the southern hemisphere. The Tresco Abbey ruins form an evocative backdrop.

6 Rosemoor
MAP H2 ■ Great Torrington
■ 01805 624067 ■ Open Apr–Sep:
10am–6pm daily; Oct–Mar: 10am–
5pm daily ■ Adm ■ www.rhs.org.uk

In North Devon's Torridge Valley, Rosemoor provides year-round interest, with snowdrops in winter, rhododendrons in spring, flower borders in summer and fiery hues in autumn. The most spectacular displays, however, are 2,000 roses with more than 200 cultivars. Woodland walks provide further interest.

7 Lanhydrock
Surrounding this grand manor house *(see pp12–13)* are a number of horticultural spectacles, including a unique yew-hedged herbaceous garden, which is at its best in summer. Other highlights are magnolias from Sikkim and southern China, as well as hybrid rhododendrons and geraniums.

8 Trebah
This subtropical garden *(see p18)* features a selection of 100-year-old tree ferns and water gardens with koi carp. Plants from around the world are grown here, including gunnera (giant rhubarb) from Brazil and Australasian tree ferns. Rhododendrons and hydrangeas lead to a private beach on the River Helford.

Glendurgan garden's maze

9 Glendurgan
This wooded valley garden *(see p104)* on the banks of the Helford has walled areas and herbaceous planting with brilliant colour and foliage. The spring-flowering magnolias and camellias are especially impressive. Children will enjoy the baffling laurel maze dating from 1833 and the Giant's Stride rope swing.

Flower from Lanhydrock

10 Mount Edgcumbe
Located on the Rame Peninsula outside Plymouth, Mount Edgcumbe *(see p66)* has Italian, French and American formal gardens and is home to the national camellia collection, which flowers from January. The grounds include follies and a deer park.

🔟 Walks

Walking the Two Moors Way

① Two Moors Way/ Coast-to-Coast Walk

MAP J1–K1

The Two Moors Way, which links Exmoor and Dartmoor, can be extended at its southern end between Ivybridge and Wembury to make a 188-km (117-mile) coast-to-coast hike. The most dramatic scenery is on Dartmoor, though Lynmouth at the northern end makes a striking end point.

② Camel Trail

The Camel River flows through some of Cornwall's most beautiful landscapes, from the edge of Bodmin Moor to the sea at Padstow. A 27-km (17-mile) bike and walking trail follows a disused railway line (much admired by John Betjeman) through wooded valleys to the wide-open tidal mudflats of the Camel Estuary (see p89).

③ Tarka Trail

Inspired by Henry Williamson's animal tale *Tarka the Otter* (see p74), this figure-of-eight route centres on Barnstaple and takes in coastal and inland areas of North Devon.

If you include the section covered by the Tarka Line between Eggesford and Barnstaple, the route is 288 km (180 miles).

④ Coast and Clay Trail

MAP D4–C5

This 75-km (45-mile) network of shorter inter-linked paths around Truro, St Austell and the Roseland Peninsula, is designed to give a taste of Cornish history – from gardens and fishing villages to the china clay industry and the Eden Project.

⑤ Saints Way

A coast-to-coast trail, this (see p35) covers about 48 km (30 miles) between Padstow and Fowey. There is no evidence that the whole route was used in the Middle Ages, but parts of it were certainly travelled by pilgrims en route to shrines, holy wells and chapels.

⑥ Dart Valley Trail

MAP J5

Experience the Dart Valley on this 26-km (16-mile) walk, which swoops high above or runs alongside the River Dart. Half of it is a circuit, involving two ferry crossings, and the other half follows the river to Totnes.

Hiker on the South West Coast Path

Dartmoor Way
MAP J4

This circular 153-km (95-mile) route crosses some of Dartmoor's most thrilling terrain, including rugged moorland, wooded valleys and disused railway tracks. Much of the trail skirts the edge of the moor, but it also takes in Princetown in the centre of Dartmoor.

 East Devon Way
MAP L4

Also known as the Foxglove Way, this undulating inland trail follows footpaths, bridleways and lanes between Exmouth and Uplyme, north of Lyme Regis over the Dorset border. It is 61 km (38 miles) long.

 St Michael's Way
MAP B5

Weaving between Lelant, near St Ives, and Marazion, this 19.5-km (12.5-mile) trail was once used by pilgrims and travellers to avoid the treacherous waters at Land's End.

 South West Coast Path

At 1,014 km (630 miles) in length, this is England's longest National Trail, used by anyone who walks for any distance along the Devon and Cornwall seaboard. Starting in Minehead in Somerset, and winding along the coasts of Devon, Cornwall and finally Dorset, this scenic trail *(see p111)* is predominantly hilly and often dramatic.

TOP 10 WATERSPORTS

Gig Racing at Salcombe

1 Gig Racing
Ex-pilot boats are raced off the coastal villages of West Cornwall in summer, most famously in the Isles of Scilly.

2 Sea Kayaking
This is a fantastic way to explore sheltered coastlines and the Isles of Scilly, as well as tidal rivers and creeks.

3 Canoeing
Enjoy the rivers of Dartmoor and the waterways of Cornwall on a canoe trip.

4 Coasteering
This increasingly popular pursuit involves negotiating rocky coasts using a variety of means.

5 Sailing
Salcombe, Dartmouth, Falmouth and Fowey offer a great range of facilities for sailors of all levels.

6 Surfing
Some of Britain's top surfing beaches can be found in the West Country, with annual competitions at Newquay.

7 Windsurfing
The region's bays and inlets are ideal for windsurfers, with rental equipment available at many places.

8 Diving
The wrecks and reefs off the coast of Devon and Cornwall attract diving enthusiasts from far and wide.

9 Stand-Up Paddleboarding
SUP is hugely popular, with boards, tuition and guided paddles offered on many beaches across the region.

10 Sea Safaris
Take to the seas on one of these organized whale-, seal- and shark-watching excursions during summer.

Train Journeys

Steam train on the privately run Bodmin and Wenford Railway

1 Bodmin and Wenford Railway
MAP D4 ▪ 01208 73555
▪ www.bodminrailway.co.uk

This railway is a great way to explore the countryside around Bodmin. The terminus at Bodmin Parkway is linked by a 3-km (2-mile) path to Lanhydrock (see pp12–13). There is direct access to the Camel Trail from Boscarne Junction and to Cardinham Woods from Colesloggett Halt.

2 Looe Valley Line
MAP E4 ▪ 01752 584777
▪ greatscenicrailways.co.uk

The fishing port of Looe is linked to Liskeard by this branch line dating from 1860. The route runs beside the river through the Looe Valley.

3 Atlantic Coast Line
MAP C4–D4 ▪ 01752 584777
▪ greatscenicrailways.co.uk

This 33-km (21-mile) coast-to-coast line runs from the English Channel at Par Station to Newquay on the Atlantic, passing through the lunar landscape of china clay country.

4 Exeter to Newton Abbot
MAP K4 ▪ 08457 484950
▪ www.nationalrail.co.uk

Between Exeter and Newton Abbot, the main line runs beside two estuaries, the Exe and the Teign, offering delightful vistas over serene mudflats populated by wading birds.

5 Tarka Line
MAP H1–H3 ▪ 01752 584777
▪ greatscenicrailways.co.uk

Named after Tarka the Otter, this 65-km (39-mile) line, centred on Barnstaple, weaves through rural Devon. After Crediton, it sticks close to the River Taw, passing through a woodland.

6 Tamar Valley Line
MAP F4 ▪ 01752 584777
▪ greatscenicrailways.co.uk

The highlight of this branch line is the Calstock Viaduct between Devon and Cornwall. A "rail ale trail" is available for those wanting to drink en route.

Calstock Viaduct, Tamar Valley Line

7 South Devon Railway

From a station outside Totnes, the steam trains of the South Devon Railway *(see p84)* depart several times daily between April and October (and some days in winter), for a scenic ride to Buckfastleigh, on the edge of Dartmoor. There is a stop at Staverton, with access to a path beside the River Dart.

8 Launceston Steam Railway

MAP F3 ▪ 01566 775665
▪ www.launcestonsr.co.uk

These narrow-gauge Victorian steam engines run for 4 km (2.5 miles) between Launceston and Newmills. At Launceston Station visitors can see restoration projects as well as vintage cars and motor-bikes at the Transport and Engineering Museum.

Launceston Steam Railway

9 Paignton and Dartmouth Steam Railway

MAP K5 ▪ 01803 555872 ▪ www. dartmouthrailriver.co.uk

This heritage line runs from Paignton Station around the Tor Bay coast, then follows the River Dart to Kingswear. A round trip ticket includes a river cruise from Dartmouth to Totnes and the coach ride back to Paignton.

10 St Erth to St Ives

MAP B5 ▪ 01752 584777
▪ greatscenicrailways.co.uk

This branch line is the best way to reach St Ives *(see pp30–31)*. It edges along the Hayle Estuary before winding around the beaches of St Ives Bay, ending up near Porthminster Beach.

TOP 10 BEAUTY SPOTS

Golitha Falls in autumn

1 Golitha Falls, Bodmin Moor
MAP E3
A series of waterfall cascades gush through oak and beech woodland.

2 Hartland Point
Cliffs and crags flank this rocky promontory, which offers spectacular views of Lundy Island *(see p76)*.

3 Roseland Peninsula
One of the region's most photogenic and least spoiled spots *(see p96)*, with two waterside churches.

4 Valley of the Rocks, Exmoor
This dry valley *(see p76)* has striking rock formations and coastal views.

5 Lydford Gorge, Dartmoor
This lovely spot *(see p17)* has riverside walks, a whirlpool and a waterfall.

6 Lizard Point
MAP C6
A wild, rocky promontory at England's southern tip, with invigorating walks to beaches and a famous lighthouse.

7 Watersmeet, Exmoor
A canopy of oaks covers this beautiful confluence *(see p76)* of the East Lyn and Hoar Oak rivers. Perfect for walks.

8 Cape Cornwall, Penwith Peninsula
MAP A5
The ocean pounds against this craggy headland, which is overlooked by an abandoned chimney stack.

9 Dartmeet, Dartmoor
The West and East Dart rivers merge here *(see p17)*, near a clapper bridge and close to a nature reserve.

10 Hell Bay, Isles of Scilly
On the island of Bryher, this dramatic, stunning bay *(see p26)* bears the full brunt of Atlantic storms.

TOP 10 Children's Attractions

Thrill ride, Flambards

1 Flambards
MAP B5 ▪ Helston ▪ 01326 573404 ▪ Open Apr–Oct: 10am–5pm daily (last entry at 3pm) ▪ Adm ▪ www.flambards.co.uk

Attractions here include a re-created Victorian village, with 50 shops and cottages, and an exhibition of Britain in the Blitz. The Hornet Roller Coaster, Sky Swinger, Sky-Force, the Log Flume as well as the Aviation Experience are popular. Some attractions remain closed during winters.

2 Kents Cavern
MAP K5 ▪ Ilsham Rd, Torquay ▪ 01803 215136 ▪ Open daily, check website for tour times ▪ Adm ▪ www.kents-cavern.co.uk

Stone Age living is brought to life in one of the country's most significant prehistoric sites, with tours of the caves, treasure hunts, foraging trails and cave painting. There

are also spooky ghost tours and special seasonal events.

3 Newquay Zoo
Cornwall's largest zoo (see p90), set in lakeside gardens, is home to lions, lynxes, meerkats and tortoises. Activities for kids include exploring the Tarzan Trail and the Dragon Maze.

4 Bodmin Jail
Built in 1779 from granite sourced from Bodmin Cuckoo Quarry, this spooky, atmospheric prison is now a major attraction (see p92). Its dark, fascinating history is brought to life through interactive displays, theatrical sound effects and storytelling. Be warned: it's not for the very young or faint-hearted. Also on site is a luxury boutique hotel, where guests can stay in converted prison cells (see p119).

5 Babbacombe Model Village
MAP K5 ▪ Hampton Ave, Babbacombe, Torquay ▪ 01803 315315 ▪ Opening times vary, check website ▪ Adm ▪ www.model-village.co.uk

This miniature world features working railways, gardens, a celebrity mansion, a naturist beach and a 4D theatre and indoor displays. After dusk, 10,000 bulbs light up the streets, homes and gardens.

Babbacombe Model Village

(6) The Monkey Sanctuary

MAP E4 ■ St Martin's, Looe ■ 01503 262532 ■ Opening times vary, check website ■ Adm ■ www. monkeysanctuary.org

This charitable sanctuary overlooking Looe Bay promotes the welfare of South American woolly and capuchin monkeys and Barbary macaques. A colony of lesser horseshoe bats housed here can be observed via cameras and infrared lights.

(7) Pirate's Quest Adventure Golf

MAP C4 ■ 22 St Michael's Rd, Newquay ■ 01637 873379 ■ Opening times vary, check website ■ Adm ■ www.piratesquest.co.uk

A pirate-themed experience that combines mini-golf with enthusiastic actors, special effects and superb sets to transport players back to the age of Cornish swashbuckling free-traders.

(8) Watermouth Castle

MAP H1 ■ Berrynarbor, Ilfracombe ■ 01271 867474 ■ Opening times vary, check website ■ Adm ■ www.watermouthcastle.com

This Victorian folly castle and adventure park includes a model railway, crazy golf and toboggan run. The castle itself displays suits of armour and a 1950s organ on which life-size figures play instruments.

(9) Crealy Theme Park & Resort

This award-winning theme park (see p80) has more than 60 rides, plus a wide range of indoor and outdoor activities, live entertainment, a farm and a small zoo.

Beer Heights Light Railway, Pecorama

(10) Pecorama

MAP M4 ■ Underleys, Beer, Seaton ■ 01297 21542 ■ Open Apr–Oct: 10am–4pm daily ■ Adm ■ www.pecorama.co.uk

Home to the manufacturers of model railway, the star attraction is a ride on the 7.25-inch-gauge Beer Heights Light Railway – running along a mile of track with coastal views. Some attractions remain closed in winters.

🔟 Pubs

The Masons Arms, Branscombe

1 The Masons Arms

Located 10 minutes from the beach, this East Devon inn *(see p77)* serves locally brewed bitter and top-notch food, including local mussels and crab. Try their raspberry mousse as well as sorbet for dessert. There is outdoor seating and rooms are also available upstairs. Set menus are available for lunch.

2 The Sloop Pub

One of Cornwall's oldest pubs *(see p106)*, with beams, benches and nooks, the Sloop is a popular St Ives haunt right on the harbour. It offers a fine range of real ales and decent pub fare. Make sure to try their signature gin; you can even take a bottle home. Punters spill out onto the cobbled harbourside in summer.

3 Ship Inn, Mousehole

This excellent inn *(see p106)* stands directly above the harbour in a tiny fishing village. The Tinners and Tribute ales and fish pie are worth sampling. If you miss out on a seat with harbour views, sit in the tiny patio garden upstairs. Accommodation is also available.

4 Turks Head

Said to be Penzance's oldest pub, the Turks Head *(see p106)* dates from 1233 and has a maze of low-ceilinged rooms, a beer garden and a smugglers' tunnel. Try the Cornish Seafood Pie stuffed with local fish.

5 Blue Anchor Inn

Dating back to the 15th century, this lovely Helston pub *(see p106)*, which was originally a monks' rest house, has been brewing its own beer, Spingo Ale, for 600 years.

6 Tinners Arms

This historic pub *(see p106)*, which dates from 1271, is where DH Lawrence *(see p48)* stayed when he came to Zennor. The food menu consists of locally sourced produce, meat and seafood. There's a log fire, and live music on most Thursdays. Children are also welcome.

The Sloop Pub

7 Prospect Inn, Exeter

MAP P3 ■ The Quay, Exeter
■ 01392 273152

The family-friendly Prospect Inn, is right on the waterfront, and has tables outside on the quay – a good spot for watching the sun set during the summer months. Well-cooked meals are served with a good range of local beers and ciders.

8 Blisland Inn
MAP E3 ■ Blisland ■ 01208 850739

A traditional country pub on Bodmin Moor, the Blisland Inn has Toby jugs hanging from wooden beams and walls festooned with photographs. A wide variety of real ales and tasty pub food is available.

Interior of the Blisland Inn

9 Warren House Inn
MAP J4 ■ 4 km (2 miles) NE of Postbridge, Dartmoor ■ 01822 880208

The third-highest pub in England stands in solitary splendour on Dartmoor. It is a welcome sight to walkers, with two hearths – one that has reputedly been kept burning since 1845 – and good food.

10 Bridge Inn
MAP K4 ■ Bridge Hill, Topsham ■ 01392 873862

The pink-walled, 16th-century Bridge Inn, with its real ales and traditional trappings, is one of Devon's best pubs. It is reputedly the first pub to have been graced by the Queen in an official capacity, when she visited the region in 1998.

TOP 10 LOCAL BREWERIES

1 St Austell
This is Cornwall's major brewer, whose traditional cask ales include the legendary HSD and Tribute.

2 Harbour Brewing Company
A progressive Cornish microbrewery offering a range of innovative beers.

3 Sharp's
The Cornish producer of fine beers such as Doom Bar, Wolf Rock, Coaster, Atlantic, Sea Fury and Orchard.

4 Otter
A Honiton-based brewery which produces five regular beers and one winter ale available throughout Devon.

5 O'Hanlon's
Located in Devon, this small, specialist brewery produces some award-winning cask and bottled beers.

6 Country Life
Bideford-based producer of ales such as Old Appledore, the light-coloured Golden Pig, and Country Bumpkin.

7 Spingo Ales
These famous brews are available only in Helston's Blue Anchor, in four distinctive varieties from 4.5 per cent to 6.5 per cent ABV.

8 Driftwood Spars Brewery
Award-winning microbrews from the Driftwood Spars brewpub at St Agnes.

9 Ales of Scilly
The producer of the Schiller golden ale and the Challenger bitter ale also offers some additional seasonal beers.

10 Skinners
This Truro-based brewery features ales named after Cornish locations and folk heroes, such as Betty Stogs.

The range of beers at Skinners

TOP10 Places to Eat

Gidleigh Park's main building amid beautiful grounds

1 Gidleigh Park
An award-winning restaurant *(see p85)* headed by Chris Eden, with a contemporary and informal approach to fine dining. The menu is constantly evolving, with unique dishes accompanied by vegetables and herbs grown in the kitchen garden. It boasts a prestigious wine cellar with 13,000 bottles from around the world.

2 The Masons Arms
This Michelin-starred pub-restaurant *(see p77)* on the edge of Exmoor is owned by chef Mark Dodson, who trained with Michel Roux. Locally sourced food is taken to new levels, and the atmosphere is relaxed. Dine outside in good weather.

Dining room at The Masons Arms

3 Kota Restaurant
New Zealand chef Jude Kereama blends Asian and European flavours with locally sourced Cornish produce in his award-winning restaurant *(see p107)*. Great location above the harbour at Porthleven.

4 The Seafood Restaurant
Rick Stein's flagship fish and seafood restaurant *(see p93)*, founded in 1975, is buzzy and unpretentious, featuring many of the dishes familiar from his books and TV programmes. The sticky, spicy Singapore crab – impossible to eat without using your fingers – is incredible. If you don't have a booking, there is a seafood bar in the middle of the restaurant where you can sit and watch chefs assembling platters of oysters, langoustines and sashimi.

5 The Elephant Restaurant and Brasserie
The informal atmosphere of the Elephant *(see p85)* suits its Torquay location. Chef Simon Hulstone has created a Michelin-starred restaurant, with a menu that features sustainably caught fish, meat as well as vegetables from his farm.

6 The Coach House

A glass window allows diners to watch the chefs at work in this restaurant *(see p77)* from Devon's culinary star, Michelin award-winning chef Michael Caines. The menu is strictly seasonal and relies on local produce.

7 Restaurant Nathan Outlaw

Two-Michelin-starred chef Nathan Outlaw, who trained with Rick Stein, has two restaurants and a pub in Cornwall. The flagship restaurant *(see p93)* is located at Port Isaac, which serves just one set tasting menu.

8 Driftwood Restaurant

A relaxed and understated Michelin-starred hotel-restaurant *(see p99)* on the Roseland Peninsula. Meat, fish and vegetables are locally sourced. The focus is on bringing out the very best in the prime ingredients.

Sea views at Driftwood Restaurant

9 The Hidden Hut

Porthcurnick Beach is home to a beach café *(see p99)* whose feast nights (two or three each month, March–October) sell out instantly. The formula is simple: there's one dish and you bring your own alcohol. It's fun and perfect for families.

10 Crab Shack

This converted cowshed *(see p106)* at Hell Bay is hung with nets and nautical paraphernalia and the tables are upcycled doors from the old abbey on Tresco. The menu features crabs, mussels or scallops, plus chips, salad and wine.

TOP 10 PLACES FOR CREAM TEAS

Picturesque Clock Tower Café

1 Clock Tower Café
MAP L4 ▪ Connaught Gardens, Sidmouth ▪ www.clocktower sidmouth.com
Enjoy the sea-views while indulging in delicious homemade cakes.

2 Falmouth Hotel
MAP C5 ▪ Castle Beach, Falmouth ▪ www.falmouthhotel.co.uk
Nibble scones on the hotel terrace.

3 Otterton Mill
MAP L4 ▪ Otterton, Budleigh Salterton ▪ www.ottertonmill.com
Fine scones are baked and served at this ancient mill.

4 Dwelling House
Scones and an excellent choice of cakes in an eclectic tearoom *(see p99)*.

5 Weavers Cottage Tea Shoppe
MAP K5 ▪ Cockington, Torquay ▪ 01803 605407
Thatched cottage serving tea-time treats.

6 Southern Cross
MAP L4 ▪ Newton Poppleford, near Sidmouth ▪ www.southerncross devon.co.uk
Perfect garden setting for afternoon tea.

7 Melinsey Mill
MAP D5 ▪ Veryan, Roseland ▪ www.melinseymill.co.uk
Scones are served beside the peaceful pond of this 16th-century watermill.

8 Watersmeet House
A lovely spot for tea and cakes *(see p77)*.

9 Polpeor Café
MAP C6 ▪ The Lizard ▪ 01326 290939
England's southernmost café has impressive seascapes and tasty scones.

10 Rectory Farm and Tea Rooms
MAP E2 ▪ Crosstown, Morwenstow, near Bude ▪ www.rectory-tearooms. co.uk
Feast on cakes and scones beside an open fire in a 13th-century farmhouse.

TOP 10 Shopping

1 Totnes Elizabethan Market

MAP K5 ■ Civic Square, Totnes ■ 01803 411183 ■ Open May–Sep ■ www.visittotnes.co.uk

Every Tuesday morning throughout summer, local traders dress up in Tudor costumes for the Elizabethan market, which runs alongside an all-day crafts market.

2 Bickleigh Mill

MAP K3

■ Bickleigh, Tiverton ■ 01884 855419 ■ www.bickleighmill.com

Set in an 18th-century watermill, this retail centre sells jewellery, ceramics, soaps, seasonal gifts and toys.

3 Tavistock Pannier Market

MAP H4 ■ Tavistock ■ 01822 611003 ■ www.visit-tavistock.co.uk

This indoor market sells antiques and collectables (Tuesdays), crafts (Wednesdays and Thursdays), local produce (Fridays), popular collectables (first Saturday of the month) and mixed markets (third and fourth Saturday of the month).

Branch of the Seasalt clothing chain

4 Seasalt

MAP C5 ■ Sale Shop: Unit 17, Kernick Business Park, Annear Rd, Penryn ■ 01326 379451 ■ www.seasaltcornwall.co.uk

This is the sale outlet of the company, which creates women's clothes inspired by the Cornish coast and landscape – including signature raincoats. Nearly a dozen branches are located across Devon and Cornwall.

5 Darts Farm

MAP K4 ■ Topsham, Exeter ■ 01392 878200 ■ www.dartsfarm.co.uk

From its launch as a farm shop, Darts has evolved into an entire shopping hub based around the concept of fresh, locally sourced food. On site you can find a food hall, butchers, deli, fish shed and cider works, and also a restaurant and health and beauty treatments.

6 Cream Cornwall

MAP C5 ■ 51 Church St, Falmouth ■ 01326 317253 ■ creamcornwall.co.uk

The flagship store of a Cornish interiors chain known for its monochrome printed china, it also sells textiles and lampshades with designs featuring fish, lobsters and jellyfish.

Tavistock Pannier Market

7 Cornwall Crafts Association

Trelissick branch: MAP C5 ■ Feock, Truro ■ 01872 864514 ■ Open 10am–5pm daily ■ www.cornwallcrafts.co.uk

A range of top quality Cornish arts and crafts are exhibited and sold at the Trelissick Gallery. The pieces, made by craftmakers living in Cornwall, are inspired by contemporary trends.

8 Duchy of Cornwall Nursery

MAP E4 ■ Cott Rd, Lostwithiel ■ 01208 872668 ■ www.duchyof cornwallnursery.co.uk

One of the largest nurseries in South West England, this place is an inspiration for gardeners, offering a range of shrubs, ornamental and fruit trees, climbers and conservatory plants. Among its specialities are various conifers, fuchsias, bamboos and camellias.

Duchy of Cornwall Nursery

9 Barnstaple Pannier Market

A lively market is held daily until around 4pm in this purpose-built hall (see p75) dating from 1855. Come for books, clothing, household goods, local produce, crafts and antiques.

10 Devon Guild of Craftsmen

MAP K4 ■ Riverside Mill, Bovey Tracey ■ 01626 832223

This consortium sells some of the region's best contemporary crafts, including ceramics, textiles, jewellery and furniture. Its base on the edge of Dartmoor holds regular exhibitions.

TOP 10 THINGS TO BUY

Creamy Cornish fudge

1 Fudge
Creamy and delicious flavoured fudge is available in almost every gift shop throughout the region.

2 Serpentine
A speciality of the Lizard Peninsula, this greenish rock is used to make a variety of local ornaments.

3 Local Art
Buy local art at small galleries, which are to Devon and Cornwall what antique shops are to the Cotswolds.

4 Ice Cream
Most resorts have at least one shop selling quality ice cream in a range of contemporary flavours.

5 Local Wine and Gin
West Country wines are among the country's finest, while historic Plymouth Gin is internationally famous.

6 Fishermen's Apparel
Fishing smocks, caps and woolly jumpers are widely available and make great mementos and souvenirs.

7 Crafts
Hand-crafted woodwork, jewellery, silverware and glassware are among the South West's specialities.

8 Fresh Seafood
Experience the thrill of buying seafood directly from the harbour. It can usually be iced and packaged if you have a long trip back home.

9 Surf Gear
All the major surf gear brands are represented at outlets in the surfing centres of Devon and Cornwall.

10 Pottery
Some of the country's most renowned potters are based in the South West and exhibit their wares in the region.

TOP10 Cornwall and Devon for Free

1 Falmouth Art Gallery

This family-friendly gallery *(see p19)* has a collection of 2,000 artworks, ranging from Pre-Raphaelite paintings to contemporary prints, photographs and children's illustrations. It also has the UK's largest public collection of automata. There are workshops for families and a changing programme of exhibitions.

Mount Edgcumbe formal gardens

2 Mount Edgcumbe

Although there is a fee to enter the house *(see p98)*, access to the grounds – with more than 350 ha (865 acres) of beautiful parkland, formal gardens and the National Camellia Collection – is free. There are walks along the seashore among rare trees and plants, as well as a good chance of glimpsing wild fallow deer.

3 Marconi Centre, Poldhu

MAP B6 ▪ Near Mullion ▪ 01326 241656 ▪ Opening times vary ▪ Donation requested ▪ www.marconi-centre-poldhu.org.uk

This small heritage centre was built on the site from which Guglielmo Marconi transmitted the first ever transatlantic radio message to Signal

Merrivale Prehistoric Settlement

Hill, St John's, Newfoundland on 12 December 1901. A short video presentation and information boards relate the fascinating story.

4 Cornish Camels

MAP B5 ▪ Rosuick Organic Farm, St Martin, Helston ▪ 01326 231302 ▪ www.cornishcamels.com

This organic livestock farm, with peacocks and a small group of camels, sits in its own beautiful valley on the Lizard Peninsula. Visitors are free to follow paths around the farm.

5 Roskilly's Ice Cream Farm

MAP C6 ▪ Tregellast Barton Farm, St Keverne ▪ 01326 280479 ▪ www.roskillys.co.uk

Roskilly's Cornish ice cream is sold throughout the county. At this organic farm you can watch the cows being milked as well as enjoy the ice cream. There are also marked trails through the wild meadows, and cows, goats, pigs, sheep, turkeys, geese, quails and chickens to be seen.

6 Merrivale Prehistoric Settlement, Dartmoor

MAP H4 ▪ On B3357, W of Princetown ▪ www.english-heritage.org.uk

The remains of a Bronze Age village of round houses and several ritual structures can be found on Dartmoor, including three stone rows, a stone circle, standing stones and a number of burial mounds. These monuments were built between 2500 and 1000 BC, but one of the most distinctive stones is medieval – a huge round of granite once used for crushing cider apples.

Buckfast Abbey and gardens

7 Buckfast Abbey

The abbey (see p84) and its grounds, including a lavender garden and a physic garden where medicinal herbs are cultivated, is home to a community of Benedictine monks. There is also a shop selling crafts and produce made by monks and nuns from all over Europe.

8 Geocaching in Devon
www.geocaching.com

Devon is a perfect location for geocaching – treasure-hunting via smartphone – with more than 25,000 geocaches scattered along its vast network of paths and cycle tracks. Geocachers use GPS to hide containers and then post clues to help others. The app is free to download.

9 Shoalstone Pool, Brixham

MAP K5 ▪ Berry Head Rd ▪ Open May–Sep ▪ www.shoalstonepool.com

This Art Deco lido was built in 1926, with a seawater swimming pool dating from 1896, and is maintained by volunteers and the local council. There is a fee for parking, and for those who decide to hire a beach hut or lounger. The use of the pool is free though donations are appreciated.

10 Heartlands, Pool

MAP B5 ▪ Robinson's Shaft, Dudnance Lane ▪ 01209 707300 ▪ www.heartlands.com

A free leisure and cultural centre created around a disused tin mine in Cornwall's UNESCO-designated mining country. There are interactive exhibitions on the history of mining, plus gardens and a good café.

TOP 10 BUDGET TIPS

1 National Trust Membership
Membership not only gives free access to the region's many NT properties, but also free parking at various beauty spots.

2 Beach Picnics
Look out for artisan breads, local cheeses and farm-grown fresh produce sold from farm shops, and enjoy your feast with a spectacular view.

3 Stay Inland
Accommodation inland and off the beaten track in Cornwall can be good value, while still within easy driving distance of the coast.

4 Wine and Cider Tastings
Look out for free tastings at vineyards and cider farms around the counties.

5 Bus Passes
In Devon, the weekly Megarider Gold ticket gives access to all routes run by Stagecoach South West.

6 Camp or Self-Cater
Staying on a campsite or in self-catering accommodation (see p115) is usually cheaper than a hotel.

7 Take the Sleeper
Save time – and a night's stay – by travelling on the Night Riviera train from London Paddington to Cornwall.

8 Cornish Heritage Trust Membership
Membership gives free entry to all English Heritage sites in Cornwall.

9 Discount Vouchers
Look out for vouchers giving discounted entry to sights or special deals in cafés and restaurants. They can be found at most regional tourist offices.

10 Multiday Tickets
Entry tickets at many attractions are valid for 7 days and some – including for the Eden Project and the National Marine Aquarium – are valid for a year.

Biomes at the Eden Project

⟨TOP 10⟩ Festivals

① Obby Oss, Padstow

MAP D3 ▪ 1 May (or 2 May if date falls on Sun)

Pagan fertility rites and local traditions unite in this May Day spectacle. The main character, the Obby Oss, garbed in a black costume draped around a 2-m- (6-ft-) wide hoop, is accompanied by a "Teazer" with music, drumming and the May Song.

② Helston's Flora Day

MAP B5 ▪ 8 May (or previous Sat if date falls on Sun or Mon) ▪ www.helstonfloraday.org.uk

This uniquely Cornish extravaganza involves a stately procession of top-hatted people in frocks performing the "Furry Dance" through the streets of Helston. Flowers and sprigs of sycamore feature too.

③ Fowey Festival of Arts and Literature

MAP E4 ▪ Mid-May ▪ www.foweyfestival.com

Run by the Daphne du Maurier Society, this 8-day literary festival celebrates the author, who lived in Fowey, and features music, drama, walks, workshops and daily talks.

④ Golowan Festival, Penzance

MAP B5 ▪ Late Jun ▪ www.golowanfestival.org

This week-long arts and dance festival features processions, circus acts, buskers and a mock mayoral election. Live music, flaming torches and fireworks are all part of the spectacle.

Sidmouth Folk Festival performers

⑤ Sidmouth Folk Festival

MAP L4 ▪ Late Jul–early Aug ▪ www.sidmouthfolkfestival.co.uk

Folk music, Northumbrian pipes and Morris dancers feature at a seaside festival in one of Devon's most elegant towns. Even non-folk fans succumb to the event's upbeat charm, with buskers lining the Esplanade and pubs jammed with carousers. Accommodation and concert tickets sell out quickly.

⑥ Cornwall Pride

MAP C4 ▪ Late Aug ▪ www.cornwallpride.org

The LGBTQ+ community in Cornwall celebrates the annual Pride festival in Newquay. Entertainment, crafts, a parade with floats, walking bands, barbecue and more add to all the fun.

Parade float, Golowan Festival

⑦ St Ives September Festival

MAP B5 ▪ Mid-Sep ▪ www.stivesseptemberfestival.co.uk

The arts have long had a strong presence in St Ives and this two-week jamboree brings them together with exhibitions, drama and poetry readings. Music ranges from cello recitals to tribute pop acts and African beats, with most performances held at the Guildhall and the Western Hotel. There are also talks and comedy performances.

8 Oyster Festival, Falmouth

MAP C5 ■ Mid-Oct ■ www.falmouth oysterfestival.co.uk

This four-day event pays homage to Cornish seafood. The event features music from the local brass band, oyster-shucking competitions, cookery demonstrations as well as boat races.

Revellers at Oyster Festival

9 Tar Barrelling, Ottery St Mary

MAP L3 ■ 5 Nov (or previous Sat if date falls on Sun) ■ www.tarbarrels. co.uk/nextbarrels

Every Bonfire Night, tar-soaked barrels are set alight and hoisted around town and there are races for men, women as well as children. The evening culminates in fireworks and a huge bonfire beside the River Otter.

10 Tom Bawcock's Eve, Mousehole

MAP A5 ■ 23 Dec

A procession and fireworks celebrate the fisherman who saved the village from starvation by going to sea in a storm and landing a huge catch of pilchards, which were served up in stargazy pie – the Cornish pie.

TOP 10 LIVE MUSIC AND THEATRE VENUES

1 Theatre Royal, Plymouth
MAP P5 ■ Royal Parade ■ 01752 267222 ■ www.theatreroyal.com
Mainstream shows are held in the main theatre, while the Drum Theatre hosts cutting-edge performances.

2 Eden Project
This is Cornwall's best outdoor music venue (see pp14–15) in summer.

3 The Poly, Falmouth
MAP C5 ■ 24 Church St ■ 01326 319461 ■ www.thepoly.org
Year-round venue for exhibitions, art cinema, theatre and concerts.

4 Hall for Cornwall, Truro
MAP C5 ■ Back Quay ■ 01872 262466 ■ www.hallforcornwall.co.uk
Drama and music are staged here.

5 Exeter Northcott Theatre
MAP N1 ■ Stocker Rd ■ 01392 726363 ■ www.exeternorthcott.co.uk
This is Exeter's principal theatrical venue.

6 Minack Theatre
This amphitheatre hosts a range of productions in summer (see pp28–9).

7 Acorn Arts Centre, Penzance
MAP B5 ■ Parade St ■ 01736 363545 ■ www.theacornpenzance.com
This former church is now a playhouse.

8 Calstock Arts Centre, Calstock
MAP F3 ■ The Old Chapel ■ 01822 833183 ■ www.calstockarts.org
Calstock's arts centre hosts a wide range of live music, theatre and comedy.

9 Barbican Theatre, Plymouth
MAP Q6 ■ Castle St ■ 01752 267131 ■ www.barbicantheatre.co.uk
A theatre specializing in new drama.

10 Exeter Phoenix
MAP P2 ■ Gandy St ■ 01392 667080 ■ www.exeterphoenix.org.uk
This is Exeter's premier arts centre.

A performance at Exeter Phoenix

Cornwall and Devon Area by Area

Hawthorn tree and granite outcrop at sunrise on Dartmoor

TOP 10 North Devon

Between the austere heights of Exmoor and the rocky pinnacles of Hartland Point, North Devon crams in a rich landscape. Two of the region's top nature reserves, Northam Burrows and Braunton Burrows, and some of the best beaches, such as Woolacombe Bay, Saunton Sands and Westward Ho!, are located on this stretch of coast. The main towns are Barnstaple, Ilfracombe and Bideford, but the true treasures are the coastal villages of Appledore and Clovelly. Inland, the Tarka Trail is ideal for cycling or walking, while out at sea, Lundy Island is home to puffins and seals.

Lighthouse on Lundy Island

① Lundy Island
MAP G1 ▪ Tourist information: 01271 863636 ▪ www.landmark trust.org.uk/lundyisland
This remote 5-km- (3-mile-) long sliver of land is located north of Hartland Point and is named after the puffins that live here ("lunde" is medieval Norse for puffin). There are options for overnight stays, including a lighthouse and a radio room. Day trips sail from Ilfracombe and Bideford in summer.

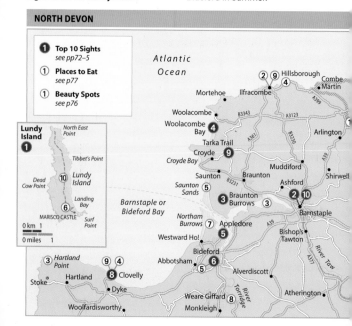

NORTH DEVON

- ① **Top 10 Sights** see pp72–5
- ① **Places to Eat** see p77
- ① **Beauty Spots** see p76

Atlantic Ocean

Lundy Island ①
North East Point
Tibbet's Point
Dead Cow Point
Lundy Island ⑩
Landing Bay
MARISCO CASTLE ⑥
Surf Point
0 km 1
0 miles 1

Hillsborough ② ⑨
Combe Martin
Mortehoe Ilfracombe ④ A399
Woolacombe B3343 A3123
Woolacombe Bay ④
Arlington
Tarka Trail ⑨
Croyde
Croyde Bay
Saunton Braunton Muddiford
Saunton Sands ⑤ B3231 Ashford Shirwell
Barnstaple or Bideford Bay ③ Braunton Burrows ③ ② ⑩
Northam Burrows ⑦ Appledore ⑤ Barnstaple
Westward Ho! ⑤ Bishop's Tawton
Bideford ⑥
③ Hartland Point ⑨ ④ Abbotsham ⑤ ⑥ Alverdiscott
Stoke Hartland ⑧ Clovelly Weare Giffard ⑧ Atherington
Dyke Monkleigh River Torridge
Woolfardisworthy River Taw
A377

2 Museum of Barnstaple and North Devon

MAP H2 ■ The Square, Barnstaple
■ 01271 346747 ■ Open Apr–Oct:
10:30am–4:30pm Tue–Sat (Nov–
Mar: until 4pm) ■ www.barnstaple
museum.org.uk

This museum has features on the
area's wildlife and a gallery devoted to
Tarka the Otter (see p74). You can walk
through a model Wellington bomber
and view timepieces and glassware.
The Barum Ware – pottery for which
this area is renowned – is superb.

3 Braunton Burrows

MAP H2

The core of a UNESCO-designated
biosphere, this area constitutes the
largest sand-dune system in the UK.
The dunes are stabilized by marram
grass and other plants. Nearly 500
species of vascular plants and a
variety of invertebrates live here.
Meandering paths traverse the
area, which can be reached on
the Tarka Trail *(see p54)* and the
South West Coast Path *(see p55)*.

Bodyboarders at Woolacombe Bay

4 Woolacombe Bay

MAP H1

Surfers know this impressive arc
of sand as one of the country's top
sites for riding the waves, but non-
surfers will find plenty of space here,
especially at the more sheltered
southern end, Putsborough. Surf
gear can be rented at shops and
stalls above the beach, where there
are also a handful of cafés and bars.

5 Appledore

MAP H2 ■ Maritime Museum:
01237 422064; open Apr–Oct:
10:30am–5pm daily; adm; www.
northdevonmaritimemuseum.co.uk

A stately air hangs over this village
of Georgian houses at the edge of
the Torridge Estuary. Behind the
seafront, narrow lanes with shops
and pubs lead uphill to the Maritime
Museum with its collection of nautical
items. For the best estuary views,
tasty seafood and a pint, head for
one of the two pubs on Irsha Street.

Bude Street in Appledore

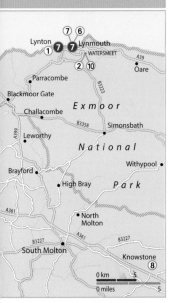

⑥ Burton Art Gallery and Museum

MAP H2 ■ Kingsley Rd, Bideford
■ 01237 471455 ■ Open 10am–4pm
Mon–Sat (Aug: to 5pm), 11am–4pm
Sun ■ www.burtonartgallery.co.uk

The "little white town" of Bideford, rich with historical associations and home of the Elizabethan mariner Sir Richard Grenville, houses the Burton Art Gallery and Museum. The gallery boasts an absorbing collection of art and artifacts, including watercolours, model ships and replicas of the famed local slipware. The museum is located in Victoria Park, where cannons taken from the Spanish Armada are exhibited.

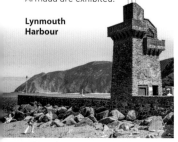

Lynmouth Harbour

⑦ Lynton and Lynmouth
MAP J1

These villages on the Exmoor coast, linked by a water-powered funicular, have drawn visitors since the 1800s when the poet Shelley spent his honeymoon here. Nestled among hills, the villages are a haven of tranquillity, though it was not always peaceful here. Lynmouth, by the sea, was devastated by a flash flood in 1952; the Glen Lyn Gorge, through which the torrent raged, holds an exhibition in memory of the event.

⑧ Clovelly
MAP G2 ■ Tourist information: 01237 431781; www.clovelly.co.uk

This picturesque settlement clings to a steep cliff and plunges down to a small harbour. The town is privately owned and there is an absence of cars, except for a Land Rover service

Clovelly's pretty harbourfront

for visitors who find the steep main street unmanageable. Some of the cottages are open to the public, including a museum dedicated to Charles Kingsley, author of *The Water Babies*, who lived here as a child.

⑨ Tarka Trail
MAP H1–H3

Henry Williamson's classic animal fable *Tarka the Otter* was set around his native North Devon. The otter's epic journeys are traced in this 288-km (180-mile) trail, which describes a figure of eight centred on the town of Barnstaple and incorporating sections of the South West Coast Path and Tarka Line railway. Over 50 km (31 miles) of the trail, between Braunton and Meeth, can be cycled. Other sections take in the scenic Taw Valley and Williamson's home village of Georgeham.

TARKA THE OTTER

North Devon's Tarka Line, Tarka Trail and Tarka Country all refer to *Tarka the Otter*, written by Henry Williamson. The book narrates the adventures of a young otter amid the beautiful landscape of North Devon – "the country of the two rivers". The book has retained its place as a classic animal tale, and was made into a film in 1979, narrated by Peter Ustinov.

⑩ Barnstaple Pannier Market

MAP H2 ∎ Butchers Row, Barnstaple
∎ 01271 379084 ∎ Open Tue–Sat
∎ barnstaple.co.uk

This covered market in the town centre is the most famous of Devon's "pannier markets" – so called because traders originally brought their wares in baskets or panniers. Antiques, crafts, local produce, household items and clothes are all on sale here. Alongside is Butchers Row, which once held butchers' shops and is now home to a variety of stores selling clothes, antiques, household items and gifts.

Barnstaple Pannier Market

A DRIVE ALONG THE NORTH DEVON COAST

▶ MORNING

Begin your tour in the sister villages of **Lynton** and **Lynmouth** at the foot of Exmoor. The upper village, Lynton, is connected by an ingenious cliff railway to Lynmouth. From here it is a short drive to Ilfracombe (see p72), a cheerfully traditional resort with a bustling harbour. On the coast south of Ilfracombe, **Woolacombe** (see p73) and **Croyde** (see p51) beaches invite a stopover. Though very different – Croyde is a sheltered inlet while Woolacombe is a long, curving bay – both are good for families as well as watersports enthusiasts. You can indulge in a beachside picnic lunch or drive inland to lunch at the restaurant in the **Broomhill Art Hotel** (see p118), where the sculpture will prove absorbing.

AFTERNOON

In the afternoon, make a stop at Barnstaple, home to the lively **Pannier Market** as well as the **Museum of Barnstaple and North Devon** (see p73). Or you could instead call in at Bideford for a visit to the **Burton Art Gallery and Museum**, which hosts regular exhibitions. Up at the mouth of the estuary, **Appledore** (see p73) has another museum you can explore, but a stroll along the riverside is equally enjoyable. Proceed west along Bideford Bay to **Clovelly**, an enchanting, well-preserved village, and stop here for a cup of tea. If time allows, continue west to **Hartland Abbey** (see p42), a majestic mansion with lovely grounds sweeping down to the sea.

See map on pp72–3

Beauty Spots

① Valley of the Rocks
MAP J1

West of Lynton, this steep heathland is dominated by rugged rock formations. Herds of wild goats still roam free as they have done here for centuries.

Watersmeet's woodland gorge

② Watersmeet
MAP J1

In a deep wooded gorge, Hoar Oak Water joins with the East Lyn River on its way down to the sea. Shady riverside walks branch out from here.

③ Hartland Point
MAP G2

On Devon's northwestern tip, overlooked by a solitary lighthouse, this remote, storm-battered headland has dramatic views of slate cliffs, jagged black rocks and swirling sea.

④ Hillsborough
MAP H1

Outside Ilfracombe, the summit of this 136-m (447-ft) hill is one of the few places in the country where you can see the sun rise and set over the sea.

⑤ Saunton Sands
MAP H2

The first view of this 6-km (4-mile) westward-facing strand is breath-taking, with ranks of Atlantic rollers advancing in stately fashion. This spot is a favourite among surfers.

⑥ Lynmouth

The East and West Lyn rivers flow placidly into the sea at this cliff-sheltered Exmoor village (see p74). The Glen Lyn Gorge has woodland walks and waterfalls.

⑦ Northam Burrows
MAP H2

Located next to Westward Ho!, this expanse of grasslands, salt marsh and sand dunes offers wonderful views across the Taw/Torridge Estuary. The broad beach in front attracts surfers and sail-boarders.

⑧ Weare Giffard
MAP H2

This graceful village in the wooded Torridge Valley has a 15th-century manor house and a weathered pub. It is accessible from the Tarka Trail.

⑨ Clovelly

One of the loveliest Devon villages, Clovelly (see p74) has neat cottages and a miniature harbour.

⑩ Lundy Island

This remote outpost (see p72) where the Atlantic meets the Bristol Channel is either tranquil or in complete uproar, depending on the sea.

Hillsborough

Places to Eat

PRICE CATEGORIES
For a three-course meal for one with half a bottle of wine, including taxes and extra charges.
....
£ under £35 ££ £35–£55 £££ over £55

1 The Coach House
MAP H2 ▪ Kentisbury Grange, Barnstaple ▪ 01271 882295 ▪ £££

A stylish country hotel on the edge of Exmoor hosts this restaurant by Devon-born chef Michael Caines.

2 Thomas Carr 1873
MAP H1 ▪ 63 Fore St, Ilfracombe ▪ 01271 867831 ▪ Open for dinner only Tue–Sat ▪ £££

Housed in Ifracombe's old harbourside Victorian police station, this elegant Michelin-starred restaurant specializes in local fish dishes.

3 Fremington Quay Café
MAP H2 ▪ Fremington Quay, Barnstaple ▪ 01271 268720 ▪ £

This café is a perfect stop on the Tarka Trail from Barnstaple to Bideford. It serves cakes, cream teas and lunch.

4 Red Lion
MAP G2 ▪ Clovelly ▪ 01237 431237 ▪ ££

A harbourside inn with great views, here (see p116) you can eat locally caught fish and game from the Clovelly Estate. There are rooms upstairs.

5 M' Rock N' Bowl
MAP H2 ▪ 1 Ennisfarne Rd, Westward Ho!, Bideford ▪ 07745 085147 ▪ ££

This friendly restaurant has stunning sea views and focuses on authentic Moroccan cuisine.

6 Marisco Tavern
MAP G1 ▪ Lundy Island ▪ 01237 431831 ▪ £

Lundy's sole pub serves island specialities using Soay lamb and venison from Sika deer. Highland cattle can be found near the tavern.

7 Rising Sun
MAP J1 ▪ Harbourside, Lynmouth ▪ 01598 753223 ▪ ££

Contemporary cuisine – featuring seafood – is served in a 14th-century inn that claims to have once accommodated poet Percy Shelley.

8 The Masons Arms
MAP J2 ▪ Knowstone, South Molton ▪ 01398 341231 ▪ Closed Mon, Sun (except first Sun of the month) ▪ £££

This welcoming Michelin-starred restaurant is set in a thatched 13th-century pub on the edge of Exmoor, with excellent food, and outside dining in good weather.

The Masons Arms

9 Lynbay Fish & Chips
MAP H1 ▪ 6 The Quay, Ilfracombe ▪ 01271 866850 ▪ £

A classic fish and chips meal awaits you at this take away spot right on the harbour. A menu for kids as well as gluten-free options are available.

10 Watersmeet House
MAP J1 ▪ Watersmeet Rd, Lynmouth ▪ 01598 753348 ▪ Closed Nov–mid-Mar ▪ ££

At a famous Exmoor beauty spot, this Victorian fishing lodge, run by the National Trust, is now an inviting tearoom and garden.

See map on pp72–3 ←

TOP **10** South Devon

A genteel atmosphere pervades much of South Devon. Verdant meadows are interspersed with cob-and-thatch villages, and rivers drift serenely through wooded valleys dotted with tidy cottages. Crumbling red cliffs rear above beaches, while in the forbidding expanse of Dartmoor, lonely tors punctuate slopes of bracken and gorse, and isolated communities are huddled around centuries-old churches. A world away from these rural scenes are the cathedral cities of Exeter and Plymouth, the region's historic power centres, both with a scattering of medieval and Elizabethan remains to explore.

A Greater Horseshoe Bat at Berry Head National Nature Reserve

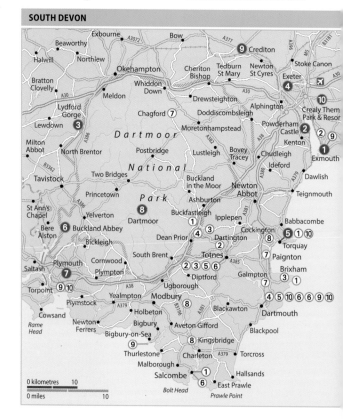

SOUTH DEVON

1 A La Ronde

MAP L4 ▪ Summer Lane, Exmouth ▪ 01395 265514 ▪ Open mid-Feb–Oct: 11am–5pm daily ▪ Adm ▪ www.nationaltrust.org.uk

When cousins Jane and Mary Parminter returned from their European travels in 1790, they brought with them trunkloads of souvenirs and a vision. They built this 16-sided house and filled it with mementos and quirky creations. These range from seaweed and sand concoctions to a frieze of game-bird and chicken feathers, and a shell-covered gallery.

Façade of Powderham Castle

2 Powderham Castle

MAP K4 ▪ Kenton ▪ 01626 890243 ▪ Open Apr–Oct: 11am–4:30pm Sun–Fri ▪ Adm ▪ www.powderham.co.uk

Surrounded by a deer park, this stately pile is the long-time seat of the earls of Devon. Tours take in the ornate music room, the majestic dining room, lavish bedrooms and the Victorian kitchen. There are kids' activity trails in the grounds.

3 Lydford Gorge

On the edge of Dartmoor, the River Lyd gushes noisily through this oak-wooded ravine (see pp16–17), home to the spectacular Devil's Cauldron whirlpool and the White Lady Waterfall that plummets 28 m (90 ft). There are walks along the river and a winding upper path but sturdy boots are required, and children must be supervised. Access may be difficult for those with impaired mobility.

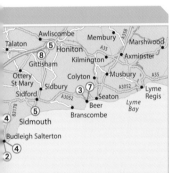

White Lady Waterfall, Lydford Gorge

4 Exeter

Devon's capital (see pp22–5) is a relaxed city with a historic core that includes the region's oldest cathedral and a treasure trove of a museum. Among other attractions is a network of underground passages and an old quayside. The city has an active cultural life, with year-round festivals and events, and a good selection of restaurants.

The Children's Holiday (1865) by William Holman Hunt, Torre Abbey

5 Torre Abbey

MAP K5 ■ King's Drive, Torquay ■ 01803 293593 ■ Open 10am–5pm Wed–Sun ■ Adm ■ www.torre-abbey. org.uk

One of Devon's best museums is housed in a mansion converted from abbey buildings after the Dissolution of the Monasteries in 1539 (see p38). Its strong 19th-century art collection includes works by Holman Hunt and Burne-Jones. The grounds hold medieval ruins and a tithe barn.

DEVON'S RESORTS

Devon's south coast benefited from the 19th-century development and extension of Britain's railway network. With the influx of visitors, villas and *cottage ornés* (thatched, rustic dwellings) sprang up in fashionable towns such as Torquay, Exmouth and Sidmouth.

6 Buckland Abbey

MAP H5 ■ Yelverton ■ 01822 853607 ■ Open mid-Feb–Oct: 10am–5pm daily; times vary in winter ■ Adm ■ www.nationaltrust.org.uk

The former home of Elizabethan mariners Richard Grenville and Francis Drake, this handsome manor house occupies beautiful grounds in the Tavy Valley. Visitors can look round the monastic Great Barn, Elizabethan Garden and the main Abbey, where galleries feature interactive displays. Exhibits include Drake's Drum which, according to legend, will sound again when England is in danger to summon Drake from his grave.

7 Plymouth
MAP H5

This historic city contains remnants of its Elizabethan glory days, notably in the harbourside Barbican quarter. Other attractions include the National Marine Aquarium (see p46) and the Plymouth Gin Distillery (see p82). Don't miss the magnificent sea views from Plymouth Hoe, a high, grassy esplanade above the harbour.

8 Dartmoor

In a region dominated by the sea, Dartmoor (see pp16–17) is a windy wasteland where semi-wild ponies roam. Prehistoric remains are scattered across the moor, while on its edges lie the market towns of Okehampton and Tavistock. Dartmoor offers opportunities for walking, canoeing and wildlife watching.

Ponies on Dartmoor

The façade of Crediton Parish Church

9 Crediton Parish Church

MAP K3 ■ Church St, Crediton
■ 01363 773226 ■ www.crediton
parishchurch.org.uk

This red sandstone structure from the 15th century is one of Devon's grandest churches. Its east window features the key points in the life of the missionary St Boniface, who was born in AD 680. The extensive and intricate memorial of 1911, occupying the east wall of the nave, is dedicated to Sir Redvers Buller. He was awarded the Victoria Cross in the 1879 Zulu War.

10 Crealy Theme Park & Resort

MAP L4 ■ Sidmouth Rd, Exeter ■ 01395 233200 ■ Opening times vary, check website ■ Adm ■ www.crealy.co.uk

This is the largest theme park in Devon. It offers a fun-filled day out, with thrilling rides such as the Maximus Rollercoaster, a Tidal Wave Log Flume and the Crealy Grand Prix electric race track.

A DRIVING TOUR IN SOUTH DEVON

▶ MORNING

Start close to the Dorset border at the fishing village of **Beer** *(see p83)*, associated with the exploits of the infamous smuggler Jack Rattenbury. You can grab a crab sandwich on the beach. Follow the A3052 west to **Sidmouth** *(see p83)*, whose seafront and esplanade are perfect for a stroll. The town is studded with well-preserved villas from the Regency period. The museum here includes a lovely display of lace. Indulge in a hearty seaside lunch by the waterfront before leaving town.

AFTERNOON

Continuing west, just outside **Exmouth** *(see p83)* off the A376, stop to admire **A La Ronde** *(see p79)*, a 16-sided folly constructed by Jane and Mary Parminter. Go north to the M5, then take the A380 and A381 south to **Totnes** *(see p83)*. Despite its free-spirited vibe, the town retains much of its Elizabethan character and has a Norman castle and a 14th-century church. The town's tearooms are a good place to stop for some refreshments. From Totnes, drive or take a river cruise along the River Dart to the sailing resort of **Dartmouth** *(see p83)*, also filled with reminders of the Elizabethan era. From Totnes or Dartmouth, it is an easy excursion to the South Hams, an area of sleepy villages and peaceful views. Unless you are based in Totnes or Dartmouth, either stay over in Kingsbridge or **Salcombe** *(see p83)*, or head back up the A381 to **Exeter** *(see pp22–5)*.

See map on pp78–9 ←

The Best of the Rest

A hiker looking out across Berry Head

① Berry Head, Torbay
MAP K5

This coastal headland and nature reserve is home to guillemots and the endangered Greater Horseshoe Bat.

② Fairlynch Museum
MAP L4 ▪ 27 Fore St, Budleigh Salterton ▪ 01395 442666 ▪ Open Apr–Oct: 2–4:30pm Tue–Sun & bank hols ▪ fair lynchmuseum.uk

This 19th-century *cottage orné* holds a collection of lace, costumes and toys.

③ Beer Quarry Caves
MAP M4 ▪ Quarry Lane, Beer ▪ 01297 680282 ▪ Open Apr–Sep: 10am–4:30pm; Oct: 10am–2:30pm ▪ Adm ▪ www.beerquarrycaves.co.uk

This limestone quarry, first established by the Romans, supplied stone for Exeter and St Paul's cathedrals.

④ Bicton Park
MAP L4 ▪ East Budleigh, Budleigh Salterton ▪ 01395 568465 ▪ Open 10am–5pm daily ▪ Adm ▪ www.bictongardens.co.uk

A horticultural idyll, Bicton includes a 1730s formal garden reputedly inspired by Versailles, and a Palm House from the 1820s.

Soay Sheep, Paignton

⑤ Allhallows Museum
MAP L3 ▪ High St, Honiton ▪ 01404 44966 ▪ Open Apr–Oct: Mon–Sat ▪ www.honitonmuseum.co.uk

Housed in the oldest building in Honiton, this museum displays fine lace.

⑥ Overbeck's Museum
MAP J6 ▪ Sharpitor, Salcombe ▪ 01548 842893 ▪ Open mid-Feb–Oct: 10:30am–4pm Sun–Thu ▪ Adm ▪ www.nationaltrust.org.uk

Inventor and scientist Otto Overbeck's collection is housed in this museum.

⑦ Paignton Zoo
MAP K5 ▪ Totnes Rd, Paignton ▪ 01803 697500 ▪ Opening times vary, check website ▪ Adm ▪ www.paigntonzoo.org.uk

This zoo is designed to mimic the natural habitats of the animals that live here.

⑧ Kingsbridge Cookworthy Museum
MAP J6 ▪ 108 Fore St, Kingsbridge ▪ 01548 853235 ▪ Open Apr–Oct: Mon–Sat ▪ Adm ▪ kingsbridgemuseum.org.uk

The museum is named after the pioneer of English porcelain made from china clay.

⑨ Burgh Island
MAP J6 ▪ Bigbury-on-Sea

This tiny isle is reached by sea tractor at high tide. Stay overnight at the ritzy Burgh Island Hotel (see p117).

⑩ Plymouth Gin Distillery
MAP P5 ▪ 60 Southside St ▪ 01752 665292 ▪ Open 11am–5:30pm Tue–Sat, noon–5:30pm Sun ▪ Adm ▪ www.plymouthdistillery.com

Tours of England's oldest working gin distillery include tastings.

Towns and Villages

1 Salcombe
MAP J6

At the mouth of the placid Kingsbridge Estuary, Devon's southernmost port is a magnet for sailors. Beaches, coastal walks and Overbeck's Museum are all nearby.

2 Totnes
MAP K5

The age of this riverside town is attested by its Norman castle and medieval remains. It is popular with craftworkers and produces some of the country's finest glass and crystal.

3 Brixham
MAP K5

Much of the seafood served in the region's restaurants is landed at this harbour. A magnificent replica of the *Golden Hind*, the vessel in which Francis Drake circumnavigated the globe, is moored here.

4 Budleigh Salterton
MAP L4

John Everett Millais painted his famous *Boyhood of Raleigh* while on this village's pebble beach. The Fairlynch Museum is well worth a visit.

5 Sidmouth
MAP L4

The queen of East Devon resorts, elegant Sidmouth has a long esplanade fronted by a shingle strand. Families prefer the more secluded Jacob's Ladder beach to the west.

Shingle beach, Sidmouth

6 Dartmouth
MAP K6

The Royal Regatta *(see p84)* and the Royal Naval College confirm this port's yachting credentials. Cobbled streets, impressive Tudor buildings and a castle add to its allure.

7 Beer
MAP M4

The village is best-known for fishing, smuggling and Beer stone, a prized building material. A culvert carries a stream along the main street, from where you descend to the beach.

Thatched cottages in Cockington

8 Cockington
MAP K5

There is no denying the rustic appeal of this well-preserved village, a peaceful contrast to the ebullience of neighbouring Torquay.

9 Exmouth
MAP L4

Primarily a family resort, Exmouth becomes quite lively during the summer. The Beacon, an elegant row of Regency houses overlooking the sea, once accommodated the wives of Byron and Nelson.

10 Torquay
MAP K5

Capital of the so-called English Riviera, engaging Torquay, with its palms and fairy lights, smacks unmistakably of the Mediterranean.

See map on pp78–9

Sights Along the River Dart

① Buckfast Abbey
MAP J5 ▪ Buckfastleigh
▪ 01364 645500 ▪ Open 9am–6pm
Mon–Sat, noon–6pm Sun ▪ www.
buckfast.org.uk

The river flows through the grounds of this Benedictine house. The monks here produce a famous tonic wine.

Dartington Hall lawns

② Dartington Hall
MAP J5 ▪ 01803 847514
▪ www.dartington.org

Founded by US heiress Dorothy Elmhirst, this arts and education centre hosts various cultural events.

③ Elizabethan Museum
MAP K5 ▪ 70 Fore St, Totnes
▪ 01803 863821 ▪ Open Apr–Sep:
10am–4pm Tue–Fri ▪ www.
totnesmuseum.org ▪ Adm (by donation)

This museum, in a cloth merchant's home from 1575, has a room devoted to Charles Babbage, who built the forerunner of the computer.

④ South Devon Railway
MAP J5 ▪ Station Rd,
Buckfastleigh ▪ 01364 644370
▪ Opening times vary ▪ Adm
▪ www.southdevonrailway.co.uk

Travel back in time in a vintage Great Western Railway coach hauled by a steam locomotive via the scenic route between Totnes and Buckfastleigh.

⑤ Totnes Guildhall
MAP K5 ▪ 5 Rampart's Walk
▪ 01803 862147 ▪ Open Apr–Oct:
11am–3pm Mon–Fri

Built on the ruins of a priory in 1553, the Guildhall later housed a courtroom and jail. It displays a table believed to have been used by Oliver Cromwell.

⑥ Riverlink Cruises
MAP K5 ▪ 5 Lower St,
Dartmouth ▪ 01803 555872 ▪ Open
Apr–Oct ▪ Adm ▪ www.dartmouth
railriver.co.uk

The most relaxing way to explore the Dart is during a 90-minute cruise between Totnes and Dartmouth.

⑦ Greenway
MAP J6 ▪ Galmpton ▪ 01803
842382 ▪ Open Mar–Dec: times vary;
book parking in advance ▪ Adm
▪ www.nationaltrust.org.uk

Set on the river bank, Agatha Christie's holiday home, furnished in 1950s style, is full of her family's collections of books, china and more.

⑧ South Devon Chilli Farm
MAP J6 ▪ Loddiswell, near
Kingsbridge ▪ 01548 550782 ▪ www.
southdevonchillifarm.co.uk

This farm cultivates over 200 types of chilli, and some can be seen growing in season. There's a café and a shop.

⑨ Dartmouth Royal Regatta
MAP K5 ▪ 01803 834912 (during the
Regatta) ▪ Late Aug ▪ www.dartmouth
regatta.co.uk

Pageantry is the order of the day at this annual jamboree celebrating the port's maritime traditions.

⑩ Dartmouth Museum
MAP K5 ▪ Duke St ▪ 01803
832923 ▪ Open Apr–Oct: 10am–4pm
Tue–Sat, 1–4pm Sun & Mon; Nov–
Mar: 1–4pm daily ▪ Adm ▪ www.
dartmouthmuseum.org

A collection of maritime models and more is housed in here.

Places to Eat

1 The Elephant Restaurant and Brasserie
MAP K5 ▪ 3 & 4 Beacon Terrace, Torquay ▪ 01803 200044 ▪ Closed Sun & Mon ▪ ££

This Michelin-starred restaurant (see p62) features local fish, seafood, meat as well as vegetables grown on the chef's farm.

2 Lympstone Manor
MAP L4 ▪ Courtlands Lane, Exmouth ▪ 01395 202040 ▪ £££

A venture by culinary genius Michael Caines, this boutique country hotel has three restaurants and a vineyard.

3 Riverford Field Kitchen
MAP J5 ▪ Wash Farm, Buckfastleigh ▪ 01803 762074 ▪ ££

A friendly, organic farm restaurant, serving hearty lunches and dinners at wooden communal tables.

Rockfish's airy dining room

4 Rockfish
MAP K6 ▪ 8 South Embankment, Dartmouth ▪ 01803 832800 ▪ ££

The first branch of chef and writer Mitch Tonks' seafood restaurant is laid-back yet chic. Try the fish tacos or go for the traditional fish and chips that comes with unlimited fries.

5 Café Alf Resco
MAP K5 ▪ Lower St, Dartmouth ▪ 01803 835880 ▪ Open for breakfast & lunch only ▪ £

A local favourite, this child-friendly café with a terrace serves pastries, baguettes and lunchtime specials.

PRICE CATEGORIES
For a three-course meal for one with half a bottle of wine, including taxes and extra charges.

£ under £35   ££ £35–£55   £££ over £55

6 The Curator Kitchen
MAP K5 ▪ 2 The Plains, Totnes ▪ 01803 865570 ▪ Closed Sun ▪ ££

An Italian osteria where local produce from Totnes and the Marche region of Italy come together with well-chosen wines. The Curator Café below serves wood-roasted coffee.

7 Gidleigh Park
MAP J4 ▪ Chagford ▪ 01647 432367 ▪ £££

Chris Simpson is the latest chef to lead this Michelin-starred kitchen (see p62). His inventive menu combines Far East influences with an excellent selection of meticulously sourced local ingredients.

8 The Pig at Combe
MAP L3 ▪ Gittisham, Honiton ▪ 01404 540400 ▪ ££

This is a romantic Elizabethan manor house hotel. It has a restaurant with a kitchen garden, sources its own vegetables and offers outdoor seating.

9 Barbican Kitchen
MAP Q6 ▪ 60 Southside St, Plymouth ▪ 01752 604448 ▪ Closed Sun & Mon ▪ ££

Set in the historic Plymouth Gin Distillery (see p82), this relaxed brasserie is famed for its Friday fish and chips, using the day's catch fresh from the boats at Looe in Cornwall.

10 Seahorse
MAP K6 ▪ 5 South Embankment, Dartmouth ▪ 01803 835147 ▪ Closed Sun & Mon ▪ £££

Mitch Tonks' flagship restaurant specializes in fresh fish and shellfish grilled on an open charcoal fire. There are excellent-value lunch and early dinner menus.

See map on pp78–9

🔟 North Cornwall

With the Atlantic hammering on its coast, North Cornwall feels harsher than the county's more sheltered southern seaboard. Abandoned engine houses and chimney stacks recall its industrial past, while numerous Wesleyan chapels reveal the faith of its mining population. Between the cliffs are some of the region's best surf beaches. You can enjoy fine seafood in Padstow, explore historic buildings at Prideaux Place and Lanhydrock, and hunt out Arthurian connections, not least the ruins at Tintagel.

Ruins of Tintagel Castle

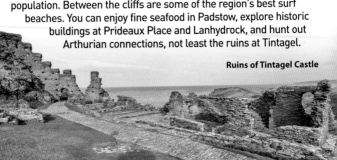

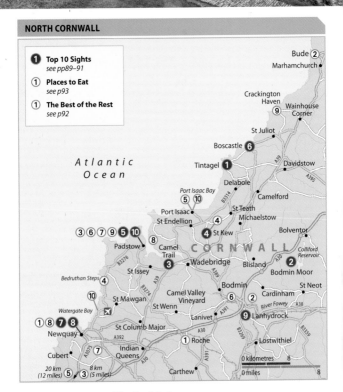

NORTH CORNWALL

① **Top 10 Sights**
see pp89–91

① **Places to Eat**
see p93

① **The Best of the Rest**
see p92

Atlantic Ocean

Bude ②
Marhamchurch

Crackington Haven
Wainhouse Corner ⑨

St Juliot

Boscastle ⑥

Tintagel ①
Davidstow

Delabole
Camelford

Port Isaac Bay ⑤ ⑩
Port Isaac
St Endellion
St Teath
Michaelstow
Bolventor

③ ⑥ ⑦ ⑨ ⑤ ⑩   St Kew ④
④ St Kew
Colliford Reservoir

⑧
Padstow   Camel Trail
③   Wadebridge   Blisland   ②
Bodmin Moor
St Neot

Bedruthan Steps ④
St Issey

Camel Valley Vineyard
Bodmin   ⑥ ②   Cardinham
River Fowey   A38

⑩
St Mawgan   St Wenn
Watergate Bay

① ⑧ ⑦ ⑧
Newquay
St Columb Major
Lanivet   ⑨ Lanhydrock
① Roche
Lostwithiel

Cubert ⑦   Indian Queens
20 km (12 miles)   ⑤ ③ 8 km (5 miles)   Carthew

C O R N W A L L

0 kilometres   8
0 miles   8

Previous pages Dramatic cliffs at Land's End

1 Tintagel Castle

MAP D2 ▪ Tintagel ▪ 01840 770328 ▪ Opening times vary, check website for details; advance booking recommended ▪ Adm ▪ www.english-heritage.org.uk

This coastal stronghold is one of the country's most romantic castle ruins. Its appeal is enhanced by its Arthurian associations; it is the supposed birthplace of the Once and Future King. The structure, however, probably dates from the 12th century, when it belonged to the Norman earls of Cornwall. There may already have been a Roman fortification and traces of a Celtic monastery have been found here too.

2 Bodmin Moor

MAP E3

Cornwall's great inland wilderness is made of the same granite mass as Dartmoor and has the same mixture of rugged grandeur interspersed with splashing rivers and shady woodland. Dotted with mysterious prehistoric remains such as the Hurlers and Trethevy Quoit, the moor has a plethora of places associated with King Arthur and his knights. The moor also has a distinction of being a World Heritage Site. The mining industry here is nearly 4,000 years old. In the midst of the desolate expanses lie appealing villages, such as Blisland, St Neot's and Altarnun.

Cyclists on the Camel Trail

3 Camel Trail

MAP E3–D3

This walking and cycling route runs for 27 km (17 miles) between Padstow and the edge of Bodmin Moor. The Padstow–Wadebridge section is on a resurfaced railway track and has abundant birdlife along Camel Estuary. From Wadebridge, the route heads southeast towards Bodmin before following the river through the woods north to Poley's Bridge. The tourist offices at Padstow, Wadebridge and Bodmin all have leaflets, detailed guides and maps of the route.

4 Camel Valley Vineyard

MAP D4 ▪ Nanstallon, Bodmin ▪ 01208 77959 ▪ Open Mon–Fri; Easter–Sep: Mon–Sat ▪ www.camel valley.com

Set on the slopes of the Camel Valley, this vineyard, founded in 1989 by an ex-RAF pilot and his wife, is the largest in Cornwall. It grows a number of grape varieties and produces sparkling wines, and red, white and rosé wines, many of them to be found in the region's top restaurants. Book ahead for weekday tours with wine tasting in season (young adults need to provide proof they are aged 18 or over).

The sprawling Bodmin Moor

Colourful fishing trawlers moored at Padstow's harbour

5 Padstow

Both fishing port and seaside resort, Padstow *(see pp34–5)* is also Cornwall's gastronomic capital, synonymous with gourmet food since seafood champion Rick Stein established a restaurant here in the 1970s. The beaches nearby attract both surfers and families, and the sheltered Camel Estuary has great walking and cycling routes.

6 Boscastle
MAP D2

The great wall of cliffs comprising much of North Cornwall's coast is sliced through here by the Valency and Jordan rivers, which twist through a ravine to a harbour. Boscastle was devastated by a flash flood in 2004, but the damage has been repaired and the village has regained its serenity. Look out for the blowhole known as Devil's Bellows, below Penally Point.

Sand Lizard, Newquay Zoo

CORNWALL'S MINEWORKS

An iconic image of the Cornish landscape is the engine house and chimney that denote the existence of a former mine. North Cornwall is dotted with these castle-like granite structures, which hark back to a time when the county was producing up to two-thirds of the world's copper and tin. The industry fell into decline in the 1870s.

7 Newquay's Beaches
MAP C4

Newquay developed as a beach resort after the railway arrived in the 1870s, and is now one of Britain's pre-eminent surf resorts, hosting numerous competitions at Fistral Beach. Holywell Bay and Perran Beach are also highly regarded surfing spots, while the more sheltered Towan Beach, Tolcarne and Lusty Glaze are better for families. Watergate Bay attracts the extreme sports crowd.

8 Newquay Zoo
MAP C4 ▪ Trenance Gardens ▪ 01637 873342 ▪ Open daily ▪ Adm ▪ www. newquayzoo.org.uk

This zoo holds more than 130 species and boasts an active conservation and education agenda. Visitors can meet the animals and watch them being fed. Look out for the graceful red pandas and comical lemurs, and have fun feeding fish to the penguins and mealy worms to the meerkats. There's also a Dragon Maze.

9 Lanhydrock

The finest house in Cornwall *(see pp12–13)* was originally Jacobean, but little of it survived a fire in 1881, which makes the Victorian interior visible today – restored by the

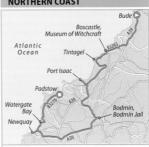

National Trust – all the more astonishing. It comprises some 50 rooms, including the maids' quarters and the lavish rooms of the Agar-Robartes family, but the highlights are the impressive kitchens and sculleries. The gardens and parkland are worth exploring.

⑩ Prideaux Place

This mansion *(see p34)* blends Elizabethan splendour with 18th-century Gothic. Highlights include the Great Chamber, with an illustrated plaster ceiling, and the oak-panelled Great Hall. Look out for the carving of Elizabeth I standing on a pig (a symbol of vice) next to the fireplace. The morning room has paintings by Cornish artist John Opie.

Library at Prideaux Place

▶ MORNING

Cornwall's northernmost resort of Bude has fine beaches for a morning dip. From here, the A39 plunges south; branch off onto the B3263 to **Boscastle** for a stroll along its harbour and to explore the **Museum of Witchcraft** *(see p46)*. On the way in or out of the village, stop at St Juliot's church, where Thomas Hardy once worked as an architect. Travel 6 km (4 miles) to **Tintagel** *(see p89)*, its ruined castle is said to have been King Arthur's birthplace. After touring the ruins, lunch in a local café, or head south to the small harbour village of **Port Isaac** *(see p92)*.

AFTERNOON

After lunch, head inland to drive to Bodmin, an ancient market town featuring Cornwall's largest parish church. You can also visit the **Bodmin Jail** *(see p92)* and the Courtroom Experience next to the tourist office, where you can cast your vote in a re-enactment of a celebrated murder trial from 1844. From Bodmin, take the A30 west to **Newquay**, which has some of Cornwall's best beaches. The zoo is located here too. You can head up the coast on the B3276 and stop at **Watergate Bay** *(see p50)*, where The Beach Hut *(see p93)* is a great spot for snacks. Surfing equipment can be rented at the Extreme Academy. For dinner, continue up the B3276 to **Padstow**, which has a wide range of top-rated seafood restaurants *(see p93)*.

See map on p88

The Best of the Rest

Ruins of a chapel atop Roche Rock

1 Roche Rock Hermitage
MAP D4

Situated on top of a dramatic granite outcrop are the ruins of a chapel built as a hermitage in 1409. It is associated with numerous Cornish folk tales.

2 Cardinham Woods
MAP E3 ▪ Bikes for hire ▪ www.forestryengland.uk

There are four forest walks and three waymarked trails for mountainbikers, plus a café and picnic areas.

3 Callestick Farm
MAP C5 ▪ Callestick, Truro ▪ 01872 573126 ▪ Open Easter–Oct: 10am–5:30pm Mon–Sat (until 5pm Sun) ▪ www.callestickfarm.co.uk

Watch ice cream being made using clotted cream from the milk of the farm's cattle – and sample it too.

4 Bedruthan Steps
MAP C3

The jagged slate outcrops on this beach were said to be the stepping stones of the giant Bedruthan. A cliffside staircase descends to the beach but bathing is unsafe.

5 Wheal Coates and East Pool Mine
MAP C4–5 ▪ Wheal Coates: St Agnes; 01872 552412 ▪ East Pool Mine: Pool; 01209 315027 ▪ Adm ▪ www.national trust.org.uk

These former tin mines are today owned by the National Trust.

6 Bodmin Jail
MAP D4 ▪ Berrycoombe Rd, Bodmin ▪ 01208 76292 ▪ Open 9:30am–6:30pm Sun–Thu (until 5pm Fri & Sat) ▪ Adm ▪ www.bodminjail.org

Visits to this 1779 jail include tours of the "execution pit" and the cells.

7 Trerice
MAP C4 ▪ Kestle Mill, Newquay ▪ 01637 875404 ▪ Open Mar–Oct: 11am–5pm daily ▪ Adm ▪ www. nationaltrust.org.uk

This Elizabethan National Trust manor has a splendid barrel-roofed Great Chamber. You can play kayles (Cornish skittles) in the grounds.

8 St Enodoc
MAP D3 ▪ Daymer Bay ▪ www.northcornwallclusterof churches.org.uk

This tiny 13th-century church appears hidden amid dunes on a golf course. Poet John Betjeman is buried here.

9 Crackington Haven
MAP E2

This beach is backed by cliffs rising upto 130 m (430 ft), with a rock strata.

10 Port Isaac
MAP D3

A North Cornish fishing village with winding lanes and a working harbour.

Clifftops above Port Isaac

Places to Eat

PRICE CATEGORIES

For a three-course meal for one with half a bottle of wine, including taxes and extra charges.

£ under £35 ££ £35–£55 £££ over £55

1 Lewinnick Lodge
MAP C4 ▪ Pentire Headland, Newquay ▪ 01637 878117 ▪ ££

Seafood is the speciality at this coastal restaurant. Take in the views from the terrace or dine in the main restaurant, bar or beer garden.

2 L.A.B
MAP E2 ▪ Summerleaze Beach, Bude ▪ 01288 355222 ▪ ££

Overlooking the Atlantic, this café serves baguettes and burgers during the day. By night it is a classy candle-lit bistro with a focus on seafood.

3 Paul Ainsworth at No. 6
MAP D3 ▪ 6 Middle St, Padstow ▪ 01841 532093 ▪ Closed Sun & Mon ▪ £££

Dress up for dining in this Georgian town house with contemporary decor and sophisticated food.

4 St Kew Inn
MAP D3 ▪ St Kew, Bodmin ▪ 01208 841259 ▪ ££

This 15th-century inn, nestled in the heart of the Cornish countryside, uses locally sourced seasonal produce in their dishes and offers cask ales.

5 Restaurant Nathan Outlaw
MAP D3 ▪ 6 New Rd, Port Isaac ▪ 01208 880896 ▪ Closed Sun & Mon ▪ £££

Chef and writer Nathan Outlaw's fish and seafood restaurant *(see p63)* serves a single set tasting menu based around the morning's catch.

6 Stein's Fish & Chips
MAP D3 ▪ South Quay, Padstow ▪ 01841 532700 ▪ £

The most affordable and relaxed of Stein's eateries, this place serves some of the most succulent fish and chips. Check out Stein's Fishmongers and Seafood Bar next door.

7 The Seafood Restaurant
MAP D3 ▪ Riverside, Padstow ▪ 01841 532700 ▪ £££

This is a lively restaurant *(see p63)* whose walls are covered with paintings. The menu features dishes familiar from Rick Stein's books and TV programmes, along with newer creations.

The Seafood Restaurant

8 Rick Stein Fistral
MAP C4 ▪ Fistral Beach, Newquay ▪ 01637 303103 ▪ Closed Mon–Wed ▪ £

The food is served here in cardboard boxes in a stunning setting. Enjoy a range of dishes, from fish and chips to pad thai and Goan chicken curry.

9 St Petroc's Bistro
MAP D3 ▪ 4 New St, Padstow ▪ 01841 532700 ▪ ££

Smaller than the Seafood Restaurant, this Stein venture has fewer choices on the menu and lower prices, but delivers the goods. Meat is given equal billing with seafood.

10 The Beach Hut
MAP C4 ▪ Watergate Bay ▪ 01637 860543 ▪ ££

With its stunning beachside location, this is a casual place for summer evenings. Fish specials and burgers are mainstays of the menu.

See map on p88

TOP 10 South Cornwall

With its undulating coastline and river estuaries interspersed with small settlements, South Cornwall is ripe for exploration. Fowey and fishing villages such as Polperro should not be missed, while Cornwall's capital, Truro, is small enough to negotiate on foot. The region's most famous attraction is the Eden Project, although South Cornwall's other major gardens, Trelissick and Heligan, are also essential stops. To the south, the Roseland Peninsula offers sandy coves and plenty of places to stay, eat and drink.

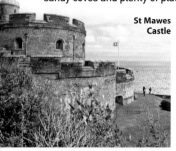

St Mawes Castle

1 St Mawes Castle

MAP C5 ■ St Mawes ■ 0370 333 1181 ■ Open Apr–Sep: 10am–6pm daily; Oct: 10am–5pm daily; Nov–Feb: 10am–4pm Sat & Sun; Mar: 10am–4pm Wed–Sun ■ Adm ■ www.english-heritage.org.uk

One of the two 16th-century artillery forts close to the Fal Estuary, this castle is better preserved than Pendennis, with heraldic devices dedicated to Henry VIII and Edward VI.

SOUTH CORNWALL

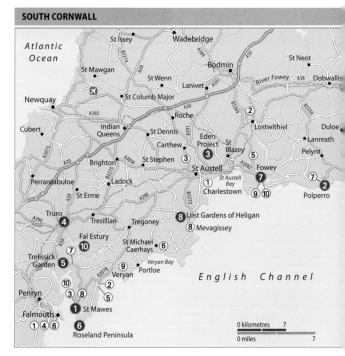

The pretty village of Polperro, set around a fishing harbour

The interior has 19th-century ships' cannons plus a cannon from c.1560, recovered off the Devon coast.

2 Polperro
MAP E4

At peak times, this Cornish fishing village is overcrowded, but visit out of season, or early in the morning, and you can appreciate its charm. A long main street leads down to a huddle of houses around the harbour. Check out the smuggling and fishing museum housed in an old pilchard factory.

3 Eden Project

Since opening in a former clay pit in 2001, this *(see pp14–15)* has been one of Cornwall's success stories. A "living theatre of plants and people", it is a great illustration of the diversity of the planet's plant life and makes for a perfect visit at any time of year.

4 Royal Cornwall Museum
MAP C5 ▪ River St, Truro ▪ 01872 272205 ▪ Open 10am–4pm Tue–Sat ▪ www.royalcornwallmuseum.org.uk

This museum is a cornucopia of Cornish culture, with everything from Bronze Age pottery to Newlyn art and minerals and fossils collections. Botanical and zoological specimens include stuffed puffins, butterflies and shells.

Exhibits at the Royal Cornwall Museum

Pensilva
Callington
St Ann's Chapel
Cotehele House 9
A390
St Mellion
Bere Alston
Bere Ferrers
Liskeard
A388
Menheniot
Landulph
A38
Deviock
A387
Saltash
A374
St Germans
Plymouth
East Looe
Looe Bay
Whitesand Bay
4
Cowsand
Rame Head

The River Fal at Trelissick Garden

5 Trelissick Garden

This lovely, extensive garden (see p19) has lawns, flowerbeds as well as hollows filled with rare plants and shrubs, sprawling parkland as well as miles of woodland paths with panoramic views of the River Fal. Late April, early May and September are the best times to visit. The King Harry chain ferry, supposedly founded by King Henry VIII after spending his honeymoon with Anne Boleyn in St Mawes (see p19), crosses the River Fal below the garden, allowing direct access to the Roseland Peninsula – the round trip by road is 43 km (27 miles).

6 Roseland Peninsula
MAP C5

A long, broad peninsula stretching south of Truro to bank the Fal Estuary, the Roseland Peninsula has lush rolling hills, subtropical gardens and unspoiled sandy coves, making it one of Cornwall's most desirable destinations. There are chic hotels and restaurants along the coast and in St Mawes, while the church of St-Just-in-Roseland is set in a lavish subtropical garden, described by the poet Sir John Betjeman as "the most beautiful churchyard on earth". Portscatho, the sandy cove of Porthcurnick, the long sands at Towan and St Anthony's Head Lighthouse are among the peninsula's coastal highlights.

7 Fowey
MAP E4

Climbing up the west bank of the River Fowey, this was one of the foremost ports of medieval England and is still a busy harbour town. Most of today's maritime activity, however, involves the pleasure boats anchored in the estuary. It is worth hiring a boat to fully enjoy the beauty of the river.

8 Lost Gardens of Heligan
MAP D4 ■ Pentewan, St Austell ■ 01726 845100 ■ Open Apr–Sep: 10am–6pm daily; Oct–Mar: 10am–5pm daily ■ Adm ■ www.heligan.com

"Lost" for 70 years and neglected for even longer, this salvaged Victorian garden is a triumph of horticultural design. Presenting a splendid pageantry of plants in a variety of habitats, including ferneries, fruit houses, Italian gardens and a kitchen garden, this subtropical "Jungle" and "Lost Valley", with its strong emphasis on conservation, appeals to both adults and kids.

Hikers on the Roseland Peninsula

9 Cotehele House

MAP H5 ■ St Dominick, Saltash ■ 01579 351346 ■ Open mid-Mar–Oct: 11am–4pm daily ■ Adm ■ www.nationaltrust.org.uk

The excellent condition of this Tudor abode is due to its abandonment by its owners, the Edgcumbe family, who left it intact for a home outside Plymouth. The National Trust took over it in 1947. The house has many original pieces of furniture, suits of armour, and a collection of embroideries and tapestries that are best seen on a bright day as the rooms have no electric light.

Façade at Cotehele House

10 Fal (Carrick Roads) Estuary

The largest of Cornwall's tidal river estuaries, the Fal *(see pp18–19)* is an ancient river valley, drowned at the end of the last ice age, when glaciers melted. From its source near St Austell, the Fal meets up with five other rivers and numerous small tidal creeks to flow into the estuary. It is 34 m (140 ft) at its deepest point. Along the river are more than 4,500 moorings for crafts, from yachts to deep water freighters, which often congregate here between contracts.

THE CHINA CLAY STORY

No one passing through the St Austell area can fail to notice the vast conical spoil heaps linked to the local china clay industry. The substance is used in a variety of products, from paint and paper to medicines. You can learn about its history and applications at the fascinating Wheal Martyn *(see p98)*.

A DRIVING TOUR IN SOUTH CORNWALL

▶ MORNING

Start your journey in Looe, a traditional resort that has gained a reputation as a shark-catch-and-release centre. A 6-km (4-mile) drive from here takes you to **Polperro** *(see p95)*, whose tightly packed houses and harbour are best appreciated before the crowds arrive. There is a small smuggling and fishing museum here. From Polperro, a scenic minor road leads you west to Bodinnick village, where ferries cross to **Fowey**. The port town has pubs and bistros that make for a good lunch stop (there is a car park near the ferry quay). Before or after eating, take a stroll around Fowey to see St Catherine's Castle, one of Henry VIII's fortifications, or follow the 6-km (4-mile) Hall Walk, climbing through woodland above the harbour to Penleath Point for tremendous views.

AFTERNOON

From Fowey, take the A3082 to St Austell, from which the A390, B3287 and A3078 will bring you to St Mawes on the **Fal (Carrick Roads) Estuary**. Here, **St Mawes Castle** *(see p94)* offers river views. Explore the **Roseland Peninsula** *(see p96)*, an area of backwaters and churches. North of St Mawes, **Trelissick Garden** offers woodland walks. The King Harry ferry crosses the river, from where it is a short drive to the county capital, Truro. Dominated by its Neo-Gothic cathedral, it has good restaurants, accommodation, and an excellent museum.

See map on pp94–5

The Best of the Rest

Elegant exterior of 19th-century Caerhays Castle, near St Austell

1 Shipwreck Treasure Museum

MAP D4 ▪ Quay Rd, Charlestown ▪ 01726 69897 ▪ Open 10am–5pm daily ▪ Adm ▪ www.shipwreckcharlestown.com

This collection has discoveries from 150 shipwrecks, including the *Titanic*.

2 Restormel Castle

MAP E4 ▪ Lostwithiel ▪ 01208 872687 ▪ Open Apr–Sep: 10am–5pm daily; Oct–Nov: 10am–4pm daily ▪ Adm ▪ www.english-heritage.org.uk

The parapet of this 13th-century keep has great views over the Fowey Valley.

3 Wheal Martyn

MAP D4 ▪ Wheal Martyn, St Austell ▪ 01726 850362 ▪ Apr–Oct: 10am–5pm daily (Nov–Mar: to 4pm) ▪ Adm ▪ www.wheal-martyn.com

This museum provides a fascinating insight into the china clay industry.

4 Mount Edgcumbe

MAP F4 ▪ Cremyll, Torpoint ▪ 01752 822236 ▪ Open Apr–Sep: 11am–4:30pm Sun–Thu ▪ Adm ▪ www.mountedgcumbe.gov.uk

Rebuilt after World War II, this 16th-century house displays Chinese porcelain and Flemish tapestries. The grounds remain open year-round.

5 Castle Dore

MAP E4 ▪ Golant

This Iron Age hillfort, with its concentric rings of defensive ridges, is considered to be the site of the palace of the legendary figure, King Mark of Cornwall.

6 Caerhays Castle

MAP D5 ▪ Gorran, St Austell ▪ 01872 501310 ▪ Tours mid-Mar–mid-Jun: 11:30am, 1pm, 2:30pm Mon–Fri ▪ Adm ▪ www.caerhays.co.uk

Take a guided tour of this 19th-century castle, an elegant backdrop to Porthluney Cove beach.

7 King Harry Ferry

MAP C5 ▪ Feock, Truro ▪ 01872 861917 ▪ www.falriver.co.uk

Shave miles off the road trip between St Mawes and Falmouth by taking this chain ferry across the Fal.

8 Mevagissey

MAP D5

With its long tradition of fishing and smuggling, this busy port is worth visiting for its good museum, pubs and seafood restaurants.

9 Veryan

MAP D5

Close to good beaches, Veryan is known for its 200-year-old circular houses designed to prevent the devil from hiding in corners.

10 Carrick Roads Estuary

MAP C5

This estuary complex is one of the world's largest natural harbours, with lovely coastal walks and sandy coves.

Places to Eat

1 The Wheel House
MAP C5 ▪ Upton Slip,
Falmouth ▪ 01326 318050
▪ Closed Sun–Tue ▪ ££
This quayside shellfish café serves simple oyster, mussel, prawn and crab dishes in *cataplanas* (Portuguese dishes), plus house wine.

2 Driftwood Restaurant
MAP C5 ▪ Rosevine, Portscatho
▪ 01872 580644 ▪ £££
Fresh seafood and local meat dishes are the mainstays of the menu at this elegant hotel-restaurant perched above the sea, offering fine views.

3 St Mawes Hotel
MAP C5 ▪ Commercial Rd,
St Mawes ▪ 01326 270 266 ▪ ££
A relaxed brasserie serving simple dishes at lunch and dinner, such as lobster and chips and homemade pizza using local ingredients. Popular for an evening prosecco or cocktail.

Bar area at St Mawes Hotel

4 Hooked on the Rocks
MAP C5 ▪ Swanpool Beach,
Falmouth ▪ 01326 311886 ▪ ££
The beachside terrace here is a great place to enjoy a selection of tapas, lobster, crab, or Cornish bouillabaisse.

5 The Hidden Hut
MAP C5 ▪ Porthcurnick Beach,
Portscatho, Truro ▪ Closed winter
▪ www.hiddenhut.co.uk ▪ £
A much-loved beach café *(see p63)* in a hut perched above sandy

Porthcurnick cove, serving simple lunches, soups, coffees and cakes, with occasional Friday feast nights.

6 Gylly Beach Café
MAP C5 ▪ Cliff Rd, Falmouth
▪ 01326 312884 ▪ ££
A heavenly place for breakfast, lunch, cakes or dinner, with splendid views over Gyllyngvase Beach. This is a Falmouth institution.

7 The Kitchen
MAP E4 ▪ The Coombes,
Polperro ▪ 01503 272812 ▪ Closed
Mon & Jan ▪ ££
This simple, intimate restaurant serves excellent fish and meat dishes, plus delicious clotted cream desserts and Cornish cheeses.

8 Hotel Tresanton
MAP C5 ▪ 27 Lower Castle Rd,
St Mawes ▪ 01326 270055 ▪ £££
Modern Mediterranean food is served in this seaside hotel *(see p118)*. A terrace offers scenic alfresco dining.

9 The Old Quay House
MAP E4 ▪ Old Quay House,
28 Fore St, Fowey ▪ 01726 833302
▪ Closed Mon & Tue lunch, Easter–Sep; times vary in winter ▪ £££
This restaurant at the Old Quay House hotel *(see p116)*, enjoys splendid views over the River Fowey and fabulous food to match.

10 Dwelling House
MAP E4 ▪ 6 Fore St, Fowey
▪ 01726 833662 ▪ £
The tiers of scrumptious cakes and delectable scones on view in the window of this period tearoom lure visitors inside. There's a menu of leaf teas to complement your chosen treat.

See map on pp94–5

TOP 10 West Cornwall and the Isles of Scilly

Egyptian House detail, Penzance

For many, the western tip of Cornwall embodies what makes the county so special. Here, you can find every kind of landscape and settlement Cornwall has to offer, from the port of Falmouth to the fishing hamlet of Mousehole, from the moorland of the Penwith Peninsula to sandy Whitesand Bay and the inhospitable cliffs at Zennor. There are prehistoric remains and the island stronghold of St Michael's Mount. Land's End and Lizard Point bring you face-to-face with the Atlantic Ocean, but you can get closer still by venturing out to the beautiful Isles of Scilly.

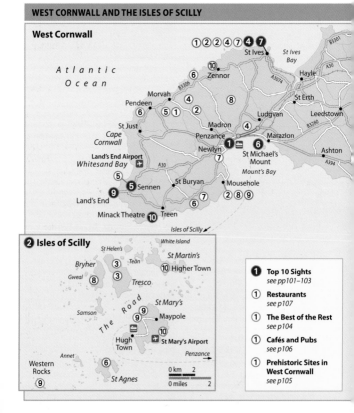

WEST CORNWALL AND THE ISLES OF SCILLY

① Top 10 Sights
see pp101–103

① Restaurants
see p107

① The Best of the Rest
see p104

① Cafés and Pubs
see p106

① Prehistoric Sites in West Cornwall
see p105

1 Penzance

Draped over a hill above a harbour, charming Penzance *(see pp32–3)* possesses two of Cornwall's best museum-galleries – Penlee House and the Exchange – and plenty of historical character in the handsome buildings of Chapel Street. From the town, all the glories of the Penwith Peninsula are easily accessible, from St Michael's Mount to the coast's rocky coves and beaches.

2 Isles of Scilly

It takes effort to reach the Isles of Scilly but few come away disappointed. Imagined by some to be the remains of the legendary lost land of Lyonnesse, which sank below the waves after the last battle

Boats off Bryer Island, Isles of Scilly

between Arthur and Mordred, this scattered archipelago is breathtakingly beautiful, sprinkled with hundreds of tiny, jagged rocks and islets. Of the five inhabited islands, the main island is St Mary's. The chicest retreat is privately owned Tresco, home to the Abbey Gardens, while Bryher, St Martin's and St Agnes appeal to those who want to escape from contemporary life.

3 Trebah Garden

Subtropical Trebah *(see p18)* is one of the most beautiful gardens in Cornwall, spilling down to the waters of the River Helford. Now owned by the Trebah Garden Trust, the gardens were created by Charles Fox, a Quaker, scientist and owner of an iron foundry, who paid meticulous attention to every detail. Highlights include valleys of hydrangeas and azaleas, a water garden and a river beach.

Footpath through Trebah Garden

4 Tate St Ives

A beacon of modern art, this gallery *(see p30)* pays homage to the local schools of art that have flourished in the area, while also showcasing contemporary work. Converted from a gasworks in 1993, the building is a modernist statement in itself, with a rooftop terrace offering stunning ocean views.

5 Barbara Hepworth Museum and Sculpture Garden

One of the foremost sculptors of the 20th century, Hepworth was inspired by the granite landscapes of West Cornwall and settled in St Ives in 1939. Her sleek, abstract sculptures can be seen in her former St Ives studio *(see p30)*. Smaller works are displayed inside, while the adjoining walled garden, laid out by Hepworth herself, provides an ideal setting for her large-scale geometric forms.

> **STARGAZY PIE**
>
> According to legend, after a winter of storms when boats had been unable to put out to sea, Mousehole's people were starving. On 23 December, fisherman Tom Bawcock braved the storm and landed a huge catch of pilchards, which were then cooked up by the villagers into stargazy pie.

6 St Michael's Mount

This castle residence in Mount's Bay *(see pp22–3)* can be reached by causeway or passenger ferry, followed by a steep climb up to the house itself. Inside, the most impressive rooms are the Tudor Great Hall and the dainty Blue Drawing Room. Other rooms hold armour, weaponry and memorabilia. Views from the battlements are stupendous.

St Michael's Mount

Boats at St Ives' sandy waterfront

7 St Ives

The Mediterranean flavour of this seaside town *(see pp30–31)* is clearly visible with its maze of flowery lanes climbing up the hill. The clear light and rugged landscape were a major draw for a succession of artists who settled here, renting studios from local fishermen. Today, tourists have replaced pilchards as the town's mainstay, thronging its numerous galleries, sandy beaches and elegant restaurants every summer. To escape the crowds, climb up to the Island, a grassy headland with views across St Ives Bay.

8 Lizard Peninsula
MAP C6–B6

As the southernmost peninsula in Britain, the Lizard is an area of extreme contrasts, stretching from the glassy waters, whitewashed villages and ancient oak woodland of the River Helford, across open heathland to serpentine cliffs, dramatic sculpted bays and unspoiled fishing villages such as Cadgwith Cove. On the southwest edge of bleak Goonhilly Downs is stunning Kynance Cove.

9 Land's End
MAP A6

The westernmost tip of the British mainland holds a perennial fascination. The headland offers panoramic views over the coast and to rocky outcrops out at sea with, intriguing names such as Dr Syntax Head and the Armed Knight. The Longships lighthouse, 2 km (1 mile) out, is also usually visible. At times you can spot Wolf Rock lighthouse, 15 km (9 miles) to the southwest, and even the Isles of Scilly, 45 km (28 miles) away.

View from Minack Theatre

10 Minack Theatre

The vision of one woman, Rowena Cade *(see p28)*, the Minack *(see pp28–9)* is a unique attraction in Cornwall. Just like a Roman amphitheatre on some Mediterranean shore, the theatre has been carved out of the cliff-face above the sea, creating a magical setting for watching plays and musicals. Shows are performed from April through to September, though the Exhibition Centre is open all year. Cancellations due to bad weather are rare, but it's advisable to wrap up warmly.

A WALK FROM NEWLYN TO PORTHCURNO

▶ MORNING

If you're in **Newlyn** *(see p104)* early enough, look in on the fish auction that takes place here every morning. Start your walk along a cycle-path running south from the harbour. After walking about 2 km (1 mile), you will reach the bijou fishing village *(see p104)* of **Mousehole** (pronounced "mowzel") . The place was ransacked by a Spanish raiding party in 1595, who reputedly left just one building standing – the 14th-century Keigwin House, which is still there. Walk through the village and pick up the coast path heading south to reach Point Spaniard where the raiders supposedly landed. The path then swerves inland before meeting the coast at Carn Du, the eastern point of Lamorna Cove. Stop for lunch at the Lamorna Cove Café *(Lamorna Cove, Penzance)*.

AFTERNOON

From Lamorna the path sticks close to the rocky coast. Follow it past Tater Du lighthouse and round Boscawen Point to St Loy's Cove. For this stretch of the walk there are no cafés, so make sure you stock up with snacks. After a short walk, mainly on the clifftop, you will reach unspoiled Penberth Cove – little more than a few cottages and fishing boats. Continue along the clifftop, past the Iron Age fort of **Treryn Dinas** *(see p28)*, where you can see the famous **Logan Rock** *(see p29)*. For dinner, follow the path down to **Porthcurno** *(see pp28–9)*, which has a café and pub, plus a museum of telegraphy and the **Minack Theatre**.

See map on pp100–101

The Best of the Rest

① Cornish Seal Sanctuary
MAP B5 ▪ Gweek, Helston ▪ 01326 221361 ▪ Open 10am–4pm daily ▪ Adm ▪ www.sealsanctuary.co.uk

Sick or injured seals are brought here from all over the country. You can tour the pools and the hospital.

Mousehole's sheltered harbour

② Mousehole
MAP A5

With its steep, cobbled alleyways and higgledy-piggledy whitewashed houses, popular Mousehole is the quintessential Cornish fishing village.

③ Helford and Frenchman's Creek
MAP C5

The village of Helford is the starting point for a walk through oak wood-land to Frenchman's Creek, named after Daphne du Maurier's novel.

④ Tremenheere Sculpture Gardens
MAP B5 ▪ Gulval, Penzance ▪ 01736 448089 ▪ Open mid-Feb–Oct: 10:30am–5:30pm daily ▪ Adm ▪ www.tremenheere.co.uk

Contemporary sculpture and art installations blend with lush sub-tropical planting in a sheltered valley.

⑤ Helford Passage
MAP C5

This pretty village lies across the river from Helford. The Ferryboat Inn terrace is a great place to watch the local gig rowers training.

⑥ Geevor Tin Mine
MAP A5 ▪ Pendeen ▪ 01736 788662 ▪ Open Apr–Oct: 9am–5pm Sun–Thu; Nov–Mar: 10am–4pm Sun–Thu ▪ Adm ▪ www.geevor.com

Tour the surface works and the 18th-century tunnels at the UK's largest preserved tin mining site.

⑦ Newlyn
MAP A5

Britain's most important fishing port, was home to an influential art move-ment in the late 19th and early 20th centuries. Works of Henry Scott Tuke and Stanhope Forbes are featured in the Newlyn Art Gallery.

⑧ Glendurgan
MAP C5 ▪ Mawnan Smith ▪ 01326 252020 ▪ Open mid-Feb–Oct: 10:30am–5pm or dusk Tue–Sun (daily in Aug) ▪ Adm ▪ www.nationaltrust.org.uk

Highlights of this lovely 19th-century wooded garden (see p53) include azalea and camellia gardens and a popular cherry laurel hedge maze.

⑨ Western Rocks, Isles of Scilly
MAP A4

These remote islands are breeding grounds for grey seals and several seabird species. Landing is prohib-ited, but there are boat trips to see shipwrecks and spot birds and seals.

⑩ Lizard Lighthouse
MAP C6 ▪ 3 Lighthouse Rd, Lizard, Helston ▪ 01326 290202 ▪ Open Apr–Oct: 10am–5pm daily ▪ Adm

Climb the southernmost lighthouse in mainland Britain for displays on morse code, semaphore and sounding foghorns. It's also a bird-watching site.

See map on pp100–101

Prehistoric Sites in West Cornwall

1 Chun Castle
MAP A5 ■ Near Morvah, off B3318

The walls of this Iron Age hillfort are mainly collapsed, but in parts they reach a height of 3 m (9 ft), and the gateposts still stand. The ruined huts inside date from the Dark Ages.

2 Lanyon Quoit
MAP A5 ■ Near Morvah

Also known as the Giant's Quoit or Giant's Table, this capped burial chamber is one of the most accessible of West Penwith's prehistoric remains.

3 Halliggye Fogou
MAP C6 ■ Trelowarren, Mawgan, Helston ■ Open daily

This is one of the most impressive of West Cornwall's *fogous* – long underground structures from the Iron Age.

4 Men-an-Tol
MAP A5 ■ Near Morvah, off Morvah–Madron Rd

The Cornish name (which means stone-with-a-hole) very accurately describes this Bronze Age monument that was long thought to have mystical healing powers. Situated on moorland, it is 2,500–4,000 years old.

5 Chun Quoit
MAP A5 ■ Near Morvah, off B3318

On open moorland, this quoit – a neolithic chamber tomb topped by a flat stone and resembling a giant granite mushroom – dates from around 2,000 BC.

6 Tregiffian Burial Chamber
MAP A6 ■ Near Lamorna, off B3315

This barrow tomb revealed a funerary urn and cremated bones when it was excavated in 1967.

7 The Merry Maidens
MAP A6 ■ Near Lamorna, off B3315

Considered Cornwall's most perfect stone circle. According to legend, it is the remains of 19 maidens turned to stone for carousing on the Sabbath.

8 Chysauster
MAP A5 ■ Near Zennor ■ 07831 757934 ■ Open Apr–Oct ■ Adm

Cornwall's most complete prehistoric monument consists of stone-walled houses arranged around courtyards, where you can discern a number of hearths, basins and drains.

9 Bant's Carn, Isles of Scilly
MAP B4 ■ Halangy Down, St Mary's

One of the Isles' many megalithic monuments, this atmospheric burial chamber on St Mary's has a roof comprising four huge slabs.

10 Porth Hellick Barrow, Isles of Scilly
MAP B4 ■ Porth Hellick Down, St Mary's

Located in the southeastern corner of St Mary's island, this is the best-preserved of the prehistoric tombs on the Isles of Scilly.

Chun Quoit

Cafés and Pubs

① Pedn Olva

This pub *(see p116)* is owned by the St Austell Brewery and is set on the promontory between St Ives' two beaches. Try the local goat's cheese with a local beer – it's unforgettable. Accommodation is also available.

② The Sloop Pub

MAP B5 ▪ St Ives ▪ 01736 796584

Enjoy a sumptuous meal at this iconic pub. Choose from homemade gin, Cornish ales and lagers, and a seafood platter to complete the meal.

③ New Inn

MAP A4 ▪ Tresco, Isles of Scilly ▪ 01720 422849

A stylish pub with dining in a courtyard as well as inside. Offers superior pub food, such as Bryher lobster and chips or Tresco beef burgers.

④ Blue Anchor Inn

MAP B5 ▪ 50 Coinagehall St, Helston ▪ 01326 562821

Enjoy the medieval atmosphere at this former monks' resthouse dating from the 15th century. Cosy nooks and home-brewed Spingo ales are the main attractions.

⑤ Kynance Cove

MAP B5 ▪ Kynance Cove, Helston ▪ 01326 290436

A beach café in a former fisherman's cottage – the decked terrace is a perfect place to relax and watch the dramatic cove change with the rise and fall of the tide.

⑥ Turks Head

MAP A4 ▪ St Agnes, Isles of Scilly ▪ 01720 422434

The most southwesterly pub in Britain has views of the sea and a community hub, serving Turks Ale, crab rolls and great Cornish pasties.

⑦ Ferry Boat Inn

MAP C5 ▪ Helford Passage ▪ 01326 250625

With a terrace overlooking the River Helford, the hearty lunches and lighter snacks here are popular with walkers on the coastal path.

⑧ Crab Shack

MAP A4 ▪ Bryher, Isles of Scilly ▪ 01722 422947 ▪ Closed Oct–Apr

Pop on a pinny, roll up your sleeves and dig into mussels, scallops or crabs, with chips, salad and wine at this simple wooden shack.

⑨ Ship Inn

MAP A5 ▪ South Cliff, Mousehole ▪ 01736 731234

You can almost feel the sea spray in this fisherman's pub above the harbour, full of maritime character. Battered catch of the day with chips is usually on the menu.

⑩ Tinners Arms

MAP A5 ▪ Zennor ▪ 01736 796927

It's the only pub in the village and it happens to be a great one. Tinner's Arms has served the locals for more than 700 years. Try the local Newlyn crab sandwich for lunch.

Kynance Cove

Restaurants

1 Kota Restaurant
MAP B5 ■ Harbour Head, Porthleven ■ 01326 562407 ■ Closed Sun & Mon ■ ££

Chef Jude adds an Asian twist to food made using organic Cornish produce at this harbourside restaurant.

2 Blas Burgerworks
MAP B5 ■ The Warren, St Ives ■ 01736 797272 ■ £

St Ives' lively gourmet burger restaurant serves some excellent chargrilled Cornish burgers. Vegetarian options include a black bean burger and grilled halloumi.

3 The Ruin Beach Café
MAP B4 ■ Tresco, Isles of Scilly ■ 01720 424849 ■ £

Beautifully styled restaurant housed in a former smugglers' cottage, with terrace seating and a contemporary Mediterranean menu, including pizzas from a wood-burning oven.

4 Porthminster Beach Café
MAP B5 ■ Porthminster Beach, St Ives ■ 01736 795352 ■ Closed Mon in winter ■ ££

A beach café by day and a smart and pricey restaurant at night, this place serves dishes such as monkfish curry or crispy squid with miso dressing.

5 The First & Last Inn
MAP A5 ■ Sennen ■ 01736 871680 ■ www.firstandlastinn.co.uk ■ ££

Just a mile from Lands End, this historic pub has been welcoming crowds since the 17th century. It now offers hearty meals and local ales beside an open fire or outside in the sheltered garden.

6 Gurnard's Head
MAP A5 ■ Zennor ■ 01736 796928 ■ ££

A stylish, relaxed gastro-pub serving Mediterranean dishes using fresh fish and locally sourced meat and produce.

Gurnard's Head, Zennor

7 Porthmeor Beach Café
MAP B5 ■ Porthmeor, St Ives ■ 01736 793366

Located just above Porthmeor Beach, the food here is inspired by far-flung cuisines and the dessert tapas are sublime.

8 2 Fore Street
MAP A5 ■ 2 Fore St, Mousehole ■ 01736 731164 ■ ££

Head to this relaxed French-style bistro right by the harbour for unfussy dishes such as Newlyn crab soufflé.

9 Juliet's Garden Restaurant
MAP B4 ■ St Mary's, Isles of Scilly ■ 01720 422228 ■ Closed Nov–Mar ■ ££

Enjoy a daytime snack or a candle-lit dinner at this spot with sea views.

10 Adam's Fish and Chips
MAP B4 ■ Higher Town, St Martin's ■ 01720 423082 ■ Closed Oct–Mar ■ £

Booking is essential at this local spot. Choose your own fish in advance.

See map on pp100–101

Streetsmart

**Surfboards at Polzeath Beach,
North Cornwall**

Getting Around

Arriving by Air

International flights arrive into London and regular flights from Europe also serve Southampton and Bristol airports. South West England's main airport is **Exeter Airport**, with direct flights from several UK and European cities. **Cornwall Airport Newquay** and **Land's End Airport** have flights to St Mary's Airport in the Scilly Isles, and there are seasonal flights from Exeter. The main airline serving the region is **Flybe**, with **Skybus** operating all flights to the Scilly Isles.

Regular buses operated by various agencies connect the airports with various points across Cornwall and Devon. A bus service from Land's End Airport to Penzance railway station is operated for Skybus passengers. Minibuses meet arrivals at St Mary's Airport, with transfers to several points on the island.

International Train Travel

St Pancras International is the London terminus for **Eurostar**, the high-speed train linking the UK with Europe. Buy tickets and passes for multiple international journeys via **Eurail** or **Interrail**. Eurostar runs a regular service from Paris, Brussels and Amsterdam to London via the Channel Tunnel. **Eurotunnel** operates a drive-on-drive-off train service between Calais and Folkestone, in South East England.

Domestic Train Travel

Great Western Railway runs trains along the main line from London's Paddington to Penzance, taking approximately 5 hours, usually calling at Exeter, Totnes, Bodmin, Plymouth, Liskeard, Truro and St Erth. The best way to travel is on a sleeper train (the Night Riviera Sleeper), but there is also a good daytime service.

Branch lines make it possible to see a fair amount of Cornwall and Devon by train. There are several useful branch lines: from Exeter, trains travel south to Torquay and Paignton and north to Barnstaple; from Liskeard, a line heads to Looe; from Par, trains run north to Newquay; and from Truro, a line goes to Falmouth.

Tickets are cheaper when they are bought well in advance. For multiple journeys, you can save money with Day Ranger tickets, which give one day's unlimited rail travel within Devon (£13) or Cornwall (£13.50), or Freedom of Devon and Cornwall passes, which offer unlimited rail travel within the region for 3 days out of 7, or 8 days out of 15.

Long-Distance Bus Travel

The **National Express** coaches run from London to Penzance, but the trip takes at least 9 hours. There are also services to destinations such as Exeter, Truro and Falmouth. Tickets are often cheaper if bought online in advance.

Buses

Regular buses operated by **Stagecoach** connect Exeter Airport with Exeter St David's railway station, Exeter bus station and Exmouth. There is also a regular bus service between Cornwall Airport Newquay, Newquay railway station and Padstow, operated by **First Kernow**.

Bus services, especially in rural areas, are infrequent, but if time is not an issue, buses can be a scenic and cheap way to tour the region.

There are numerous companies in Devon (all listed on the **Devon County Council** website), while in Cornwall most services are run by First Kernow, with a few local operators (listed on the **Cornwall County Council** website). Several companies offer passes for unlimited travel over 1, 3 or 7 days.

Driving

For visitors from abroad, driving in England is a challenge simply because you drive on the left. The measurement of distances in miles can add to the confusion, as can narrow roads, the many roundabouts, and scarce parking in urban areas. But in rural areas driving can be a pleasure and the key way to get around.

In summer and on Bank Holiday weekends, large numbers of drivers – many towing caravans (trailers) – travel along the M5 motorway and A38 trunk road through Devon, and on the A30 and A39 through Cornwall, so progress can be slow.

Once within Devon and Cornwall, most major roads are inland, away from the coastline of the north, and the river valleys and peninsulas of the south. Allow plenty of time if travelling by car. Satnavs often don't work, and many minor roads do not appear on road maps, so it's best to use an OS 1:25,000 map. There is a toll charged to cross the Tamar Bridge from Cornwall into Devon.

Ferries

Brittany Ferries links Plymouth with Roscoff in France and Santander in Spain. From mid-March to October, **Isles of Scilly Travel** runs ferries from Penzance to the islands. The **MS Oldenberg**, operated by the **Lundy Shore Office**, sails to Lundy Island from Ilfracombe and Bideford from April to October.

Local car ferries across rivers and estuaries often save drivers a detour. The **Kingswear Ferry** connects to Dartmouth, while the **King Harry** chain ferry between the Roseland Peninsula and Trelissick saves drivers 43 km (27 miles). **C Toms & Son** runs a car ferry between Fowey and Bodinnick. **Padstow Ferry** shuttles passengers between Padstow and Rock, and in the summer months **Mevagissey**

Ferries runs a passenger ferry between Fowey and Mevagissey.

Cycling

Cycle routes are plentiful. Off-road routes include the Granite Way on Dartmoor, the Tarka Trail, the flat Camel Trail and the Saints Way (see pp54–5). Excellent cycle maps and guides of the National Cycle Network are published by **Sustrans**.

Walking

The **South West Coast Path** borders the entire South West Peninsula, while Bodmin Moor, Exmoor and Dartmoor are ideal for inland hikes. There are a number of coast-to-coast walks (see pp54–5).

DIRECTORY

ARRIVING BY AIR

Cornwall Airport Newquay
🖥 cornwallairport newquay.com

Exeter Airport
🖥 exeter-airport.co.uk

Flybe
🖥 flybe.com

Land's End Airport
🖥 landsendairport. co.uk

Skybus
🖥 islesofscilly-travel. co.uk/skybus

INTERNATIONAL TRAIN TRAVEL

Eurail
🖥 eurail.com

Eurostar
🖥 eurostar.com

Eurotunnel
🖥 eurotunnel.com

Interrail
🖥 interrail.eu

DOMESTIC TRAIN TRAVEL

Great Western Railway
🖥 gwr.com

LONG-DISTANCE BUS TRAVEL

National Express
🖥 nationalexpress.com

BUSES

Cornwall County Council
🖥 cornwall.gov.uk

Devon County Council
🖥 devon.gov.uk

First Kernow
🖥 firstgroup.com/ cornwall

Stagecoach
🖥 stagecoachbus.com

FERRIES

Brittany Ferries
🖥 brittany-ferries.co.uk

C Toms & Son
🖥 ctomsandson.co.uk

Isles of Scilly Travel
🖥 islesofscilly-travel. co.uk

King Harry
🖥 falriver.co.uk

Kingswear Ferry
🖥 dkfb.co.uk

Lundy Shore Office
🖥 landmarktrust.org.uk

Mevagissey Ferries
🖥 mevagissey-ferries. co.uk

Padstow Ferry
🖥 padstow-harbour. co.uk

CYCLING

Sustrans
🖥 sustrans.org.uk

WALKING

South West Coast Path
🖥 southwestcoastpath. org.uk

Practical Information

Passports and Visas

For entry requirements, including visas, consult your nearest British embassy or check the **UK Government** website. Citizens of Australia, New Zealand, Canada and the US do not need visas for stays of up to six months. Post-Brexit arrangements for citizens from EEA countries will vary depending on the terms agreed; rights of Irish citizens will not change.

Government Advice

Now more than ever, it is important to consult both your and the UK government's advice before travelling. The **UK Foreign and Commonwealth Office**, the **US State Department** and the **Australian Department of Foreign Affairs and Trade** offer the latest information on security, health and local regulations.

Customs Information

You can find information on the laws relating to goods and currency taken in or out of the UK on the **UK Government** website.

Insurance

We recommend that you take out a comprehensive insurance policy covering theft, loss of belongings, medical care, cancellations and delays, and read the small print carefully.

Emergency treatment is usually free from the National Health Service (**NHS**) for UK residents, and there are reciprocal arrangements with Australia, New Zealand and some others (check the NHS website for the latest details). Healthcare arrangements for EEA citizens are subject to change; check the NHS website for the most up-to-date information.

Health

The UK has a world-class healthcare system and emergency medical care is generally free. Visitors from abroad may have to pay upfront for medical treatment and reclaim on insurance at a later date. It is therefore important to arrange comprehensive medical insurance before you travel.

For minor ailments go to a pharmacy or chemist. These are plentiful in towns and cities. You may need a doctor's prescription to obtain certain pharmaceuticals; the pharmacist can inform you of the closest doctor's surgery or medical centre where you can see a GP (General Practitioner).

If you have an accident or a medical problem requiring non-urgent medical attention, find details of your nearest non-emergency medical service on the NHS website. Alternatively, contact **NHS 111** (the NHS emergency care service) at any hour online or by phone. If things are serious, call 999 or go to your nearest Accident and Emergency (A&E) department.

For information regarding COVID-19 vaccination requirements, consult government advice. No other inoculations are needed for the UK.

England has no special health issues, but hikers might pick up ticks, which can carry Lyme disease; if you see a tick on your body, contact a doctor or pharmacist promptly.

Unless otherwise stated, tap water in England is always safe to drink.

Smoking, Alcohol and Drugs

Smoking and "vaping" are banned in all public spaces. However, many bars and restaurants have outdoor areas where smoking is permitted.

Alcohol may not be sold to or bought for anyone under 18. The UK legal limit for drivers is 80 mg of alcohol per 100 ml of blood, or 0.08 per cent BAC (blood alcohol content). This is roughly equivalent to one small glass of wine or a pint of regular-strength lager. It is best to avoid drinking altogether if you plan to drive.

Possession of all recreational drugs is an offence and could result in a prison sentence.

ID

There is no requirement for visitors to carry ID, but in the case of a routine check you may be asked to show your passport and visa documentation. Anyone who looks under 18 (and in some cases, under 25) may be asked for photo ID to prove their age when buying alcohol.

Personal Security

Cornwall and Devon are both safe areas to visit; use your common sense and take the usual precautions.

For **emergency police**, **ambulance** or **fire brigade** services dial 999 – the operator will ask you which service you require. If you need medical help but the situation is not an emergency call the NHS 111 service.

If you have anything stolen, report the crime as soon as possible to the nearest police station. Get a copy of the crime report in order to claim your insurance. Contact your embassy or consulate immediately if your passport is stolen, or in the event of a serious crime or accident.

Be careful around the sea – currents can change quickly. Never enter the water when a red warning flag is flying. To locate beaches supervised by a lifeguard, visit the **Royal National Lifeboat Institution** (RNLI) website.

On the whole, England is a welcoming and inclusive country, with many nationalities calling it home and some of the most progressive LGBTQ+ rights in Europe. Homosexuality was legalized in England in 1967 and the UK recognized the right to legally change your gender in 2004. Even so, acceptance is not necessarily a given and communities can feel quite homogenous outside of major cities. If you do feel unsafe, the **Safe Space Alliance** pinpoints your nearest place of refuge.

Travellers with Specific Requirements

The best guide for wheelchair users is *Holidays in the British Isles* published by **Disability Rights UK**. Many modern buildings and infrastructure have been designed with wheelchairs in mind, while most trains and buses have been adapted for wheelchair use. Accessibility information for public transport is available from regional public transport websites.

Many major museums and galleries offer audio tours and induction loops for those with impaired sight and hearing. **Action on Hearing Loss** and the **Royal National Institute for the Blind** offer information and advice.

Tourism for All's website has information on accommodation, attractions, transport and places to eat. **Countryside Mobility South West** is a not-for-profit organization that rents mobility equipment – all-terrain trampers – at several sites. They also have wheelyboats for hire at several inland lakes.

DIRECTORY

PASSPORTS AND VISAS

UK Government
w gov.uk/check-uk-visa
w gov.uk/guidance/
visiting-the-uk-after-brexit

GOVERNMENT ADVICE

Australian Department of Foreign Affairs and Trade
w smartraveller.gov.au

UK Foreign and Commonwealth Office
w gov.uk /foreign-travel-advice

US State Department
w travel.state.gov

CUSTOMS INFORMATION

UK Government
w gov.uk/duty-free-goods

INSURANCE

NHS
w nhs.uk

HEALTH

NHS 111
☎ 111
w 111.nhs.uk

PERSONAL SECURITY

Emergency Number
☎ 999

Royal National Lifeboat Institution
w rnli.org

Safe Space Alliance
w safespacealliance.com

TRAVELLERS WITH SPECIFIC REQUIREMENTS

Action on Hearing Loss
w actionhearingloss.org.uk

Countryside Mobility South West
w countrysidemobility.org

Disability Rights UK
w disabilityrightsuk.org

Royal National Institute for the Blind
w rnib.org.uk

Tourism for All
w tourismforall.co.uk

Time Zone

The UK is on Greenwich Mean Time (GMT) from late October to late March. For the rest of the year it operates on British Summer Time (BST), which is one hour ahead of GMT. GMT is five hours ahead of US Eastern Standard Time and one hour behind Central European Time.

Money

The currency in England is the pound sterling (GBP). Major credit and debit cards, plus contactless payments, are widely accepted. Some smaller businesses, markets and local public transport, however, operate a cash-only policy. Cash machines are located at banks, train stations and main high streets.

Tipping in England is discretionary. In restaurants it's customary to tip 10–12.5 per cent for good service. It is usual to tip taxi drivers 10 per cent, and concierge, hotel porters and housekeeping £1–2 per bag or day.

Electrical Appliances

Electricity in the UK is 230 volts 50 Hz. Plugs have three square pins; most overseas visitors will need a plug adaptor. North American visitors will need a converter too.

Mobile Phones and Wi-Fi

Free Wi-Fi hotspots are widely available in town and city centres. Cafés and restaurants may give you their Wi-Fi password, providing you make a purchase. Many train stations in Cornwall and Devon offer free Wi-Fi, as will most hotels.

Visitors from outside the UK should check whether they are affected by data roaming charges; it may be cheaper to buy a SIM card in the UK.

Do not rely on mobile phones or other devices for navigation or emergency communications in remote areas where reception can be intermittent or non-existent.

Postal Services

Standard post in the UK is handled by **Royal Mail**. Post office branches and counters, plus England's distinctive red post boxes, are found in most towns and cities. They generally open 9am–5.30pm Monday–Friday and until 12:30pm Saturday. Stamps – 1st class, 2nd class and international – are available in post offices, shops, supermarkets and newsagents. Post offices and the Royal Mail website provide full details on postal charges.

Weather

The best times to visit Cornwall and Devon are in spring and autumn – weather in September and October is often better than it is in August. However, the weather, as throughout the UK, is unpredictable. The weather conditions here can change with alarming rapidity. Hikers especially should be careful. Make sure you check the weather forecast on TV and radio, in newspapers, at tourist offices or on the website of the **British Meteorological Office**.

The tide comes in very fast, and beach walkers have been cut off or drowned in the past – always check the tide tables before heading out. They are prominently displayed in coastal towns and villages, and can be checked online on the **BBC**, **Beach Guide** or **Windfinder** websites.

Opening Hours

Major supermarkets are generally open 8am–8pm. Other shops usually open between 9am and 10am and close at 5 or 5:30pm. On Sundays, all shops (except for small food shops) are restricted to opening for only six hours, generally 10am–4pm.

Banks usually open 9am or 9:30am to 3:30 or 4pm weekdays. Some branches also open on Saturday mornings.

Museums usually open between 9 and 10am and close between 4 and 6pm. Some close on Mondays.

On public holidays, banks close and some shops and attractions either close or operate shorter hours.

COVID-19 Increased rates of infection may result in temporary opening hours and/or closures. Always check ahead before visiting museums, attractions and hospitality venues.

Visitor Information

The official tourist board websites **Visit Devon** and **Visit Cornwall** are an excellent first stop for information, including help with accommodation. They also provide details of all the region's visitor centres. The **Dartmoor National Park** and **Exmoor National Park** websites list details of their network of visitor centres, which have useful information and books and maps on the area.

Most attractions offer concessionary rates for children, seniors and students. If you are a student, the International Student Identity Card (**ISIC**) is recommended. If you intend to visit several castles, historic homes and gardens, an annual **National Trust** membership may be worthwhile. Also worth considering is a **Cornish Heritage Trust** membership, which gives free entry to all attractions in Cornwall that are owned by English Heritage.

A useful app to download is **what3words**. This is a geocode system that divides the world into 3 m x 3 m squares and pinpoints your exact location – ideal when exploring the region's expansive countryside.

Visiting Places of Worship

Show respect by dressing modestly, especially when entering churches and religious buildings.

Responsible Tourism

Be sure to familiarize yourself with England's **Countryside Code** before you set off. This sets out the responsibilities of visitors to the countryside and includes such things as taking away your litter, keeping dogs under effective control, and leaving gates and property as you found them.

Language

English is spoken throughout Cornwall and Devon. Accents vary tremendously, however, and can at times be stronger in certain areas.

Taxes and Refunds

Value Added Tax (VAT) is charged at 20 per cent and almost always included in the marked price. Stores offering tax-free shopping display a distinctive sign and (for non-EU residents) will provide you with a VAT 407 form to validate in order to get a refund when you leave the country.

Accommodation

Cornwall and Devon offer a huge variety of accommodation, from grand Victorian seaside hotels and country retreats to B&Bs and budget hostels. There are also many camp sites and caravan sites, as well as plenty of self-catering options.

Lodgings can fill up quickly and prices become inflated during the summer, so it is worth booking well in advance. The lists of accommodation maintained by local tourist boards are useful but international booking engines have the best coverage.

DIRECTORY

POSTAL SERVICES

Royal Mail
w royalmail.com

WEATHER

BBC
w bbc.co.uk/weather/coast_and_sea/tide_tables

Beach Guide
w thebeachguide.co.uk

British Meteorological Office
w metoffice.gov.uk/public/weather/forecast

Windfinder
w windfinder.com

VISITOR INFORMATION

Cornish Heritage Trust
w cornwallheritagetrust.org

Dartmoor National Park
w dartmoor.gov.uk

Exmoor National Park
w exmoor-nationalpark.gov.uk

ISIC
w isic.org

National Trust
w nationaltrust.org.uk

Visit Cornwall
w visitcornwall.com

Visit Devon
w visitdevon.co.uk

what3words
w what3words.com

RESPONSIBLE TOURISM

Countryside Code
w gov.uk/government/publications/the-countryside-code

Places to Stay

PRICE CATEGORIES

For a standard, double room per night (with breakfast if included), taxes and extra charges.

£ under £100 ££ £100–£200 £££ over £200

Coastal

Boscastle YHA

MAP D2 ▪ Palace Stables, Boscastle ▪ 0345 3719006 ▪ www.yha.org.uk ▪ £

Set right on Boscastle's quayside, this hostel has dorms, private rooms with en suite facilities and a four-bed room with its own bathroom and kitchen. Perfect for walks on the South West Coast Path.

Lizard YHA

MAP C6 ▪ Lizard Point ▪ 0345 3719550 ▪ www. yha.org.uk ▪ £

Located on Britain's most southerly point, this hostel occupies a former four-star Victorian hotel. Choose between dorm rooms or bigger family rooms, many with sea views. There's a kitchen, sitting room and garden.

Lundy House Hotel

MAP H1 ▪ Chapel Hill, Mortehoe ▪ 01271 8703 72 ▪ www.lundyhouse hotel.webvilla.net ▪ £

Each room is different at this B&B overlooking Woolacombe Bay. Great sea views accompany the hearty breakfasts. There is a family room and a self-catering apartment.

The Beach

MAP E2 ▪ Summerleaze Crescent, Bude ▪ 01288 389800 ▪ www.thebeach atbude.co.uk ▪ ££

This lively seaside hotel, features a very cool bar with a decked terrace overlooking the beach, and rooms with limed oak furniture and king-size beds. Popular with surfers.

Norbury House

MAP H1 ▪ Torrs Park, Ilfracombe ▪ 01271 863888 ▪ www.norbury house.co.uk ▪ ££

Contemporary rooms in a stylish Victorian B&B overlooking the sea. Visitors can help themselves to drinks in the cocktail bar, or tea and biscuits in the lounge.

The Old Quay House

MAP E4 ▪ 28 Fore St, Fowey ▪ 01726 833302 ▪ theoldquayhouse.com ▪ ££

This elegant hotel is set in a whitewashed Victorian building on the banks of the River Fowey. Some of its bedrooms have balconies that overlook the estuary. Guests aged 12 and above are welcome.

Old Success Inn

MAP A5 ▪ Cove Hill, Sennen Cove ▪ 01736 871232 ▪ www.old success.co.uk ▪ ££

An unpretentious seaside pub right on Sennen Cove, with rooms decorated in Cornish coastal style. Rooms feature plantation shutters and furnishings in calming shades of sand, pebble and blue. This cosy pub also has a great terrace.

Pedn Olva

MAP B5 ▪ West Porthminster Beach, St Ives ▪ 01736 796222 ▪ www.pednolva.co.uk ▪ ££

Situated on the cliffs between the beaches at St Ives, Pedn Olva has a chic boutique feel. Many rooms have balconies, and there are terraces for alfresco drinking, or for wallowing in the plunge pool. An informal restaurant serves Modern British food.

Red Lion

MAP G2 ▪ The Quay, Clovelly ▪ 01237 431237 ▪ www.clovelly.co.uk ▪ ££

A welcoming inn with cosy rooms and lovely views of Clovelly's picturesque harbour, plus superior renditions of traditional pub grub. The Sail Loft annexe has larger bedrooms with sea views that cost only a fraction more.

Rosevine

MAP C5 ▪ Rosevine, Nr Portscatho ▪ 01872 580206 ▪ www.rosevine. co.uk ▪ ££

This country house, a stone's throw from the sea, combines the comforts offered by a luxury hotel with the independence of self-catering. Set in luxuriant gardens above a sheltered sandy cove, it has a playroom, an indoor heated pool, an adults-only lounge and a good restaurant. The studios, apartments and suites all have a kitchen and dining area.

St Petroc's
MAP D3 ■ New St, Padstow
■ 01841 532700 ■ www.
rickstein.com ■ ££
A sociable town house
hotel above a buzzy Rick
Stein bistro and bar, with
a labyrinth of stylish sitting
and reading rooms. The
ten bedrooms are not
huge, but are comfortable,
and have a nautical New
England decor.

Watersmeet Hotel
MAP H1 ■ Woolacombe
■ 01271 870333 ■ www.
watersmeethotel.co.uk
■ ££
Perched on a cliff above
the sandy Combesgate
beach, this boutique hotel
offers luxurious rooms
with stunning views of
the sea. Other facilities
include indoor and out-
door pools, a restaurant,
and a relaxing spa.

Burgh Island Hotel
MAP J6 ■ Burgh Island,
Bigbury-on-Sea ■ 01548
810514 ■ www.burgh
island.com ■ £££
Art Deco elegance on an
island reached by a tidal
causeway. Former guests
include Winston Churchill,
Noël Coward and Agatha
Christie. There's a 1930s
billiards room, cocktail
bar and swimming lagoon.
Murder mystery parties
are regularly hosted.

Hell Bay
MAP A4 ■ Bryher, Isles
of Scilly ■ 01720 422947
■ www.hellbay.co.uk
■ £££
This chic, contemporary
hotel is set above a rug-
ged bay on tiny, remote
Bryher island. There's an
outdoor heated swimming
pool, some fabulous art
and locally sourced food
in the informal restaurant.

It's excellent for families:
a games room has table
football, a pool table, a TV
and video games, including
an outdoor play area.

Idle Rocks
MAP C5 ■ Harbourside, St
Mawes ■ 01326 270270
■ www.idlerocks.com ■ £££
A lovely conversion of an
Edwardian waterfront inn,
in chic St Mawes. The
interior here is fabulous,
adorned with driftwood
sculptures, collections of
vintage bathing suits and
the like. The hotel restaurant uses the freshest local
ingredients and the south
facing terrace is perfect
for admiring the view.

The Nare
MAP C5 ■ Veryan-in-
Roseland ■ 01872 501111
■ www.narehotel.co.uk
■ £££
A family-run country
house on the Roseland
Peninsula, with warm,
traditional styling – plenty
of antiques and heirlooms.
Spectacular views can be
taken in from the relaxed
Quarterdeck and the more
formal dining room. There
is also an outdoor swim-
ming pool and a private
launch. It's ideal for
families with children,
particularly as it has
direct beach access.

The Scarlet
MAP C4 ■ Tredragon Rd,
Mawgan Porth ■ 01637
861800 ■ www.scarlet
hotel.co.uk ■ £££
This super-indulgent,
super-chic, eco hotel
is embedded in the cliffs
above Mawgan Porth
beach. There are log-
fired hot tubs, an Ayurvedic
spa, a natural swimming
pool, and a restaurant
serving Modern European

food using local produce.
It's strictly for grown-ups
only, and is the ultimate
romantic retreat.

Soar Mill Cove
MAP J6 ■ Soar Mill Cove,
Salcombe ■ 01548
561566 ■ www.soarmill
cove.co.uk ■ £££
Set in its very own
cove, a short drive from
Salcombe, this friendly
hotel has been in the
same family for three
generations. There's
plenty to entertain
adults and kids, with
an indoor saltwater
pool, tennis court, games
room, great food and a
champagne bar. The
beach and rock pools
are on the doorstep.

South Sands Hotel
MAP J6 ■ Bolt Head,
Salcombe ■ 01548 845
900 ■ www.southsands.
com ■ £££
Waves practically lap right
up to this New England-
style contemporary hotel.
It has a grand spiral staircase and an excellent
restaurant. The blue and
white theme with nautical
touches runs throughout
the 22 bedrooms.

St Edmunds
MAP D3 ■ St Edmunds
Ln, Padstow ■ 01841
532700 ■ www.rickstein.
com ■ £££
A refined Padstow retreat
in an elegant town house
with a garden and views
over the estuary – just a
couple of minutes' walk
from all the Rick Stein
restaurants. Designed
by Jill Stein, these are
the most luxurious of the
Stein rooms, with oak
floors, French windows,
plantation shutters and
bespoke oak furniture.

St Enodoc

MAP D3 ■ Rock ■ 01208 863394 ■ www.enodoc-hotel.co.uk ■ £££
One of Cornwall's pioneering seaside chic hotels, set in spacious grounds right next to a golf course, across the river from Padstow, St Ednoc can be reached by the passenger ferry. Rooms are modern with a cosy Scandinavian theme, and many have extensive estuary views. There's a spa, a beach on the doorstep, and the hotel is very family-friendly. The on-site restaurant serves fresh and healthy local dishes prepared by Masterchef winner James Nathan and his team.

Tresanton

MAP C5 ■ 27 Lower Castle Rd, St Mawes ■ 01326 270055 ■ www.tresanton.com ■ £££
Created by Olga Polizzi within the buildings of a 1940s yacht club, this hotel has sweeping views across the bay to St Anthony's lighthouse. The hotel's wooden yacht, *Pinuccia*, is available for skippered sails around the sheltered waters of the Fal Estuary and Helford River.

Watergate Bay Hotel

MAP C4 ■ Watergate Bay ■ 01637 860543 ■ www.watergatebay.co.uk ■ £££
Watergate Bay is a prime surfing location and this contemporary, family-run hotel has a very relaxed beachside vibe. Extreme Academy here is one of the best watersports schools in the country. Self-catering is available.

Country

St Benet's Abbey

MAP D4 ■ Truro Rd, Lanivet, Bodmin ■ 01208 831352 ■ www.stbenetsabbey.co.uk ■ £
Constructed in 1411, this medieval house is now a B&B located in the heart of the Cornish country-side. On offer here are comfortable rooms, one of which has a fabulous four-poster bed.

Broomhill Art Hotel

MAP H2 ■ Muddiford, Barnstaple ■ 01271 850 262 ■ www.broomhill-estate.com ■ £
The eight individually styled rooms of this hotel are set in a Victorian house surrounded by a sculpture garden. The Terra Madre restaurant serves Mediterranean food.

East Dyke Farmhouse

MAP G2 ■ Higher Clovelly ■ 01237 431216 ■ www.bedbreakfastclovelly.co.uk ■ £
A 15-minute walk above the beautiful Clovelly, this 200-year-old farmhouse offers three spacious bedrooms of which two have splendid sea views. Breakfast is served in the lovely flagstoned dining room. The Clovelly Dykes hill fort is nearby.

Okehampton YHA

MAP H3 ■ Klondyke Rd, Okehampton ■ 01837 53916 ■ www.yha.org.uk ■ £
Set in a converted railway goods shed on the northern edge of Dartmoor, this hostel caters to various pursuits, including rock climbing, abseiling, gorge scrambling, geocaching and pony trekking.

Cider House

MAP H5 ■ Buckland Abbey, Yelverton ■ 01822 259062 ■ www.cider-house.co.uk ■ ££
This boutique B&B is located on the 700-acre estate of Buckland Abbey, occupying the building where the monks used to make cider. Guests have access to the estate and abbey with waymarked trails, and to the kitchen gardens, hens and beehives. There is also glamping in two super-stylish shepherds' huts.

Coombeshead Farm

MAP E3 ■ Lewannick ■ 01566 782009 ■ www.coombesheadfarm.co.uk ■ ££
The perfect farmstay for sociable foodies, run by two chefs in a Georgian farmhouse surrounded by 66 acres of woodland and meadows, with kitchen gardens, hens, beehives, a firepit and more. Rooms are comfy, and every evening a communal three-course dinner is served using the farm's own livestock and vegetables. Guests over the age of 12 are welcome.

The Old Rectory

MAP D2 ■ St Juliot, Boscastle ■ 01840 250225 ■ Closed Dec–mid-Feb ■ www.stjuliot.com ■ ££
The writer Thomas Hardy once stayed in this rural guesthouse located on Boscastle's outskirts. All rooms are preserved in their Victorian splendour and there are some lovely wooded gardens. Children over 12 are welcome.

Gidleigh Park
MAP J4 ■ Chagford ■ 01647 432367 ■ www.gidleigh.co.uk ■ £££
A romantic haven in a striking half-timbered Tudor-style house, this hotel is set amid 107 acres of private woodland in Dartmoor National Park. The style is traditional, with plenty of antiques. while the restaurant here *(see p62)* is one of the region's most exceptional.

Hotel Endsleigh
MAP H4 ■ Milton Abbot, Tavistock ■ 01822 870000 ■ www.hotelendsleigh.com ■ £££
Created by Olga Polizzi in a 19th-century hunting lodge, Hotel Endsleigh is set in the glorious Tamar Valley. The grounds of this hotel were landscaped by Sir Humphry Repton and cover 100 acres of formal gardens, streams, woodlands, follies and grottoes. It has 19 bedrooms, many of which have views of the gardens and the river Tamar. The house retains many of its original features and is decorated with a seamless fusion of old and new, including walk-in showers and large, comfortable beds.

Town

Falmouth Lodge Backpackers
MAP C5 ■ 9 Gyllyngvase Terrace, Falmouth ■ 01326 319996 ■ www.falmouthbackpackers.co.uk ■ £
This homely hostel, in an Edwardian semi-detached house, is just a street away from Gyllyngvase beach. It has a comfy living room, a conservatory, kitchen, and outdoor spaces. Three out of six rooms can be rented as dorms or family rooms, two doubles or twins, and an en suite attic room.

Highcliffe
MAP C5 ■ 22 Melvill Rd, Falmouth ■ 01326 314466 ■ www.highcliffefalmouth.com ■ £
Engaging owners and fantastic breakfasts feature at this B&B on a residential road between the estuary and the sea. Beaches and the town are close by, and the rooms at the back have views over the roofscape of Victorian Falmouth to the estuary.

Penzance YHA
MAP B5 ■ Castle Horneck, Penzance ■ 0345 3719653 ■ www.yha.org.uk ■ £
This hostel occupies a Georgian mansion which is walking distance from the centre of Penzance. Within its grounds are a barbecue area and a camp site. Open all year, it has a self-catering kitchen and dining room, plus bunks, double and family rooms.

Chapel House PZ
MAP B5 ■ Chapel St, Penzance ■ 01736 362024 ■ www.chapelhousepz.co.uk ■ ££
This Georgian town house with views across the bay to St Michael's Mount is furnished with a mix of antiques and iconic 20th-century designer pieces. Children and dogs are welcome.

The Greenbank
MAP C5 ■ Harbourside, Falmouth ■ 01326 312440 ■ www.greenbank-hotel.co.uk ■ ££
Set on the banks of the Fal, this hotel has evolved over 400 years, with its 50 rooms across four interlinked buildings. The lounge-bar is the perfect place to sit, and there are two outdoor terraces, as well as the Working Boat pub.

Southernhay House
MAP K3 ■ 36 Southernhay East, Exeter ■ 01392 439000 ■ www.southernhayhouse.com ■ ££
This luxurious town house hotel in the city's Georgian quarter features monsoon showers and mid-room rolltop baths, giving the rooms a boudoir feel. There's also a cocktail bar and a restaurant.

Bodmin Jail Hotel
MAP D4 ■ Scarlett's Well Rd, Bodmin ■ 01208 822844 ■ www.bodminjailhotel.com ■ £££
Luxury and history are perfectly combined at this hotel, where guests stay in beautiful rooms converted from 250-year-old prison cells. Each room is en suite and features deep free-standing baths.

Star Castle
MAP B4 ■ St Mary's, Isles of Scilly ■ 01720 422317 ■ www.star-castle.co.uk ■ £££
This star-shaped fortress, built at the order of Elizabeth I, has great views from its turrets and ramparts. Inside, it's all wood-beamed ceilings, creaky staircases, and crooked rooms furnished with a miscellany of Persian rugs, Jacobean-style furniture, and comfy old sofas. There are more conventional, spacious rooms in the castle garden, along with a lovely indoor pool.

For a key to hotel price categories see p116

Index

Acknowledgments

Author

Robert Andrews has been travelling and writing travel guidebooks for 20 years. His main areas of interest are the West Country in England and southern Italy. Based in Bristol, he also writes articles, compiles anthologies and takes photographs.

Additional contributor
Ros Belford

Publishing Director Georgina Dee

Publisher Vivien Antwi

Design Director Phil Ormerod

Editorial Sophie Adam, Ankita Awasthi Tröger, Kate Berens, Rachel Fox, Lucy Richards, Sally Schafer, Anuroop Sanwalia

Cover Design Maxine Pedliham, Vinita Venugopal

Design Tessa Bindloss, Bharti Karakoti

Commissioned Photography Tim Draper, John Harrison, Nigel Hicks

Picture Research Subhadeep Biswas, Taiyaba Khatoon, Ellen Root, Rituraj Singh

Cartography Ashutosh Bharti, Suresh Kumar, James Macdonald, Casper Morris, John Plumer

Mapping based on data from the People's Map

DTP Jason Little

Production Igrain Roberts

Factchecker Elizabeth Dale

Proofreader Laura Walker

Indexer Hilary Bird

Revisions Avanika, Parnika Bagla, Dipika Dasgupta, Kate Hughes, Sumita Khatwani, Shikha Kulkarni, Alison McGill, Meghna, Azeem Siddiqui, Beverly Smart, Priyanka Thakur, Stuti Tiwari, Vaishali Vashisht, Lisa Voormeij, Tanveer Zaidi

Picture Credits

The publisher would like to thank the following for their kind permission to reproduce their photographs:
Key: a-above; b-below/bottom; c-centre; f-far; l-left; r-right; t-top

123RF.com: Brian Scantlebury 4cr.

4Corners: Pietro Canali 20–1, 50b, 51br, 60b, 102–3; Arcangelo Piai 79br; Dave Porter 82tl; Maurizio Rellini 24tr, 94cla, 96b.

Alamy Stock Photo: A.F. ARCHIVE 49br; Herb Bendicks 73tr; Kevin Britland 4cla, 18–9, 34cla, 58tl, 64bl, 68bc, 107cra; Adam Burton 4crb; E.J.Westmacott 35tc; Economic Images 58b; Greg Balfour Evans 32cl; Guy Edwardes Photography 81tl; Nick Hanna 3tr, 108–9; David Hastilow 34bl; Holmes Garden Photos 25tr; i on the world 28cb; Ian Dagnall Commercial Collection 93cr; incamerastock 29tl, 76b, 83bl; International Photobank 68tr; Christopher Jones 42t; Ian Kingsnorth 31crb; LatitudeStock 57cl; Geraint Lewis / Seed (2003–7) by Peter Randall-Page 14cb, Mary Evans Picture Library/ D H Lawrence by Jeffrey Morgan 48tl; Paul Melling 30bl; MSP Travel Images 61tr; The National Trust Photolibrary National Trust Images 96tl; Christopher Nicholson 59crb; David Pearson 4clb; Lee Pengelly 23cr; Ben Ramos 100tl; Matthias Riedinger 106b; Robertharding 2tr, 36–7; Steve Taylor ARPS 11cra, 54tl, 60tl; Anna Stevenson 56br; Derek Stone 3tl, 66b, 70–1; Peter Titmuss 40b; VIEW Pictures Ltd 15tl; Paul Washer 4cl; Washington Imaging 75bl; way out west photography 26-27ca; Westmacott 46b; Kathleen Whit 69cl.

AWL Images: Robert Birkby 73br, 101tr; Adam Burton 16–7, 29crb, 76cla; Danita Delimont Stock 103cl; Travel Pix Collection 11clb.

Depositphotos Inc: linfernum 12cl.

Dreamstime.com: Acceleratorhams 11crb, 55tr; Adeliepenguin 11cr; Alexirina27000 11b; Steve Allen 51cl; Gordon Bell 50tl; Dan Breckwoldt 4b; Colinboylett 97cl; Darrensharvey 12–3; Davidmartyn 89tr; Dreambigphotos 65tr; Hannah6d 7br; Helen Hotson 1, 10bl, 17tl, 38t, 44–5b, 57tr, 66cla, 89bl; Darren Howe 74–5; Clare Jackson 104cl; Anthony Jacobs 58c; Valerijs Jegorovs 45cr; Johnhill118 102tr; Aagje De Jong 10cl, 14–5, 39tr, 67br; Keatsy3 56t; Denis Kelly 67tl; Shahid Khan 10crb; Lymey 33clb; Sue Martin 24bl; Chris Moncrieff 10tr, 13tl; Mycolors 90c; Colin & Oksana Phillipson 53c, 90–1; Craig Russell 15cla; Andrew Roland 26br; Sharpshot 6cla; Kiril Stanchev 98t; Sally Stap 82c; Stevieuk 13crb; Petr Švec 19crb; Jennifer Thompson 83cr; Travelling-light 63tr; Vaclav Volrab 28cla; Ian Woolcock 11tl, 30–1, 33tl, 41crb, 86–7, 92b, 105b; Pavla Zakova 80–1.

Driftwood: 61clb.

English Heritage: Dorling Kindersley /Nigel Hicks 44tl.

Getty Images: AFP 49tl; Dave Porter Peterborough Uk 16bl; Andreas von Einsiedel 91bl; Fox Photos 48br; Franz-Marc Frei 27cra; Hulton Deutsch 39clb; Loop Images 84cla, / Sebastian Wasek 4t; Nature Picture Library / Laurent Gesli 78cla; James Osmond 54–5; Print Collector 38br; Olaf Protze 2tl, 8–9, 22br,

24c, 25bl, 32–3, 101br; Robertharding / Peter Barritt 27tl; Andy Sheppard 69br; Paul Thompson 14cla, 30crb; Peter Unger 88ca; Sebastian Wasek 17bc.

Gidleigh Park, Andrew Brownsword Hotels: 60t.

©HeliganGardensLtd: 52t.

iStockphoto.com: George Clerk 64tr; csfotoimages 74cl; fieldwor 61br; PaulMaguire 92tl; 95t; George Standen 34–5.

Masons Arms: 60bl.

National Maritime Museum Cornwall: 19tl.

National Trust Images: Lynda Aiano 46ca, 42c; Andrew Butler 52clb; Andreas von Einsiedel 61br; Angelo Hornak 43tr; John Millar 53tr.

PENGUIN and the Penguin logo are trademarks of Penguin Books Ltd: *Lorna Doone* by R. D. Blackmore 48c.

Penlee House: 47tr.

Rex Shutterstock: Bill Bradshaw 80cl.

Robert Harding Picture Library: Ashley Cooper 28bl, 72cla; J. Kruse 79tr.

Rockfish: 85clb.

The Royal Cornwall Museum: 95br.

The St Mawes Hotel: David Griffen Photography 99clb.

SuperStock: age fotostock /Craig Joiner 16cl, /Olaf Protze 22cla, /Sebastian Wasek 35crb.

Trebah: David Chapman 18bl.

Cover

Front and spine: **Dreamstime.com:** Helen Hotson.

Back: **123RF.com:** valeryegorov crb; **Alamy Stock Photo:** Manfred Gottschalk tr; **AWL Images:** Adam Burton cla; **Dreamstime. com:** Helen Hotson b; **Shutterstock:** Alexey Lobanov tl.

Pull Out Map Cover

Dreamstime.com: Helen Hotson

All other images © Dorling Kindersley

For further information see:
www.dkimages.com

First edition 2009

First published in Great Britain by
Dorling Kindersley Limited
DK, One Embassy Gardens, 8 Viaduct
Gardens, London SW11 7BW, UK

The authorised representative in the EEA is
Dorling Kindersley Verlag GmbH. Arnulfstr.
124, 80636 Munich, Germany

Published in the United States by
DK US, 1450 Broadway, Suite 801,
New York, NY 10018, USA

Copyright © 2009, 2022 Dorling
Kindersley Limited

A Penguin Random House Company

21 22 23 24 10 9 8 7 6 5 4 3 2 1

**Reprinted with revisions 2011, 2013,
2015, 2018, 2020, 2022**

A CIP catalogue record is available
from the British Library.

A catalogue record for this book is available
from the Library of Congress.

ISSN 1479-344X
ISBN 978 0 2415 5930 7

Printed and bound in China

www.dk.com

*As a guide to abbreviations in visitor information
blocks: **Adm** = admission charge; **D** = dinner.*

MIX
Paper from
responsible sources
FSC™ C018179

This book was made with Forest
Stewardship Council ™ certified
paper – one small step in DK's
commitment to a sustainable future.
For more information go to
www.dk.com/our-green-pledge

21982320318821

Selected Town Index

PENGUIN BOOKS

SHARPE'S GOLD

Bernard Cornwell was born in London and educated at London University. He worked for several years as a producer and writer for BBC Television before becoming, in 1978, the editor of Thames Television's "Thames at Six" program. Since the completion of his first novel, *Sharpe's Eagle*, Mr. Cornwell has been writing full-time, producing a rousing historical adventure series that has won readers and acclaim worldwide.

SHARPE'S GOLD

RICHARD SHARPE AND THE
DESTRUCTION OF
ALMEIDA, AUGUST 1810

Bernard Cornwell

PENGUIN BOOKS

PENGUIN BOOKS
Viking Penguin Inc., 40 West 23rd Street,
New York, New York 10010, U.S.A.
Penguin Books Ltd, Harmondsworth,
Middlesex, England
Penguin Books Australia Ltd, Ringwood,
Victoria, Australia
Penguin Books Canada Limited, 2801 John Street,
Markham, Ontario, Canada L3R 1B4
Penguin Books (N.Z.) Ltd, 182–190 Wairau Road,
Auckland 10, New Zealand

First published in Great Britain by
William Collins & Co. Ltd. 1981
First published in the United States of America by
the Viking Press 1982
Published in Penguin Books 1987

Copyright © Rifleman Productions, Ltd., 1981
All rights reserved

Printed in the United States of America by
Offset Paperback Mfrs., Inc., Dallas, Pennsylvania
Set in Linotype Baskerville

This book is for
ANDREW GARDNER
with much gratitude

For a soldier I listed, to grow great in fame.
And be shot at for sixpence a day.

Charles Dibdin, 1745–1814

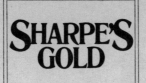

CHAPTER 1

The war was lost; not finished, but lost. Everyone knew it, from Generals of Division to the whores of Lisbon: that the British were trapped, trussed, ready for cooking, and all Europe waited for the master chef himself, Bonaparte, to cross the mountains and put his finishing touch to the roast. Then, to add insult to imminent defeat, it seemed that the small British army was not worthy of the great Bonaparte's attention. The war was lost.

Spain had fallen. The last Spanish armies had gone, butchered into the history books, and all that was left was the fortress harbour of Cádiz and the peasants who fought the *guerrilla*, the 'little war'. They fought with Spanish knives and British guns, with ambush and terror, till the French troops loathed and feared the Spanish people. But the little war was not the war, and that, everyone said, was lost.

Captain Richard Sharpe, once of His Majesty's 95th Rifles, now Captain of the Light Company of the South Essex Regiment, did not think that the war was lost, although, despite that, he was in a foul mood, morose and irritable. Rain had fallen since dawn and had turned the dust of the road's surface into slick, slippery mud and made his Rifleman's uniform clammy and uncomfortable. He marched in solitary silence, listening to his men chatter, and Lieutenant Robert Knowles and Sergeant Patrick Harper, who both would normally have sought his company, let him alone. Lieutenant Knowles had commented on Sharpe's mood, but the huge Irish Sergeant had shaken his head.

'There's no chance of cheering him up, sir. He likes being miserable, so he does, and the bàstard will get over it.'

Knowles shrugged. He rather disapproved of a Sergeant calling a Captain a 'bastard', but there was no point in

9

protesting. The Sergeant would look innocent and assure Knowles that the Captain's parents had never married, which was true, and anyway Patrick Harper had fought beside Sharpe for years and had a friendship with the Captain that Knowles rather envied. It had taken Knowles months to understand the friendship, which was not, as many officers thought, based on the fact that Sharpe had once been a private soldier, marching and fighting in the ranks, and now, elevated to the glories of the officers' mess, still sought out the company of the lower ranks. 'Once a peasant, always a peasant,' an officer had sneered, and Sharpe had heard, looked at the man, and Knowles had seen the fear come under the impact of those chilling, mocking eyes. Besides, Sharpe and Harper did not spend off-duty time together; the difference in rank made that impossible. But still, behind the formal relationship, Knowles saw the friendship. Both were big men, the Irishman hugely strong, and both confident in their abilities. Knowles could never imagine either out of uniform. It was as if they had been born to the job and it was on the battlefield, where most men thought nervously of their own survival, that Sharpe and Harper came together in an uncanny understanding. It was almost, Knowles thought, as if they were at home on a battlefield, and he envied them.

He looked up at the sky, at the low clouds touching the hilltops either side of the road. 'Bloody weather.'

'Back home, sir, we'd call this a fine day!' Harper grinned at Knowles, the rain dripping off his shako, and then turned to look at the Company, who followed the fast-marching figure of Sharpe. They were straggling a little, slipping on the road, and Harper raised his voice. 'Come on, you Protestant scum! The war's not waiting for you!'

He grinned at them as he shouted, proud they had outmarched the rest of the Regiment, and happy that, at last, the South Essex was marching north to where the summer's battles would be fought. Patrick Harper had heard the rumours – everyone had – of the French armies and their new commander, but Patrick Harper did not intend to lose any sleep over the future even though the South Essex was pitifully under strength. Replacements had sailed from Portsmouth in March, but the convoy had been hit by a storm, and, weeks later, rumours came of hundreds of bodies washed ashore on the southern Biscay beaches, and now the Regiment must fight with less than half its proper number. Harper did not mind. At Talavera the army had been outnumbered two to one, and tonight, in the town of Celorico, where the army was gathering, there would be women in the streets and wine in the shops. Life could be a lot worse for a lad from Donegal, and Patrick Harper began whistling.

Sharpe heard the whistling and checked his impulse to snap at the Sergeant, recognizing it as pure irritation, but he was annoyed by Harper's customary equanimity. Sharpe did not believe the rumours of defeat, because, to a soldier, defeat was unthinkable. It was something that happened to the enemy. Yet Sharpe despised himself because, like a walking nightmare, the remorseless logic of numbers was haunting him. Defeat was in the air, whether he believed it or not, and as the thought came to him again he marched even faster, as if the aching pace could obliterate the pessimism. But at least, at long last, they were doing something. Since Talavera the Regiment had patrolled the bleak southern border between Spain and Portugal, and it had been a long, boring winter. The sun had risen and set, the Regiment had trained, they had watched the empty hills, and there had been too much leisure, too much softness. The officers had found a discarded French cavalryman's breastplate and used it as a shaving bowl, and to his disgust Sharpe had found himself taking the luxury of hot water in a bowl as a normal daily occurrence! And weddings. Twenty alone in the last three months, so that, miles behind, the other nine companies of the South Essex were leading a motley procession of women and children, wives and whores, like a travelling fairground. But now, at last, in an unseasonably wet summer, they were marching north, to where the French attack would come, and where the doubts and fears would be banished in action.

The road reached a crest, revealing a shallow valley with a small village at its centre. There were cavalry in the village, presumably summoned north, like the South Essex, and as Sharpe saw the mass of horses, he let his irritation escape by spitting on the road. Bloody cavalry, with their airs and

11

graces, their undisguised condescension to the infantry, but then he saw the uniforms of the dismounted riders and felt ashamed of his reaction. The men wore the blue of the King's German Legion, and Sharpe respected the Germans. They were fellow professionals, and Sharpe, above everything else, was a professional soldier. He had to be. He had no money to buy promotion, and his future lay only in his skill and experience. There was plenty of experience. He had been a soldier for seventeen of his thirty-three years, first as a Private, then a Sergeant, then the dizzy jump to officer's rank, and all the promotions had been earned on battlefields. He had fought in Flanders, in India, and now in the Peninsula, and he knew that should peace arrive the army would drop him like a red-hot bullet. It was only in war that they needed professionals like himself, like Harper, like the tough Germans who fought France in Britain's army.

He halted the Company in the village street under the curious gaze of the cavalrymen. One of them, an officer, hitched his curved sabre off the ground and walked over to Sharpe. 'Captain?' The cavalryman made it a question because Sharpe's only signs of rank were the faded scarlet sash and the sword.

Sharpe nodded. 'Captain Sharpe. South Essex.'

The German officer's eyebrows went up; his face split into a smile. 'Captain Sharpe! Talavera!' He pumped Sharpe's hand, clapped him on the shoulder, then turned to shout at his men. The blue-coated cavalry grinned at Sharpe, nodded at him. They had all heard of him: the man who had captured the French Eagle at Talavera.

Sharpe jerked his head towards Patrick Harper and the Company. 'Don't forget Sergeant Harper, and the Company. We were all there.'

The German beamed at the Light Company. 'It was well done!' He clicked his heels to Sharpe and gave the slightest nod. 'Lossow. Captain Lossow at your service. You going to Celorico?' The German's English was accented but good. His men, Sharpe knew, would probably speak no English.

Sharpe nodded again. 'And you?'

Lossow shook his head. 'The Coa. Patrolling. The enemy are getting close, so there will be fighting.' He sounded pleased and Sharpe envied the cavalry. What fighting there was to be had was all taking place along the steep banks of the river Coa and not at Celorico. Lossow laughed. 'This time we get an Eagle, yes?'

Sharpe wished him luck. If any cavalry regiment were likely to break apart a French battalion, it would be the Germans. The English cavalry were brave enough, well mounted, but with no discipline. English horsemen grew bored with patrols, with picquet duty, and dreamed only of the blood-curdling charge, swords high, that left their horses blown and the men scattered and vulnerable. Sharpe, like all infantry in the army, preferred the Germans because they knew their job and did it well.

Lossow grinned at the compliment. He was a square-faced man, with a pleasant and ready smile and eyes that looked out shrewdly from the web of lines traced on his face by staring too long at the enemy-held horizons. 'Oh, one more thing, Captain. The bloody provosts are in the village.' The phrase came awkwardly from Lossow's lips, as if he did not usually use English swearwords except to describe the provosts, for whom any other language's curse would be inadequate.

Sharpe thanked him and turned to the Company. 'You heard Captain Lossow! There are provosts here. So keep your thieving hands to yourselves. Understand?' They understood. No one wanted to be hung on the spot for being caught looting. 'We stop for ten minutes. Dismiss them, Sergeant.'

The Germans left, cloaked against the rain, and Sharpe walked up the only street towards the church. It was a miserable village, poor and deserted, and the cottage doors swung emptily. The inhabitants had gone south and west, as the Portuguese government had ordered. When the French advanced they would find no crops, no animals, wells filled with stones or poisoned with dead sheep: a land of hunger and thirst.

Patrick Harper, sensing that Sharpe's mood had lightened after the meeting with Lossow, fell into step beside his Captain. 'Nothing here to loot, sir.'

Sharpe glanced at the men stooping into the cottages. 'They'll find something.'

The provosts were beside the church, three of them, mounted on black horses and standing like highwaymen waiting for a plump coach. Their equipment was new, their faces burned red, and Sharpe guessed they were fresh out from England, though why the Horse Guards sent provosts instead of fighting soldiers was a mystery. He nodded civilly to them. 'Good morning.'

One of the three, with an officer's sword jutting from beneath his cloak, nodded back. He seemed, like all of his kind, to be suspicious of any friendly gesture. He looked at their green Riflemen's jackets. 'There aren't supposed to be any Riflemen in this area.'

Sharpe let the accusation go unanswered. If the provost thought they were deserters, then the provost was a fool. Deserters did not travel the open road in daylight, or wear uniforms, or stroll casually up to provosts. Sharpe and Harper, like the other eighteen Riflemen in the Company, had kept their old uniforms out of pride, preferring the dark green to the red of the line battalions.

The provost's eyes flicked between the two men. 'You have orders?'

'The General wants to see us, sir.' Harper spoke cheerfully.

A tiny smile came and went on the provost's face. 'You mean Lord Wellington wants to see you?'

'As a matter of fact, yes.'

Sharpe's voice had a warning in it, but the provost seemed oblivious. He was looking Sharpe up and down, letting his suspicions show. Sharpe's appearance was extraordinary. The green jacket, faded and torn, was worn over French cavalry overalls. On his feet were tall leather boots that had originally been bought in Paris by a Colonel of Napoleon's Imperial Guard. On his back, like most of his men, he carried a French pack, made of ox hide, and on his shoulder, though he was an officer, he slung a rifle. The officer's epaulettes had gone, leaving broken stitches, and the scarlet sash was stained and faded. Even Sharpe's sword, his other badge of rank, was irregular. As an officer of a Light Company he should have carried the curved sabre of the British Light Cavalry, but Richard Sharpe preferred the sword of the Heavy Cavalry, straight-bladed and ill balanced. Cavalrymen hated it; they claimed its weight made it impossible to parry swiftly, but Sharpe was six feet tall and strong enough to wield the thirty-five inches of ponderous steel with deceptive ease.

The provost officer was unsettled. 'What's your Regiment?'

'We're the Light of the South Essex.' Sharpe made his tone friendly.

The provost responded by spurring his horse forward so he could see down the street and watch Sharpe's men. There was no immediately apparent reason to hang anyone, so he looked back at the two men and his eyes stopped, with surprise, when they reached Harper's shoulder. The Irishman, with four inches more height than Sharpe, was a daunting sight at the best of times, but his weapons were even more irregular than Sharpe's big sword. Slung with his rifle was a brute of a gun – a seven-barrelled, squat menace. The provost pointed. 'What's that?'

'Seven-barrelled gun, sir.' Harper's voice was full of pride in his new weapon.

'Where did you get it?'

'Christmas present, sir.'

Sharpe grinned. It had been a present, given at Christmas time, from Sharpe to his Sergeant, but it was obvious that the provost, with his two silent companions, did not believe it. He was still staring at the gun, one of Henry Nock's less successful inventions, and Sharpe realized that the provost had probably never seen one before. Only a few hundred had ever been made, for the Navy, and at the time it had seemed like a good idea. Seven barrels, each twenty inches long, were all fired by the same flintlock, and it was thought that sailors, perched precariously in the fighting tops, could wreak havoc by firing the seven barrels down on to the enemy's crowded decks. One thing had been overlooked. Seven half-inch barrels fired together made a fearful discharge, like a small cannon's, that not only wreaked havoc but also broke the shoulder of any man who pulled the trigger. Only Harper, in Sharpe's acquaintance, had the brute strength to use the gun, and even the Irishman, in trying it out, had been astonished by the crashing recoil as the seven bullets spread from the flaming muzzles.

The provost sniffed. 'A Christmas present.'

'I gave it to him,' Sharpe said.

'And you are?'

'Captain Richard Sharpe. South Essex. You?'

The provost stiffened. 'Lieutenant Ayres, sir.' The last word was spoken reluctantly.

'And where are you going, Lieutenant Ayres?'

Sharpe was annoyed by the man's suspicions, by the pointless display of his power, and he edged his questions with a touch of venom. Sharpe carried on his back the scars of a flogging that had been caused by just such an officer as this: Captain Morris, a supercilious bully, with his flattering familiar, Sergeant Hakeswill. Sharpe carried the memory along with the scars and a promise that one day he would revenge himself on both men. Morris, he knew, was stationed in Dublin; Hakeswill was God knows where, but one day, Sharpe promised himself, he would find him. But for now it was this young puppy with more power than sense. 'Where, Lieutenant?'

'Celorico, sir.'

'Then have a good journey, Lieutenant.'

Ayres nodded. 'I'll look round first, sir. If you don't mind.'

Sharpe watched the three men ride down the street, the rain beading the wide, black rumps of the horses. 'I hope you're right, Sergeant.'

'Right, sir?'

'That there's nothing to loot.'

The thought struck both together, a single instinct for trouble, and they began running. Sharpe pulled his whistle from the small holster on his crossbelt and blew the long blasts that were usually reserved for the battlefield when the Light Company was strung out in a loose skirmish line, the enemy was pressing close, and the officers and Sergeants whistled the men back to rally and re-form under the shelter of the Battalion. The provosts heard the whistle blasts, put spurs to their horses, and swerved between two low cottages to search the yards as Sharpe's men tumbled from doorways and grumbled into ranks.

Harper pulled up in front of the Company. 'Packs on!'

There was a shout from behind the cottages. Sharpe turned. Lieutenant Knowles was at his elbow.

'What's happening, sir?'

'Provost trouble. Bastards are throwing their weight around.'

They were determined, he knew, to find something, and as Sharpe's eyes went down his ranks he had a sinking feeling that Lieutenant Ayres had succeeded. There should have been forty-eight men, three Sergeants, and the two officers, but one man was missing: Private Batten. Private bloody Batten, who was dragged by his hair from between the cottages by a triumphant provost.

'A looter, sir. Caught in the act.' Ayres was smiling.

Batten, who grumbled incessantly, who moaned if it rained and made a fuss when it stopped because the sun was in his eyes. Private Batten, a one-man destroyer of flintlocks, who thought the whole world was conspiring to annoy him, and who now stood flinching beneath the grasp of one of Ayres's men. If there were any one member of the Company whom Sharpe would gladly have hanged, it would be Batten, but he was damned if any provost was going to do it for him.

Sharpe looked up at Ayres. 'What was he looting, Lieutenant?'

'This.'

Ayres held up a scrawny chicken as if it were the Crown of England. Its neck had been well wrung, but the legs still jerked and scrabbled at the air. Sharpe felt the anger come inside him, not at the provosts but at Batten.

'I'll deal with him, Lieutenant.' Batten cringed away from his Captain.

Ayres shook his head. 'You misunderstand, sir.' He was talking with silky condescension. 'Looters are hung, sir. On the spot, sir. As an example to others.'

There was a muttering from the Company, broken by Harper's bellowed order for silence. Batten's eyes flicked left and right as if looking for an escape from this latest example of the world's injustice. Sharpe snapped at him. 'Batten!'

'Sir?'

'Where did you find the chicken?'

'It was in the field, sir. Honest.' He winced as his hair was pulled. 'It was a wild chicken, sir.'

There was a rustle of laughter from the ranks that Harper let go. Ayres snorted. 'A wild chicken. Dangerous beasts, eh, sir? He's lying. I found him in the cottage.'

Sharpe believed him, but he was not going to give up. 'Who lives in the cottage, Lieutenant?'

Ayres raised an eyebrow. 'Really, sir, I have not exchanged cards with every slum in Portugal.' He turned to his men. 'String him up.'

'Lieutenant Ayres.' The tone of Sharpe's voice stopped any movement in the street. 'How do you know the cottage is inhabited?'

'Look for yourself.'

'Sir.'

Ayres swallowed. 'Sir.'

Sharpe raised his voice. 'Are there people there, Lieutenant?'

'No, sir. But it's lived in.'

'How do you know? The village is deserted. You can't steal a chicken from nobody.'

Ayres thought about his reply. The village was deserted, the inhabitants gone away from the French attack, but absence was not a relinquishing of ownership. He shook his head. 'The chicken is Portuguese property, sir.' He turned again. 'Hang him!'

'Halt!' Sharpe bellowed and again movement stopped. 'You're not going to hang him, so just go your way.'

Ayres swivelled back to Sharpe. 'He was caught red-handed and the bastard will hang. Your men are probably a pack of bloody thieves and they need an example and, by God, they will get one!' He raised himself in his stirrups and shouted at the Company. 'You will see him hang! And if you steal, then you will hang too!'

A click interrupted him. He looked down and the anger in his face was replaced by astonishment. Sharpe held his Baker rifle, cocked, so that the barrel was pointing at Ayres.

'Let him go, Lieutenant.'

'Have you gone mad?'

Ayres had gone white, had sagged back into his saddle.

Sergeant Harper, instinctively, came and stood beside Sharpe and ignored the hand that waved him away. Ayres stared at the two men. Both tall, both with hard, fighters' faces, and a memory tickled at him. He looked at Sharpe, at the face that appeared to have a perpetually mocking expression, caused by the scar that ran down the right cheek, and he suddenly remembered. Wild chickens, bird-catchers! The South Essex Light Company. Were these the two men who had captured the Eagle? Who had hacked their way into a French regiment and come out with the standard? He could believe it.

Sharpe watched the Lieutenant's eyes waver and knew that he had won, but it was a victory that would cost him dearly. The army did not look kindly on men who held rifles on provosts, even empty rifles.

Ayres pushed Batten forward. 'Have your thief, Captain. We shall meet again.'

Sharpe lowered the rifle. Ayres waited until Batten was clear of the horses, then wrenched the reins and led his men towards Celorico. 'You'll hear from me!' His words were flung back. Sharpe could sense the trouble like a boiling, black cloud on the horizon. He turned to Batten.

'Did you steal that bloody hen?'

'Yes, sir.' Batten flapped a hand after the provost. 'He took it, sir.' He made it sound unfair.

'I wish he'd bloody taken you. I wish he'd bloody spread your guts across the bloody landscape.' Batten backed away from Sharpe's anger. 'What are the bloody rules, Batten?'

The eyes blinked at Sharpe. 'Rules, sir?'

'You know the bloody rules. Tell me.'

The army issued regulations that were inches thick, but Sharpe gave his men three rules. They were simple, they worked, and if broken the men knew they could expect punishment. Batten cleared his throat.

'To fight well, sir. Not to get drunk without permission, sir. And –'

'Go on.'

'Not to steal, sir, except from the enemy or when starving, sir.'

'Were you starving?'

Batten clearly wanted to say he was, but there were still two days' rations in every man's haversack. 'No, sir.'

Sharpe hit him, all his frustration pouring into one fist that slammed Batten's chest, winded him, and knocked him gasping into the wet road. 'You're a bloody fool, Batten, a cringing, miserable, whoreson, slimy fool.' He turned away from the man, whose musket had fallen into the mud. 'Company! March!'

They marched behind the tall Rifleman as Batten picked himself up, brushed ineffectively at the water that had flowed into the lock of his gun, and then shambled after the Company. He pushed himself into his file and muttered at his silent companions. 'He's not supposed to hit me.'

'Shut your mouth, Batten!' Harper's voice was as harsh as his Captain's. 'You know the rules. Would you rather be kicking your useless heels now?'

The Sergeant shouted at the Company to pick up their feet, bellowed the steps at them, and all the time he wondered what faced Sharpe now. A complaint from that bloody provost would mean an enquiry and probably a court-martial. And all for the miserable Batten, a failed horse-coper, whom Harper would gladly have killed himself. Lieutenant Knowles seemed to share Harper's thoughts, for he fell in step beside the Irishman and looked at him with a troubled face. 'All for one chicken, Sergeant?'

Harper looked down at the young Lieutenant. 'I doubt it, sir.' He turned to the ranks. 'Daniel!'

Hagman, one of the Riflemen, broke ranks and fell in beside the Sergeant. He was the oldest man in the Company, in his forties, but the best marksman. A Cheshireman, raised as a poacher, Hagman could shoot the buttons off a French General's coat at three hundred yards. 'Sarge?'

'How many chickens were there?'

Hagman flashed his toothless grin, glanced at the Company, then up at Harper. The Sergeant was a fair man, never demanding more than a fair share. 'Dozen, Sarge.'

Harper looked at Knowles. 'There you are, sir. At least sixteen wild chickens there. Probably twenty. God knows what they were doing there, why the owners didn't take them.'

'Difficult to catch, sir, chickens.' Hagman chuckled. 'That all, Sarge?'

Harper grinned down at the Rifleman. 'A leg each for the officers, Daniel. And not the stringy ones.'

Hagman glanced at Knowles. 'Very good, sir. Leg each.' He went back to the ranks.

Knowles chuckled to himself. A leg each for the officers meant a good breast for the Sergeant, chicken broth for everyone, and nothing for Private Batten. And for Sharpe? Knowles felt his spirits drop. The war was lost, it was still raining, and tomorrow Captain Richard Sharpe would be in provost trouble, real trouble, right up to his sabre-scarred neck.

CHAPTER 2

If anyone needed a symbol of impending defeat, then the Church of São Paulo in Celorico, the temporary head-quarters of the South Essex, offered it in full. Sharpe stood in the choir watching the priest whitewash a gorgeous rood-screen. The screen was made of solid silver, ancient and intricate, a gift from some long-forgotten parishioner whose family's faces were those of the grieving women and disciples who stared up at the crucifix. The priest, standing on a trestle, dripping thick lime paint down his cassock, looked from Sharpe to the screen, and shrugged.

'It took three months to clean off last time.'

'Last time?'

'When the French left.' The priest sounded bitter and he dabbed angrily with the bristles at the delicate traceries. 'If they knew it was silver they would carve it into pieces and take it away.' He splashed the nailed, hanging figure with a slap of paint and then, as if in apology, moved the brush to his left hand so that his right could sketch a perfunctory sign of the cross on his spattered gown.

'Perhaps they won't get this far.'

It sounded unconvincing, even to Sharpe, and the priest did not bother to reply. He just gave a humourless laugh and dipped the brush into his bucket. They know, thought Sharpe; they all know that the French are coming and the British falling back. The priest made him feel guilty, as if he were personally betraying the town and its inhabitants, and he moved down the church into the darkness by the main door where the Battalion's commissariat officer was supervising the piling of fresh baked bread for the evening rations.

The door banged open, letting in the late-afternoon

sunlight, and Lawford, dressed in his glittering best uniform, beckoned at Sharpe. 'Ready?'

'Yes, sir.'

Major Forrest was waiting outside and he smiled nervously at Sharpe. 'Don't worry, Richard.'

'Worry?' Lieutenant Colonel the Honourable William Lawford was angry. 'He should damned well worry.' He looked Sharpe up and down. 'Is that the best you can do?'

Sharpe fingered the tear in his sleeve. 'It's all I've got, sir.'

'All? What about that new uniform! Good Lord, Richard, you look like a tramp.'

'Uniform's in Lisbon, sir. In store. Light Companies should travel light.'

Lawford snorted. 'And they shouldn't threaten provosts with rifles either. Come on, we don't want to be late.' He crammed the tricorne hat on to his head and returned the salute of the two sentries who had listened, amused, to his outburst.

Sharpe held up his hand. 'One moment, sir.' He brushed an imaginary speck of dust from the gold regimental badge that the Colonel wore on his white diagonal sash. It was a new badge, commissioned by Lawford after Talavera, and showed an eagle in chains – a message to the world that the South Essex was the only regiment in the Peninsula that had captured a French standard. Sharpe stood back satisfied. 'That's better, sir.'

Lawford took the hint, and smiled. 'You're a bastard, Sharpe. Just because you captured an Eagle doesn't mean you can do what you like.'

'While just because some idiot is dressed up as a provost, I suppose, means that he can?'

'Yes,' Lawford said. 'It does. Come on.'

It was strange, Sharpe thought, how Lawford was the sum of all he disliked about privilege and wealth, yet he liked Lawford and was content to serve him. They were the same age, thirty-three, but Lawford had always been an officer, had never worried about promotion, because he could afford the next step, and never concerned himself where the next year's money would come from. Seven years ago, Lawford had been a Lieutenant and Richard Sharpe his Sergeant, both fighting the Mahrattas in India, and the Sergeant had kept the officer alive in the dungeons of the Tippoo Sultan. In return, Lawford taught the Sergeant to read and write and thus qualified him for a commission if ever he were foolish enough to perform some act of bravery on a battlefield that could hoist a man from the ranks into the officers' exalted company.

Sharpe followed Lawford through the crowded streets towards Wellington's headquarters, and seeing the Colonel's exquisite uniform and expensive accoutrements, he wondered where they would be in another seven years. Lawford was ambitious, as was Sharpe, but the Colonel had the birth and the money for great things. He'll be a general, Sharpe thought, and he grinned because he knew that Lawford would still need him or someone like him. Sharpe was Lawford's eyes and his ears, his professional soldier, the man who could read the faces of the failed criminals, drunks, and desperate men who had somehow become the best infantry in the world. And more than that, Sharpe could read the ground, could read the enemy, and Lawford, for whom the army was a means to a glorious and exalted end, relied on his ex-Sergeant's instinct and talent. Lawford, Sharpe decided, had done well in the last year. He had taken over an embittered, brutalized, and frightened Regiment and turned them into a unit as good as any battalion in the line. Sharpe's Eagle had helped. It had wiped out the stain of Valdelacasa, where the South Essex, under Sir Henry Simmerson, had lost a colour and their pride; but it was not just the Eagle. Lawford, with his politician's instincts, had trusted the men while he worked them hard, had given them back their confidence. And the badge, which every man wore on his shako, shared the glory of Talavera with every soldier in the Regiment.

Lawford led them through the press of officers and townspeople. Major Forrest kept glancing at Sharpe with an avuncular smile that made him look, more than ever, like a kindly country vicar dressed as a soldier for the village pageant. He tried to reassure Sharpe. 'It won't come to a court-martial, Richard; it can't! You'll probably have to apologize, or something, and it will all blow over.'

Sharpe shook his head. 'I won't bloody apologize, sir.'

Lawford stopped and turned round, his finger pushed into Sharpe's chest. 'If you are ordered to apologize, Richard Sharpe, you will damned well apologize. You will grovel, squirm, cringe and toady to order. Do you understand?'

Sharpe clicked the heels of his tall French boots. 'Sir!'

Lawford exploded in rare anger. 'Christ Almighty, Richard, don't you bloody understand? This is a general-court-martial offence. Ayres has screamed his head off to the Provost Marshal and the Provost Marshal has screamed to the General that the authority of the provost must not be undermined. And the General, Mr Sharpe, is rather sympathetic to that point of view.' Lawford's passion had attracted a small crowd of interested spectators. His anger faded as suddenly as it had erupted, but he still jabbed his finger into Sharpe's chest. 'The General wants more provosts, not fewer, and he is understandably not happy with the thought that Captain Richard Sharpe is declaring open season on them.'

'Yes, sir.'

Lawford was not placated by Sharpe's crestfallen expression, which the Colonel suspected was not motivated by true regret. 'And do not think, Captain Sharpe, that just because the General ordered us here he will look kindly on your action. He's saved your miserable skin often enough in the past and he may not be of a mind to do it again. Understand?'

There was a burst of applause from a group of cavalry officers standing by a wine shop. Lawford shot them a withering look and strode on, followed by someone's ironic mimicry of the bugle call for the full charge. Sharpe followed. Lawford could be right. The General had summoned the South Essex, no one knew why, and Sharpe had hoped that it was for some special task, something to wipe out the memory of the winter's boredom. But the scene with Lieutenant Ayres could change that for Sharpe, condemn him to a court-martial, to a future far more dreary even than patrol work on an empty border.

Four ox-carts stood outside Wellington's headquarters, another reminder that the army would move soon, but otherwise everything was peaceful. The only unusual object was a tall mast that jutted from the roof of the house, topped by a crosspiece, from which hung four tarred sheep bladders. Sharpe looked at them curiously. This was the first time he had seen the new telegraph and he wished that it was working so that he could watch the black, inflated bladders running up and down on their ropes and sending messages, via other similar stations, to the far-off fortress of Almeida and to the troops guarding the river Coa. The system had been copied from the Royal Navy and sailors had been sent to man the telegraph. Each letter of the alphabet had its own arrangement of the four black bags, and common words, like 'regiment', 'enemy', and 'general', were abbreviated to a single display that could be seen, miles away, through a huge naval telescope. Sharpe had heard that a message could travel twenty miles in less than ten minutes and he wondered, as they came close to the two bored sentries guarding the General's headquarters, what other modern devices would be thrown up by the necessity of the long war against Napoleon.

He forgot the telegraph as they stepped into the cool hallway of the house and he felt a twinge of fear at the coming interview. In a curious fashion his career had been linked to Wellington. They had shared battlefields in Flanders, India, and now in the Peninsula, and in his pack Sharpe carried a telescope that had been a present from the General. There was a small, curved, brass plate let into the walnut tube and on it was inscribed IN GRATITUDE. AW. SEPTEMBER 23RD, 1803. Sir Arthur Wellesley believed that Sergeant Sharpe had saved his life, though Sharpe, if he was honest, could remember little of the event except that the General's horse had been piked and the Indian bayonets and curved tulwars were coming forward and what else did a Sergeant do except get in the way and fight back? That had been the battle of Assaye, a bastard of a fight, and Sharpe had watched his officers die in the shot from the ornate guns and, his blood up, he had taken the survivors on and the enemy had been beaten. Only just, by God, but victory was victory. After that he was made into an officer, dressed up like a prize bull, and the same man who had rewarded him then must decide his fate now.

'His Lordship will see you now.' A suave young Major smiled at them through the door as though they had been invited for tea. It had been a year since Sharpe had seen Wellington, but nothing had changed: still the table covered with papers, the same blue eyes that gave nothing away above the beak of a nose, and the handsome mouth that was grudging with a smile. Sharpe was glad there were no provosts in the room so at least he would not have to grovel in front of the General, but even so he felt apprehensive of this quiet man's anger and he watched, cautiously, as the quill pen was laid down and the expressionless eyes looked up at him. There was no recognition in them.

'Did you threaten Lieutenant Ayres with a rifle, Captain Sharpe?' There was the faintest stress on the 'Captain'.

'Yes, sir.'

Wellington nodded. He looked tired. He stood up and moved to the window, peering through as though expecting something. There was silence in the room, broken only by the jingle of chains and rumbling of wheels as a battery of artillery drove by in the street. It struck Sharpe that the General was on edge. Wellington turned back to him.

'Do you know, Captain Sharpe, the damage it does our cause if our soldiers thieve or rape?' His voice was scathingly quiet.

'Yes, sir.'

'I hope you do, Captain Sharpe, I hope you do.' He sat down again. 'Our enemies are encouraged to steal because that is the only way they can be fed. The result is that they are hated wherever they march. I spend money – my God, how much money – on providing rations and transport and buying food from the populace so that our soldiers have no need to steal. We do this so they will be welcomed by the local people and helped by them. Do you understand?'

Sharpe wished the lecture would end. 'Yes, sir.'

There was suddenly a strange noise overhead, a shuffling and rattling, and Wellington's eyes shot to the ceiling as if he could read what the noise might mean. It occurred to Sharpe that the telegraph was working, the inflated bladders running up and down the ropes, bringing a coded message from the troops facing the French. The General listened for a few seconds, then dropped his face to Sharpe again. 'Your gazette has not yet been ratified.'

There were few things the General could have said more calculated to worry Sharpe. Officially he was still a Lieutenant, only a Lieutenant, and his Captaincy had been awarded by a gazette from Wellington a year ago. If the Horse Guards in Whitehall did not approve, and he knew they usually rejected such irregular promotions, then he was soon to be a Lieutenant again. He said nothing as Wellington watched him. If this were a warning shot, then he would take it in silence.

The General sighed, picked up a piece of paper, put it down again. 'The soldier has been punished?'

'Yes, sir.' He thought of Batten, winded, on the ground.

'Then do not, pray, let it happen again. Not even, Captain Sharpe, to wild chickens.'

My God, thought Sharpe, he knows everything that happens in this army. There was silence. Was that the end of it? No court-martial? No apology? He coughed and Wellington looked up.

'Yes?'

'I was expecting more, sir. Court-martials and drumheads.'

Sharpe heard Lawford stir in embarrassment but the General did not seem worried. He stood up and used one of his few, thin smiles.

'I would quite happily, Captain Sharpe, string up you and that damned Sergeant. But I suspect we need you. What do you think of our chances this summer?'

Again there was silence. The change of tack had taken them all by surprise. Lawford cleared his throat. 'There's clearly some concern, my lord, about the intentions of the enemy and our response.'

Another wintry smile. 'The enemy intend to push us into the sea, and soon. How do we respond?' Wellington, it occurred to Sharpe, was using up time. He was waiting for something or someone.

Lawford was feeling uncomfortable. The question was one he would rather hear answered by the General. 'Bring them to battle, sir?'

'Thirty thousand troops, plus twenty-five thousand untried Portuguese, against three hundred and fifty thousand men?'

Wellington let the figures hang in the air like the dust that shifted silently in the slanting sunlight over his desk. Overhead the feet of the men operating the telegraph still shuffled. The figures, Sharpe knew, were unfair. Masséna needed thousands of those men to contain the Guerrilleros, the Partisans, but even so the disparity in numbers was appalling. Wellington sniffed. There was a knock on the door.

'Come in.'

'Sir.'

The Major who had shown them into the room handed a slip of paper to the General, who read it, closed his eyes momentarily, and sighed.

'The rest of the message is still coming?'

'Yes, sir. But the gist is there.'

The Major left and Wellington leaned back in his chair. The news had been bad, Sharpe could tell, but not, perhaps, unexpected. He remembered that Wellington had once said that running a campaign was like driving a team of horses with a rope harness. The ropes kept breaking and all a General could do was tie a knot and keep going. A rope was unravelling, here and now, an important one, and Sharpe watched the fingers drum on the edge of the table. The eyes came up to Sharpe again, flicked to Lawford.

'Colonel?'

'Sir?'

'I am borrowing Captain Sharpe from you, and his Company. I doubt whether I need them for more than one month.'

'Yes, my lord.' Lawford looked at Sharpe and shrugged.

Wellington stood again. He seemed to be relieved, as if a decision had been made. 'The war is not lost, gentlemen, though I know my confidence is not universally shared.' He sounded bitter, angry with the defeatists whose letters home were quoted in the newspapers. 'We may bring the French to battle, and if we do we will win.' Sharpe never doubted it. Of all Britain's generals this was the only one who knew how to beat the French. 'If we win we will only delay their advance.' He opened a map, stared at it blankly, and let it snap shut again into a roll. 'No, gentlemen, our survival depends on something else. Something that you, Captain Sharpe, must bring me. Must, do you hear? Must.'

Sharpe had never heard the General so insistent. 'Yes, sir.'

Lawford coughed. 'And if he fails, my lord?'

The wintry smile again. 'He had better not.' He looked at Sharpe. 'You are not the only card in my hand, Mr Sharpe, but you are...important. There are things happening, gentlemen, that this army does not know about. If it did it would be generally more optimistic.' He sat down again, leaving them mystified. Sharpe suspected the mystification was on purpose. He was spreading some counter-rumours to the defeatists, and that, too, was part of a general's job. He looked up again. 'You are now under my orders, Captain Sharpe. Your men must be ready to march this night. They must not be encumbered with wives or unnecessary baggage, and they must have full ammunition.'

'Yes, sir.'

'And you will be back here in one hour. You have two tasks to perform.'

Sharpe wondered if he was to be told what they were. 'Sir?'

'First, Mr Sharpe, you will receive your orders. Not from me but from an old companion of yours.' Wellington saw Sharpe's quizzical look. 'Major Hogan.'

Sharpe's face betrayed his pleasure. Hogan, the engineer, the quiet Irishman who was a friend, whose sense Sharpe had leaned on in the difficult days leading to Talavera. Wellington saw the pleasure and tried to puncture it. 'But before that, Mr Sharpe, you will apologize to Lieutenant Ayres.' He watched for Sharpe's reaction.

'But of course, sir. I had always planned to.' Sharpe looked shocked at the thought that he might ever have contemplated another course of action and, through his innocently wide eyes, wondered if he saw a flicker of amusement behind the General's cold, blue gaze.

Wellington looked away, to Lawford, and with his usual disarming speed suddenly became affable. 'You're well, Colonel?'

'Thank you, sir. Yes.' Lawford beamed with pleasure. He had served on Wellington's staff, knew the General well.

'Join me for dinner tonight. The usual time.' The General looked at Forrest. 'And you, Major?'

'My pleasure, sir.'

'Good.' The eyes flicked at Sharpe. 'Captain Sharpe will be too busy, I fear.' He nodded a dismissal. 'Good day, gentlemen.'

Outside the headquarters the bugles sounded the evening and the sun sank in magnificent crimson. Inside the quiet room the General paused a moment before plunging back into the paperwork that must be done before the dinner of roast mutton. Hogan, he thought, was right. If a miracle were needed to save the campaign, and it was, then the rogue he had just seen was the best man for the job. More than a rogue: a fighter, and a man who looked on failure as unthinkable. But a rogue, thought Wellington, a damned rogue all the same.

CHAPTER 3

Sharpe had spent the hour between leaving and returning to Wellington's headquarters conjuring all kinds of quixotic answers to the mystery of what he was supposed to bring back to the General. Perhaps, he had thought as he stirred the Company into activity, it would be a new French secret weapon, something like the British Colonel Congreve's rocket system, of which there were so many tales but so little evidence. Or, more fanciful still, perhaps the British had secretly offered refuge to Napoleon's divorced Josephine, who might have smuggled herself to Spain to become a pawn in the high politics of the war. He was still wondering as he was shown into a large room of the headquarters, to find a reception committee, formal and strained, flanking a wretchedly embarrassed Lieutenant Ayres.

The unctuous young Major smiled at Sharpe as though he were a valued and expected guest. 'Ah, Captain Sharpe. You know the Provost Marshal, you've met Lieutenant Ayres, and this is Colonel Williams. Gentlemen?' The Major made a delicate gesture as if inviting them all to sit down and take a glass of sherry. It seemed that Colonel Williams, plump and red-veined, was deputed to do the talking.

'Disgraceful, Sharpe. Disgraceful!'

Sharpe stared a fraction of an inch over Williams's head and stopped himself from blinking. It was a useful way of discomfiting people, and, sure enough, Williams wavered from the apparent gaze and made a helpless gesture towards Lieutenant Ayres.

'You imperilled his authority, overstepped your own. A disgrace!'

'Yes, sir. I apologize!'

'What?' Williams seemed surprised at Sharpe's sudden

apology. Lieutenant Ayres was squirming with uneasiness, while the Provost Marshal seemed impatient to get the charade done. Williams cleared his throat, seemed to want his pound of flesh. 'You apologize?'

'Yes, sir. Unreservedly, sir. Terrible disgrace, sir. I utterly apologize, sir, regret my part very much, sir, as I'm sure Lieutenant Ayres does his.'

Ayres, startled by a sudden smile from Sharpe, nodded hastily and agreed. 'I do, sir. I do.'

Williams whirled on his unfortunate Lieutenant. 'What do you have to regret, Ayres? You mean there's more to this than I thought?'

The Provost Marshal sighed and scraped a boot on the floor. 'I think the purpose of this meeting is over, gentlemen, and I have work to do.' He looked at Sharpe. 'Thank you, Captain, for your apology. We'll leave you.'

As they left, Sharpe could hear Colonel Williams interrogating Ayres as to why he should have any regrets, and Sharpe let a grin show on his face which widened into a broad smile as the door opened once more and Michael Hogan came into the room. The small Irishman shut the door carefully and smiled at Sharpe.

'As graceful an apology as I expected from you. How are you?'

They shook hands, pleasure on both their faces. The war, it turned out, was treating Hogan well. An engineer, he had been transferred to Wellington's staff, and promoted. He spoke Portuguese and Spanish, and added to those skills was a common sense that was rare. Sharpe raised his eyebrows at Hogan's elegant, new uniform.

'So what do you do here?'

'A bit of this and the other.' Hogan beamed at him, paused, then sneezed violently. 'Christ and St Patrick! Bloody Irish Blackguard!'

Sharpe looked puzzled and Hogan held out his snuff-box. 'Can't get Scotch Rappee here, only Irish Blackguard. It's like sniffing grapeshot straight up the nostrils.'

'Give it up.'

Hogan laughed. 'I've tried; I can't.' His eyes watered as another sneeze gathered force. 'God in heaven!'

'So what do you do?'

Hogan wiped a tear from his cheek. 'Not so very much, Richard. I sort of find things out, about the enemy, you understand. And draw maps. Things like that. We call it "intelligence", but it's a fancy word for knowing a bit about the other fellow. And I have some duties in Lisbon.' He waved a deprecating hand. 'I get by.'

Lisbon, where Josefina was. The thought struck Hogan as it came to Sharpe, and the small Irishman smiled and answered the unspoken question. 'Aye, she's well.'

Josefina, whom Sharpe had loved so briefly, for whom he had killed, and who had left him for a cavalry officer. He still thought of her, remembered the few nights, but this was no time or place for that kind of memory. He pushed the thought of her away, the jealousy he had for Captain Claud Hardy, and changed the subject.

'So what is this thing that I must bring back for the General?'

Hogan leaned back. '*Nervos belli, pecuniam infinitam.*'

'You know I don't speak Spanish.'

Hogan gave a gentle smile. 'Latin, Richard, Latin. Your education was sadly overlooked. Cicero said it: "The sinews of war are unlimited money."'

'Money?'

'Gold, to be precise. Bucketfuls of gold. A King's bloody ransom, my dear Richard, and we want it. No, more than we want it, we need it. Without it –' He did not finish the sentence, but just shrugged instead.

'You're joking, surely!'

Hogan carefully lit another candle – the light beyond the windows was fading fast – and spoke quietly. 'I wish I was. We've run out of money. You wouldn't believe it, but there it is. Eighty-five million pounds is the war budget this year – can you imagine it? – and we've run out.'

'Run out?'

Hogan gave another shrug. 'A new government in London, bloody English, demanding accounts. We're paying all Portugal's expenses, arming half the Spanish nation, and now we need it.' He stressed the 'we'. 'It's what, I think, you would call a local embarrassment. We need some money fast,

34

in a matter of days. We could force it out of London in a couple of months, but that will be too long. We need it now.'

'And if not?'

'If not, Richard, the French will be in Lisbon and not all the money in the world will make any difference.' He smiled. 'So you go and get the money.'

'I go and get the money.' Sharpe grinned at the Irishman. 'How? Steal it?'

'Shall we say "borrow"?' Hogan's voice was serious. Sharpe said nothing and the Irishman sighed, leaned back. 'There is a problem, Richard, which is that the gold belongs to the Spanish government, in a manner of speaking.'

'What manner?'

Hogan shrugged. 'Who knows where the government is? Is it in Madrid, with the French? Or in Cádiz?'

'And where's the gold? Paris?'

Hogan gave a tired smile. 'Not quite that far. Two days' march.' His voice became formal, reciting instructions. 'You leave tonight, march to Almeida. The crossing of the Coa is guarded by the Sixtieth; they're expecting you. In Almeida you meet Major Kearsey. From then on you are under his orders. We expect you to take no longer than one week, and should you need help, which pray God you do not, here is all you're going to get.'

He pushed a piece of paper over the table. Sharpe unfolded it. *Captain Sharpe is directed by my orders and all Officers of the Allied Armies are requested and instructed to offer Captain Sharpe any assistance he may require.* The signature was a simple *Wellington.*

'There's no mention of gold?' Sharpe had expected elucidation at this meeting. He seemed to find only more mysteries.

'We didn't think it wise to tell too many people about a great pile of gold that's looking for an owner. It sort of encourages greed, if you follow me.'

A moth flew crazy circles round the candle flames. Sharpe heard dogs barking in the town, the tramping of horses in the stables behind the headquarters.

'So how much gold?'

'Kearsey will tell you. It can be carried.'

'Christ Almighty! Can't you tell me anything?'

Hogan smiled. 'Not much. I'll tell you this much, though.' He leaned back, locked his fingers behind his head. 'The war's going bad, Richard. It's not our fault. We need men, guns, horses, powder, everything. The enemy gets stronger. But there's only one thing can save us now, and that's this money.'

'Why?'

'I can't tell you.' Hogan sighed, pained by hiding something from a trusted friend. 'We have something that is secret, Richard, and it must stay that way.' He waved down an interruption. 'It's the biggest damned secret I've ever seen, and we don't want anyone to know – anyone. You'll know in the end, I promise you; everyone will. But for the moment, get the gold; pay for the secret.'

They had marched at midnight. Hogan had waved them farewell, and now with the dawn bleaching the sky the Light Company was climbing the gorge of the river Coa towards the fortress town of Almeida. A shadowy picquet had waved them across the narrow, high bridge that spanned the river, and it had seemed to Sharpe, in that moment, that he was marching into the unknown. The road from the river zigzagged up the side of the gorge. Jagged rocks loomed over the path; the creeping dawn showed a savage landscape half hidden by mist from the water. The men were silent, saving their breath for the steep road.

Almeida, a mile or so ahead, was like an island in French territory. It was a Portuguese fortress town, manned by the Portuguese army under British leaders, but the countryside around was in French hands. Soon, Sharpe knew, the French would have to take Almeida by siege, batter their way through its famous walls, storm the breach, drown the island in blood so they could march safely towards Lisbon. The sentries on the bridge had stamped their feet and waved at the dark hills. 'No patrols yesterday. You should be all right.'

The Light Company were not worried by the French. If Richard Sharpe wanted to lead them to Paris they would go, blindly confident that he would see them through, and they had grinned when he had told them they were to march behind the enemy patrols, across the Coa, across the river

Agueda – for Hogan had known that much – and then back again. But something in Sharpe's voice had been wrong; no one had said anything, but the knowledge was there that the Captain was worried. Harper had picked it up. He had marched alongside Sharpe as the road dropped towards the Coa, its surface still sticky from the rain.

'What's the problem, sir?'

'There isn't one.' Sharpe's tone had shut off the conversation, but he was remembering Hogan's final words. Sharpe had been pushing and probing, trying for information that Hogan was not giving. 'Why us? It sounds like a job for cavalry.'

Hogan nodded. 'The cavalry tried, and failed. Kearsey says the country's not good for horses.'

'But the French cavalry use it?'

Another tired nod. 'Kearsey says you'll be all right.' There was something constrained about Hogan's voice.

'You're worried about it.'

Hogan spread his hands. 'We should have fetched the gold out days ago. The longer it's there, the riskier it gets.'

There had been a fraction of silence in the room. The moth had burned its wings, was flapping on the table, and Sharpe crushed it. 'You don't think we'll succeed, do you.' It was a statement, not a question.

Hogan looked up from the dead moth. 'No.'

'So the war's lost?' Hogan nodded. Sharpe flicked the moth on to the floor. 'But the General says there are other tricks up his sleeve. That this isn't the only hope.'

Hogan's eyes were tired. 'He has to say that.'

Sharpe had stood up 'So why the hell don't you send three bloody regiments in? Four. Send the bloody army! Make sure you get the gold.'

'It's too far, Richard. There are no roads beyond Almeida. If we attract attention, then the French will be there before us. The regiments could never get across both rivers without a fight, and they'd be outnumbered. No. We're sending you.'

And now he was climbing the tight bends of the border road, watching the dull horizon for the telltale gleam of a drawn enemy sabre, and marching in the knowledge that he was expected to fail. He hoped Major Kearsey, who waited for the Company in Almeida, had more faith, but Hogan had been diffident about the Major. Sharpe had probed again. 'Is he unreliable?'

Hogan shook his head. 'He's one of the best, Richard, one of the very best. But he's not exactly the man we'd have chosen for this job.'

He had refused to elaborate. Kearsey, he had told Sharpe, was an exploring officer, one of the men who rode fast horses behind enemy lines, in full uniform, and sent back a stream of information, despatches captured from the French by the Partisans and maps of the countryside. It was Kearsey who had discovered the gold, informed Wellington, and only Kearsey knew its exact location. Kearsey, suitable or not, was the key to success.

The road flattened on the high crest of the Coa's east bank, and ahead, silhouetted in the dawn light, was Portugal's northern fortress, Almeida. It dominated the countryside for miles around, a town built on a hill that rose to the huge bulk of a cathedral and a castle side by side. Below those buildings, massive and challenging, the thick-tiled houses fell away down the steep streets until they met Almeida's real defences. In this early light, at this distance, it was the castle that impressed, with its four huge turrets and crenellated walls, but Sharpe knew that the high battlements had long been out of date, replaced by the low, grey ramparts that spread a vast, grim pattern round the town. He did not envy the French. They would have to attack across open ground, through a scientifically designed maze of ditches and hidden walls, and all the time they would be enfiladed by dozens of masked batteries that could pour canister and grape into the killing-ground between the long, sleek arms of the star-like fortifications. Almeida had been fortified, its defences rebuilt only seven years before, and the old, redundant castle looked down on the modern, unglamorous, granite monster that was designed only to lure, to trap, and to destroy.

Closer, the defences seemed less threatening. It was an illusion. The old days of sheer, high walls were past and the best modern fortresses were surrounded by smooth hummocks, like the ones the Light Company approached, that were so gently sloping that even a cripple could walk up without losing breath. The hummocks were there to deflect the besiegers' cannon shots, to send the balls and shells ricocheting into the air, over the defences, so that when the infantry attacked, up the gentle, innocent grass slopes, they would find the murderous traps intact. At the top of that slope was hidden a vast ditch, at the far side of which was a granite-faced wall, topped by belching guns, and even if that were taken there was another behind, and another, and Sharpe was glad he was not summoning the strength to attack a fortress like this. It would come, he knew, because before the French were spat out of Spain the British would have to take towns like this, and he pushed away the thought. Sufficient unto the day was that evil.

The Portuguese defenders were as impressive as their walls. The Company marched through the first gate, a tunnel that took two right turns beneath the first massive wall, and Sharpe was pleased at the look of the Portuguese. They were nothing like the shambles that had called itself the army of Spain. The Portuguese looked confident, with the arrogance of soldiers secure in their own strength and unafraid of the French storm that would soon lap round the walls of their huge, granite star. The town's steep streets were virtually empty of civilians, most of the houses barred shut, and to Sharpe it was as if Almeida were waiting, empty, for some great event. It was certainly prepared. From the guns on the inner walls to the bales of food stacked in courtyards, the fortress was supplied and ready. It was Portugal's front door and Masséna would need all his fox-like cunning and strength to open it.

Brigadier Cox, the English Commander of the garrison, had his headquarters at the top of the hill, but Sharpe found him outside, in the main Plaza, watching his men roll barrels of gunpowder into the door of the cathedral. Cox, tall and distinguished, returned Sharpe's salute.

'Honoured, Sharpe, honoured. Heard about Talavera.'

'Thank you, sir.' He glanced at the barrels going into the dark interior of the cathedral. 'You seem well prepared.'

Cox nodded happily. 'We are, Sharpe, we are. Filled to the gunwales and ready to go.' He nodded at the cathedral. 'That's our magazine.'

Sharpe showed his surprise and Cox laughed. 'The best defences in Portugal and nowhere to store the ammunition. Can you imagine that? Luckily they built that cathedral to last. Walls like Windsor Castle and crypts like dungeons. Hey presto, a magazine. No, I can't complain, Sharpe. Plenty of guns, plenty of ammunition. We should hold the Froggies up for a couple of months.' He looked speculatively at Sharpe's faded green jacket. 'I could do with some prime Riflemen, though.'

Sharpe could see his Company being ordered on to the main ramparts and he swiftly changed the subject. 'I understand I'm to report to Major Kearsey, sir.'

'Ah! Our exploring officer! You'll find him in the place nearest to God.' Cox laughed.

Sharpe was puzzled. 'I'm sorry, sir?'

'Top of the castle, Sharpe. Can't miss it, right by the telegraph. Your lads can get breakfast in the castle.'

'Thank you, sir.'

Sharpe climbed the winding stairs of the mast-topped turret and, as he came into the early sunlight, understood Cox's reference to nearness to God. Beyond the wooden telegraph with its four motionless bladders, identical to the arrangement in Celorico, Sharpe saw a small man on his knees, an open Bible lying next to a telescope at his side. Sharpe coughed and the small man opened a fierce, battling eye.

'Yes?'

'Sharpe, sir. South Essex.'

Kearsey nodded, shut the eye, and went back to his prayers, his lips moving at double speed until he had finished. Then he took a deep breath, smiled at the sky as if his duty were done, and turned an abruptly fierce expression on Sharpe. 'Kearsey.' He stood up, his spurs clicking on the stones. The cavalryman was a foot shorter than Sharpe, but he seemed to compensate for his lack of height with a look of Cromwellian fervour and rectitude. 'Pleased to meet you, Sharpe.' His voice was gruff and he did not sound in the least pleased. 'Heard about Talavera, of course. Well done.'

'Thank you, sir.' Kearsey had succeeded in making the

compliment sound as if it had come from a man who had personally captured two or three dozen Eagles and was encouraging an apprentice. The Major closed his Bible.

'Do you pray, Sharpe?'

'No, sir.'

'A Christian?'

It seemed a strange conversation to be having on the verge of losing the whole war, but Sharpe knew of other officers like this who carried their faith to war like an extraordinary weapon.

'I suppose so, sir.'

Kearsey snorted. 'Don't suppose! Either you're washed in the blood of the Lamb or not. I'll talk to you later about it.'

'Yes, sir. Something to look forward to.'

Kearsey glared at Sharpe, but decided to believe him. 'Glad you're here, Sharpe. We can get going. You know what we're doing?' He did not wait for an answer. 'One day's march to Casatejada, pick up the gold, escort it back to British lines, and send it on its way. Clear?'

'No, sir.'

Kearsey had already started walking towards the staircase, and, hearing Sharpe's words, he stopped abruptly, swivelled, and looked up at the Rifleman. The Major was wearing a long, black cloak, and in the first light he looked like a malevolent small bat.

'What don't you understand?'

'Where the gold is, who it belongs to, how we get it out, where it's going, do the enemy know, why us and not cavalry, and most of all, sir, what it's going to be used for.'

'Used for?' Kearsey looked puzzled. 'Used for? None of your business, Sharpe.'

'So I understand, sir.'

Kearsey was walking back to the battlement. 'Used for! It's Spanish gold. They can do what they like with it. They can buy more gaudy statues for their Romish churches, if they want to, but they won't.' He started barking, and Sharpe realized, after a moment's panic, that the Major was laughing. 'They'll buy guns, Sharpe, to kill the French.'

'I thought the gold was for us, sir. The British.'

Kearsey sounded like a dog coughing, Sharpe decided, and

he watched as Kearsey almost doubled over with his strange laugh. 'Forgive me, Sharpe. For us? What a strange idea. It's Spanish gold, belongs to them. Not for us at all! Oh, no! We're just delivering it safely to Lisbon and the Royal Navy will ship it down to Cádiz.' Kearsey started his strange barking again, repeating to himself, 'For us! For us!'

Sharpe decided it was not the time, or place, to enlighten the Major. It did not matter much what Kearsey thought, as long as the gold was taken safely back over the river Coa. 'Where is it now, sir?'

'I told you. Casatejada.' Kearsey bristled at Sharpe, as though he resented giving away precious information, but then he seemed to relent and sat on the edge of the telegraph platform and riffled the pages of his Bible as he talked. 'It's Spanish gold. Sent by the government to Salamanca to pay the army. The army gets defeated, remember? So the Spaniards have a problem. Lot of money in the middle of nowhere, no army, and the countryside crawling with the French. Luckily a good man got hold of the gold, told me, and I came up with the solution.'

'The Royal Navy.'

'Precisely! We send the gold back to the government in Cádiz.'

'Who's the "good man", sir?'

'Ah. Cesar Moreno. A fine man, Sharpe. He leads a guerrilla band. He brought the gold from Salamanca.'

'How much, sir?'

'Sixteen thousand coins.'

The amount meant nothing to Sharpe. It depended how much each coin weighed. 'Why doesn't Moreno bring it over the border, sir?'

Kearsey stroked his grey moustache, twitched at his cloak, and seemed unsettled by the question. He looked fiercely at Sharpe, as if weighing up whether to say more, and then sighed. 'Problems, Sharpe, problems. Moreno's band is small and he's joined up with another group, a bigger group, and the new man doesn't want us to help. This man's marrying Moreno's daughter, has a lot of influence, and he's our problem. He thinks we just want to steal the gold! Can you imagine that?' Sharpe could, very well, and he suspected that

Wellington had more than imagined it. Kearsey slapped at a fly. 'Wasn't helped by our failure two weeks ago.'

'Failure?'

Kearsey looked unhappy. 'Cavalry, Sharpe. My own regiment, too. We sent fifty men and they got caught.' He chopped his hand up and down as if it were a sabre. 'Fifty. So we lost face to the Spanish. They don't trust us, and they think we're losing the war and planning to take their gold. El Católico wants to move the gold by land, but I've persuaded them to give us one more chance!'

After a dearth of information Sharpe was suddenly being deluged with new facts. 'El Católico, sir?'

'I told you! The new man. Marrying Moreno's daughter.'

'But why El Católico?'

A stork flapped its way up into the sky, legs back, long wings edged with black, and Kearsey watched it for a second or two.

'Ah! See what you mean. The Catholic. He prays over his victims before he kills them. The Latin prayer for the dead. Just as a joke, of course.' The Major sounded gloomy. His fingers riffled the pages as if he were drawing strength from the psalms and stories that were beneath his fingertips. 'He's a dangerous man, Sharpe. Ex-officer, knows how to fight, and he doesn't want us to be involved.'

Sharpe took a deep breath, walked to the battlement, and stared at the rocky northern landscape. 'So, sir. The gold is a day's march from here, guarded by Moreno and El Católico, and our job is to fetch it, persuade them to let us take it, and escort it safely over the border.'

'Quite right.'

'What's to stop Moreno already taking it, sir? I mean, while you're here.'

Kearsey gave a single snorting bark. 'Thought of that, Sharpe. Left a man there, one of the Regiment, good man. He's keeping an eye on things, keeping the Partisans sweet.' Kearsey stood up and, in the growing heat of the sun, shrugged off his cloak. His uniform was blue with a pelisse of silver lace and grey fur. At his side was the polished-steel scabbard of the curved sabre. It was the uniform of the Prince of Wales Dragoons, of Claud Hardy, of Josefina's lover,

Sharpe's usurper. Kearsey pushed the Bible into his slung sabretache. 'Moreno trusts us; it's only El Católico we have to worry about, and he likes Hardy. I think it will be all right.'

'Hardy?' Sharpe had somehow sensed it, the feeling of an incomplete story.

'That's right.' Kearsey glanced sharply at the Rifleman. 'Captain Claud Hardy. You know him?'

'No, sir.'

Which was true. He had never met him, just watched Josefina walk away to Hardy's side. He had thought that the rich young cavalry officer was in Lisbon, dancing away the nights, and instead he was here! Waiting a day's march away. He stared westward, away from Kearsey, at the deep, dark-shadowed gorge of the Coa that slashed across the landscape. Kearsey stamped his feet.

'Anything else, Sharpe?'

'No, sir.'

'Good. We march tonight. Nine o'clock.'

Sharpe turned back. 'Yes, sir.'

'One rule, Sharpe. I know the country, you don't, so no questions, just instant obedience.'

'Yes, sir.'

'Company prayers at sunset, unless the Froggies interfere.'

'Yes, sir.' Good Lord!

Kearsey returned Sharpe's salute. 'Nine o'clock, then. At the north gate!' He turned and clattered down the winding stairs and Sharpe went back to the battlement, leaned on the granite, and stared unseeing at the huge sprawl of defences beneath him.

Josefina. Hardy. He squeezed the silver ring, engraved with an eagle, which she had bought for him before the battle, but which had been her parting gift when the killing had finished along the banks of the Portina stream north of Talavera. He had tried to forget her, to tell himself she was not worth it, and as he looked up at the rough countryside to the north he tried to force his mind away from her, to think of the gold, of El Católico, the praying killer, and Cesar Moreno. But to do the job with Josefina's lover? God damn it!

A midshipman, far from the sea, came on to the turret to man the telegraph, and he looked curiously at the tall, dark-haired Rifleman with the scarred face. He looked, the midshipman decided, a dangerous beast, and he watched as a big, tanned hand fidgeted with the hilt of an enormous, straight-bladed sword.

'She's a bitch!' Sharpe said.

'Pardon, sir?' The midshipman, fifteen years old, was frightened.

Sharpe turned, unaware he had been joined. 'Nothing, son, nothing.' He grinned at the bemused boy. 'Gold for greed, women for jealousy, and death for the French. Right?'

'Yes, sir. Of course, sir.'

The boy watched the tall man go down the stairs. Once he had wanted to join the army, years before, but his father had simply looked up and said that anyone who joined the army was stark mad. He started untying the ropes that secured the bladders. His father, as ever, had been undoubtedly right.

CHAPTER 4

On foot Kearsey was busy and, to Sharpe's eyes, ludicrous. He strutted with tiny steps, legs scissoring quickly, while his eyes, above the big, grey moustache, peered acutely at the mass of taller humanity. On horseback, though, astride his huge roan, he was at home as if he had been restored to his true height. Sharpe was impressed by the night's march. The moon was thin and cloud-ridden, yet the Major led the Company unerringly across difficult country. They crossed the frontier somewhere in the darkness, a grunt from Kearsey announcing the news, and then the route led downhill to the river Agueda, where they waited for the first sign of dawn.

If Kearsey was impressive he was also annoying. The march had been punctuated with advice, condescending advice, as if Kearsey were the only man who understood the problems. He certainly knew the countryside, from the farmlands along the road from Almeida to Ciudad Rodrigo, to the high country that was to the north, the chaos of the valleys and hills that dropped finally to the river Duero, into which the Coa and the Agueda flowed. He knew the villages, the paths, the rivers and where they could be crossed; he knew the high hills and the sheltered passes, and within the lonely countryside he knew the guerrilla bands and where they could be found. Sitting in the mist that ghosted up from the Agueda, he talked, in his gruff voice, about the Partisans. Sharpe and Knowles listened, the unseen river a sound in the background, as the Major talked of ambushes and murders, the secret places where arms were stored, and the signal codes that flashed from hilltop to hilltop.

'Nothing can move here, Sharpe, nothing, without the Partisans knowing. The French have to escort every messenger with four hundred men. Imagine that? Four hundred sabres to protect one despatch and sometimes even that's not enough.'

Sharpe could imagine it, and even pity the French for it. Wellington paid hard cash for every captured despatch; sometimes they came to his headquarters with the crusted blood of the dead messenger still crisp on the paper. The messenger who died clean in such a fight was lucky. The wounded were taken not for the information but for revenge, and the war in the hills between French and Spanish was a terrible tale of ghastly pain. Kearsey was riffling the pages of his unseen Bible as he talked.

'By day the men are shepherds, farmers, millers, but by night they're killers. For every Frenchman we kill, they kill two. Think what it's like for the French, Sharpe. Every man, every woman, every child, is an enemy in the countryside. Even the catechism has changed. "Are the French true believers?" "No, they are the devil's spawn, doing his work, and must be eradicated."' He gave his barking laugh.

Knowles stretched his legs. 'Do the women fight, sir?'

'They fight, Lieutenant, like the men. Moreno's daughter, Teresa, is as good as any man. She knows how to ambush, to pursue. I've seen her kill.'

Sharpe looked up and saw the mist silvering overhead as the dawn leaked across the hills. 'Is she the one who's to marry El Católico?'

Kearsey laughed. 'Yes.' He was silent for a second. 'They're not all good, of course. Some are just brigands, looting their own people.' He was silent again. Knowles picked up his uncertainty.

'Do you mean El Católico, sir?'

'No.' Kearsey still seemed uncertain. 'But he's a hard man. I've seen him skin a Frenchman alive, inch by inch, and praying over him at the same time.' Knowles made a sound of disgust, but Kearsey, visible now, shook his head. 'You must understand, Lieutenant, how much they hate. Teresa's mother was killed by the French and she did not die well.' He peered down at the Bible, trying to read the print, then looked up at the lightening mist. 'We must move. Casatejada's a two-hour march.' He stood up. 'You'll find it best to tie your boots round your neck as we cross the river.'

47

'Yes, sir.' Sharpe said it patiently. He had probably crossed a thousand rivers in his years as a soldier, but Kearsey insisted on treating them all as pure amateurs.

Once over the Agueda, waist-high and cold, they were beyond the farthest British patrols. From now on there was no hope of any friendly cavalry, no Captain Lossow with his German sabres, to help out in trouble. This was French territory, and Kearsey rode ahead, searching the landscape for signs of the enemy. The hills were the French hunting-ground, the scene of countless small and bloody encounters between cavalrymen and Partisans, and Kearsey led the Light Company on paths high up the slopes so that should an enemy patrol appear they could scramble quickly into the high rocks where horsemen could not follow. The Company seemed excited, glad to be near the enemy, and they grinned at Sharpe as he watched them file past on the goat track.

He had only twenty Riflemen now, including himself and Harper, out of the thirty-one survivors he had led from the horror of the retreat to Corunna. They were good men, the Green Jackets, the best in the army, and he was proud of them. Daniel Hagman, the old poacher, who was the best marksman. Parry Jenkins, five feet and four inches of Welsh loquaciousness, who could tease fish out of the most reluctant water. Jenkins, in battle, partnered Isaiah Tongue, educated in books and alcohol, who believed Napoleon was an enlightened genius, England a foul tyranny, but nevertheless fought with the cool deliberation of a good Rifleman. Tongue wrote letters for the other men in the Company, read their infrequent mail when it arrived, and dearly wanted to argue his levelling ideas with Sharpe, but dared not. They were good men.

The other thirty-three were all Redcoats, armed with the smoothbore Brown Bess musket, but they had proved themselves at Talavera and in the tedious winter patrols. Lieutenant Knowles, still awed by Sharpe, but a good officer, decisive and fair. Sharpe nodded at James Kelly, an Irish Corporal, who had stunned the Battalion by marrying Pru Baxter, a widow who was a foot taller and two stones heavier than the skinny Kelly, but the Irishman had hardly stopped smiling in the three months since the marriage. Sergeant

Read, the Methodist, who worried about the souls of the Company, and so he should. Most were criminals, avoiding justice by enlisting, and nearly all were drunks, but they were in Sharpe's Company and he would defend them, even the useless ones like Private Batten or Private Roach, who pimped his wife for a shilling a time.

Sergeant Harper, the best of them all, moved alongside Sharpe. Next to the seven-barrelled gun he had slung two packs belonging to men who were falling with tiredness after the night's march. He nodded ahead. 'What's next, sir?'

'We pick up the gold and come back. Simple.'

Harper grinned. In battle he was savage, crooning the old stories of the Gaelic heroes, the warriors of Ireland, but away from the fighting he covered his intelligence with a charm that would have fooled the devil. 'You believe that, sir?'

Sharpe had no time to reply. Kearsey had stopped, two hundred yards ahead, and dismounted. He pointed left, up the slope, and Sharpe repeated the gesture. The Company moved quickly into the stones and crouched while Sharpe, still puzzled, ran towards the Major. 'Sir?'

Kearsey did not reply. The Major was alert, like a dog pointing at game, but Sharpe could see from his eyes that Kearsey was not sure what had alarmed him. Instinct, the soldier's best gift, was working, and Sharpe, who trusted his own instinct, could sense nothing. 'Sir?'

The Major nodded at a hilltop, half a mile away. 'See the stones?'

Sharpe could see a heap of boulders on the peak of the hill. 'Yes, sir.'

'There's a white stone showing, yes?' Sharpe nodded, and Kearsey seemed relieved that his eyes had not deceived him. 'That means the enemy are abroad. Come on.'

The Major led his horse, Marlborough, into the tangle of rocks, and Sharpe followed patiently, wondering how many other secret signs they had passed in the night. The Company were curious, but silent, and Kearsey led them over the crest, into a rock-strewn valley, and then eastwards again, back on course for the village where the gold should be waiting.

'They won't be up here, Sharpe.' The Major sounded certain.

Where, then?'

Kearsey nodded ahead, past the head of the valley. He looked worried. 'Casatejada.'

To the north, over the hilltops, a bank of cloud was ominous and still on the horizon, but otherwise the sky was arching an untouched blue over the pale grass and rocks. To Sharpe's eyes there was nothing strange in the landscape. A rock thrush, startled and noisy, flew from the Company's path, and Sharpe saw Harper smile with enjoyment. The Sergeant could have spent his life watching birds, but he gave the thrush only a few seconds' attention before searching the skyline again. Everything seemed innocent, a high valley in morning sunshine, yet the whole Company was alert because of the Major's sudden knowledge.

A mile up the valley, as the sides began to flatten out into a bleak hilltop, Kearsey tethered Marlborough to a rock. He talked to the horse and Sharpe knew that on many lonely days, behind French lines, the small Major would have only the big, intelligent roan for company. The Major turned back to Sharpe, the gruffness back in his voice. 'Come on. Keep low.'

The skyline proved to be a false crest. Beyond was a gully, shaped like a bowl, and as Sharpe ran over the lip he realized that Kearsey had brought them to a vantage point high in the hills that was overlooked only by the peak with its white, warning stone. It was a steep scramble over the edge, impossible for a horse, and the Company tumbled into the bowl and sat, grateful for the rest, as Kearsey beckoned Sharpe to the far side. 'Keep low!' The two officers used hands and feet to climb the bowl's inner face and then they were peering over the edge. 'Casatejada.' Kearsey spoke almost grudgingly, as if not wanting to share this high and secret village with another Englishman.

Casatejada was beautiful: a small village in a high valley that was built where two streams met and irrigated enough land to keep forty or so houses filled with food. Sharpe began to memorize the layout of the village, two miles away, from the old fortress-tower at one end of the main street, a reminder that this was border country, past the church, to the one large house at the far end of the street. He dared not use his telescope, pointing it eastwards towards the rising sun that might flash on the lens, but even without it, he could see that the house was built round a lavish courtyard and that within its outer walls were stables and outbuildings. He asked Kearsey about the house.

'Moreno's house, Sharpe.'

'He's rich?'

Kearsey shrugged. 'Used to be. The family own the whole valley and a lot of other land. But who's rich with the French here?' Kearsey's eyes flicked left, down the street. 'The *castillo*. Ruins now, but they used to take refuge there from the raids over the hills.'

There were no animals in sight, no humans, just the wind stirring the barley that should have been harvested. The single village street was empty and Sharpe let his eyes travel beyond the church, across a flat pasture to some stunted fruit trees, and there, half hidden by the orchard, was another church and a bell-tower.

'What's the far church?'

'Hermitage.'

'Hermitage?'

Kearsey grunted. 'Some holy man lived there, long ago, and they built the shrine. It's not used now, except that the graveyard's there.' Sharpe could see the walled cemetery through the trees. Kearsey nodded at the hermitage. 'That's where the gold is.'

'Where's it hidden?'

'In the Moreno vault, inside the hermitage.'

The village street ran left and right across Sharpe's vision. To the right, to the south, the street became a road that disappeared in the purple shadows at the far end of the valley, miles away, but to the left the road came nearer to the hills before disappearing into the slopes. He pointed.

'Where does it go?'

'Ford at San Anton.' Kearsey was chewing his grey moustache, glancing up at the white stone on the hilltop, back to the village. 'They must be there.'

'Who?'

'The French.'

Nothing moved, except the wind on the heavy barley. Kearsey's eyes flicked up and down the valley. 'An ambush.'

'What do you mean, sir?' Sharpe was beginning to understand that in this kind of warfare he knew nothing.

Kearsey spoke quietly. 'The weathervane on the church. It's moving. When the Partisans are in the village they jam it with a metal rod so you know they're there. There are no animals. The French have butchered them for food. They're waiting, Sharpe, in the village, and they want the Partisans to think they've gone.'

'Will they?'

Kearsey gave his asthmatic bark. 'No. They're too clever. The French can wait all day.'

'And us, sir?'

Kearsey flashed one of his fierce glances on Sharpe. 'We wait, too.'

The men had piled their arms on the floor of the bowl, and as the sun rose they used the weapons to support spread greatcoats to give themselves shade. The water in the canteens was brackish but drinkable, and the Company grumbled because, before leaving Almeida, Sharpe, Harper and Knowles had virtually stripped each man and taken away twelve bottles of wine and two of rum. Even so, Sharpe knew, someone would have drink, but not enough to do any harm. The sun's heat increased, baking the rocks, while most of the Company slept, heads pillowed on haversacks, and single sentries watched the empty landscape around the hidden gully. Sharpe was frustrated. He could climb the gully's rim, see where the gold was stored, see where the survival of the army was hidden in a seemingly uninhabited valley, yet he could do nothing. As midday approached he slept.

'Sir!' Harper was shaking him. 'We've got action.'

He had slept no more than fifteen minutes. 'Action?'

'In the valley, sir.'

The Company were stirring, looking eagerly at Sharpe, but he waved them down. They must stifle their curiosity and watch, instead, as Sharpe and Harper climbed up beside Kearsey and Knowles on the rock rim. Kearsey was grinning. 'Watch this.'

From the north, from a track that led down from high pastures, five horsemen trotted slowly towards the village. Kearsey had his telescope extended and Sharpe found his own. 'Partisans, sir?'

Kearsey nodded. 'Three of them.'

Sharpe pulled out his glass, his fingers feeling the inset brass plate, and found the small group of horsemen. The Spaniards rode, straight-backed and easy, looking relaxed and comfortable, but their two companions were quite different. Naked men, tied to the saddles, and through the glass Sharpe could see their heads jerking with fear as they wondered what was to happen to them.

'Prisoners.' Kearsey said the word fiercely.

'What's going to happen?' Knowles was fidgeting.

'Wait.' Kearsey was still grinning.

Nothing stirred in the village. If the French were there they were well hidden. Kearsey chuckled. 'The ambushers ambushed!'

The horsemen had stopped. Sharpe swung the glass back. One Spaniard held the reins of the prisoners' horses while the others dismounted. The naked men were pulled from their saddles and the ropes that had tied their legs beneath the horses' bellies were used to lash their ankles tightly together. Then more rope was produced, thick loops hanging from the Partisans' saddles, and the two Frenchmen were tied behind the horses. Knowles had borrowed Sharpe's telescope and beneath his tan he paled, shocked by the sight.

'They won't run far,' the Lieutenant said half in hope.

Kearsey shook his head. 'They will.'

Sharpe took the glass back. The Partisans were unfastening their saddle-bags, going back to the horses with the roped men. 'What are they doing, sir?'

'Thistles.'

Sharpe understood. Along the paths and in the high rocks huge purple thistles grew, often as high as a man, and the Spanish, a horse at a time, were thrusting the heads of the spiny plants beneath the empty saddles. The first horse began fighting, rearing up, but was held firm, until with a final crack over its rump the beast was released and it sprung off, infuriated by the pain, the prisoner jerked by the legs and scraped in a cloud of dust behind the angry horse.

The second horse followed, pulling left and right, zigzagging behind the first towards the village. The three Spaniards mounted and stood their horses quietly. One had a long cigar, and through the telescope Sharpe saw the smoke drift over the fields.

'Good God.' Knowles stared unbelieving.

'No need for blasphemy.' Kearsey's gruff reprimand did not hide the excitement in his voice.

The two naked, tied men were invisible in the dust, but, as the horses swerved at a rock, Sharpe caught a glimpse, a flash through the cloud, of a body streaked red, and then the horse was running again. By now the Frenchmen would be unconscious, the pain gone, but the Partisans had guessed right and Sharpe saw the first movement in the village as the gates of Cesar Moreno's big house were thrown open and cavalry, hidden all morning, rode on to the street. Sharpe saw sky-blue trousers, brown jackets, and the tall fur helmet. 'Hussars.'

'Wait. This is the clever bit.' Kearsey could not hide this admiration.

The Hussars, sabres drawn, cantered down the street to meet the two horses with their terrible attachments. It seemed that the Spanish plan was to end in anti-climax, for the Hussars would rescue the two bloody and battered Frenchmen at the northern end of the village, but then the two horses became aware of the cavalry. They stopped.

'Jesus,' Harper muttered. He was using Sharpe's glass. 'One of those buggers is moving.'

Sharpe could see him. Far from unconscious, one of the two naked Frenchmen was trying to sit up, a writhing mass of blood, but suddenly he was whirled back to the roadway, wrenched terribly about, and the horses were moving, away from the Hussars, splitting apart in a mad, panicked gallop. Kearsey nodded in satisfaction. 'They won't go near French cavalry, not unless they're ridden. They're too used to running from it.'

There was chaos in the valley. The horses, with their thistle-driven pain, circled crazily in the fields; the Hussars, all order gone, tried to ride them down, and the nearer the French came to them the more the Spanish horses took the disorganized mass northwards. Sharpe guessed there were a hundred Frenchmen, in undisciplined groups, crossing and recrossing the fields. He looked back to the village, saw more horsemen standing in the street, watching the chase, and he wondered how he would feel if those two bodies were his men, and he knew that he would do what the French were doing: try to rescue them.

'Good.' Knowles seemed to have sided, instinctively, with the French.

One of the horses had been caught and quieted, and dismounted French cavalrymen were unbuckling the girth and untying the prisoner. A trumpet sounded, calling order to the scattered Hussars who still raced after the other horse, and at that exact moment, as the trumpet notes reached the gully, El Católico launched his own horsemen from the northern hills. They came down on to the scattered and outnumbered French in a long line, blacks and browns and greys, swords of all descriptions held over their heads, the dust spurting behind them, while from the rocks on the hillside Sharpe saw muskets firing over their heads at the surprised French.

Kearsey almost jumped over the rim with joy. His fist slammed into the rock. 'Perfect!'

The ambushers had been ambushed.

CHAPTER 5

El Católico, the Catholic, led the horsemen from the cover of the hills, and Sharpe found him in the telescope. Kearsey barked out a description, but even without it Sharpe would have recognized the tall man as the leader. 'Grey cloak, grey boots, long rapier, black horse.'

Kearsey was thumping his fist on the rock, willing the Partisans on, closer and closer to the wheeling French. Sharpe scanned the guerrilla line, looking for the blue and silver of a Prince of Wales Dragoon, but he could see no sign of Captain Hardy. He remembered Kearsey saying that El Católico's fiancée, Teresa, fought like a man, but he could see no woman in the charging line, just men screaming defiance as the first horses met and the swords chopped down on the out-numbered French.

In the village the trumpets split the quiet; men scrambled on to nervous mounts, sabres hissed from scabbards, but El Católico was no fool. He was not going to fight a regiment and lose. Sharpe saw him waving at his men, turning them back, and the Rifleman searched with the telescope in the obscuring dust for clues to what was happening. The French had been hard-punished. Outnumbered two to one, they had fallen back, taking casualties, and the Spanish charge had given them no time to form a disciplined line. Sharpe saw prisoners, dragged by the arms, going back with the horsemen who had been disciplined, presumably by El Católico, to make the one killing charge and then get out of danger's way. Sharpe admired the action. The French had been baited, had fallen for the lure, and then been savagely hurt in one quick charge. It was hardly two minutes since the Spanish had appeared and already, hidden by dust, they were returning to the hills and taking with them more prisoners whose fate would be worse than that of the two men who had drawn the Hussars from the safety of the village walls. One man alone stayed in the valley.

El Católico stood his horse and watched the Hussars stretching out from the village. Closer to him were the survivors of the Spanish charge and they now spurred their horses to attack the lone Partisan. El Católico seemed unconcerned. He urged his horse into a canter, away from the safety of the hills, circled in the uncut barley and looked over his shoulder as the French came close. A dozen men were chasing him, leaning over their horses' manes, sabres stretched out, and it was certain that the tall Partisan leader must be taken until, at the last moment, his horse sidestepped, the thin rapier flashed, one Frenchman was down and the big, black horse with its grey rider was in full gallop to the north and the Hussars were milling in uncertainty where their leader lay dead. Sharpe whistled softly.

Kearsey smiled. 'He's the finest swordsman on the border. Probably in Spain. I've seen him take on four Frenchmen and he never stopped saying the prayer for their death.'

Sharpe stared into the valley. A hundred horsemen had ridden out to rescue the two prisoners and now two dozen of the Hussars were dead or captured. The Partisans had lost none; the speed of their charge and withdrawal had ensured that, and their leader, staying till the end, had slapped French pride in the face. The black horse was cantering to the hills, its strength obvious, and the French would never catch El Católico.

Kearsey slid down from the skyline. 'That's how it's done.'

Sharpe nodded. 'Impressive. Except for one thing.'

The fierce eyebrow shot up. 'What?'

'What are the French doing in the village?'

Kearsey shrugged. 'Clearing out a hornet's nest.' He waved southwards. 'Remember their main road is down there. All the supplies for the siege of Almeida go through this area, and when they invade Portugal proper, then everything will come through here. They don't want Partisans in their rear. They're clearing them out, or trying to.'

The answer made sense to Sharpe, but he was worried. 'And the gold, sir?'

'It's hidden.'

'And Hardy?'

Kearsey was annoyed by the questions. 'He'll be some-where, Sharpe; I don't know. At least El Católico's here, so we're not friendless!' He gave his bark of a laugh and then pulled at his moustache. 'I think it would be sensible to let him know we've arrived.' He slid down the inner side of the gully. 'Keep your men here, Sharpe. I'll ride to El Católico.'

Knowles looked worried. 'Isn't that dangerous, sir?'

Kearsey gave the Lieutenant a pitying look. 'I was not planning to go through the village, Lieutenant.' He gestured towards the north. 'I'll go round the back. I'll see you again tonight sometime, probably late. Don't light any fires!' He strode away, small legs urgent, and Harper waited till he was out of earshot.

'What did he think we were going to do? Borrow a light from the French?' He looked at Sharpe and raised his eyebrows. 'Bloody muddle, sir.'

'Yes.'

But it was not too bad, Sharpe decided. The French could not stay forever; the Partisans would be back in the village, and then there was only the small problem of persuading El Católico to let the British 'escort' the gold towards Lisbon. He turned back towards the valley, watched as the Hussars walked their horses disconsolately towards the village, one of them bearing the bloody horror that had been one of the naked prisoners, then raised his eyes and looked at the hermitage. It was a pity it was the far side of the valley, beyond the village, or else he would have been tempted to search the place that night, Kearsey or no Kearsey. The idea refused to go away and he lay there, the sun hot on his back, and thought of a dozen reasons why he should not make the attempt, and one huge, overriding reason why he should.

The valley settled in peace. The sun burned down on the grass, turning it a paler brown, and still, on the northern horizon, the great cloud bank loomed. There would be rain in a couple of days, Sharpe thought, and then he went back to the route he had planned in his head, down the slope to the road that led to the ford at San Anton, proceed to the big rock that would be a natural marker and then follow the edge of the barley field as far as the stunted fruit trees. Beyond the trees was another barley field that would give good cover and from there it was just fifty yards of open ground to the cemetery and the hermitage. And if the hermitage were locked? He dismissed the idea. A dozen men in the Company had once earned a living by opening up locks they had no right to be near; a lock was no problem, but then there was the task of finding the gold. Kearsey had said it was in the Moreno vault, which should be easy enough to find, and he let his imagination play with the idea of finding the gold in the middle of the night, just two hundred yards from a French regiment, and bringing it safely back to the gully by daybreak. Harper lay beside him, thinking the same thoughts.

'They won't move out the village, sir. Not at night.'

'No.'

'Be a bit difficult finding our way.'

Sharpe pointed to the route he had planned. 'Hagman will lead.'

Harper nodded. Daniel Hagman had an uncanny ability to find his way in the darkness. Sharpe often wondered how the old poacher had ever been caught, but he supposed that one night the Cheshireman had drunk too much. It was the usual story. Harper had one more objection. 'And the Major, sir?' Sharpe said nothing and Harper nodded. 'As you say, sir. A pox on the bloody Major.' The Irish Sergeant grinned. 'We can do it.'

Sharpe lay in the westering sun, looking at the valley, following the course he had planned until he agreed. It could be done. A pox on Kearsey. He imagined the vault as having a vast stone lid; he saw it, in his mind, being heaved back, to reveal a heap of gold coins that would save the army, defeat the French, and he wondered again why the money was needed. He would have to take all the Company, post a string of guards to face the village, preferably Riflemen, and the gold would have to go in their packs. What if there was more than they could carry? Then they must carry what they could. He wondered about a diversion, a small group of Riflemen in the southern end of the valley to distract the French, but he rejected the idea. Keep it simple. Night attacks could go disastrously wrong and the smallest complication could turn a well-thought plan into a horrid mess that cost lives. He felt the excitement grow. They could do it!

At first the trumpet was so faint that it hardly penetrated Sharpe's consciousness. Rather it was Harper's sudden alertness that stirred him, dragged his mind from the gold beneath the Moreno vault, and made him curse as he looked at the road disappearing to the north-east. 'What was that?'

Harper stared at the empty valley. 'Cavalry.'

'North?'

The Sergeant nodded. 'Nearer to us than the Partisans were, sir. Something's happening up there.'

They waited, in silence, and watched the valley. Knowles climbed up beside them. 'What's happening?'

'Don't know.' Sharpe's instinct, so dormant this morning, was suddenly screaming at him. He turned and called to the sentry on the far side of the gully. 'See anything?'

'No, sir.'

'There!'

Harper was pointing to the road. Kearsey was in sight, cantering the roan towards the village and looking over his shoulder, and then the Major turned off the road, began covering the rough ground towards the slopes where the Partisans had disappeared in a hidden entry to one of the twisted valleys that spilled into the main valley.

'What the devil?'

Sharpe's question was answered as soon as he had spoken. Behind Kearsey was a regiment, rank upon rank of horsemen in blue and yellow, each one wearing a strange, square yellow hat, but that was not their oddest feature. Instead of swords the enemy were carrying lances, long, steel-tipped weapons with their red and white pennants, and as the Major turned off the road the lancers kicked in their heels, dropped their points and the race was on. Knowles shook his head. 'What are they?'

'Polish lancers.'

Sharpe's voice was grim. The Poles had a reputation in Europe: nasty fighters, effective fighters. These were the first he had encountered in his career. He remembered the moustachioed Indian face behind the long pole, the twisting, the way the man had played with him, and the final thrust that had pinned Sergeant Sharpe to a tree and held him there till the Tippoo Sultan's men had come and pulled the needle-sharp blade from his side. He still carried the scar. Bloody lancers.

'They won't get him, sir.' Knowles sounded very sure.

'Why not?'

'The Major explained to me, sir. Marlborough's fed on corn and most cavalry horses are grass-fed. A grass-fed horse can't catch a corn-fed horse.'

Sharpe raised his eyebrows. 'Has anyone told the horses?'

The lancers were catching up, slowly and surely, but Sharpe suspected Kearsey was saving the big horse's strength. He watched the Poles and wondered how many regiments of cavalry the French had thrown up into the hills to wipe out the guerrilla bands. He wondered how long they would stay.

Sharpe had snapped his glass open, found Kearsey, and saw the Major look over his shoulder and urge Marlborough to go faster. The big roan responded, widening the gap from the nearest lancers, and Knowles clapped his hands. 'Go on, sir!'

'They must have caught him crossing the road, sir,' Harper said.

Marlborough was taking the Major out of trouble, stretching the lead, galloping easily. Kearsey had not even bothered to unsheath his sabre and Sharpe was just relaxing when suddenly the big horse reared up, twisted sideways, and Kearsey fell.

'What the —'

'Bloody nightjar!' Harper had seen a bird fly up, startled, right beneath the horse's nose. Sharpe wondered, irrelevantly, how the Irishman could possibly have identified the bird at such a distance. He focused the glass again. Kearsey was on his feet, Marlborough was unhurt, and the little man was reaching up desperately to put his foot in the stirrup. The trumpet sounded again, the sound delayed by the distance, but Sharpe had already seen the lancers spurring their horses, reaching out with their nine-foot weapons, and he gritted his teeth as Kearsey seemed to take an age in swinging himself into the saddle.

'Where's El Católico?' Knowles asked.

'Miles away.' Harper sounded gloomy.

The horse went forward again, Kearsey's heels raking back, but the lancers were desperately close. The Major turned the roan downslope towards the village, letting his speed build up before turning back, but his horse seemed winded or frightened. The roan's head tossed nervously, Kearsey urged it, and at the moment when Sharpe knew the lancers must catch him the Major realized it as well. He circled back, sword drawn, and Knowles groaned.

'He might do it yet.' Harper spoke gently, as if to a nervous recruit on the battlefield.

Four lancers were closest to the Major. He spurred towards them, singled one out, and Sharpe saw the sabre, point downwards, high in Kearsey's hand. Marlborough had calmed, and as the lancers thundered in, Kearsey touched the spurs, the horse leapt forward, and the Major had turned the right-hand lance to one side, swivelled his wrist with the speed of a trained swordsman, and one Pole lay beheaded on the ground.

'Beautiful!' Sharpe was grinning. Once a man got past the razor tip of a lance he was safe.

Kearsey was through, crouching on Marlborough's neck, urging the horse on towards the hills, but the first squadron of lancers were close behind their fellows, at full gallop, and the effort was useless. A dust cloud engulfed the Englishman, the silver points disappeared in the storm, and Kearsey was trapped with only his sword to save him. A man reeled out of the fight holding his stomach, and Sharpe knew the sabre had laid open the horseman's guts. The dust billowed like cannon smoke. The lance points were forced upwards in the press and once – Sharpe was not sure – he thought he saw the slashing light of the lifted sabre. It was magnificent, quite hopeless, one man against a regiment, and Sharpe watched the commotion subside, the dust drift towards the night-jar's treacherous nest, and the lance points sink to rest. It was over.

'Poor bastard.' Harper had not been looking forward to

company prayers, but he had never wanted lancers to take away the unpleasant prospect.

'He's alive!' Knowles was pointing. 'Look!'

It was true. Sharpe rested the glass on the rock rim of the gully and saw the Major riding between two of his captors. There was blood on his thigh, a lot, and Sharpe saw Kearsey trying to stem the flow with his two fists where a lance point had gouged into his right leg. It was a good capture for the Poles. An exploring officer whom they could keep for a few months before exchanging for a Frenchman of equal rank. They could well have recognized him. The exploring officers often rode in sight of their enemy, their uniforms distinct, relying on their fast horses to carry them from trouble, and it was possible that the French would decide not to exchange Kearsey for months; perhaps, Sharpe thought with a sinking feeling, till the British had been driven from Portugal.

The depressing thought made him stare at the hermitage, half hidden by trees, the unlikely place where Wellington's hopes were pinned. Without Kearsey it was even more important that the Company should try to find the gold that night, but then those hopes, too, were dashed. Half the lancers rode with their prisoner to the village, but the other half, in a curving column, trotted towards the graveyard and its hermitage. Sharpe cursed beneath his breath. There was no hope now of finding the gold that night. The only chance left was to wait until the French had gone, till they had stopped using the village and the hermitage as their base for the campaign against the Partisans in the hills. And when the French did go, El Católico would come, and Sharpe had no doubt that the tall, grey-cloaked Spaniard would use every effort to stop the British from taking the gold. Only one man stood a chance of persuading the Partisan leader, and that man was a prisoner, wounded, in the hands of the lancers. He slid back from the skyline, turned and stared at the Company.

Harper slid down beside him. 'What do we do, sir?'

'Do? We fight.' Sharpe gripped the hilt of the sword. 'We've been spectators long enough. We get the Major out, tonight.'

Knowles heard him, turned an astonished face on them. 'Get him out, sir? There's two regiments there!'

'So? That's only eight hundred men. There are fifty-three of us.'

'And a dozen Irish.' Harper grinned at the Lieutenant.

Knowles scrambled down the slope, looking at them with a disbelieving stare. 'With respect, sir. You're mad.' He began to laugh. 'Are you serious?'

Sharpe nodded. There was no other choice. Fifty-three men must take on eight hundred, or else the war was lost. He grinned at Knowles. 'Stop worrying! It'll be simple!'

And how the hell, he thought, do we do it?

CHAPTER 6

Sharpe mocked himself. So simple. Just release the Major when two of the finest regiments in the French army were expecting a night attack. The wise course, he thought, was to go home. The French probably had the gold by now, the war was lost, and a sensible man would shoulder his rifle and think about making a living at home. Instead, like a gambler who had lost all but a handful of coins, he was staking everything on one last throw, a throw against odds of sixteen to one.

Which was not, he told himself as the Company filed down a goat track in the darkness, quite true. He had lain on the gully's rim as the sun westered and watched the French preparations. They were thorough, but in their defence was their weakness, and Sharpe had felt the excitement well up inside, the incipient knowledge of success. The French expected an attack by Partisans, by small groups of silent men who would carry knives, or else who would fire muskets from the darkness, and they had prepared themselves for that ordeal. The village did not help them. The houses either side of the narrow street were jostled by low, ragged outbuildings; the whole making a maze of alleyways and dark corners where a silent assassin held the advantage. The French had no outlying sentries. To put a small group of men out in the fields was to write their death sentence, and the French, accustomed to this kind of fighting, had drawn themselves into makeshift fortresses. Most of the cavalry were in Cesar Moreno's house with its ample stabling and high, encircling wall. The other fortress, the only other building with a wall high and strong enough, was the hermitage with its cemetery. Both buildings would be crowded, but both safe from the silent knives, and to make them safer the French had embarked on a crusade of systematic destruction. The cottages nearest the Moreno house had been flattened, the ringing of the big hammers on their stone walls carrying up into the gully, and every tree, every door, every stick of furniture, had been cut and splintered and piled into heaps that could be lit so an attacking Partisan would be denied the gift of darkness. The French held the advantage, but only against Partisans. In their wildest dreams they would not imagine the sudden appearance of British infantry, crossbelts vivid in the defensive firelight, muskets flaming disciplined death. Or so Sharpe hoped.

He had one other advantage, slight but important. Kearsey had obviously given his parole, his gentleman's promise, to his captors that he would not attempt to escape, and Sharpe had seen the small Major limping round the village. Each time, Kearsey had gone back to Moreno's house, and finally, as the light faded, Sharpe had seen the Major sitting on a balcony, on one of the few pieces of furniture left, so at least the rescuers knew where their goal lay. All that remained was to break into the house and for that speed was vital.

The march in the darkness seemed to take forever, but Sharpe dared not hurry the men, for fear of getting lost. They slipped and cursed on the stones; their musket stocks banged hollowly on rock; they squinted in the tiny light that came from the sickle moon hazed by the northern clouds. To the east the stars pricked at the outline of the hills, and as they neared the valley floor and midnight approached, the French lit fires that beckoned the Company like a beacon in the dark night.

Harper was beside Sharpe. 'They'll blind themselves, sir.'

The French, in the security of their firelight, would see nothing beyond a musket shot from their walls. The circling night would be a place of fantasy and strange shapes. Even for Sharpe the landmarks, that had seemed so clear by day, now took on monstrous shapes, even disappeared, and he stopped often, crouched, and tried to filter the real from the imaginary. The men's guns were loaded, but not cocked, their white belts hidden beneath greatcoats; their breathing loud in the darkness. They neared the village, angling north away from the house, going past the heavy barley and feeling naked and obvious in the wide valley. Sharpe strained his senses for a telltale sign that a sentry, high on Moreno's house, had been alerted: the click of a carbine-lock, the scrape of an officer's sword, or worst of all the sudden stab of flame as a picquet saw the dark shapes in the field. The crunching of the dry soil beneath his feet seemed to be magnified into a terrible loudness, but he knew it was the same for the enemy guards. This was the worst time of night, when fears took over, and the Hussars and lancers inside their walls would hear the wolves in the hills, the nightjars, and each sound would be a knelling for their death until the senses were blunted, distrusted, and the night merely became a horror to survive.

A flash of light. 'Down!' Sharpe hissed. Christ! Flames whipped crazily into the night, spewed sparks that spiralled away in the breeze, and then he realized that the cavalrymen had lit another fire, one of the timber piles out in the cleared space, and Sharpe stayed on the ground, listening to the pounding of his heart, and searched the dark shapes of the deserted cottages to his front. Or were they deserted? Had the French been clever and let any watcher in the hills think that they were all inside the protective, well-lit walls? Had the small cottages, the dark alleyways, been salted with men, waiting with sabres? He took a breath. 'Sergeant?'

'Sir?'

'You and me. Lieutenant?'

'Sir?'

'Wait here.'

Sharpe and Harper went forward, dark uniforms blending with the night, and Sharpe could hear every rustle of his jacket, creak of his belt, and the looming walls seemed to hold danger in every shadow. He felt himself tense with anticipation, his teeth gritted, waiting for the mocking shot, but instead his hand reached out and touched a dry-stone wall, and Harper was beside him, and Sharpe went on, into an alleyway that stank of manure, and his instinct began to come back.

There was no one in the village. Harper, a vast shadow, crossed the alley and crouched by the main street. A fire flickered at its end, sending crazy shadows, but the cottages were deserted and Sharpe felt the relaxation of relief. They went back to the outer wall and Harper whistled softly, three small sounds, and the shadows in the barley humped and moved, the Company coming forward to the shelter of the wall.

Sharpe found Knowles. 'We stay on this side of the house. Rifles first. Wait for the signals.'

Knowles nodded and his teeth flashed white as he grinned. Sharpe could feel the excitement of the Company, their confidence, and he marvelled at it. They were enjoying it, taking on sixteen times their number, and he did not understand that it was because of him. Harper knew, Knowles knew, that the tall Rifle Captain who was not given to rousing speeches could nevertheless make men feel that the impossible was just a little troublesome and that victory was a commonplace where he led.

They went in fits and starts beside the outer walls, the Riflemen scouting the dark shadows, the Company catching up, and the only breath-stopping moment was as they passed beneath the tall, dark tower of the church. A sound came from the belfry, a musical whisper, and the men froze, their eyes suddenly scared, and then came the sound of beating wings, receding in the blackness, and the Company sighed together as the owl, which had brushed a wing against the hanging bell, disappeared on its own hunt. Harper glanced up, saw the white flash, and thought of the barn owls that ghosted down the valley at Tangaveane, of the stream that leaked from the peat beds, of Ireland.

'Halt!' Sharpe's voice was scarcely above a whisper. He pointed. 'In there.'

The Company crowded into an alley, the firelight uncomfortably close, and Sharpe peered cautiously into the street, at the pile of new rubble, and for the first time he could properly see the front of Moreno's house. The wall was high, eight or nine feet, but the great double gate through which the farm animals could be driven was wide open. Inside he could see white faces staring at the fires that were the main defence and behind those faces the dim shadows of mounted men. Knowles had not understood that the gate would be open, but it was obvious to Sharpe. He had seen through the telescope that the front wall of the courtyard had no fire-step, no platform on which men could stand and keep watch or fire down on attacking Partisans, so the French had little choice. They would, he knew, keep the gate open and light the area in front so that should any Partisan be foolish enough to attack, the lancers could sweep out into the killing-ground with their long, searching blades. And no Partisan would be foolish enough to attack the gate. The front of the house was brightly lit, the courtyard armed and ready, and the only danger from the front was an attack by trained troops, and that, the French knew, was an impossibility. Sharpe grinned.

The fire in front of the gate crackled and roared and its noise covered the scuffling and grunts in the alley. The Redcoats of the South Essex were struggling from their greatcoats, rolling them up and strapping the bundles to their packs. He grinned at them. The Riflemen, without white crossbelts to startle the enemy, crouched near him, some fidgeting with excitement, all wanting to start the action, to dispel the nervous thoughts of anticipation.

Knowles pushed through the men. 'Ready, sir.'

Sharpe turned to the Riflemen. 'Remember. Go for officers.'

The Baker rifle was a deadly weapon, slow to load but more accurate than any gun on the battlefield. The muskets, under Lieutenant Knowles, could spread death in a wide arc, but the rifles were instruments of precision. Once in the building, the Green Jackets should seek for enemy officers, kill them, and leave the cavalry leaderless. Sharpe turned again towards the house. He could hear the mutter of voices, the trampling of hooves in the yard, a man coughing, and then he touched Harper's shoulder and the Riflemen slithered into the street, crawling on their bellies, hiding in the shadows till they had formed a line behind the rubble. The Rifles would go first, to draw the enemy fire, to start the chaos, and the rest was up to Knowles, to lead the Company into the cavalry's nightmare. Sharpe waited. He inched his sword out of its scabbard, laid it in front of him, and waited as his men put the long bayonets on their rifles. It had been so long since he had faced the enemy.

'Come on!' He had ordered them to scream, to shout, to sound like the fiends of hell, and they scrambled over the rubble, the long rifles silent, and the guards at the gate whirled, jerked up carbines and fired too soon. Sharpe heard a bullet strike stone, saw Harper run forward to the fire and grab, with both hands, the unburnt end of a baulk of timber. The Sergeant whirled it around, and hurled the flaming wood at the waiting horsemen. It struck the ground, exploded in sparks, and the horses reared up, and Sharpe's sword was reaching for the first guard who was trying to drop an empty carbine and snatch up his sabre. The sword took the Hussar in the throat; the man grabbed at the blade, seemed to shake his head, and slumped. Sharpe turned to the Riflemen. 'Come on!'

The gate was empty, the cavalry frightened by Harper's missile, and the Riflemen knelt at its edges and aimed at the fire-lit space. Voices shouted in strange languages, bullets chipped at the cobbled entrance, and Sharpe, desperately searching the courtyard for signs of its organized defence, heard the first distinctive cracks of the Baker rifles. Where the hell was Knowles? He turned round and saw the Redcoats running round the fire, being formed, their muskets deliberately untipped by bayonets, so as not to slow the loading of fresh rounds, and then Harper's voice bellowed at him.

He heard a couple of rifle shots, turned, and saw a lancer riding for him. The horse was tossing its head, eyes reflecting firelight, the rider crouched on its neck, the steel blade reaching for Sharpe, and Sharpe slammed himself to one side, hitting the gatepost, saw the spear go past, and the horse smelt in his nostrils. Another rifle spat, and the beast screamed. The Pole's arms went up and man and horse fell sideways, and Sharpe was running forward, into the courtyard.

Everything was too slow! Horses were tethered and he hacked at the ropes. 'Hup! Hup! Hup!' A man swung a sabre at him, missed, and Sharpe rammed his sword into the Hussar's chest. It stuck. Riflemen ran past, screaming incoherently, long bayonets driving scattered Frenchmen into dark doorways, and Sharpe put his foot on the body and twisted his sword free. He saw Harper stamping forward, bayonet outstretched, driving back an officer who screamed for help against the giant Irishman. The man tripped, fell backwards, the screams becoming panic as he fell into a fire and Harper turned, forgot him, and Sharpe yelled to him to get out of the way. 'Rifles!'

He blew his whistle, shouted at them, brought them over to the building where he stood. Stray horses skittered in the yard, galloped at the entrance, reared as the Company, white belts gleaming, filled the entrance, and Lieutenant Robert Knowles began the terrible commands that would chill any Frenchman who knew the firepower of British infantry. 'Present! Front rank only! Fire!'

It was the last thing the Hussars and lancers could have expected. Instead of brigands and silent knives they were fighting a clockwork machine that could spit out four volleys a minute. The muskets flamed, smoke gouted into the courtyard, the three-quarter-inch musket balls hammered between the walls. 'Rear rank! Look to the roof!' The front rank were already taking the next cartridge from their ammunition pouch, biting the bullet from the paper-wrapped cylinder, pouring the powder into the gun, but saving a pinch for the pan. The left hand held the top of the barrel; the right poured the powder; the left gripped the paper and tore off most of it while the right kept the priming between finger and thumb. The paper was pushed loosely into the muzzle, the other three fingers of the right hand had the ramrod up in the air, a bullet spat into the gun, and down with the steel rod. Once was enough, and the ramrod was taken out, the gun swung up, and all the time they had to ignore the shouts of the enemy, the carbine bullets, the screaming horses, the fires, and put the pinch of powder into the pan after the flint was dragged back, and the rear rank had fired, flash and explosion in their ears, and Lieutenant Knowles, his voice calm, was ordering the slaughter. 'Present! Fire!' It was a mechanical job and no infantry in the world did it better, because no infantry in the world, except the British, ever practised with real ammunition. The clockwork killing. Fire, reload, present, fire, until their faces were blackened, their eyes smarting with the grains of powder thrown up by the priming just inches from their cheeks, their shoulders bruised by the kick of the gun, and the courtyard ahead was littered with the bodies of their enemy, sifted with smoke, and all the time Knowles had taken them forward, two steps at a time, and the maddened horses had escaped behind them and Sharpe had watched as Hagman's group of four Riflemen had shut the gates. Hardly a minute had passed.

'Inside!' Sharpe kicked at a door, Harper hit it, and the Rifles were inside the house. Someone fired at them, a pistol, but the bullet went wide and Sharpe was hacking with the sword. 'Bayonets!' The Riflemen formed line, snarled forward, and Sharpe saw they were in a hall which was officer country, the table littered with used bottles, stairs leading to bedrooms where men were waking to the sounds of battle.

Outside, in the courtyard, Lieutenant Knowles counted to himself, keeping the rhythm of the volleys, and at the same time looking desperately round to see where danger might threaten. He could see Hagman, kneeling to one side, the other Riflemen in his party loading for the small Cheshireman, and knew that any officer who showed his face on balcony or rooftop would be cut down by a rifle bullet. His own men, sweating in the firelight, advanced step by step, scouring the walls and windows, and it occurred to the Lieutenant that this was only his third real fight. He was pushing down the panic, the impulse to run for shelter, but his voice was calm and in the noise he hardly heard the carbine bullets that struck near him. He saw Redcoats falling, struck by enemy fire, saw Sergeant Read tending to them and then, with a ghastly realization, suddenly identified the bubbling and screaming noise that had been nagging at his eardrums for the last minute. He had stepped to one side, to avoid a fire, and saw, kicking in the flames, a French officer. The man seemed to be reaching for the Lieutenant, blackened hands curled like claws, and from his throat came the terrible noise. Knowles suddenly remembered the sword in his hand, the blade bought by his father, and with a grimace he stepped close to the man and shut his eyes as he pushed the tip at the dying man's throat. He had stopped his orders, but the men neither noticed nor missed them. They fired their volleys into the shadows, and Knowles opened his eyes to see he had killed his first man with a sword, and then the voice of Sergeant Harper was dominating the courtyard. 'In here, sir!'

Sharpe guessed a minute and a half had gone by since the Riflemen had first cleared the gate. He had counted, unconsciously, the volleys from the courtyard, reckoning that in this light the men would fire a shot every fifteen seconds. Now, in the main hallway of Moreno's house, there was trouble. Officers at the top of the stairs had seen what was happening, found mattresses and the furniture they'd kept for their own use and thrown up a barricade. Sharpe needed firepower, quick and overpowering, to clear the stair's top.

'Sergeant!'

It would be suicide on the stairs. The huge Irishman took a pace towards the steps, but Sharpe stopped him. 'Give me the gun!'

Harper looked at the seven-barrelled gun, grinned, and shook his head. Before Sharpe could stop him the Sergeant had leapt to the bottom step, pointed the fearful weapon upwards, and pulled the trigger. It was as if a small cannon had gone off in the room. It belched smoke and flame, stunned the eardrums, and to Sharpe's horror the Sergeant fell backwards, thrown back, and he ran to him, fearing the worst.

Harper grinned. 'Bloody kick!'

Sharpe took the stairs two at a time, the sword ahead, seeing where the blast had thrown back the barrier, smeared blood on a wall, and then an officer was aiming a pistol. There was nothing Sharpe could do. He saw the trigger pulled, the cock fall forward, and nothing happened. In his haste and panic the Frenchman had forgotten to prime the pan. It was a death sentence. The sword slammed down, cutting skull and brain, and Sharpe had seized the mattresses, thrown them aside, and the sword was beating at the slim sabres of the two men who had survived the seven-barrelled gun.

'Rifles!' Harper had shouted, was pounding up the stairs. Sharpe lunged, wounded a man, stepped aside as the other swung wildly, and then Harper was beside him, sword-bayonet stabbing upwards, and the landing was clear.

'Kearsey!' Sharpe yelled, forgetting niceties of rank. For God's sake, where was the bastard? 'Kearsey!'

'Sharpe?' The Major was standing in a doorway, buckling his trousers. 'Sharpe?'

'Get out of here, Major!'

'My parole!'

'You're rescued!' Damn his parole.

A door opened at the end of the passage, a rifle fired, the door shut. Kearsey suddenly seemed to wake up. 'That way!' He pointed at closed doors across the passage. 'You drop outside the house.'

Sharpe nodded. The landing seemed safe. An officer had opened a door at the end of the passage, but a rifle bullet had dissuaded him from further risk. The Green Jackets were reloading, waiting for orders, and Sharpe went to the stairhead. Downstairs was chaos. The room was filled with musket smoke that was lanced, second by second, with flames as the Redcoats fired at windows, doors and passageways. Knowles had long stopped controlling the volleys. Now each man fired as fast as he could and the burning paper wads, spat after the musket balls, were setting fire to rush mats and hanging curtains. Sharpe cupped his hands. 'Lieutenant! Up here!'

Knowles nodded and turned back to his men. Sharpe found Kearsey at his side, hopping on one leg as he pulled on a boot. 'The rifles will cover them, Major! Take over!'

Kearsey nodded, showed no surprise at Sharpe's peremptory commands, and the tall Rifleman turned to the closed doors. The first was not locked. The room was empty, the window invitingly open, and Harper went through to knock out the remaining glass and frame. Sharpe tried the other door, it resisted, and he hit it with his shoulder, the wood round the lock splintering easily, and he stopped.

On the bed, hands and feet tied to the four stubby posts, was a girl. Dark hair on a pillow, a white dress, a reminder of Josefina, and eyes that glared at him over a gag. She was jerking and writhing, struggling to free herself, and Sharpe was struck by the sudden beauty, the fierceness of the face. The shots still sounded downstairs, a sudden cry, the smell of flames catching wood, and he stepped to the bed and cut at the ropes with the unwieldy sword. She jerked her head sideways, towards the room's shadowed corner, and Sharpe saw the movement, flung himself down, heard the explosion and felt the wind of the pistol ball as a man reared up from beside the bed. A Colonel, no less, in Hussar uniform, whose pleasure had been interrupted before it could begin. There was fear on the man's face. Sharpe smiled, climbed on to the bed, watched as the Colonel tried to wriggle from the corner, and then, with cold determination, pinned him prisoner against the wall.

'Sergeant!'

Harper came in, seven-barrelled gun in hand, and saw the girl. 'God save Ireland.'

'Cut her free!'

Sharpe heard Kearsey's voice on the landing. 'Steady now!' He could hear Knowles downstairs, counting off the men, sending the wounded up first. The French Colonel was babbling at Sharpe, pointing at the girl, but the sword held him and Sharpe wished he had killed the man straightaway. This was no place to take prisoners and he was trapped, not knowing what was happening outside. The girl was free, rubbing her wrists, and Sharpe dropped the sword. 'Watch him, Sergeant!'

He ran to the window, smashed panes with the sword, and saw the empty darkness outside. They could make it! The first Redcoats were at the head of the stairs, and then the French Colonel screamed, a terrible agony, and Sharpe whipped round to see that the slim, dark-haired girl had taken the Frenchman's own sabre and plunged it, point first, into his groin. She was smiling, and she was beautiful enough to catch the breath.

Harper was staring aghast. Sharpe ignored the Frenchman. 'Patrick!'

'Sir?'

'Get the men in here. Through the window! And next door!'

The girl spat at the Colonel, who had collapsed in his own blood, swore at him, and then looked at Sharpe with a glance that seemed to convey pure disdain because he had not killed the Frenchman himself. Sharpe was reeling from her, thrown off balance by her hawk-like beauty, hardly hearing the commands from the landing, the banging muskets. He snapped his attention back, despising himself, but the girl was faster. She had the Colonel's sabre, her freedom, and she ran out the door, ignoring the fight, and turned right. Sharpe followed, caution gone, just the instinct left that some things, just one thing perhaps, could turn a man's life inside out.

CHAPTER 7

Knowles had done well. The hall was on fire but empty of the enemy, and the Redcoats backed up the stairs, still loading and firing their muskets, ignoring the fresh blood that made the steps slippery, and then the Riflemen took over, the Bakers spitting into the hallway below, and Major Kearsey, sabre in hand, was pushing the men into a bedroom, towards a window, and shouting, 'Jump!'

'Aim low! Aim low!' Harper's voice bellowed at the Riflemen. Hussars were coming into the hall, choking on the smoke. Redcoats were pouring from the first-floor windows, forming up in the field beneath, and only Sharpe was absent.

Knowles looked round. 'Captain!'

'He's missing!' Major Kearsey grabbed Knowles. 'Get outside! There may be cavalry!'

The girl had run through a door and Sharpe followed, noticing, irrelevantly, a small statue of the Virgin Mary with a host of candles flickering at its base. He remembered the Catholics in the Company deciding that today – no, yesterday – was the fifteenth of August, the Assumption of the Blessed Virgin Mary, and he was grateful because the stairs beyond the door were pitch dark and he grabbed a candle and followed the fading footsteps. He hurried, heels sliding over steps, banging down the stairs. He cursed himself. His place was with his men, not chasing some girl because she had Josefina's long black hair, a slim body, and a beauty that had overcome him. But this was not a night for sensible action; it was a mad darkness, a gambler's last throw, and he reasoned that she had been kept a prisoner and that made her important to the enemy, and so important to him.

The rationalization lasted to the bottom of the stairs. The stairway was four-sided and he knew it had plunged below ground level, into the cellars, and he was still hurtling down, almost out of control, with the candle flame blown out, when a white arm shot out and her voice hushed him. They were by a door, light leaking through its gaping planks, but there was no point in pretending that anyone on the far side had not heard their feet on the stairway. Sharpe pushed it open, ignoring her caution, and in the cellar a lantern hung from a hook, and beneath it, fear across his face, was a lancer holding a musket and bayonet. He lunged at Sharpe, thinking perhaps that he could kill with a blade point more easily than by pulling a trigger, but Sharpe had cut his teeth on just such fighting. He let the bayonet come, stepped aside, and used his enemy's own motion to run the sword blade into his stomach. Then Sharpe nearly gagged.

The cellar was spattered with blood, with bodies that showed death in a dozen horrid ways. Wine-racks stood by the walls, looted empty, but the floor was black with Spanish blood, strewn with mutilations obscene as nightmare. Young, old, men and women, all killed horribly. It struck Sharpe that these people must have died the day before, as he watched from the hilltop, killed as the French pretended the village was empty. He had lain in the gully, the sun warm on his back, and in the cellar the Spanish had died, slowly and with exquisite pain. The bodies lay in the crumpled way of the dead, their number impossible to count, or to tell the ways in which they had died. Some were too young even to have known what had happened, killed no doubt before their mothers' eyes, and Sharpe felt an impotent rage as the girl stepped past him, searching the shambles, and from far away, as if across a whole town, Sharpe heard a volley of shots. They must get out! He grabbed the girl's arm.

'Come on!'

'No!'

She was searching for one person, pulling at the bodies, oblivious of the horror. Why would there be a guard on dead men? Sharpe pushed past her, took the lantern, and then heard the moaning from the far, dark end of the old wine cellar. The girl heard, too.

'Ramon!'

Sharpe stepped on dead flesh, flinched from a spider's web,

and then, dimly at first, he saw a man manacled to the far wall. He did not ask himself why a wine cellar should be equipped with manacles; there was no time. He took the lantern closer and saw that what he had thought were chains were blood trails. The man was not manacled but nailed to the stone wall, alive.

'Ramon!' The girl was past Sharpe, pulling ineffectively at the nails, and Sharpe put down the lantern and hammered at the nail-heads with his sword's brass hilt. He knocked them left and right, hearing the thunder of hooves outside, shouts and a volley, and then the nail was loose, blood trickling afresh, and he pulled it out and started on the second hand. Another volley, more hooves, and he hammered desperately until the prisoner was free. He gave the girl his sword and heaved Ramon, if that were his name, on to his shoulder.

'Go on!'

The girl led him past the doorway they had come through, past the welter of blood and bodies, to the far corner of the cellar. A trapdoor was revealed by the lantern she was holding and she gestured at it. Sharpe dropped his moaning burden, reached up, heaved, and a sudden breeze of welcome night air dispelled the foul stench of the blood and dead. He pulled himself up, surprised to find that the trapdoor emerged outside the house walls, and then realized it was so supplies could reach the house without being trampled through the courtyard and kitchens. He looked round and there was the Company, marching steadily in three ranks.

'Sergeant!'

Harper turned, relief visible on his face in the light from the burning house. Sharpe dropped back into the cellar, heaved the wounded man on to the ground, leaped up himself, and reached down for the girl. She ignored him, pulled herself up, rolled into the grass, and Sharpe had a glimpse of long legs. There were cheers from the men and Sharpe realized they were for him. Harper was there, thumping his back, saying something unintelligible about thinking Sharpe was lost, and then the Sergeant had the wounded man and they were running towards the Company and Sharpe, for the first time, saw horsemen in the darkness. Harper gave the wounded man into the ranks. Knowles was grinning at Sharpe, Kearsey gesturing to the girl.

'Are they loaded?' Sharpe gestured at the muskets, screamed at Knowles over the sound of the burning house.

'Most, sir.'

'Keep going!'

Sharpe pushed Knowles on, driving the Company towards the barley field and the comforting darkness, and turned to face the house and see what the cavalry were doing. Harper was already there, running backwards, the seven-barrelled gun threatening any horsemen. Sharpe wondered how long it had been since they had burst through the gate. No more than seven or eight minutes, he decided. Enough time for his men to have fired seven or eight hundred shots into the astonished French, set fire to the house, rescued Kearsey, the girl and the prisoner, and he grinned in the darkness.

'Watch right!' Harper called. A dozen lancers, in line, with the wicked points held low so that they glittered by the ground were coming at a trot, to take the Company in the flank. But there was still time. 'Right wheel!'

The Company turned, three ranks swivelling. 'Halt!' A ragged line, but it would do. 'Rear rank about turn. Hold your fire!' That looked after the rear. 'Present! Aim at their stomachs; give them a bellyache! Fire!'

It was inevitable. The enemy became a turmoil of falling horses and tumbling lancers. 'Right turn! Forward! Double!' He had the small company in a column now. Running for the barley, for the unharvested crop that would give them a little cover. There were more hoof-beats behind, but not enough loaded muskets to fight off another charge. Time only to run. 'Run!'

The Company ran, sprinting despite their burdens, and Sharpe heard a wounded man groan. Time later to count the wounded. Now he turned, saw lancers coming in desperate chase, one aiming at Harper, but the Irishman dashed the lance aside with the squat gun and reached up a huge hand that plucked the Pole clean out of the saddle. The Sergeant was screaming insults in his native Gaelic. He held the lancer effortlessly, his huge strength making the man seem to be weightless, and then threw him at the feet of another horse. A rifle cracked behind Sharpe, another horse down, and Hagman's voice came through the din. 'Got him.'

'Back!' Harper was shouting, the other horses still yards away, and suddenly the barley was under Sharpe's feet, and he ran into the field, and for a moment the trumpets meant nothing to him. He was just running, remembering the Indian with the razor point, the desperate and futile attempt to run from the lance, and then he heard Harper's triumphant voice.

'The recall! Bastards have had enough!' Harper was grinning, laughing. 'You did it, sir!'

Sharpe slowed down, let the breath heave in his chest. It was strangely quiet in the field, the hooves muted, the gunfire stopped, and he guessed that the French refused to believe that just fifty men had attacked the village. The sight of red jackets and crossbelts would have convinced them that more British troops would be out in the darkness and it would be madness to throw the lancers into the massed volley of a hidden regiment. He listened to the men panting, some moaning as they were carried, the excited mutterings of victorious troops. He wondered what the price would be and turned to Harper. 'Are you all right?'

'Yes, sir. Yourself?'

'Bruised. What's the bill?'

'Don't know for certain, sir. Jim Kelly's bad.' Harper's voice was sad and Sharpe remembered the wedding, only weeks ago, when the massive Pru Baxter had woven daisies into her hair to marry the small Irish Corporal. Harper went on. 'Cresacre was bleeding, says he's all right. We lost a couple, though. Saw them in the courtyard.'

'Who?' He should have known.

'Don't know, sir.'

They climbed, up into the hills, up where horses could not go, back to the gully, which they reached as the far hills were lined with the faintest grey of dawn. It was a time for sleep and the men crumpled like the bodies in the cellar. Some were posted as picquets at the gully's rim, their eyes red with exhaustion, smeared with powder, grinning at Sharpe, who had brought them through. The girl sat with Kearsey,

81

binding up his leg, while Knowles looked after the other wounded. Sharpe stood over him.

'How bad?'

'Kelly's going, sir.'

The Corporal had a chest wound and Knowles had picked away the shreds of jacket to show a mangled horror of glistening ribs and bubbling blood. It was a wonder he had lived this long. Cresacre had been shot in the thigh, a clean wound, and he dressed it himself, swore he would be all right, and apologized to Sharpe as if he were making a nuisance of himself. Two others were badly wounded, both cut with sabres, but they would live, and there was hardly a man who did not have a scratch, a bruise, some memento of the night. Sharpe counted heads. Forty-eight men, three Sergeants, and two officers had left the gully. Four men had not come back. Sharpe felt the tiredness wash through him, tinged with relief. It was a smaller bill than he dared hope for. Once Kelly died, his body kept from the vultures by a shallow grave, he would have lost five men. The lancers must have lost three times that number. He went round the Company, to those who were awake, and praised them. The men seemed embarrassed by the thanks, shaking as the sweat dried on their bodies in the cold air, their heads jerking as some tried to stay awake and look, red-eyed, into the dawn.

'Captain Sharpe!' Kearsey was standing in a clear patch of the gully. 'Captain!'

Sharpe went down the side of the gully. 'Sir?'

Kearsey stared at him, his small eyes fierce. 'Are you mad, Sharpe?'

For a second the meaning did not percolate into Sharpe's head.

'I beg your pardon, sir?'

'What were you doing?'

'Doing, sir? Rescuing you.' Sharpe had expected thanks.

Kearsey winced, whether from the pain of his leg or from Sharpe's ingenuousness it was difficult to tell. The dawn was revealing the details of the gully: the collapsed men, the blood, the anger on Kearsey's face. 'You fool!'

Sharpe bit back his anger. 'Sir?'

Kearsey waved at the wounded. 'How do you get them back?'

'We carry them, sir.'

'Carry them, sir.' Kearsey mimicked him. 'Over twenty miles of country? You were only here to help carry the gold, Sharpe! Not fight a battle in the back of beyond!'

Sharpe took a deep breath, suppressing the urge to shout back. 'Without you, sir, we would have had no chance of persuading El Católico to let us take the gold. That was my judgment.'

Kearsey looked at him, shook his head and pointed at Jim Kelly. 'You think it was worth that?'

'The General told me the gold was important, sir.' Sharpe spoke quietly.

'Important, Sharpe, only because it is a gesture to the Spanish.'

'Yes, sir.' It was no time for an argument.

'At least you rescued them.' The Major waved at the two Spaniards.

Sharpe looked at the girl's dark beauty. 'Them, sir?'

'Moreno's children. Teresa and Ramon. The French were holding them as bait, hoping Moreno or El Católico would try a rescue. At least we've earned their thanks and that's probably more valuable than carrying the gold for them. Besides, I doubt if the gold is there.'

The sun split across the gully's rim. Sharpe blinked. 'Pardon, sir?'

'What do you expect? The French are there. They probably have the gold. Or hadn't that occurred to you?'

It had, but Sharpe was not in a mood to give Kearsey his thoughts. If the French had found the gold he suspected they would have ridden it straight to Ciudad Rodrigo, but doubtless Kearsey would not be convinced. Sharpe nodded. 'Did they say anything about it to you, sir?'

Kearsey shrugged, not liking the reminder that he had been captured. 'I was unlucky, Sharpe. Not to know lancers were there.' He shook his head, sounded suddenly tired. 'No, they said nothing.'

'So there's hope, sir?'

The Major looked bitter, waved at Kelly. 'Tell him that.'

'Yes, sir.'

Kearsey sighed. 'I'm sorry, Sharpe. Undeserved.' He seemed to think for a moment. 'You do know, though, don't you, that they'll be after us today?'

'The French, sir?'

The Major nodded. 'Who else? You'd better sleep, Sharpe. In a couple of hours you'll have to defend this place.'

'Yes, sir.'

He turned away, and as he did he caught Teresa's eyes. She looked at him without interest, without recognition, as if the rescue and the two shared killings meant nothing. El Católico, he thought, is a lucky man. He slept.

CHAPTER 8

Casatejada was like a shattered ants' nest. All morning the patrols left, searched the valley, then galloped in their dust clouds back to the houses and the thin spires of smoke that were the only signs left of the night's activity. Others rounded up stray horses, circling the valley floor, reminding Harper of the pony drives on his native Donegal moors. In the gully the men moved slowly, quietly, as if their sound could carry to the village, but in truth the elation of the attack had given way to weariness and sadness. Kelly's breath bubbled through the morning, a constant pink froth at the corner of his mouth, and the men avoided him as if death were contagious. Sharpe woke up, told Harper to sleep, replaced the picquets, and struggled to scrape the clotted blood from his sword with a handful of wiry grass. They dared not light a fire to heat the water that could scour out their muskets, so the men used the battlefield expedient, urinating into the barrels, and grinned self-consciously at the girl as they sloshed the liquid around to loosen the caked powder deposits of the night. The girl did not react, her face seemed unmovable, and she sat holding her brother's hand, talking quietly to him and giving him sips of tepid water from a wooden canteen. The heat bounced from the rocky sides of the gully, attacked from all sides, roasting the living and the dying alike.

Kearsey climbed up to lie alongside Sharpe and took the telescope so that he could spy down on the French. 'They're packing up.'

'Sir?'

Kearsey nodded at the village. 'Mules, Sharpe. String of them.'

Sharpe took his telescope back and found the village street. Kearsey was right, a string of mules with men lashing ropes

85

over their burdens, but it was impossible to tell whether there was gold or just forage in the packs.

'Perhaps they won't look for us.'

The Major had calmed down since dawn. 'Bound to. Look at the track we left.' Running across the barley field, like a giant signpost, was the trampled spoor of the Light Company's retreat. 'They'll want to look over the ridge, just to make sure you've gone.'

Sharpe looked at the bare rocks and turf of the hillside. 'Should we move?'

Another shake of the head. 'Best hiding place for miles, this gully. You can't see it from any side; even from above it's difficult. Keep your heads down and you'll be all right.'

Sharpe thought it strange that Kearsey should talk of 'you', as if the Major himself were not part of the British army, or as if the survival of Sharpe in enemy territory were not his concern. He said nothing. The Major nibbled nervously at a strand of his moustache; he seemed to be deep in thought, and when he spoke he sounded as if he had come to the end of long deliberation.

'You must understand why it's important.'

'Sir?' Sharpe was puzzled.

'The gold, Sharpe.' He stopped and Sharpe waited. The small man flicked at his moustache. 'The Spanish have been let down badly, Sharpe, very badly. Think what happened after Talavera, eh? And Ciudad Rodrigo. A shameful business, Sharpe, shameful.'

Sharpe still kept silent. After Talavera the Spanish had forfeited Wellington's support by failing to provide the food and supplies they had promised. A starving British army was of no use to Spain. Ciudad Rodrigo? Five weeks ago the Spanish fortress town had surrendered, after an heroic defence, and Wellington had sent no help. The town had been an obstacle to Masséna's advance, Almeida was the next, and Sharpe had heard savage criticism that the British had let their allies down, but Sharpe was no strategist. He let the Major go on.

'We must prove something to them, Sharpe, that we can help, that we can be useful, or else we must forfeit their support. Do you understand?' He turned his fierce gaze on Sharpe.

'Yes, sir.'

The jauntiness and confidence crept back into the Major's voice. 'Of course, we lose the war if we don't have the Spanish! That's what Wellington has come to understand, eh, Sharpe? Better late than never!' He gave his laugh. 'That's why Wellington wants us to bring the gold, so that the British are seen to deliver it to Cádiz. It proves a point, Sharpe, shows that we made an honest effort. Helps to cover up the betrayal at Ciudad Rodrigo! Ah, politics, politics!' He said the last two words much as an indulgent father might talk about the rowdy games of his children. 'Do you understand?'

'Yes, sir.'

It was no time to argue, even though Sharpe disbelieved every word Kearsey had uttered. Of course the Spanish were important, but so were the British to the Spanish, and delivering a few bags of gold would not restore the amity and trust that had been shattered by Spanish inefficiency the year before. Yet it was important that Kearsey believed Wellington's motives to be honest. The small Major, Sharpe knew, was passionately engaged on the Spanish side, as if, after a lifetime of soldiering, he had found in the harsh hills and white houses of the Spaniards a warmth and trust he had found nowhere else.

Sharpe turned and nodded at Teresa and Ramon. 'Do they know anything about the gold? About Captain Hardy?'

'They say not.' Kearsey shrugged. 'Perhaps El Católico moved the gold and Hardy went with it. I ordered him to stay with it.'

'Then surely the girl would know?'

Kearsey turned and spoke in staccato Spanish to her. Sharpe listened to the reply; her voice was deep and husky, and even if he could not understand the language he was glad to look at her. She had long, dark hair, as black as Josefina's, but there the resemblance ended. The Portuguese girl had been a lover of comfort, of wine drunk by candlelight, of soft sheets, while this girl reminded Sharpe of a wild beast with eyes that were deep, wary, and set either side of a hawk-like

87

nose. She was young. Kearsey had told him twenty-three, but at either side of her mouth were curved lines. Sharpe remembered that her mother had died at the hands of the French, God knows what she herself had suffered, and he remembered the smile after she had skewered the Colonel with his own sabre. She had aimed low, he recalled, and he laughed at the remembrance. She looked at Sharpe as if she would have liked to claw out his eyes with her long fingers.

'What's funny?'

'Nothing. You speak English?'

She shrugged and Kearsey looked at Sharpe. 'Her father's fluent; that's what makes him so useful to us. They've picked up a bit, from him, from me. Good family, Sharpe.'

'But do they know anything about Hardy? The gold?'

'She doesn't know a thing, Sharpe. She thinks the gold must still be in the hermitage, and she hasn't seen Hardy.' Kearsey was happy with the answer, confident that no Spaniard would lie to him.

'So the next thing we must do, sir, is search the hermitage.'

Kearsey sighed. 'If you insist, Sharpe. If you insist.' He winced again and slid down from the edge of the gully. 'But for now, Sharpe, watch for that patrol. It won't be long.'

The Major was right, at least, about that. Three hundred lancers rode from the village, trotting their horses along a track that paralleled the broken stalks of barley, and Sharpe watched them come. They carried carbines instead of lances and he knew they intended to search the hillsides on foot. He turned to the gully and ordered silence, explained that a patrol was coming, and then turned back to see the Poles dismounting at the foot of the rock-strewn slope.

A fly landed on his cheek. He wanted to crush it but dared not, as the lancers had started their climb up the steep slope, their horses left with picquets below. They were stringing into a line, a crude skirmish order, and he could hear the distant voices grumbling at the heat and the exertion. There was a chance that they would miss the gully, that by climbing obliquely up the slope they would emerge on the crest near the pile of rocks and never suspect that a whole Company was in dead ground behind them. He breathed slowly, willed them to stay low on the slope, and watched the officers trying to force the line higher with the flat side of their drawn sabres.

He could hear Kelly's breathing, someone else clearing his throat, and he flapped with his free hand for silence. A tall lancer, suntanned and with a black moustache, was climbing higher than the others. As he clawed his way up, carbine slung, Sharpe saw a tarnished gold band on the man's sleeve. A Sergeant. He was a big man, almost as big as Harper, and his face was scarred from battlefields on the other side of Europe. Go down, Sharpe urged silently, go down, but the man kept coming on his lone, perverse climb. Sharpe moved his head slowly, saw the faces staring at him, and found Harper. He beckoned slowly, put a finger to his lips, pointed at the foot of the inner slope of the gully.

The Polish Sergeant stopped, looked up, wiped his face, and turned to look at his comrades. An officer shouted at him, waved his sabre to make the Sergeant join the line, which had gone ahead, but the Sergeant shook his head, shouted back, and gestured at the skyline, which was just a few, steep feet away. Sharpe cursed him, knew that if the Light Company were discovered they would be harried eastwards, away from the gold, from victory, and this one veteran was putting it all at risk. He was climbing just below Sharpe, who craned forward as far as he dared to see the yellow, square top of the headgear come closer and closer. He could hear the man grunting, the sound of his fingernails scraping on rock, the scrabble of his boots searching for a foothold, and then, as if in a nightmare, a large brown hand with bitten nails appeared right by Sharpe's face and he summoned all his strength for a desperate act. He waited – it could only have been for a half-second, but it seemed forever – until the man's face appeared. The eyes widened in surprise and Sharpe put out his right hand and gripped the Sergeant by the windpipe, his fingers closing like a man-trap on the throat. He thrust his left hand forward, found the belt, and, half turning on to his back, he pulled the lancer up and over the rim, holding the huge man in the air with a strength he hardly knew he possessed, and he threw him, arms and carbine flailing, to the tender mercy of Sergeant Harper. The Irishman kicked the lancer as he landed, had his seven-barrelled gun reversed and brought it down, sickeningly, on the man's head. Sharpe whirled back to face the slope. The line was still advancing! No one had seen, no one had noticed, but it was still not over. The lancer was tough, and Harper's blows, that would have killed a fair-sized bullock, seemed to have done nothing more than knock off the yellow and blue hat.

The enemy Sergeant had Harper round the waist, was squeezing, and the Irishman was trying to twist the other man's head clean off his shoulders. The Pole's teeth were gritted; he should have shouted, but he must have been dazed, and all he could think of was trying to stand up, to face his opponent, and use his own massive fists to beat at Harper. The men in the gully were frozen, appalled by the enemy who had suddenly landed in their midst, and it was Teresa who reacted. She picked up a musket, turned it, took four steps and swung its brass-tipped butt into the man's forehead. He slumped, tried to rise, but she swung again and Sharpe saw the fierce joy on her face as the weapon felled the Sergeant, his face bloodied, and suddenly it was quiet again in the gully.

Harper shook his head. 'God save Ireland.'

The girl gave Harper the kind of pitying look that Sharpe thought she had reserved only for him, and then, without so much as a glance at Sharpe, she scrambled up the slope to lie beside him and peer at the enemy. They had at last missed the Sergeant. Men from the top of the line stopped and bunched uncertainly, called down to their officer, waiting as he cupped his hands and shouted up the slope. The voice echoed and faded. He called again, stopped the rest of the line, and Sharpe knew that in a few moments they would be discovered. Damn the Sergeant! He looked round, wondering if there were cover to be had on the far slope beyond the gully, knowing it was hopeless, and then he saw the girl was moving, crossing the gully and climbing out the far side. His face must have betrayed his alarm, for Kearsey, sitting by Ramon, shook his head. 'She'll manage.' The whisper just reached Sharpe.

The search-line had sat down, glad of the rest, but the officer still called to the missing Sergeant. He was climbing the hill in short, erratic bursts, uncertain what to do and annoyed by those of his men who shouted with him. He had no choice, though; he would have to come and look for his

Sergeant, and Sharpe, the sweat pouring off his face, could not imagine what one girl could do that would deflect the lancers from the search.

A scream startled him, piercing, and was cut off and repeated. He slid down the rocks a few inches and turned his face up the ridge where the sound had come from. Harper looked at him, puzzled. It had to be the girl. Sharpe peered over the edge again and saw the lancers pointing up the slope. Teresa screamed again, a terrifying sound, and Sharpe's men looked at each other, then up at Sharpe, as if to ask him what they could do to rescue her. Sharpe watched the lancers, saw their uncertainty, and then he heard them shout and point up the slope. He looked to see what had excited them, and his men, watching him, were reassured by a smile that seemed to Harper to be the biggest he had ever seen on Sharpe's face. None of them down in the gully could see what was happening, but Sharpe, up on the rim, picked up the telescope and gave up caring if anyone saw the flash of light or not.

Not that anyone would be watching, not while a naked girl ran wildly along the ridge, stopping to turn and hurl stones at an imagined pursuer on the slope hidden from the lancers. Drink or women, Sharpe thought, the bait for soldiers, and Teresa was leading the lancers in a mad rush ever further from the gully. He had her in the glass, shamelessly, and he could hear the excited shouts of the lancers who would be lost to the control of the strung-out officers. They would assume that the Sergeant had found the girl, stripped her, let her get away, and was now pursuing her. Sharpe acknowledged her cleverness and bravery, but for the moment he had time only for the slim, muscled body, for a beauty that he wanted.

Kearsey had limped to the edge of the gully's floor and was looking up at Sharpe. 'What's happening?'

'She's leading them away, sir.' He talked normally, the lancers were way beyond earshot.

Kearsey nodded, as if he had expected the answer. Harper still looked curious. 'How, sir?'

The girl had disappeared behind the summit, and the lancers, all discipline shredded, were panting up the slope a good fifty yards behind. Sharpe grinned at his Sergeant. 'She took her clothes off.'

Kearsey whipped round, aghast. 'You looked!'

'Only to see if I could help, sir.'

'What kind of a man are you, Sharpe?' Kearsey was furious, but Sharpe turned away. What kind of a man was it that would not have looked?

Harper still stood over the unconscious lancer and he sounded aggrieved. 'You might have told me, sir.'

Sharpe turned back. Kearsey had limped away. 'I promised your mother I'd keep you out of trouble. Sorry.' He grinned at the Sergeant again. 'If I'd told you, then the whole damn Company would have wanted a look. Yes? And by now we'd be back in the war instead of being safe.'

Harper grinned. 'Privilege of rank, eh, sir?'

'Something like that.' He thought of the beauty, the shadowed body with its hard stomach, long thighs, and the challenges of the disinterested, almost antagonistic glances that she had given him.

It was two hours before she returned, as silently as she had left, and wearing her white dress. She had done her work well, for the lancers had been recalled, the Sergeant given up, and Casatejada was thronged with Frenchmen. Sharpe guessed that the village had been the centre of a huge operation to clear the Partisans from Masséna's supply areas. Kearsey agreed, and the two men watched as other cavalry units came from the north to join the Polish lancers. Dragoons, chasseurs, the uniforms of empire, stirring a dust cloud that would have befitted a whole army, and all spent on chasing Partisans through dry hills.

The girl came up the rim and watched, silently, as the cavalry left her village. Their weapons flashed needles of light through the brown haze of the dust; the ranks seemed endless, the glorious might of France that had ridden down the best cavalry in Europe but could not defeat the Guerrilleros. Sharpe looked at the girl, at Kearsey, who talked with her, and was glad once more that he did not have to fight the Partisans. The only way to win was to kill them all, every one, young and old, and even that, as the French were finding, did not work. He thought of the bodies in the blood of the basement. It was not the war of Talavera.

They spent the night in the gully, cautious lest the French should still be watching, and some time in the small hours the bubbles stopped in Kelly's throat. Pru Kelly, though she did not know it, was a widow again, and Sharpe remembered the small Corporal's smile, his willingness. They buried him at dawn, in a grave scratched from the soil, and they heaped it with rocks that would be forced apart by a fox and perched on by the vultures who would tear his chest further apart.

Kearsey said the words, from memory, and the men stood round the heaped stones awkwardly. Dust to dust, ashes to ashes, and in a few weeks, Sharpe thought, Pru Kelly would marry again because that was the way with the women who marched with soldiers. The Polish Sergeant, tied up with musket slings, watched the burial and, for a few moments, stopped his struggles. The new day came, still hot, the rain still keeping away, and the Light Company marched into the empty valley to find their gold.

CHAPTER 9

It was a sweet smell, sticky-sweet, that left a foul deposit somewhere at the top of the nostrils, yet it was impossible to describe why it was so unpleasant. Sharpe had smelt it often enough, so had most of the Company, and they knew it fifty yards from the village. It was not so much a smell, Sharpe thought, as a state of the air, like an invisible mist. It seemed, like a mist, to thicken the air, make breathing difficult, yet all the time to have that sweet promise, as if the corpses the French had left behind were made of sugar and honey.

Not even the dogs had been left alive. A few cats, too difficult to catch, had survived the French, but the dogs, like their owners, had been killed, splayed open with desperate savagery, as if the French thought that death by itself was not enough and a body must be turned inside out if it was not to come magically alive to ambush them again. Only one man lived in the village, one of Sharpe's men left behind in the attack, and the French, true to the curious honour that prevailed between the armies, had left John Rorden propped on a mattress, with bread and water to hand and a bullet somewhere in his pelvis that would kill him before this new day was done.

Ramon, in slow English, told Sharpe that four dozen people had been left in the village, mostly the old or the very young, but they had all died. Sharpe stared at the wrecked houses, the blood splashed on low, white walls.

'Why were they caught?'

Ramon shrugged, waved a bandaged hand. 'They were good.'

'Good?'

'Francese.' He was lost for a word and Sharpe helped.

'Clever?'

The young man nodded. He had his sister's nose, the same dark eyes, but there was a friendliness to him that Sharpe had not seen in Teresa. Ramon shook his head hopelessly. 'They were not all Guerrilleros, yes?' Each group of words was a question, as if he wanted assurance that his English was adequate. Sharpe kept nodding. 'They want peace? But now.' He spoke two quick sentences in Spanish, his tone bitter, and Sharpe knew that those people of the uplands who had tried to stay aloof from the war would be drawn in whether they wanted it or not. Ramon blinked back tears; the dead had been of his village. 'We went there?' He pointed north. 'They were before us, yes? We were . . .' He described a circle with his two bandaged hands.

'Surrounded?'

'*Sí*.' He looked down at his right hand, at the fingers that poked from the grey bandage, and Sharpe saw the index finger moving as if it were pulling a trigger. Ramon would fight again.

The bodies were not just in the cellar. Some, perhaps for the amusement of the lancers, had been taken to the hermitage to meet their bitter end, and on the steps of the building Sharpe found Isaiah Tongue, the admirer of Napoleon, throwing up the dry bread that had been his breakfast. The Company waited by the hermitage. The prisoner, tall and proud, stood by Sergeant McGovern, and Sharpe stopped by the Scotsman.

'Look after him, Sergeant.'

'Aye, sir. They'll not touch him.' The sturdy face was twisted as if in pain. McGovern, like Tongue, had looked inside the hermitage. 'Savages, sir, that's what they are. Savages!'

'I know.'

There was nothing to say that would reach McGovern's pain, the hurt of a father far from his children who had just seen small, dead bodies. The stench was thick by the hermitage, buzzing with flies, and Sharpe paused by the steps. There was almost a reluctance to go inside, not just because of the bodies but because of what the hermitage might not contain. The gold. So close, so near to the war's survival, and instead of a feeling of triumph he felt stained, touched by a horror that brought an anger against his job. He climbed the steps, his face a mask, and wondered what his men would do if they found themselves, as they probably would, in a place where the rules no longer counted. He remembered the uncontrollable savagery that followed a siege, the sheer, exploding rage that he had felt after death had touched him a score of times in one small breach and he knew, as the cold air of the hermitage struck him, that this war in Spain, if it should go on, would not be won until British infantry had been fed into the narrow meat grinder of a small gap in a city wall.

'Out! Get them out!' The men, pale-faced, looked shocked at Sharpe's anger, but he knew no other way to react to the small bodies. 'Bury them!'

Harper was crying, tears running down his cheeks. So much innocence, so much waste, as if a baby had earned this. Kearsey stood there, with Teresa, and neither cried. The Major flicked at his moustache. 'Terrible. Awful.'

'So is what they do to the French.' Sharpe surprised himself by saying it, but it was true. He remembered the naked prisoners, wondered how the other captured Hussars had died.

'Yes.' Kearsey used the tone of a man trying to avoid an argument.

The girl looked at Sharpe and he saw she was holding back tears, her face rigid with an anger that was frightening. Sharpe swatted at a fly. 'Where's the gold?'

Kearsey followed him, spurs clicking on stone, and pointed at a stone slab that was flush with the hermitage floor. The building was not used for services. Even despite the ravages worked by the Poles it had the air of disuse, of being little more than storage for the village cemetery. It was a place that was consecrated only to death. The Major poked the stone slab with his toe. 'Under there.'

'Sergeant!'

'Sir!'

'Find a bloody pick! Smartly!'

There was a comfort in orders, as if they could recall a war in which small babies did not die. He looked at the slab engraved with the name Moreno and beneath the letters an ornate and eroded coat of arms. Sharpe tried to forget the sound of the bodies being dragged outside. He tapped his toe on the shield.

'Noble family, sir?'

'What? Oh.' Kearsey was subdued. 'I don't know, Sharpe. Perhaps once.'

The girl had her back to them and Sharpe realized that this was her family's vault. It made Sharpe wonder, with an irritating gesture, where his own body would finally rest. Beneath the ashes of some battlefield, or drowned like the poor reinforcements in their transport ships? 'Sergeant!'

'Sir?'

'Where's that pick?'

Harper kicked at the debris left by the Poles, then grunted and stooped. He had the pick, minus its handle, and he thrust it into the gap between the stones. He heaved, the veins on his face standing out, and with a shudder the slab moved, lifted, and there was a space large enough for Sharpe to slide a piece of broken stone beneath.

'You men!' Faces looked round from the door of the hermitage. 'Come here!'

Teresa had gone to a second door, opening into the cemetery, and stood there as if she was not interested. Harper found another spot, levered again, and this time it was easier and there was enough space for a dozen hands to take hold of the slab and pull it from the floor, swinging it like a trapdoor, while Kearsey fussed that they would let it fall and bequeath to the Morenos a broken vault. Dark steps led down into the blackness. Sharpe stood at the top, claiming the right to be first down.

'Candle? Come on, someone! There's got to be a candle!'

Hagman had one in his pack, a greasy but serviceable stump, and there was a pause while it was lit. Sharpe stared into the blackness. Here was where Wellington's hopes were pinned? It was ludicrous.

He took the candle and began the slow descent into the tomb and to a different kind of smell. This was not a sweet smell, not rank, but dusty because the bodies had been here a long time, some long enough for the coffins to have collapsed and to show the gleam of dry bones. Others were newer, still intact, the stonework below their niches stained with seeping liquid, but Sharpe was not looking at coffins. He held the miserable light high, sweeping it round the small space and saw, bright in the corruption, the flash of metal. It was not gold, just a discarded piece of brass that had once bound the corner of a casket.

Sharpe turned to look at Kearsey. 'There's no gold.'

'No.' The Major looked round, as if he might have missed sixteen thousand gold coins on the empty floor. 'It's gone.'

'Where was it stored?' Sharpe knew it was hopeless, but he would not give up.

'There. Where you are.'

'Then where's it gone, sir?'

Kearsey sniffed, drew himself up to his full height. 'How would I know, Sharpe? All I know is that it is not here.' He sounded almost vindicated.

'And where's Captain Hardy?' Sharpe was angry. To have come this far, for nothing.

'I don't know.'

Sharpe kicked the vault's wall, a petty reaction, and swore. The gold gone, Hardy missing, Kelly dead and Rorden dying. He put the candle on the ledge of a niche and bent down to look at the floor. The dust had been disturbed by long, streaking marks, and he congratulated himself ironically for guessing that the smears had been made when the gold was removed. The knowledge was not much use now. The gold was gone. He straightened up.

'Could El Católico have taken it?'

The voice came from above them, from the top of the steps, and it was a rich voice, deep as Kearsey's but younger, much younger. 'No, he could not.' The owner of the voice wore long grey boots and a long grey cloak over a slim silver scabbard. As he descended the steps into the dim light, he proved to be a tall man with dark, thin good looks. 'Major. How good to see you back.'

Kearsey preened himself, flicked at his moustache, gestured at Sharpe. 'Colonel Jovellanos, this is Captain Sharpe. Sharpe, this is –'

'El Católico.' Sharpe's voice was neutral, no pleasure in the meeting.

The tall man, perhaps three years older than Sharpe, smiled. 'I am Joaquím Jovellanos, once Colonel in the Spanish army, and now known as El Católico.' He bowed slightly. He seemed amused by the meeting. 'They use my name to frighten the French, but you can see that I am really harmless.' Sharpe remembered the man's extraordinary speed with the sword, his bravery in facing the French charge alone. The man was far from harmless. Sharpe noticed the hands, long-fingered, that moved with a kind of ritual grace when he gestured. One of them was offered to Sharpe. 'I hear you rescued my Teresa.'

'Yes.' Sharpe, as tall as El Católico, felt lumpish beside the Spaniard's civilized languor.

The other hand came from behind the cloak, briefly touched Sharpe's shoulder. 'Then I am in your debt.' The words were given the lie by eyes that remained watchful and wary. El Católico moved back and smiled deprecatingly as if in admission that Spanish manners could be a trifle flowery. A slim hand gestured at the tomb. 'Empty.'

'So it seems. A lot of money.'

'Which it would have been your pleasure to carry for us.' The voice was like dark silk. 'To Cádiz?'

El Católico's eyes had not left Sharpe. The Spaniard smiled, made the same gesture round the vault. 'Alas, it cannot be. It is gone.'

'Do you know where?' Sharpe felt like a grubby street-sweeper in the presence of an exquisite aristocrat.

The eyebrows went up. 'I do, Captain. I do.'

Sharpe knew he was being tantalized, but ploughed on. 'Where?'

'Does it interest you?' Sharpe did not reply and El Católico smiled again. 'It is our gold, Captain, Spanish gold.'

'I'm curious.'

'Ah. Well, in that case, I can relieve your curiosity. The French have it. They captured it two days ago, along with your gallant Captain Hardy. We captured a straggler who told us so.'

Kearsey coughed, looked to El Católico as if for permission to speak, and received it. 'That's it, Sharpe. Hunt's over. Back to Portugal.'

Sharpe ignored him, continued to stare at the watchful Spaniard. 'You're sure?'

El Católico smiled, raised amused eyebrows, spread his hands. 'Unless our straggler lied. And I doubt that.'

'You prayed with him?'

'I did, Captain. He went to heaven with a prayer, and with all his ribs removed, one by one.' El Católico laughed.

It was Sharpe's turn to smile. 'We have our own prisoner. I'm sure he can deny or confirm your straggler's story.'

El Católico pointed a finger up the stairs. 'The Polish Sergeant? Is that your prisoner?'

Sharpe nodded. The lies would be nailed. 'That's the one.'

'How very sad.' The hands came together with a graceful hint of prayerful regret. 'I cut his throat as I arrived. In a moment of anger.'

The eyes were not smiling, whatever the mouth did, and Sharpe knew this was not the moment to accept, or even acknowledge, the delicate challenge. He shrugged, as if the death of the Sergeant meant nothing to him, and followed the tall Spaniard up the steps and into the hermitage that was noisy with newcomers who quietened as their leader appeared. Sharpe stood, in the thick, sweet smell, and watched the grey-cloaked man move easily among his followers: the figure of a leader who disbursed favour, reward, and consolation.

A soldier, Sharpe knew, was judged not merely by his actions but by the enemies he destroyed, and the Rifleman's fingers reached, unconsciously, for his big sword. Nothing had been admitted, nothing openly said, but in the gloom of the vault, in the wreckage of British hopes, Sharpe had found the enemy, and now, in the scent of death, he groped for the way to victory in this sudden, unwanted, and very private little war.

CHAPTER 10

The rapier moved invisibly, one moment on Sharpe's left, the next, as if by magic, past his guard and quivering at his chest. There was enough pressure to bend the blade, to feel the point draw a trace of blood; then El Católico stepped backwards, flicked the slim blade into a salute, and took up his guard again.

'You are slow, Captain.'

Sharpe hefted his blade. 'Try changing weapons.'

El Católico shrugged, reversed his blade, and held it to Sharpe. Taking the heavy cavalry sword in return, he held it level, turned his wrist, and lunged into empty air. 'A butcher's tool, Captain. *En garde!*'

The rapier was as delicate as a fine needle, yet even with its balance, its responsiveness, he could do nothing to pierce El Católico's casual defence. The Partisan leader teased him, led him on, and with a final contemptuous flick he beat Sharpe's lunge aside and stopped his hand half an inch before he would have laid open Sharpe's throat.

'You are no swordsman, Captain.'

'I'm a soldier.'

El Católico smiled, but the blade moved just enough to touch Sharpe's skin before the Spaniard dropped the sword on the ground and held out a hand for his own blade.

'Go back to your army, soldier. You might miss the boat.'

'The boat?' Sharpe bent down, pulled his heavy blade towards him.

'Didn't you know, Captain? The British are going. Sailing home, Captain, leaving the war to us.'

'Then look after it. We'll be back.'

Sharpe turned away, ignoring El Católico's laugh, and walked towards the gate leading into the street. He was in the ruins of Moreno's courtyard, where Knowles had smashed the volleys into the lancers, and all that was left were bullet marks on the scorched walls. Cesar Moreno came through the gate and stopped. He smiled at Sharpe, raised a hand to El Católico, and looked round as if frightened that someone might be listening.

'Your men, Captain?'

'Yes?'

'They're ready.'

He seemed a decent enough man, Sharpe thought, but whatever power and prowess he had once had seemed to have drained away under the twin blows of his wife's death and his daughter's love for the overpowering young El Católico. Cesar Moreno was as grey as his future son-in-law's cloak: grey hair, grey moustache, and a personality that was a shadow of what he had once been. He gestured towards the street.

'I can come with you?'

'Please.'

It had taken a full day to clear up the village, to dig the graves, to wait while Private Rorden died, the agony unbearable, and now they walked to where he and the other dead of the Company would be buried, out in the fields. El Católico walked with them, seemingly with inexhaustible politeness, but Sharpe sensed that Moreno was wary of his young colleague. The old man looked at the Rifleman.

'My children, Captain?'

Sharpe had been thanked a dozen times, more, but Moreno explained again.

'Ramon was ill. Nothing serious, but he could not travel. That was why Teresa was here, to look after him.'

'The French surprised you?'

El Católico interrupted. 'They did. They were better than we thought. We knew they would search the hills, but in such strength? Masséna is worried.'

'Worried?'

The grey-cloaked man nodded. 'His supplies, Captain, all travel on roads to the south. Can you imagine what we will do to them? We ride again tomorrow, to ambush his ammunition, to try to save Almeida.' It was a shrewd thrust. El

Católico would risk his men and his life to save Almeida when the British had done nothing to rescue the Spanish garrison of Ciudad Rodrigo. He turned his most charming smile on Sharpe. 'Perhaps you will come? We could do with those rifles of yours.'

Sharpe smiled back. 'We must rejoin our army. Remember? We might miss the boat.'

El Católico raised an eyebrow. 'And empty-handed. How sad.'

The guerrilla band watched them pass in silence. Sharpe had been impressed by them, by their weaponry, and by the discipline El Católico imposed. Each man, and many of the women, had a musket and bayonet, and pistols were thrust into their belts alongside knives and the long Spanish swords. Sharpe admired the horses, the saddlery, and turned to El Católico.

'It must be expensive.'

The Spaniard smiled. It was as easy as parrying one of Sharpe's clumsier lunges. 'They ride for hatred, Captain, of the French. Our people support us.'

And the British give you guns, Sharpe thought, but he said nothing. Moreno led them past the *castillo*, out into the field.

'I'm sorry, Captain, that we cannot bury your man in our graveyard.'

Sharpe shrugged. The British could fight for Spain, but their dead could not be put in a Spanish cemetery in case the Protestant soul would drag all the others down to hell. He stood in front of the Company, looked at Kearsey, who stood by the graves in his self-appointed role of chaplain, and nodded to Harper.

'Hats off!'

The words rang thin in the vastness of the valley. Kearsey was reading from his Bible, though he knew the words by heart, and El Católico, his face full of compassion, nodded as he listened. 'Man that is born of a woman is of few days, and full of trouble. He cometh forth like a flower, and is cut down.' And where's the gold? Sharpe wondered. Was it likely that the French, having killed the old and young, smashed the crucifix, smeared excreta on the walls of the hermitage, would carefully replace the stone lid of the family tomb? High over the valley an exaltation of larks tumbled in their song flight, and Sharpe looked at Harper. The Sergeant was looking up, at his beloved birds, but as Sharpe watched him the Irishman glanced at his Captain and away. His face had been impassive, unreadable, and Sharpe wondered what he had found. He had asked him to look round the village, explaining nothing but knowing that the Sergeant would understand.

'Amen!' The burial service was over and Kearsey glared at the Company. 'The salute, Captain!'

'Sergeant!'

'Company!' The words rang out confidently, discipline in chaos, the muskets rising together, the faces of the men anonymous in the ritual. 'Fire!'

The volley startled the larks, drifted white smoke over the graves, and the decencies had been done. Sharpe would have buried the men without ceremony, but Kearsey had insisted, and Sharpe acknowledged that the Major had been right. The drill, the old pattern of command and obey, had reassured the men, and Sharpe had heard them talking, quietly and contentedly, about marching back to the British lines. The trip across the two rivers, out into enemy country, was being called a 'wild-chicken chase', diverting and dangerous but not part of the real war. They were missing the Battalion, the regular rations, the security of a dozen other battalions on the march, and the thought of gold that had once excited them was now seen in perspective, as another soldier's dream, like finding an unlooted wine shop full of pliant women.

Kearsey marched across to stand beside Sharpe. He faced the Company, the Bible still clasped in his hand. 'You've done well. Very well. Difficult countryside and a long way from home. Well done.' They stared back at him with the blank look soldiers keep for encouraging talks from unpopular officers. 'I'm sorry that you must go back empty-handed, but your efforts have not been in vain. We have shown, together, that we do care about the Spanish people, about their future, and your enthusiasm, your struggle, will not be forgotten.'

El Católico clapped, beamed at the Company, smiled at Kearsey. Sharpe's Company stared at the two men as if wondering what new indignity would be heaped on them, and Sharpe suppressed a smile at the thought of the Spanish people remembering the enthusiasm and struggle of Private Batten.

Kearsey flicked at his moustache. 'You will march tomorrow, back to Portugal, and El Católico, here, will provide an escort.'

Sharpe kept his face straight, hiding his fury. Kearsey had told him none of this.

The Major went on. 'I'm staying, to continue the fight, and I hope we will meet again.' If he had expected a cheer he was disappointed.

Then, as El Católico had visited the burial of the British dead, it was the officers' turn to stand in the walled graveyard as the dead villagers were put into a common grave. El Católico had a tame priest, a moth-eaten little man, who rushed through the service as Sharpe, Knowles, and Harper stood awkwardly by the high wall. The French had been here, too, as disturbed graves and burst-open sepulchres showed. The dead had been reburied, the damage patched up, but Sharpe wondered yet again at the savagery of such a war.

He looked at Teresa, dressed in black, and she gave him one of her unconcerned stares, as if she had never seen him before, and he told himself that there was already enough trouble looming on the horizon without planning to pursue El Católico's woman. The Spanish officer, his sword still tucked under his arm, caught the glance Teresa gave Sharpe and he smiled slightly, or at least twitched the corners of his mouth, as if he recognized Sharpe's desire and pitied him for wanting something as unattainable as Teresa. Sharpe remembered the golden body running up the rocks, the shadows on the skin, and he knew he would as soon give up his search for the gold as give up his desire for the girl.

Harper crossed himself, the hats went on, and people stirred in the graveyard. Ramon limped over to Sharpe and smiled.

'You go tomorrow?'

'Yes.'

'I am sad.' He was genuine, the one friendly face in Casatejada. He pointed to Sharpe's rifle. 'I like it.'

Sharpe grinned, gave him the rifle to handle. 'Come with us; you could become a Rifleman.' There was a laugh and El Católico stood there, Kearsey loyally shadowing the tall man, and he watched as Ramon felt with his little finger, poking from the bandage, the seven rifled grooves that spun the ball and made the weapon so accurate.

El Católico cleared his throat. 'A sad day, Captain.'

'Yes, sir.' Surely he had not come to tell Sharpe it had been a sad day.

El Católico looked round the graveyard with an imperious eye. 'Too many dead. Too many graves. Too many new graves.'

Sharpe followed his eyes round the small graveyard. There was something strange here, something out of place, but it could have been his reaction to the burials, to the French damage in the graveyard. One wall, beside the hermitage, was made of niches, each sized to receive a coffin, and the French had torn off the sealed doors and spilt the rotting contents to the ground. Had the French heard of the gold, Sharpe wondered, or did they treat all cemeteries this way? To defile the dead was a taunt almost as callous as man could devise, but Sharpe guessed it was commonplace in the war between Partisans and French.

Sergeant Harper, unexpectedly, took a pace forward. 'They didn't open all the graves, sir.' He stated it consolingly, with his surprising compassion.

El Católico smiled at him, saw that Harper was pointing at a fresh grave, neatly piled with earth and waiting for its headstone. The tall man nodded. 'Not all. Perhaps there was not time. I buried him six days ago. A servant, a good man.'

There was a snap and they all looked at Ramon, who was still fumbling with the Baker rifle. He had the small trap open, in the butt, and seemed impressed by the cleaning tools hidden inside. He handed the rifle back to Sharpe. 'One day I have one, yes?'

'One day I'll give you one. When we're back.'

Ramon lifted his eyebrows. 'You come back?'

Sharpe laughed. 'We'll be back. We'll chase the French all the way to Paris.'

He slung the rifle and walked away from El Católico, across the cemetery and through a wrought-iron side gate that opened on to the wide fields. If he had hoped for fresh air, untainted with death, he was unlucky. Beside the gate, half hidden by dark-green bushes, was a vast manure heap, stinking and warm, and Sharpe turned back to see that El Católico had followed him.

'You think the war is not lost, Captain?'

Sharpe wondered if he detected a trace of worry in the Spaniard. He shrugged. 'It's not lost.'

'You're wrong.' If the Spaniard had been worried, it was gone now. He spoke loudly, almost sneeringly. 'You've lost, Captain. Only a miracle can save the British now.'

Sharpe copied the sneering tone. 'We're all bloody Christians, aren't we? We believe in miracles.'

Kearsey's protest was stopped by a peal of laughter. It checked them all, swung them round, to see Teresa, her arm through her father's, standing at the hermitage door. The laugh stopped, the face became stern again, but for the first time, Sharpe thought, he had seen that she was not completely bound to the tall, grey-cloaked Spaniard. She even nodded to the Rifleman, in agreement, before turning away. Miracles, Sharpe decided, were beginning to happen.

CHAPTER 11

The elation had worn thin. Failure, like a hangover, imposed
its mocking price of depression and regret as Sharpe marched
westward from Casatejada towards the two rivers that barred
the Light Company from a doomed British army. Sharpe felt
sour, disappointed, and cheated. There had been little
friendliness in the farewells. Ramon had embraced him,
Spanish fashion, with a garlic kiss on both cheeks, and the
young man had seemed genuinely sad to be parting from the
Light Company. 'Remember your promise, Captain. A rifle.'

Sharpe had made the promise, but he wondered, gloomily,
how it was to be kept. Almeida must soon be under siege, the
French would dominate the land between the rivers, and the
British would be retreating westward towards the sea, to final
defeat. And all that stood between survival and a silent, bitter
embarkation was his suspicion that the gold was still in
Casatejada, hidden as subtly as the Partisans hid their food
and their weapons. He remembered Wellington's words.
'*Must*, do you hear? *Must!*' There had to be more gold,
Sharpe thought: gold in the cellars of London, in the
merchant banks, the counting-houses, in the bellies of
merchant ships. So why *this* gold? The question could not be
answered and the threat of defeat, like the rain-clouds that
still built in the north, accompanied the Light Company on
its empty march towards the river Agueda.

The Partisans were also going westward and for the first
hour Sharpe had watched the horsemen as they rode on the
spine of a low chain of hills to the south. El Católico had
talked of ambushing the French convoys that would be
lumbering with ammunition towards Almeida. But, often as
Sharpe saw Kearsey's blue coat among the horsemen, he
could not see El Católico's grey cloak. He had asked José, one

of El Católico's Lieutenants and the leader of the Company's escort, where the Partisan leader was, but José shrugged.

'Went ahead.' The Spaniard spurred his horse away.

Patrick Harper caught up with Sharpe, glanced at his Captain's face. 'Permission to speak, sir?'

Sharpe looked at him sourly. 'You don't usually ask. What is it?'

Harper gestured at the escorting horsemen. 'What do they remind you of, sir?'

Sharpe looked at the long black cloaks, wide hats, and long-stirruped saddlery. He shrugged. 'So tell me.'

Harper looked up at the northern sky, at the heavy clouds. 'I remember, sir, when I was a recruit. It was like this, so it was, marching from Derry.' Sharpe was used to the Sergeant's circumlocutions. If there were a way of imparting information by a story, then the Irishman preferred to use it, and Sharpe, who had learned that it was worth listening, did not interrupt. 'And they gave us an escort, sir, just like this. Horsemen before, beside, behind, and all the way round, so that not one mother's son would get the hell off the road. It was like being a prisoner, sir, so it was, and all the way! Locked up at night, we were, in a barn near Maghera, and on their side, we were!'

The Sergeant's face had the fleeting look of sadness that sometimes came when he talked of home, his beloved Ulster, of a place so poor that he had ended up in the army of its enemy. The look passed and he grinned again. 'Do you see what I'm telling you, sir? This is a bloody escort for prisoners. They're seeing us off their own land, so they are.'

'And what if they are?' The two men had quickened their pace so they were ahead of the Company, out of earshot.

'The bastards are lying through their teeth.' Harper said it with a quiet relish, as if confident that he could defeat their lies as easily as he saw through them.

José paused on a ridge ahead and searched the ground before spurring his horse onwards. The Company was isolated in a vastness of pale grass, rocks, and dried streambeds. The sun baked it all, hazed it with shimmering air, cracking the soil open with miniature chasms. Sharpe knew they must stop soon and rest, but his men were uncomplaining, even the wounded, and they trudged on in the heat and dust towards the far blue line that was the hills around Almeida.

'All right. Why are they lying?'

'What did your man say yesterday?' Harper meant El Católico, but the question did not demand an answer from Sharpe. The Sergeant went on with enthusiasm. 'We were standing by that grave, you remember, and he said that he had buried the man six days before. Would you remember that?'

Sharpe nodded. He had been thinking of that grave himself, but his Sergeant's words were opening up new ideas. 'Go on.'

'Yesterday was a Saturday. I asked the Lieutenant; he can always remember the day and date. So that means he buried his servant on the Sunday.'

Sharpe looked at Harper, mystified by the meaning of his statement. 'So?'

'So he buried the man last Sunday.'

'What's wrong with that?'

'God save Ireland, sir, they would not do that. Not on a Sunday and not on a holy day. They're Catholics, sir, not your heathen Protestants. On a Sunday? Not at all!'

Sharpe grinned at his vehemence. 'Are you sure?'

'Am I sure? If my name's not Patrick Augustine Harper, and we were all good Catholics in Tangaveane despite the bastard English. Now would you look at that, sir?'

'What?' Sharpe was alarmed by the Sergeant's suddenly pointing to the north, as if a French patrol had appeared.

'A red kite, sir. You don't see many of those.'

Sharpe saw a bird that looked like a hawk, but to him most birds, from cuckoos to eagles, looked like hawks. He walked on. Harper had reinforced his suspicions, added to them, and he let his mind wander over the vague feelings that were causing him disquiet. The stone over the crypt that had not even prompted the faintest mistrust from Kearsey. Then there was the speed with which El Católico had killed the Polish Sergeant, forgoing the usual pleasure of torturing the man, and surely, Sharpe reasoned, that had been done so that the man did not have time in his dying to blurt out the awkward fact that the French knew nothing about the gold. It was not much of a reason for suspicion. In the short time that the lancer had been their prisoner Sharpe had not even found a common language, but El Católico was not to know that.

The stone, the sudden death of the lancer, and, added to those, Sharpe's first suspicions that the French, if they had found the treasure, would not have lingered in the high valley but would have ridden fast with their booty to Ciudad Rodrigo. Now there was Harper's idea that, if El Católico had told the truth, the grave in the churchyard had been created on a Sunday, which, by itself, was reason for suspicion. Sharpe walked on, feeling the sweat trickling down his back, and tried to remember El Católico's words. Had he said something like 'I buried him less than a week ago'? But if Harper was right, exact about the six days? Once again his suspicion was drifting free and had nothing to pin it and justify the plan that was in his mind. Yet El Católico was lying. He had no proof, just a certainty. He turned back to Harper.

'You think the gold is in that grave?'

'There's something there, sir, and it's as sure as eternal damnation that it's no Christian burial.'

'But he could have buried the man on the Saturday.'

'He could, sir, he could. But there's the point that the thing is not disturbed. Strange.' Again Sharpe did not follow the Irishman's reasoning. Harper grinned at him. 'Say you wanted to steal a few thousand gold coins, sir, and they were hidden in the vault. Now, would you want to share the good news with everyone that you were taking them away? Not if you have a grain of sense, sir, so you move it a short way, hidden by the walls of the burial yard, and you hide it again. In a good fresh grave.'

'And if I was a French officer' – Sharpe was thinking out loud – 'the first place I would look for anything hidden – guns, food, anything – is a good fresh grave.'

Harper nodded. He was no longer smiling. 'And if you found the corpse of a British officer, sir? What would you do then?'

The Sergeant had gone way ahead of Sharpe's thinking

and he let the idea thread itself into his suspicions. Where the hell was Hardy? If the French found a British officer in a grave they would not disturb it; they would replace the earth, even say a prayer. He whistled softly. 'But –'

'I know, sir.' Harper interrupted him. This was the Sergeant's theory, well thought over, and he raced ahead with it. 'There's the funny thing. They won't bury you heathen English in holy ground in case you spoil it for us good Catholics. But would you think sixteen thousand gold coins might overcome their fear of eternal perdition, sir? I'd be tempted. And you can always move the body when you dig up the gold, and with two Hail Marys you're back on the golden ladder.' Harper nodded in satisfaction with his theory. 'Did you talk, sir, with the girl's father?'

'Yes, but he knew nothing.' Which was not true, Sharpe reflected. He had talked with Cesar Moreno, in the burnt courtyard of the widower's house, and the grey head bowed when Sharpe had asked what had happened to Captain Hardy. 'I don't know.' Moreno had looked up, almost pleading with Sharpe not to go on.

'And the gold, sir?'

Teresa's father had jerked away from Sharpe. 'The gold! Always the gold! I wanted it to go to Lisbon. El Católico wants it to go by road! The French have it! If your cavalry had not blundered, Captain, it would be on its way to Cádiz. There is no gold any more.'

There had been a note of desperation in the man's voice that had made Sharpe want to go on prying, to let the gentle questions release Moreno's honesty, but El Católico, Teresa with him, had appeared at the gate and the chance had gone. Yet now Harper was offering a new thought, one that Sharpe would never have found for himself: that the grave in the walled cemetery held the treasure, and, like the mysterious old mounds in the British countryside, the body was surrounded by gold. There was another superstition attached to those mounds, one Sharpe remembered well, that each was guarded by a sleeping dragon, a dragon that would wake at the first scrape of a thieving pickaxe. The dragon would have to be risked.

Sharpe let the idea take wings, spin itself into the air, a

fragile sequence of possibilities on which to suspend the hope of victory. Could the gold be in Casatejada? So easy? That the gold was in the graveyard, sitting there till the armies had moved on, and El Católico could dig it up without fear of French patrols or zealous exploring officers. Then why had El Católico encouraged Kearsey to stay on with the Partisans? Or, he remembered, invited Sharpe to stay with his rifles? Yet if Harper were right, if his own suspicions were right, then the grave had been dug on a Sunday, which was against the law of the Church, and in it were the gold and the body of Josefina's lover. And perhaps El Católico had invited them to stay with the Partisans because that only lessened their suspicions, and because El Católico had all the time in the world and was in no particular hurry to dig up the coins. It was all too fantastic, a delicate web of frail surmise, but he knew that if he did not take a decision, then all would be irrevocably lost. He laughed out loud, at the absurdity of it all, at his worries that he might cause himself trouble if he were in the wrong, as if that mattered against the outcome of the summer's campaign. José looked round, startled by the sudden laugh.

'Captain?'

'We must take a rest. Ten minutes.'

The men sat down gratefully, stripped off their packs, and lay full length on the ground. Sharpe walked back along the line to talk to the wounded men who were being helped by their comrades. He heard Batten grumbling and stopped.

'Don't worry, Batten, there's not much farther to go.'

The suspicious eyes looked up at Sharpe. 'It's a hot day, sir.'

'You'd complain if it was any colder.' The men nearby grinned. 'Anyway, you'll be in Almeida tomorrow and back with the Battalion the day after.'

He spoke loudly for the escort's benefit, and as he spoke he knew that the decision had been taken. They would not be in Almeida tomorrow, or the day after, but back in Casatejada, where there was some gravedigging to do. It was the only way to allay the suspicions, but by doing it Sharpe knew he was taking on enemies that were more dangerous than the French. If the gold were there, and for a second his mind sneered away from the terrifying prospect that it was not, then the Company would have to carry it across twenty miles of hostile country, avoiding the French, but, worse than that, fighting off the Partisans, who knew the territory and how to fight it. For the moment all he could do was to convince the surly José that he had every intention of going straight back to the army, and Sharpe, to his men's surprise, suddenly waxed voluble and jolly.

'Boiled beef tomorrow, lads. No more vegetable stew! Army rum, your wives, the Regimental Sergeant Major, all the things you've missed. Aren't you looking forward to it?' They grinned at him, happy that he was happy. 'And for us unmarried men the best women in Portugal!' There were rude cheers for that and the Partisan, resting in his saddle, looked on disapprovingly.

'Your men fight for women, Captain?'

Sharpe nodded cheerfully. 'And for drink. Plus a shilling a day with deductions.'

Knowles walked up from the rear with his watch open. 'Ten minutes are up, sir.'

'On your feet!' Sharpe clapped his hands. 'Come on, lads! Let's go home. Parades, rations, and Mrs Roach to do the washing!'

The men stood up in good moods, heaved on their packs, shouldered their weapons, and Sharpe saw José's disdainful look. He had created the impression, a fairly accurate impression, that the Light Company cared only for drink and women, and such allies were not to José's taste. Sharpe wanted to be despised, to be under-rated, and if the Spaniard went back to Casatejada thinking that the men of the South Essex were clumsy, crude, and hell-bent on reaching the cat-houses of Lisbon, then that suited Sharpe.

Patrick Harper, the seven-barrelled gun hitched high on his shoulder, fell into step with Sharpe once more. 'So we're going back?'

Sharpe nodded. 'Not that anyone else needs to know. How did you guess?'

Harper laughed. He looked shrewdly at Sharpe, as if gauging the wisdom of his answer, but he seemed to think it safe. 'Because you want the bastard's woman.'

Sharpe smiled. 'And the gold, Patrick. Don't forget the gold.'

They reached the Agueda at dusk, when gnats gathered in clouds over the slow northward flow of the river. Sharpe was tempted to bivouac on the eastern bank, but knew that such an action would arouse the Partisans' suspicions, so the Light Company waded the river and went half a mile into the trees that fringed the western hills. The escort did not leave but stood on the far bank watching them, and for a moment Sharpe wondered if the Spaniards suspected that the British soldiers would try to return to Casatejada in the night. He turned to a shivering Lieutenant Knowles. 'Light a fire.'

'A fire?' Knowles looked astonished. 'But the French –'

'I know. Light it. A big one.'

The men were enthusiastic. Those who had the wicked saw-backed bayonets attacked cork-oak branches, others gathered kindling, and within minutes the blue wood-smoke rose like a wavering signal in the evening sky. Patrick Harper, standing in dripping shirt-tails and holding his sodden trousers to the fire, cocked an inquisitive look towards his Captain as if suggesting that the blaze was dangerous. It was deliberately so, because seeing it would further convince the Partisans of the ineptness of the British infantry. Any man who lit a fire in countryside patrolled by the enemy could not expect to live long.

Whether prompted by the sight of the fire or by the lateness of the hour, José decided to leave, and Sharpe, crouching in the shadows at the tree-line, watched as the horsemen wheeled and spurred their horses back to the east. The Company was alone.

'Lieutenant!'

Knowles came from the fire. 'Sir.'

'We're going back. Tonight.' He watched Knowles to see if there was any reaction, but the north countryman nodded as if the news was not unexpected. Sharpe was obscurely disappointed. 'We won't take the wounded. Sergeant Read can take them on to Almeida. Give him three men to help and tell him to find a convoy going back over the Coa. Understand?'

'Yes, sir.'

'And we'll split up tonight. I'll go ahead with the Riflemen; you follow. You'll find us in the graveyard at Casatejada.'

Knowles scratched his head. 'You reckon the gold's in there, sir?'

Sharpe nodded. 'Maybe. I want to look, anyway.' He grinned at the Lieutenant, infecting him with his enthusiasm. 'Arrange that, Robert; then let me know if there are any problems.'

Night dropped swiftly and the darkness seemed to Sharpe to be doubly thick. The moon was hidden behind looming clouds that slowly, infinitely slowly, blotted out the stars, and a small, chill breeze that came from the north reminded Sharpe that the weather had to break. Let it not be tonight, he thought, for rain would slow them, make the difficult journey even more hazardous, and he needed to be in Casatejada while the darkness still reigned. To his surprise, his pleasure, the news that they were not going on to Almeida seemed to excite the men. They grinned at him, muttered that he was a bastard, but there was a restlessness about the Company that spoke of a need to fulfil their job. Knowles came back, a shadow in the darkness.

'Any problems?'

'Only Read, sir. Wants a paper.'

Sharpe laughed. Sergeant Read was as fussy as a broody hen and doubtless thought that his small band was in more danger from their own side than from the French. If the provosts found a small group wandering away from their battalion they could assume they had found deserters and get out their long ropes. Sharpe scribbled with a pencil on a page from Knowles's notebook, not knowing in the darkness if the words were even legible. 'Give him that.' Knowles did not leave and Sharpe could hear him moving restlessly. 'What is it?'

The Lieutenant's voice was low, worried. 'Do you know the gold is there, sir?'

'You know I don't.'

There was a pause; Knowles shifted from foot to foot. 'It's a risk, sir.'

'How?' Sharpe knew that his Lieutenant was not lacking in courage.

'I thought Major Kearsey ordered you back to the army, sir. If he comes back and finds us poking round Casatejada he won't exactly be happy. And El Católico won't welcome us with open arms. And...' His voice trailed away.

'And what?'

'Well, sir.' Knowles crouched down so he was closer to Sharpe, his voice even lower. 'Everyone knows you were in trouble with the General after those provosts, sir. If Kearsey complains about you, sir, well...' He ran out of words again.

'I could be in even more trouble, yes?'

'Yes, sir. And it's not just that.' His words suddenly tumbled out as if he had been storing the speech for days, or even weeks. 'We all know the gazette hasn't come through, sir, and it's so unfair! Just because you were once a Private they seem to be doing nothing, and the Eagle counts for nothing.'

'No, no, no.' Sharpe stopped the flow. He was embarrassed, touched, even surprised. 'The army isn't unfair, just slow.'

He did not believe that himself, but if he let himself express his real thoughts, then the bitterness would show. He remembered the elation of the moment, a year before, when the General had gazetted him a Captain, but since then there had been only silence from the Horse Guards. He wondered whether the gazette had already been refused and no one dared tell him; that had happened before and battalion commanders had made up the pay themselves. Damn the army, damn the promotion system. He looked at Knowles.

'How long have you been a Lieutenant?'

'Two years and nine months, sir.' Sharpe was hardly surprised that the answer was given so fully and so quickly. Most Lieutenants counted the days till they had three years' seniority. 'So you'll be a Captain by Christmas?'

Knowles sounded embarrassed. 'My father's paying, sir. He promised me the money after Talavera.'

'You deserve it.' Sharpe felt the pang of jealousy. He could never afford fifteen hundred pounds for a Captaincy, and Knowles was lucky in his father. Sharpe laughed, disguising his mood. 'If my gazette fails, Robert, then by Christmas we'll have changed places!' He stood up, looked across the dark valley. 'Time to go. God knows how we find the way. But good luck.'

A thousand miles away, north and east, a small man with an untidy hank of hair and an insatiable appetite for work looked at the pile of papers he had dealt with and grunted approvingly as he re-read the last paragraphs of the latest despatch from Marshal André Masséna. He wondered if the Marshal, whom he himself had made into the Prince of Essling, was losing his touch. The British army was so small -- the newspapers from London said a mere twenty-three thousand with twenty-two thousand Portuguese allies – while the French armies were so big, and Masséna seemed to be taking the devil of a long time. But the despatch said that he was going forward, into Portugal, and soon the British would have their backs to the sea and would face nothing but terror, shame, and defeat. The small man yawned. He knew everything that happened in his huge Empire, even that the Prince of Essling had taken a young woman to the war to keep his bed warm at night, but he would be forgiven. A man needed that, especially as the years went on, and victory forgave all. He laughed out loud, startling a servant and flickering the candles, as he remembered a secret agent's report that said Masséna's mistress was disguised in Hussar uniform. But what did that matter? The Empire was safe and the small man went to his bed, to his Princess, in utter ignorance of the Company that marched through his territory in the hope of giving him many sleepless nights in the months to come.

CHAPTER 12

It was a nightmare journey and only Hagman's instincts, honed by years of poaching dark countryside, took the Riflemen safely back over the paths where they had been escorted earlier in the day. Sharpe wondered how Knowles, with the larger number of men, was surviving, but there were poachers not unlike Hagman in the Redcoats and there was no point in worrying. The Riflemen made good time, cursing through the rocks, stumbling on the streambeds, going faster than the less well-trained men of the South Essex could travel. The Rifles were the elite of the army, the best trained, the best equipped, the finest infantry of an army which boasted the best foot soldiers in the world, but none of their training, their vaunted self-reliance, had prepared them for the job of sneaking into Casatejada under the noses of suspicious Partisans.

Perversely the moon made an appearance as the green-jacketed men reached the final crest before the village. It sailed clear of the ragged cloud-edge and showed the village, innocent and silent, in the centre of the valley. The men dropped to the ground, pushed their rifles forward, but nothing moved in the moonlight except the barley rippling in the breeze and the maize clattering on its long stalks. Sharpe stared at the village, reliving the hopelessness of trying to get near it unseen, and tonight there would be no hope of persuading its defenders to light fires, dazzle themselves, and thus give the attackers an advantage. He stood up. 'Come on.'

They made a wide circuit, round the southern end of the valley, moving fast in the moonlight and hoping that if their shadowed bodies were dimly seen against the dark background of the hills the sentries in the village would think that it was one of the wolf-packs that ran in the uplands. Twice on the journey the Riflemen had heard the wolves near them, once seen a ragged profile on a crest, but they had not been troubled. The cemetery was on the eastern side of the street and the Riflemen had to circle the village so they could approach from the darkness. Sharpe kept looking towards the east, fearing the first sliver of dawn, fearing the approach to the village. 'Down!'

They dropped again, panting, in a field of half-cut barley that the French had trampled with their horses, criss-crossing the field so that, in the darkness, it was made of fantastic patterns and strangely shadowed curves. 'Come on.' They wriggled forward, the hermitage a quarter-mile away with its bell-tower staring at them, picking paths through the stalks where the crop had been flattened and where standing clumps gave them cover. No one spoke; each man knew his job, and each knew, too, that the Spaniards, who talked to one another with white stones on hilltops, could have watched them for the last five miles. Yet why should they be suspicious? Sharpe was haunted by the question, by the possible answers, by the knife-edge on which he had balanced the Company.

Two hundred yards to go and he stopped, raised a hand, and turned to Hagman. 'All right?'

The man nodded, grinned his toothless grin. 'Perfect, sir.'

Sharpe looked at Harper. 'Come on.'

Now it was just the two of them, creeping forward into the growing stench of the manure, listening for the tiny sounds that could betray an alert sentry. The barley, crushed and tortuous, grew almost to the wall of the graveyard, but as they twisted their way closer to the high white wall Sharpe knew they could not hope to climb it unseen. He let Harper wriggle alongside and put his mouth close to the Sergeant's ear.

'You see the bell-tower?'

Harper nodded.

'There has to be someone up there. We can't cross here. We'll be seen.'

The Sergeant put out a hand and curved it to the left. Sharpe nodded. 'Come on.'

The bell-tower, with its arches facing the four points of the compass, was the most obvious sentry post in the village. Sharpe could see nothing in the shadowed space at the top of the tower, but he knew a man was there, and as they crawled, the stalks of the barley deafening, he felt like a small animal creeping towards a trap. They reached the corner of the cemetery, stood against the wall with a false sense of relief, and then, hidden from the tower, edged slowly down its left-hand side towards the gate, the bushes, and the rank heap of manure.

Nothing stirred. It was as if Casatejada were deserted, and for a moment Sharpe let his mind dwell on the luxurious possibility that El Católico had ridden with all his followers and that the village truly was empty. Then he remembered Ramon, who could not yet ride, and his sister, Teresa, who had stayed to look after him, and he knew that the village was lived in, was guarded, yet somehow they had reached the gate into the cemetery and no one had shouted, no one had clicked back the lock of a musket, and still the village had the blank look of a sleeping community. Sharpe peered through the wrought-iron gate. The graves were lit by the moon. It was quiet, the hairs on the back of his neck prickled, and suddenly the idea of sixteen thousand gold coins hidden in the grave was ridiculous. He twitched Harper's elbow, forcing the Sergeant into the thick shadow of the bushes by the gate.

'I don't like it,' he whispered. There was no point in trying to dissect his fears; a soldier had to trust instinct and the moment he tried to pin it down it would vanish like smoke in a mist. 'You stay here. I'll go in. If anyone interferes with me use that damned gun.'

Patrick Harper nodded. He had unslung the seven-barrelled gun and he pulled back the flint, slowly and evenly, so that the heavily greased pawl slid silently into place. The Sergeant shared his officer's apprehension, though whether it was the sight of the empty graveyard in the thin moonlight or that their enemies mockingly watched them he was not sure. He watched Sharpe jump for the top of the wall, not trusting the hinges of the gate, and then he looked into the hills and saw the faintest edge on the horizon, the harbinger of dawn, and felt a chill breeze disturb the thick stench of the manure. He heard Sharpe's scabbard scrape on the stones. There was a thump as he hit the ground; then Harper was alone, in the thick cover of the bush, and gripping the stock of the killer gun.

Sharpe crouched inside the graveyard, his ears ringing with the noise he had made as he dropped over the wall. He had been a fool! He should have slipped his sword and rifle through the bars of the gate, but he had not thought of it, and he had made a noise like a lover fleeing from a returning husband as he slithered and bumped his way over the high stone barrier. But nothing moved; nothing sounded except a curious deep background sighing where the wind passed through the bell-tower and caressed the huge metal instrument. Across the graveyard he could see the wall sepulchres, little boxes in the thin light, and he thought of the putrefaction dripping down the mortar, and the bodies that lay in this yard, and then he was on his belly and crawling between the graves towards the spot, across the yard, where the fresh grave waited for him. He could be seen, he knew, from the bell-tower as he made his way across, but the die was cast, there was no going back, and he could only hope that the man in the tower was sleeping, his head on his chest, while the enemy sneaked in beneath. His belt buckle, crossbelt, and buttons all snagged on the dry earth as he crawled towards the heap of earth. The grave did look suspicious, he decided, higher than the others and somehow more neatly sculptured into a squared ridge of pale soil. He had smeared his face with a mixture of dirt and spittle, but he dared not look up, much as he wanted to, to see if a face was leaning out of the archway.

In the stillness, he cursed his stupidity. Should he have marched straight in, bayonets fixed, and insisted on digging up the grave? If he had been certain he could have done that, instead of coming like a thief in the night, but nothing was certain. A suspicion, that was all, a flimsy, damned suspicion that was buttressed by nothing more than Patrick Harper's insistence that a man would not be buried on a Sunday. He suddenly remembered that the Sergeant's middle name was Augustine and he grinned, senselessly, as at last he came up beside the object he had marched so far and hard to explore.

Nothing moved. The bell moaned gently, but there were no other sounds. It would have been easy to think that he was utterly alone, completely unseen, but his instinct was still sending danger signals that he could do nothing about. He began to dig, awkwardly, lying flat with a crooked arm and dragging back handfuls of earth from the grave. It was harder than he had thought. Every handful of dry earth and flinty stone brought down a miniature landslide from the top of the ridge, and each time it seemed that the noise was deafening, but he dared do nothing except keep scrabbling at the grave while the muscles of his arm, bent unnaturally, shrieked with agony. Once he thought he heard a noise, a foot on stone, but when he froze there was nothing. He looked up, saw the tinge of grey light that limited his time, and he dug deeper, forcing his hand into the soil and trying to make a tunnel down to whatever was buried in this hard, shallow land. The light was improving, disastrously, and what before had been mere humped shadows in the moonlight could now be seen as distinct, ornate gravestones. He could even read the writing on the nearest stone – Maria Uracca – and the carved angel that guarded her rest seemed to leer at him in the thin light. He risked a look upwards, throwing caution away, but there was nothing to be seen in the arched opening at the top of the tower, except for the grey, dim shape of the bell. He pushed his hand in harder, still meeting nothing but soil and stone, and enlarged the crater he had made, which looked as if a dog had been scrabbling for a bone. Then there was a voice, clear and distinct, somewhere in the village, and he knew there was no more time. The voice had not sounded alarmed, just someone getting up, but there was no point in trying to hide any more. He knelt up and used both hands, pulling back the soil, delving down to whatever was in the grave. And there it was. Sackcloth. He scraped more frantically, the soil caving in on the patch of sacking, and his mind whipped ahead to the thought of gold coins in thin sacks, buried six inches below the surface. He cleared the patch again, could see the sacking clearly, and he thrust at it with stiff fingers, splitting it, forcing his hand into the coins. But there were no coins. Just the filthy, desperate, rotten smell of corpse, and a horrifying slime on his fingers, a gagging in his throat, and he knew instantly that this body, shrouded in plain, brown cloth, was not Captain Hardy but El Católico's servant, who, for a reason he would never know, had been undisturbed by the marauding Frenchmen. Failure, utter, complete, total failure, the end of a thousand hopes, and fingers covered in rotting tissue. And no gold.

'Good morning.' The voice was mocking, even and steady, and Sharpe spun round to see El Católico standing in the door of the hermitage. The Spanish officer was in shadow, but there was no mistaking the long uniform cuffs beneath the grey cloak, the slim sword, or the silken voice. 'Good morning, Captain Sharpe. Were you hungry?'

Sharpe stood up, conscious of the filth on his uniform. He bent down to pick up his rifle, but checked as he saw a musket barrel point at him from behind El Católico, and suddenly, on quiet feet, a dozen men were in a line either side of the Spaniard who still looked at Sharpe with a mocking eye.

'Do you often dig up corpses, Captain Sharpe?'

There was nothing to say. He let the rifle stay on the ground and straightened up.

'I asked if you often dug up corpses, Captain.'

The tall man walked a few more feet into the cemetery. Sharpe wiped the filth from his right hand on his overall trousers. Why the devil had Harper not appeared? Had they found him, too? Sharpe had heard nothing, no footsteps, no creaking door, but he had been scraping at the soil and the noise had been enough to cover El Católico's quiet approach to the back door of the hermitage.

The Spaniard chuckled, waved a hand in one of his elegant gestures. 'You're not going to answer my question. I suppose you are searching for the gold? Am I right?' Sharpe said nothing and El Católico's voice became insistent. 'Am I right?'

'Yes.'

'You have a voice!' El Católico turned and spoke to one of his men, waited, and turned back holding a spade. 'Then dig, Captain. Dig. We never had time to bury Carlos properly. We did it in a hurry last Saturday night, so you can do us a service.' He threw the spade at Sharpe, the blade catching the light, and it thumped into the soil next to the Rifleman's feet.

Sharpe did not move. Part of him damned Harper, unfairly, for the suspicions about a Sunday burial, but he knew that he would have come back anyway. And where was the big Irishman? He could not have been captured, not without a struggle that would have been audible a mile away, and Sharpe felt the faintest stirring of hope.

El Católico took a step forward. 'You won't dig?'

The tall Spaniard chopped down with his left hand and Sharpe saw the musket barrel come up, heard the bang, saw the stab of flame in the gout of smoke, and the ball flattened itself on the wall behind him. Had the bastards cut Harper's throat? There was no hope of a rescue from Hagman; Sharpe had drummed it into the group that they were not to come into the village unless summoned. Damn everything! And Knowles would lumber into the same trap, and everything, every last bloody thing, had collapsed around him because he had been too clever. He picked up the spade – there was no choice – and he thrust its blade into the earth beside the body, and his mind, refusing to take the finality of utter defeat, still hoped that beneath the rotting corpse he might find bags of gold. Beneath the body was flinty soil, full of sharp rocks, hard-packed and jarring as he thrust down with the spade.

El Católico laughed. 'Have you found your gold, Captain?' He turned to his men, spoke in quick Spanish, and they laughed at the Englishman, mocked the Rifle Captain with the dirty face who was being forced to dig a grave like a peasant.

'Joaquím?' Teresa's voice, and suddenly she was there, dressed in a long white dress, and she stood beside her man, put her arm through his, and asked what was happening. Sharpe heard her laughter as El Católico explained.

'Dig, Captain, dig! The gold! You must have the gold!' El Católico was enjoying himself.

Sharpe threw down the spade. 'There is no gold.'

'Ah!' El Católico's face showed mock horror; his hands flew up, releasing the girl, and he translated to his men. He turned back, ignoring their laughter. 'Where are your men, Captain?'

'Watching you.'

It was a feeble answer and El Católico treated it with the contempt it deserved. He laughed. 'You were seen crawling to the grave, Captain, all alone and in the darkness. But you're not alone, are you?'

'No. And I didn't expect to find you here.'

El Católico bowed. 'An unexpected pleasure, then. Teresa's father is leading the ambush. I decided to come back.'

'To protect your gold?' It was a futile attempt, but everything was futile now.

El Católico put an arm round Teresa's shoulders. 'To protect my treasure, Captain.' He translated again, and the men laughed. The girl's face stayed enigmatic as ever. El Católico waved a hand at the gate. 'Go, Captain. I know your men are near. Go home, little gravedigger, and remember one thing.'

'Yes?'

'Watch your back. Very carefully. It's a long road.' El Católico laughed, watched Sharpe bend down to retrieve his rifle. 'Leave the rifle, little gravedigger. It will save us picking it up from the road.'

Sharpe picked it up, slung it defiantly on his shoulder, and swore uselessly at the Spaniard. El Católico laughed, shrugged, and gestured again at the gate.

'Go, Captain. The French have the gold, as I told you. The French.'

The gate was not locked; it could have been opened easily, but Patrick Harper, with the blood of Irish heroes in his veins, chose to stand back and kick it with one enormous foot. It exploded inwards, the hinges tearing from the dry mortar, and there he stood, six feet four inches of grinning Irishman, filthy as a slaughterer, and with seven barrels held in one hand that pointed casually at El Católico and his men.

'Top of the morning! And how's our lordship this morning?'

Sharpe was rarely given a glimpse of Harper's imitation of what the rest of the world thought of as Irish mannerisms, but this was obviously a rich performance. The dreadful shroud of failure vanished because Sharpe knew, with an absolute certainty, that Patrick Harper was boiling with good news. There was the grin, the jigging walk, and the inane words that bubbled from the huge soldier.

'And a fine morning it is, to be sure, your honour.' He was looking at El Católico. 'I wouldn't move, your grace, not while I've got the gun on you. It could go off with a desperate bang, so it could, and take the whole of your precious head off.' He glanced at Sharpe. 'Morning, sir! Excuse my appearance.'

Sharpe smiled, began to laugh with the relief of it. Harper was disgusting, covered with glistening and decaying muck, and the Sergeant grinned through the mask of manure.

'I fell in the shit, sir.' Only one thing about the Sergeant was not smothered in manure – the gun – and that, despite his excitement, was held very steadily on El Católico. The Irishman glanced quickly again at Sharpe. 'Would you mind calling the lads, sir?'

Sharpe drew the whistle from its holster on his leather crossbelt and blew the signal that would bring the Riflemen running to the village. Harper still looked steadily at El Católico. 'Thank you, sir.' This was his moment, his victory, and Sharpe was not going to spoil it for him.

The Sergeant smiled at El Católico. 'You were saying, your holiness, that the French have the gold?'

El Católico nodded, said nothing. Teresa looked defiantly at Harper, then at Sharpe, who now pointed his rifle at the small group of Partisans.

'The French have the gold.' Her voice was firm, her tone almost contemptuous of the two men with the guns. The Spaniards had guns, but none of them dared move while the vast muzzle of the seven-barrelled gun stared at them from the flank. Teresa repeated herself. 'The French have the gold.'

'That's good, miss, so it is.' Harper's voice was suddenly gentle. 'Because what you don't know about, as my old mother used to say, you won't miss. And look what I found in the dung-heap.' He grinned at them all, raised his free hand, and from it, trickling in a glittering cascade, fell thick gold coins. The grin became wider.

'The Good Lord,' said Patrick Augustine Harper, 'has been kind to me this morning.'

CHAPTER 13

Sharpe pointed at a stunted olive tree, apparently a marker between two fields, and shouted up at Hagman. 'See the tree, Daniel?'

The voice came down from the bell-tower. 'Sir?'

'Olive tree! Four hundred yards away. Beyond the big house!'

'Got it, sir.'

'Shoot that hanging branch off!'

Hagman muttered something about bloody miracles, El Católico sneered at the impossibility of the marksmanship, and Sharpe smiled at him.

'If any of your men try to leave the village, they get shot. Understand?'

The Spaniard did not reply. Sharpe had put four Riflemen in the bell-tower with orders to shoot any horsemen spurring away from Casatejada. For the moment he needed all the time he could gain before El Católico's whole band of hardened Partisans began the pursuit of the Light Company through the hills. The Baker rifle banged, the hanging branch leaped into the air, hinged on a strip of bark, and then fell back. Hagman had not fully severed the pale bark, but the demonstration was more than enough, and El Católico watched the ragged branch swaying like a pendulum. He said nothing. His men, disarmed and perplexed, sat by the cemetery wall and watched five other Riflemen, led by Harper, raking at the huge pile of manure with their bayonets. They were pulling out leather bags, filled with coins, and dumping them at Sharpe's feet; bag after bag, thick with gold, more money than Sharpe had ever seen in one place, a fortune beyond his imaginings.

The Riflemen were awed by the gold, elated at its

discovery, and disbelieving in their excitement as the warm, reeking bags thumped down at Sharpe's feet. El Católico's face was as rigid as a child's mask sold at a country fairground, but Sharpe knew the controlled muscles hid a raging anger. The Spaniard crossed to Sharpe, gestured at the bags.

'Our gold, Sharpe.'

'Ours?'

'Spanish.' The dark eyes searched the Rifleman's face.

'So we take it to Cádiz for you. Do you want to come?'

'Cádiz!' For a moment the mask slipped and the voice was a snarl of anger. 'You won't take it to Cádiz! It will go back to England with your army, to buy comforts for your Generals.'

Sharpe hoped his own face mirrored the scorn on El Católico's. 'And what were you going to do with it?'

The Spaniard shrugged. 'Take it to Cádiz. By land.'

Sharpe did not believe him; every instinct told him that El Católico had planned to steal the gold, keep it, but he had no proof except that the gold had been hidden. He shrugged back at the guerrilla leader. 'Then we'll save you a journey. It will be our pleasure.'

He smiled at El Católico, who turned away and spoke rapidly to his men, gesturing at Sharpe, and the seated fighters by the wall muttered angrily so that Sharpe's men had to heft their rifles and step one pace forward.

Patrick Harper stopped beside Sharpe and stretched his back muscles. 'They're not happy, sir.'

Sharpe grinned. 'They think we're stealing their gold. I don't think they want to help us take it to Cádiz.'

Teresa was staring at Sharpe as a cat might look at a bird. Harper saw her expression.

'Do you think they'll try to stop us, sir?'

Sharpe raised innocent eyebrows. 'We're allies.' He raised his voice and spoke slowly so that any of the Spaniards with a smattering of English would understand. 'We take the gold to Cádiz, to the Junta.'

Teresa spat on the ground and raised her eyes again to Sharpe. He wondered if they had all known that the gold was hidden in the manure, but doubted it. If too many of the Partisans had known, then there was always a danger that someone would talk and the secret would be gone. But there was no doubting the fact that now the gold had been revealed, they were determined to stop him taking it away. It was an undeclared war, nasty and private, and Sharpe wondered how the Light Company was to carry the coins through a countryside that was familiar hunting territory to El Católico's men.

'Sir!' Hagman was calling from the bell-tower. 'Mr Knowles in sight, sir!'

Knowles had evidently lost his way, strayed hopelessly in the dark, and the young Lieutenant's face was exasperated and tired as the red-jacketed men straggled into the village. He stopped when he saw the gold, and then turned to Sharpe again. His expression went to one of joy.

'I don't believe it.'

Sharpe picked up one of the coins and casually tossed it to him. 'Spanish gold.'

'Good God!' The newcomers pressed round the Lieutenant, leaned over and fingered the coin. Knowles looked up. 'You found it!'

Sharpe nodded at Harper. 'Harps did.'

'Harps!' Knowles used the Sergeant's nickname quite unconsciously. 'How the devil did you do it?'

'Easy, sir. Easy!'

Harper launched himself on the retelling of his exploit. Sharpe had heard it four or five times already, but this was the Sergeant's achievement, and he must hear it again. Harper had been in the bushes, as Sharpe had told him, and listening to the sound of his Captain scrabbling at the grave. 'Noisy! I thought he'd woken the dead, so I did, scratch, and all the time the light coming up.' Then there had been noises, footsteps from the village. Harper nodded at Sharpe. 'I knew he hadn't heard a thing, still scratching away like the graveyard had fleas, so he was, and I thought I'm not going to move. The bastards might know about the Captain, but I was hidden away and better off there.' He pointed at El Católico, who stared back expressionless. 'Then your man there comes round here, all on his own. Buttoning up his trousers, he was, and he peeks through the gate. So, I thought, going to jump on the Captain, are you? I was about to do a wee bit of

...d, felt one solitary raindrop splash on his cheek. H...
...ed, but there were no more, though he knew that soon
...in the hour, the clouds would burst and the streams and
...rs would rise with unimaginable speed.

...Harper came back, scrubbed clean, his clothes soaking we...
...e nodded at the Partisans. 'What do we do with them, sir?'
...'Lock them up when we go.' It would gain a little time, no...
...uch, but every minute was valuable. He turned to Knowle...
...Are we ready?'

'Nearly, sir.'

Knowles was splitting open the bags while two me...
Sergeant McGovern and Rifleman Tongue, poured the coi...
into packs. Sharpe was grateful that so many of his men ha...
looted French cowhide packs at Talavera; the British canv...
and wood ...cks would have split open under the weight. Th...
men hated the British packs, made by the firm of Trotter'...
with their terrible chest straps, which, at the end of a lon...
march, made the lungs feel as if they were filled with aci...
'Trotter's pains', it was called, and all but a couple of the me...
had captured French equipment on their backs.

Rifleman Tongue looked up at Sharpe. 'Shouldn't there b...
sixty-four bags, sir?'

'Sixty-four?'

Tongue pushed back a hank of hair that continually fe...
over ...eyes. 'Supposed to be sixteen thousand coins, si...
Ne...ot sixty-three bags, two hundred and fifty in tha...
...pointed to the opened bag. 'That makes fiftee...
...seven hundred and fifty. Two hundred and fifty...

...not all that's missing.' Harper's voice was soft and i...
...oment for Sharpe to understand. Hardy. He ha...
...Captain Hardy in the excitement of finding the...
...ooked at El Católico. 'Well?'

...niard shrugged. 'We used one bag, yes. We mus...
...ns, powder, shot, even food.'

...talking about gold.'

...n?' El Católico was very still.

...op of rain, and another, and Sharpe glanced up...
...It would be a hard march. 'Captain Hardy is...

jumping myself, but then he turns round, draws out his fancy
sword, and pokes the bloody manure! So I knew then, sure
enough, and when the bastard has gone off I poked in there
myself.' He grinned broadly, seemed to wait for applause,
and Knowles laughed.

'But how did you know?'

Sharpe interrupted. 'This is the clever bit. Honest Sergeant
Harper at work.'

Harper grinned, happy to bask in the approbation. 'Would
you ever have seen a pickpocket at work, sir?' Knowles shook
his head, muttered something about moving in different
circles, and Harper's grin grew even wider. 'It's like this, sir,
so it is. There are two of you, right? One brushes against a
wealthy man in the street, jostles him, you know how it is?
You don't hurt the man, but you wobble him off balance. So
what does he do? He thinks you may have lifted his money so
he immediately puts a hand on his pocket to see if it's there. So
your other man's watching, sees which pocket he pats, and it's
as good as picked!' He jerked a thumb at the Partisan leader.
'Silly bastard falls right into it. Hears that the Captain's
disturbing the worms so he can't resist sneaking round to
make sure that the stuff is still safe! And here it is!'

Knowles laughed. 'How does a simple Irish lad from
Donegal know about pickpockets?'

Harper raised a sage eyebrow. 'We learn a lot of things in
Tangaveane, sir. It's surprising, sir, so it is, what you learn at
your mammy's knee.'

Sharpe walked over to the strewn manure. 'How many
more bags?'

Harper brushed his hands together. 'That's it, sir. Sixty-
three bags; can't see any more.'

Sharpe looked at his ebullient Sergeant. He was covered in
dung, animal and human, his clothes slimy with liquid. He
grinned.

'Go and wash, Patrick. And well done.'

Harper clapped his hands. 'Right, lads! Clean up time!'

Sharpe walked back to the gold and picked up another coin
from the bag he had opened. It was a thick coin, he guessed
weighing near to an ounce, and on one side was the arms of
Spain, surmounted by a crown, and with a legend chased

round its perimeter. He read it aloud, working his way slowly through the syllables. ' "*Initium sapientiae timor domini.*" Do you know what that means, Lieutenant?'

Knowles looked at his coin and shook his head. Rifleman Tongue, the educated one, chimed in with a translation.

'The beginning of wisdom, sir, is the fear of the Lord.'

Sharpe grinned. He turned the coin over. On the other side was the profile of a man, his head covered in a wig of profuse curls, and the legend was easily understood. Philip the Fifth, by the Grace of God King of Spain and the Indies. At the foot of the profile was a date: 1729. Sharpe looked at Knowles.

'Know what it is?'

'Doubloon, sir. Eight escudo piece.'

'What's it worth?'

Knowles thought about it, hefted the coin in his hand, tossed it into the air. 'About three pounds ten shillings, sir.'

Sharpe looked disbelieving. 'Each?'

Knowles nodded. 'Each.'

'Sweet Jesus.'

Sixteen thousand coins, each worth three pounds and ten shillings, and Sharpe tried to work it out in his head. Isaiah Tongue beat them all, his voice full of wonder as he gave the figure.

'Fifty-six thousand pounds, sir.'

Sharpe started to laugh, feeling almost hysterical in his reaction. He could buy well over thirty Captaincies with this money. It would pay a day's wages to more than a million men. If Sharpe should live for a hundred years he would never earn the amount that was sagging in the leather bags at his feet: fat, great, thick, yellow-gold coins with their pictures of a fancy-haired, hook-nosed, soft-looking King. Money, gold, more than he could comprehend on his salary of ten shillings and sixpence a day, less two shillings and eightpence for the mess charge, and then more deductions for washing and the hospital levy, and he stared disbelieving at the pile. As for the men, they were lucky if in a year they earned as much as just two of these coins. A shilling a day, less all the deductions, brought them down to the Three Sevens: seven pounds, seven shillings, and sevenpence a year. But there were few men who made even that much. They were charged

for lost equipment, broken equipment, ¦¦¦¦¦¦ ment, and men had deserted for less th¦¦ handful of this gold.

'A thousand pounds, sir.' Knowles was lo¦¦

'What?'

'I guess that's what it weighs, sir. A thous¦ more.'

Nearly half a ton of gold, to be carried throug¦ hills, and probably in weather that was abou¦ disastrously. The clouds were overhead now, heavy¦ moving south so that soon there would be no blue sky¦ pointed at the bags.

'Split them up, Lieutenant. Thirty piles. Fill thirty¦ throw away everything except ammunition, and we¦ have to take it in turns to carry them.'

El Católico stood up, walked slowly towards Sha¦ keeping an eye on the Riflemen, who still covered ¦¦¦ Spaniards with their guns.

'Captain.'

'Yes?'

'It's Spanish gold.' He spoke with pride, making o¦ effort.

'I know.'

'It belongs to Spain. It must stay here.'

Sharpe shook his head. 'It belongs to the Sup¦¦ Cádiz. I am merely delivering it.'

'It does not need to go.' El Católico had ¦ his dignity. He spoke quietly, persuasively¦ fight the French, Captain. To kill Fren¦¦ then Britain will steal it; it will go ¦ should stay here.'

'No.' Sharpe smiled at the Spa¦ 'It goes with us. The Royal Nav¦ don't believe me, why don't yo¦ more backs to pile it on.'

El Católico returned the ¦ Captain.'

Sharpe knew what he ¦ a nightmare of fear, fea¦ was the imperative in ¦

jumping myself, but then he turns round, draws out his fancy sword, and pokes the bloody manure! So I knew then, sure enough, and when the bastard has gone off I poked in there myself.' He grinned broadly, seemed to wait for applause, and Knowles laughed.

'But how did you know?'

Sharpe interrupted. 'This is the clever bit. Honest Sergeant Harper at work.'

Harper grinned, happy to bask in the approbation. 'Would you ever have seen a pickpocket at work, sir?' Knowles shook his head, muttered something about moving in different circles, and Harper's grin grew even wider. 'It's like this, sir, so it is. There are two of you, right? One brushes against a wealthy man in the street, jostles him, you know how it is? You don't hurt the man, but you wobble him off balance. So what does he do? He thinks you may have lifted his money so he immediately puts a hand on his pocket to see if it's there. So your other man's watching, sees which pocket he pats, and it's as good as picked!' He jerked a thumb at the Partisan leader. 'Silly bastard falls right into it. Hears that the Captain's disturbing the worms so he can't resist sneaking round to make sure that the stuff is still safe! And here it is!'

Knowles laughed. 'How does a simple Irish lad from Donegal know about pickpockets?'

Harper raised a sage eyebrow. 'We learn a lot of things in Tangaveane, sir. It's surprising, sir, so it is, what you learn at your mammy's knee.'

Sharpe walked over to the strewn manure. 'How many more bags?'

Harper brushed his hands together. 'That's it, sir. Sixty-three bags; can't see any more.'

Sharpe looked at his ebullient Sergeant. He was covered in dung, animal and human, his clothes slimy with liquid. He grinned.

'Go and wash, Patrick. And well done.'

Harper clapped his hands. 'Right, lads! Clean up time!'

Sharpe walked back to the gold and picked up another coin from the bag he had opened. It was a thick coin, he guessed weighing near to an ounce, and on one side was the arms of Spain, surmounted by a crown, and with a legend chased round its perimeter. He read it aloud, working his way slowly through the syllables. ' "*Initium sapientiae timor domini.*" Do you know what that means, Lieutenant?'

Knowles looked at his coin and shook his head. Rifleman Tongue, the educated one, chimed in with a translation.

'The beginning of wisdom, sir, is the fear of the Lord.'

Sharpe grinned. He turned the coin over. On the other side was the profile of a man, his head covered in a wig of profuse curls, and the legend was easily understood. Philip the Fifth, by the Grace of God King of Spain and the Indies. At the foot of the profile was a date: 1729. Sharpe looked at Knowles.

'Know what it is?'

'Doubloon, sir. Eight escudo piece.'

'What's it worth?'

Knowles thought about it, hefted the coin in his hand, tossed it into the air. 'About three pounds ten shillings, sir.'

Sharpe looked disbelieving. 'Each?'

Knowles nodded. 'Each.'

'Sweet Jesus.'

Sixteen thousand coins, each worth three pounds and ten shillings, and Sharpe tried to work it out in his head. Isaiah Tongue beat them all, his voice full of wonder as he gave the figure.

'Fifty-six thousand pounds, sir.'

Sharpe started to laugh, feeling almost hysterical in his reaction. He could buy well over thirty Captaincies with this money. It would pay a day's wages to more than a million men. If Sharpe should live for a hundred years he would never earn the amount that was sagging in the leather bags at his feet: fat, great, thick, yellow-gold coins with their pictures of a fancy-haired, hook-nosed, soft-looking King. Money, gold, more than he could comprehend on his salary of ten shillings and sixpence a day, less two shillings and eightpence for the mess charge, and then more deductions for washing and the hospital levy, and he stared disbelieving at the pile. As for the men, they were lucky if in a year they earned as much as just two of these coins. A shilling a day, less all the deductions, brought them down to the Three Sevens: seven pounds, seven shillings, and sevenpence a year. But there were few men who made even that much. They were charged

for lost equipment, broken equipment, repla t equipment, and men had deserted for less than lue of a
handful of this gold.

'A thousand pounds, sir.' Knowles was look erious.

'What?'

'I guess that's what it weighs, sir. A thous probably
more.'

Nearly half a ton of gold, to be carried throu the enemy
hills, and probably in weather that was ab t to break
disastrously. The clouds were overhead now, he vy with r
moving south so that soon there would be no blu ky. Sh
pointed at the bags.

'Split them up, Lieutenant. Thirty piles. Fill thirty
throw away everything except ammunition, and we
have to take it in turns to carry them.'

El Católico stood up, walked slowly towards Snarpe,
keeping an eye on the Riflemen, who still covered the
Spaniards with their guns.

'Captain.'

'Yes?'

'It's Spanish gold.' He spoke with pride, making one last
effort.

'I know.'

'It belongs to Spain. It must stay here.'

Sharpe shook his head. 'It belongs to the Supréme Junta in
Cádiz. I am merely delivering it.'

'It does not need to go.' El Católico had summoned up all
his dignity. He spoke quietly, persuasively. 'It will be used to
fight the French, Captain. To kill Frenchmen. If you take it,
then Britain will steal it; it will go home in your ships. It
should stay here.'

'No.' Sharpe smiled at the Spaniard, trying to annoy him.
'It goes with us. The Royal Navy is sending it to Cádiz. If you
don't believe me, why don't you come, too? We could do with
more backs to pile it on.'

El Católico returned the smile. 'I will be coming with you,
Captain.'

Sharpe knew what he meant. The journey home would be
a nightmare of fear, fear of ambush, but Wellington's 'must'
was the imperative in Sharpe's head. He turned away and, as

he did one solitary raindrop splash on his cheek. He waited there were no more, though he knew that soon, within our, the clouds would burst and the streams and rivers wrise with unimaginable speed.

Harper back, scrubbed clean, his clothes soaking wet. He nodded the Partisans. 'What do we do with them, sir?'

'Lock them up when we go.' It would gain a little time, not much, but every minute was valuable. He turned to Knowles. 'Are we ready?'

'Nearly, sir.'

Knowles was splitting open the bags while two men, Sergeant McGovern and Rifleman Tongue, poured the coins into packs. Sharpe was grateful that so many of his men had looted French cowhide packs at Talavera; the British canvas and wood packs would have split open under the weight. The men hated the British packs, made by the firm of Trotter's, with their terrible chest straps, which, at the end of a long march, made the lungs feel as if they were filled with acid: 'Trotter's pains', it was called, and all but a couple of the men had captured French equipment on their backs.

Rifleman Tongue looked up at Sharpe. 'Shouldn't there be sixty-four bags, sir?'

'Sixty-four?'

Tongue pushed back a hank of hair that continually fell over his eyes. 'Supposed to be sixteen thousand coins, sir. We've got sixty-three bags, two hundred and fifty in that one.' He pointed to the opened bag. 'That makes fifteen thousand seven hundred and fifty. Two hundred and fifty short.'

'That's not all that's missing.' Harper's voice was soft and it took a moment for Sharpe to understand. Hardy. He had forgotten Captain Hardy in the excitement of finding the gold. He looked at El Católico. 'Well?'

The Spaniard shrugged. 'We used one bag, yes. We must buy weapons, powder, shot, even food.'

'I wasn't talking about gold.'

'What then?' El Católico was very still.

Another drop of rain, and another, and Sharpe glanced up at the clouds. It would be a hard march. 'Captain Hardy is missing.'

'I know.'

'What else do you know?'

El Católico's tongue flicked out, licked his lips. 'We think he was captured by the French.' He dropped into his sneering tone. 'No doubt they will exchange him, politely. You do not understand real war, Captain.'

Harper growled, stepped forward. 'Let me ask the questions, sir. I'll break him apart.'

'No.' It was the girl who spoke. 'Hardy tried to escape the French. We don't know where he is.'

'They're lying.' The Irishman's hands clenched.

The rain was beating on the dry ground, big, warm drops. Sharpe turned to the Company. 'Wrap your locks! Stop muzzles!'

Rain was the enemy of gunpowder and the most they could do was try to keep the rifles and muskets dry. Sharpe saw the ground soaking up the water. They had to leave soon, before the dust turned to mud.

'Sir!' Hagman again, calling from the tower.

'Daniel?'

'Horsemen, sir. Couple of miles south.'

'French?'

'No. Dagoes, sir.'

Now time was everything. Sharpe turned to Harper.

'Lock them up. Find somewhere, anywhere.' They must forget Captain Hardy and march fast, try to build a lead over the Partisans' pursuit, but Sharpe knew it was impossible. The gold was heavy. El Católico understood. As the Spaniards were herded unceremoniously ː ˑards the village he pushed his way past a Rifleman.

'You won't get far, Captain.'

Sharpe walked up to him. 'Why not?'

El Católico smiled, gestured at the rain, the gold. 'We'll chase you. Kill you.'

It was true. Sharpe knew that even by using the horses that were still in the village he could not travel fast enough. The rain was falling harder, bouncing up from the ground so that the earth seemed to have a sparkling mist an inch or two above its surface. Sharpe smiled, pushed past the Spaniard.

'You won't.' He put out his hand, took hold of Teresa's

collar, and pulled her out of the group. 'She dies if even one of us gets hurt.'

El Católico lunged for him, the girl twisted away, but Harper brought his fist into the Spaniard's stomach and Sharpe grabbed Teresa with a choking hold on her neck.

'Do you understand? She dies. If that gold does not reach the British army, she dies!'

El Católico straightened up, his eyes furious. 'You will die, Sharpe, I promise you, and not an easy death.'

Sharpe ignored him. 'Sergeant?'

'Sir?'

'Rope.'

The Spaniard watched, silent, as Harper found a scrap of rope and, at Sharpe's directions, looped and tightened it round Teresa's neck.

Sharpe nodded. 'Hold her, Sergeant.' He turned to El Católico. 'Remember her like that. If you come near me, she's dead. If I get back safely, then I'll release her to marry you.'

He gestured and the Company pushed the Spaniards away. Sharpe watched them go, knowing that soon they would be on his tracks, but he had bought more than time now. He had his hostage. He looked at her, seeing the hatred in her proud face, and knew he could not kill her. He hoped El Católico did not know that, or else, in the seething rain, the Light Company were all dead men.

They started out, silent and wet, on the long journey home.

CHAPTER 14

Six horses had been in the village and for the first two miles, back along the same track they had come, the going was easy enough. The horses carried the packs of gold, the men climbed the slope, the rain hissed in their ears, and there was the elation of success, of being at least on the road home, but it could not last. The direct route westwards, the path they were using, was not the most sensible route. It was the obvious track, the one that El Católico would search first, and it led straight towards Almeida and the burgeoning French army that was concentrating on the town. Sharpe felt the temptation to stay on the easy route, to make the march easier, but once the village was out of sight he turned the men north, up into the hills, and abandoned the horses. Lieutenant Knowles with three men took them on, further westward, and Sharpe hoped the continuing hoof-marks would delay the pursuit while the Company, astonished at the weight of the coins, struggled into the northern wasteland, up rocks and slopes that no horse could have climbed. The rain kept on steadily, soaking their uniforms, driving their tired, aching, sleepless bodies to new layers of discomfort.

Teresa seemed unafraid, as if she knew Sharpe would not kill her, and she refused the offer of a greatcoat with a disdainful shake of her head. She was cold, soaked through, humiliated by the rope round her neck, but Sharpe left it on because it would have been simple for her to run away, unencumbered, into the slippery rocks where the heavily laden men of the Light Company would never have caught her. Harper held the other end looped round his wrist.

'Where are you heading, sir?' He had to shout over the rain.

'The ford at San Anton. You remember? The Major told us about it.' Sharpe wondered where Kearsey was, what his reaction would be.

It took Knowles an hour and a half to catch up, his men worn out by the effort but glad to be back in the safety of the full Company. Knowles shook his head. 'Didn't see a thing, sir. Nothing.'

Sharpe was not reassured. These hills could have been full of hidden watchers and the ploy of laying the false trail might not delay El Católico for one minute, but as the day went on, and their tiredness became a numbness beyond pain, Sharpe let his hopes rise. They were walking a nightmare landscape on a plateau that was criss-crossed with ravines, streambeds, and rock. No horse would make fast time up here and Sharpe forced the men on pitilessly, cracking his anger like a whip, driving them north and west, through the relentless weather, kicking the men who fell, and carrying two of the packs of gold to prove to them it could be done.

Teresa watched it all, her mouth curved in an ironic smile, as her captors slipped, crashed painfully into the rocks, and blundered onwards in the storm. Sharpe prayed that the wind stayed in the north; he had lost all bearings and his only guide was the rain on his face. He stopped occasionally, let the men rest, and searched the wind-scoured plateau for the sign of a horseman. There was nothing, just the rain sweeping in slow curtains towards him, the bounce of drops from the rocks, and the grey horizon where air and stone became indistinguishable. Perhaps the ploy had worked, he thought, and El Católico was searching miles away on the wrong road, and the longer they stayed undetected the more Sharpe dared to hope that the crude ploy of the false tracks had worked.

Every half hour or so the Company stopped and the men who had not been carrying the gold-filled packs took over from those who had. It was a painfully slow march. The packs chafed their shoulders, rubbed them raw, and the gold, far from being something from their wildest dreams, became a loathed burden that the men would happily have thrown away if Sharpe had not taken his position at the rear, driving them on, forcing the Company across the bleak plateau. He had no idea how far they had come, even what time of day it was, only that they must keep marching, putting distance between themselves and El Católico, and his anger snapped when the Company suddenly stopped, dropped, and yelled at them, 'Get up!'

'But, sir!' Knowles, leading the Company, waved ahead. 'Look!'

Even in the rain, in the crushing weather, it was a beautiful sight. The plateau suddenly ended, dropped to a wide valley through which meandered a stream and a track.

The Agueda. It had to be the river Agueda, off to the left, and the stream at the bottom of the valley flowed east to west to join the river where the track led to the ford. Sharpe's heart leapt. They had made it! He could see the road start again at the far side of the river; it was the ford at San Anton, and beside the track, on this side of the river, was an ancient fort on a rock bluff that once must have guarded the crossing. At this distance, he guessed a mile and a half, the walls looked broken, stubbled in the grey light, but the fortress had to mark the site of the ford. They had done it!

'Five minutes' rest!'

The Company sat down, relieved, cheered up. Sharpe perched on a rock and searched the valley. Second by second his hopes revived. It was empty. No horsemen, no Partisans, nothing but the stream and the track going to the river. He took out his telescope, praying that the driving rain would not seep through the junctions of its cylinders, and searched the valley again. A second road, running north and south, ran this side of the river, but it, too, was empty. By God! They had done it!

'Come on!' He clapped his hands, pulled men up and pushed them on. 'To the river! We cross tonight! Well done!'

The rain still fell, blinding the men as they stumbled down the slope, but they had made it! They could see their goal, feel pride in an achievement, and tomorrow they would wake up on the west bank of the Agueda and march to the Coa. There were British patrols on the far bank, to be sure not as many as there were French, but the river Agueda marked some kind of limit, and after a day's effort like this they needed that limit. They almost ran the last part of the slope, splashed through the stream, boots crunching on its gravel bed, and then stamped on to the wet track as if it were a paved highway in the centre of London. The ford was a mile ahead, trees on both banks, and the Company knew that once they crossed they could rest, let the tiredness flow, and shut their eyes against the grey horror of the day and its journey.

'Sir.' Harper spoke quietly, with a desperate resignation. 'Sir. Behind.'

Horsemen. Bloody horsemen. Partisans who had ridden not over the plateau but up the direct road from Casatejada and who now appeared on the track behind them. Teresa smiled, gave Sharpe a look of victory, and he ignored it. He called wearily to the Company to halt.

'How many, Sergeant?'

There was a pause. 'Reckon it's just a small party.'

Sharpe could see no more than twenty or thirty horsemen, standing in the rain just three hundred yards behind the Company. He took a deep breath.

'They can't hurt us, lads. Bayonets. They won't charge bayonets!'

There was something strangely comforting about the sound of the blades scraping from the scabbards, the sight of the men crouching with bent knees as they fixed on the long blades, to be doing something that was aimed at their enemy instead of the muscle-racking tramp through the rain. The band of horsemen came forward, spurred into a trot, and Sharpe stood with his men in the front rank.

'We'll teach them to respect the bayonet! Wait for it! Wait for it!'

The Partisans had no intention of charging the small Company. The horsemen split into two groups and galloped either side of the bedraggled soldiers, almost ignoring them. El Católico was there, a smile of triumph on his face, and he swept off his hat in an ironic gesture as he went past, thirty yards away and untouchable. Teresa jerked towards him, but Harper held her firm, and she watched as the horsemen went on towards the fortress and the river. Sharpe knew what they were doing. The Company would be blocked in, trapped in the valley, and El Católico would wait until the rest of the Partisans, summoned from the south, came to his support.

He wiped rain from his face. 'Come on.' There was

nowhere to go, so the best thing was to go on. Perhaps El Católico could be threatened, a bayonet at Teresa's throat, but in Sharpe's mind he could envisage only failure, defeat. El Católico had never been fooled. They must have known Sharpe had gone north, and while the Company struggled over the foul uplands the Spaniard had brought his followers along the easy road. Sharpe cursed himself for a fool, for an optimistic fool, but there was nothing to be done. He listened to the boots scuffing on the wet surface, the hiss of the rain, the splashing of the ever-rising stream, and he let his eyes look at the far, shrouded hills across the river, then at the stone of the small fort that had been built, centuries before, to protect the upland valleys from marauders crossing from Portugal, and then he looked right, farther north, at the spur of the hills that almost reached the river, and saw, on the blurred horizon, the shape of a horseman who had a strange, square hat.

'Down! Down! Down!'

Something, an instinct, a half-perceived blur, told him the French patrol had only just arrived on the skyline. He forced the men down, into the streambed, burying the Light Company into cover. They scrambled behind the shallow turf-bank, wet faces looking to him for explanation, receiving none as he pushed them down.

El Católico was much, much slower. Sharpe, lying next to Harper and the girl, watched the Partisans ride towards the ford, and it was not until the French lancers were moving, trotting almost sedately down the slope, that the grey figure wheeled, waved his arm, and the Partisans urged their tired mounts into a gallop. The Spaniards rode back into the valley, scattering as they picked their own course, and the lancers, a different regiment from the Poles', chose their targets and went for them with levelled blades and spurs of bright water from their hooves. Sharpe, peering between tufts of grass, could see twenty lancers, but, looking back to the northern skyline, he saw more appear, and then a group at the place where the hills almost met the river, and he realized that a full French regiment was there, coming south, and as he tried to find rhyme or reason in their presence he saw the girl jerk the rope free, scrabble backwards, and she was up, white dress brilliant in the murk, and running south towards the hills, to where El Católico and his men were desperately fleeing. He pushed Harper down.

'Stay there!'

The girl stumbled on the far bank of the stream, lost her balance, turned and saw Sharpe coming. She seemed to panic, for she ran downstream, past a wide bend in the water, and turned south again. They must see her! Sharpe shouted at her to get down, but the wind snatched away the words and he forced himself on, getting closer, and leapt at her. He crashed into her as she turned to look where he was and his weight drove her into the gravel beside the stream. She fought at him, snarling, her fingernails scratching at his eyes, but he bore her down, his weight crushing her, took her wrists and forced them apart, ground them into the small sharp stones, and used all his strength to keep them still. She kicked at him and he hooked his legs over hers, hammered them down, not caring if he hurt her, thinking only of the eight feet ten inches of lance that could pin them both like wriggling insects. The stream ran cold round his ankles and he knew that Teresa must be lying in water to her waist, but there was no time to care about that because there were hooves near, and he thrust down his head, cracking her forehead, as a horse splashed by them in the stream.

He looked up, saw José, the man who had escorted them to the river, shouting down at the girl, his words lost in the whipping rain; then the Partisan's elbows and heels moved, the horse spurred into a frantic gallop, and Sharpe saw three lancers, their mouths open in the gaping, silent scream of a cavalry charge, galloping across to trap the Spaniard.

José twisted, slashed at his horse, found level ground and put his head down, but the lancers were too close. Sharpe watched, saw a Frenchman rise in his stirrups, draw back his lance, and lunge forward so the lance had all the rider's weight behind the steel point that rammed into José's back. He arched, screamed into the wind, fell with the pelting rain, and his hands fumbled at his spine to pull at the great spear that was ridden over him. The other two lancers leaned into the dying man, thrust down as they slowed their horses, and Sharpe heard the snatch of a laugh on the wind.

Teresa took a breath, twisted violently, and Sharpe knew

she was about to scream. She had not seen José's death, knew only that El Católico was near, and there was only one thing for Sharpe to do. His legs were across hers, hooking hers flat, his hands were on her wrists, so he jammed his mouth on top of hers and forced her head down. She bit at him; their teeth clashed jarringly, but he twisted his mouth so that his was at a right angle to hers and, using his teeth, forced her down into the gravel. One eye glared at him, she jerked beneath him, twisted, but his weight smothered her and, very suddenly, she lay still.

The voice was close; it seemed almost on top of them, and she could hear, as he could, the crunch of hooves in the gravel.

'*Ici!* Jean!'

There was a shout from further away, more hooves, and the girl lay utterly still. Sharpe could see the sudden fear in her eye, feel her heart beating beneath his chest, her breath suddenly checked in his mouth. He raised his mouth, with its bloodied lip, from hers, turned his head, infinitely slowly, so that he could see all her face, and whispered, 'Lie still. Still.'

She nodded, almost imperceptibly, and Sharpe let go of her wrists, though his hands stayed on top of them. The rain seethed down, smashed on his back, dripped from his hair and shako on to her face. The voice came again, still shouting, and Sharpe heard through the hissing rain the creak of saddlery and the snorting of a horse. Her eyes stayed on his. He dared not look up, though he desperately wanted to see how close the lancer was, and he saw her eyes flick upwards and back to his and there was a new fear in them. She must have seen something; the Frenchman could not be far, looking not for a couple lying in a stream but for horsemen who had scattered into the rainstorm. Her hand gripped at his; she jerked with a tiny movement of her head as if to tell him that the Frenchman was close, but he shook his head very slowly, and then, telling himself that a raised head increased the chance of discovery, he lowered his head towards her. The hooves crunched again. The Frenchman laughed, shouted something at his friends, and she kept her eyes open as Sharpe kissed her. She could have moved, but she did not; her eyes still watched as her tongue explored his cut lip, and Sharpe, looking at the huge, dark eyes, thought that she was watching him because what was happening to her was so unbelievable that only the evidence of her eyes could confirm it. He watched her, too.

The lancer shouted again, much closer, and then there was a reply, mocking and imperative, suggesting that the closest lancer had been deceived: a bird, perhaps, in the streambed, or a running rabbit, and he was being called back. Sharpe could hear the horses' hooves crashing in the streambed, and once, by a break in the wind, the sound seemed so close that the girl's eyes widened in fear, and then the sound receded, the voices faded, and she shut her eyes, kissed him fiercely, and, almost in the same movement, thrust his head away. The three lancers were going, their horses' wet rumps glistening, and Sharpe let out a sigh of relief, and of regret.

'They've gone.'

She began to move, but he shook his head. 'Wait!'

She turned her head, raised it so that her cheek touched his, and she hissed when she saw what was at the end of the valley: a convoy, with rows of ox-carts whose ungreased axles screamed piercingly through the foul weather, and either side of the plodding carts were the shapes of more horsemen, sabres and lances, escorting the carts southwards towards the Almeida road. It could take an hour for the convoy to pass, but at least it had driven away El Católico and his men, and Sharpe realized, with one of the sudden bursts of elation that had punctuated the sense of growing failure for the last week, that as long as the Light Company was not discovered they should safely reach the ford when the French had gone. He looked at the girl.

'Will you be still?'

She nodded. He asked again, she nodded again, and he slowly eased himself off her and lay down beside her. She turned over on to her stomach and the wet dress clung to her and he remembered the sight of her naked body, its shadowed, slim beauty, and he reached out a hand and took the rope at her neck, turning it so he found the knot, and fumbling at it with wet fingers. The tight, sodden rope yielded slowly, but it was off and he dropped it to the gravel.

'I'm sorry.'

She shrugged as if it was no matter. There was a chain

round her neck and Sharpe, his hand already close, pulled it, to find a square locket, made of silver. She watched, her dark eyes utterly expressionless, as he put a thumbnail under the catch and it sprang open. There was no picture and she gave the hint of a smile because she understood that he had expected one. The inside of the lid was engraved: my love to you. J. It took him a few seconds to realize that Joaquím, El Católico, would never have inscribed a piece of silver in English, and he knew, with a sick certainty, that it had belonged to Hardy. 'J' for Josefina, and he looked at the silver ring, engraved with an eagle, that she had bought before Talavera, before Hardy, and with a superstition he did not understand he touched the locket on to the ring.

'He's dead, isn't he?'

For a moment her face did not move, but then she nodded. Her eyes dropped to the ring on his finger, back to his face.

'The gold?'

'Yes?'

'You go to Cádiz?'

It was Sharpe's turn to think, to watch her eyes through the rain dripping from the peak of his shako. 'No.'

'You keep it?'

'I think so. But to fight the French, not to take home. I promise.'

She nodded and turned to watch the French convoy. Guns, coming from the French Army of the North, and going to Almeida. Not field guns or even siege artillery but Bonaparte's favourite eight-inch howitzers, with obscene little muzzles that squatted like cooking-pots in their wooden beds and which could throw explosive shells high into the air to fall into the packed houses of a besieged town. There were carts as well, presumably with ammunition, and all pulled by slow oxen who were prodded with long goads and thrashed by irate cavalrymen. Their progress was not helped by the wind getting under the canvas covers of the carts, whipping the ropes free so that the tarpaulins flapped and writhed like pinioned bats, and the cavalrymen, doubtless cursing the war, fought to cover the precious powder-kegs from the unending rain. The solid axles, turning with the wheels, screeched over the sodden valley. Sharpe could feel the rain beating on his back, the water in the stream rising to his knees, and he knew that the river would be rising as well, and that with every passing moment his chance of crossing the ford was receding. The water would be too deep. He turned to the girl again.

'How did Hardy die?'

'El Católico.' She gave the answer readily enough and Sharpe knew that her loyalty was changing. It was not the kiss.

'Why does he want the gold?'

She shrugged as though it were a stupid question. 'To buy power.'

For a moment Sharpe wondered if she meant soldiers, and then saw she had spoken the truth. The Spanish armies were gone; the government, if it could be called a government, was in faraway Cádiz, and El Católico had an unparalleled chance to build his own empire. From the hills of Old Castile he could fashion a fiefdom that would rival that of the ancient barons who had built the fortresses that dotted the border area. For a ruthless man the whole country of Spain was one big opportunity. He was still staring at the girl.

'And you?'

'I want the French dead.' The words were spoken with a terrible vehemence. 'All of them.'

'You need our help.'

She looked at him very steadily, not liking the truth, but finally nodded. 'I know.'

He kept his eyes open and leaned forward, kissed her again as the rain lashed at them and the stream soaked them and the carts of the French convoy screeched in their ears. She shut her eyes, put a hand behind his head, held him, and he knew it was not a dream. He wanted her.

She pulled away, smiled at him for the first time. 'You know the river rises?'

He nodded. 'Can we cross?'

She glanced at the stream, shook her head. 'If the rain stops tonight? Yes.' Sharpe had seen the extraordinary speed with which rivers, in these dry hills, rose and fell. She nodded at the fort. 'You can spend the night there.'

'And you?'

She smiled again. 'Can I leave?'

He felt a fool. 'Yes.'

'I'll stay. What's your name?'

'Richard.'

She nodded. She looked again at the fortress.

'You will be safe. We use it. Ten men can stop the entrance.'

'And El Católico?'

She shook her head. 'He's frightened of you. He'll wait till tomorrow, when his men come.'

Rain lashed across the valley, ran from rock and grass and swelled the stream as the wind tore at the landscape. Half in the water, half out, they waited for the convoy to pass, and for what the next day would bring. The war would have to wait.

CHAPTER 15

'Sir, sir!' A hand was shaking his shoulder and Sharpe opened his eyes, to see grey daylight on grey walls. 'Sir?'

'All right!' The girl was waking as well, the eyes blinking in surprise before she remembered where she was. He smiled at her. 'Stay here.'

He crawled out of the space beneath the stairs, past the soldier who had wakened him, and went over to the gaping hole in the south wall of the tower. Dawn was like a grey mist on the countryside, blurring the trees, the grassland across the river, but he could see white flecks on the water surface where there had been none the evening before. The water level was sinking fast and the rocks which marked the ford of San Anton were foaming the river surface. They could cross today, and he lifted his eyes to stare into the western hills as if hoping to see a friendly patrol. He remembered the guns going south the day before and he paused, motionless, in the broken gap to listen for the crumping sound of the giant, iron siege guns. Silence. The siege of Almeida had not yet started.

'Sir!' Lieutenant Knowles stood in the tower doorway.

'Lieutenant?'

'Visitors, sir. Coming down the valley.'

Sharpe grunted, scrambled to his feet, and strapped on his huge sword as he followed Knowles into the courtyard. There was a fire blazing, surrounded by men, and Sharpe looked at them.

'Do you have tea?'

One of them promised to bring him a cup and he joined Knowles on the raised rampart that formed the south-eastern corner of San Anton's courtyard. He looked into the valley, up past the stream where the girl had lain beneath his body and the French lancers had first been seen.

'We're bloody popular this morning.'

A line of horsemen was riding on the track from Casatejada, El Católico's men, in force, and among them Kearsey's blue coat. Sharpe spat over the rampart into the stream far below.

'Keep them out, Robert. Don't let anyone, even the Major, inside the walls.'

His uniform was damp and uncomfortable and he unstrapped his sword and belts, and stripped naked.

'Get that fire bigger! Use the thorns!'

Rifleman Jenkins draped Sharpe's clothes on stones near the blaze and Sharpe stood shivering, a mug of tea held in his hands, and stared at the two hundred horsemen who were aiming for the oak groves where El Católico and his men had spent the night. Sharpe looked up at the sky, saw the ragged clouds and knew that the storm had passed. Soon it would be hot, under a shadowless blue, and he wondered how much water the Company had.

'Sergeant McGovern!'

'Sir?'

'Take six men down to the river with all the canteens. Fill them up.'

McGovern looked at Knowles, back to Sharpe. 'We've already done it, sir. The Lieutenant sent us down.'

'Oh.' He looked at Knowles and growled an apology. 'No one interfered with you?'

Knowles shook his head. 'It's as you said, sir. They're guarding the ford, not the castle.'

'Any food?'

Knowles sighed. He had half hoped, against all experience, that Sharpe's morning temper would have been moderated by Teresa. 'Just hard tack, sir. And not much of that.'

Sharpe swore, flung the dregs of tea far out towards the oak trees that sheltered El Católico's men.

'Right! All weapons cleaned!' He ignored the grumbles, turned and leaned against the rampart. Everyone was better for some sleep, a few hours between sentry duty, but there had not been time or opportunity in the night for the Company to check their weapons. The night had gone quietly. Some time after midnight the rain had stopped, though the wind still

149

blew cold, and Harper had got a small fire going in the shelter of the broken tower, burning the thorn bushes that grew like weeds in the old courtyard. Teresa had been right. The fortress was approached by a single precipitous track, easy to defend, and El Católico had left them in peace.

Scraps of wispy cloud cleared away from the rising sun, shadows stretched over the courtyard, and a touch of warmth came which soon would bake the earth dry and sap the Company of its small energy. Sharpe leaned over the rampart. The spate was well over, the water sinking, and the rocks that marked the ford had broken the surface and collected ragged bundles of twigs and debris that the sudden flood had scoured from the banks. He saw Kearsey leave the oak grove and head his borrowed horse towards the path which led to the castle.

Sharpe pulled on his clothes, still damp, and nodded towards the tower. 'Keep the girl inside, Robert.' Knowles nodded. Sharpe was pulling on a damp boot that refused to go over his heel bone. 'Damn!' It slipped on. 'I'll meet the Major outside. Inspect the weapons and get ready to move.'

'Already?' Knowles seemed surprised.

'Can't stay here forever.' Sharpe buttoned his jacket, picked up his sword. 'I'll go and give Major Kearsey the good news.'

Sharpe walked briskly down the slope and waved cheerfully at Kearsey. 'Morning, sir! A nice one!'

Kearsey reined his horse, stared down at Sharpe with unfriendly eyes. 'What have you done, Sharpe?'

Sharpe stared up at the small Major who was silhouetted by the sun. He had expected anger, but not at him: he had expected Kearsey to be disillusioned at the Partisans and instead the Major's opening words, spoken with a suppressed rage, were spat at Sharpe. He replied quietly.

'I've brought the gold, sir, nearly all of it, as I was ordered.'

Kearsey nodded impatiently, as if it were the answer he expected. 'You kidnapped the girl, locked up our allies; you have disobeyed my orders; you have turned men who fought for us into men who simply want to kill you.' He paused, taking breath, but Sharpe interrupted.

'And the men who killed Captain Hardy?'

Kearsey seemed to slump on his pommel. He stared at Sharpe.

'What?'

'El Católico killed him. Stabbed him in the back. He's buried beneath a manure-heap in the village.' Teresa had told him the story during the night. 'He found El Católico moving the gold. It seems he made a protest. So they killed him. You were saying, sir?'

Kearsey shook his head. 'How do you know?'

For an instant Sharpe was about to tell him, and then remembered that no one, outside the Company, knew that Teresa was no longer a prisoner. 'I was told, sir.'

Kearsey was not prepared to give up. He shook his head, as if trying to clear a bad dream. 'But you stole the gold!'

'I obeyed orders, sir.'

'Whose orders? I am the ranking officer!'

Sharpe suddenly felt sorry for the Major. Kearsey had found the gold, told Wellington, and had never been told of the General's plans. Sharpe felt in his pocket, found the square of paper, and hoped that the rain had not soaked through the folds. It had, but the writing was still legible. He handed it up to Kearsey.

'There, sir.'

Kearsey read it, his anger growing. 'It says nothing!'

'It orders all officers to assist me, sir. All.'

But Kearsey was not listening. He waved the scrap of damp paper towards Sharpe. 'It says nothing about the gold! Nothing! You could have kept this for months!'

Sharpe laughed. 'It hardly would mention gold, would it, sir? I mean, suppose the Spanish saw the orders; suppose they guessed what the General intended to do with the gold?'

Kearsey looked at him. 'You know?'

Sharpe nodded. 'It's not going to Cádiz, sir.' He said it as gently as he could.

Kearsey's reaction was extraordinary. For a few seconds he sat motionless, his eyes screwed tight, and then he tore the paper into shreds, violent gesture after violent gesture.

'God damn it, Sharpe!'

'What?' Sharpe had tried to save the paper, but too late.

Kearsey suddenly realized he had sworn. Remorse and

anger fought on his face. Anger won. 'I have worked. God knows I have worked to help the Spanish and the British to work together. And I am rewarded by this!' He held the scraps of paper up and then, with a sudden jerk, scattered them into the wind. 'Are we to steal the gold, Sharpe?'

'Yes, sir. That's about the long and short of it.'

'We can't.' Kearsey was pleading.

'Whose side are you on?' Sharpe made the question brutal.

For an instant he thought that Kearsey's rage would come back, would explode into a blow aimed at the Rifleman, but Kearsey controlled it, and when he spoke his words were low and measured.

'We have honour, Sharpe. That is our private strength, our honour. We're soldiers, you and I. We cannot expect riches, or dignity, or continual victory. We will die, probably, in battle, or in a fever ward, and no one will remember us, so all that is left is honour. Do you understand?'

It was strange, standing in the growing warmth of the sun, and listening to the words that were wrenched from the centre of Kearsey's soul. He must have been disappointed, Sharpe thought, somewhere in his life. Perhaps he was lonely, spurned by the officers' mess, or perhaps once in his life the small man had been turned down by a woman he loved and now, growing old in his honour, he had found a job he loved. Kearsey loved Spain, and the Spanish, and the task of riding alone behind the enemy lines like a Christian who kept the faith in a world of heretics and persecution. Sharpe spoke gently.

'The General spoke to me, sir. He wants the gold. Without it the war is lost. If that's stealing, then we're stealing it. I assume that you will help us?'

Kearsey seemed not to hear. He was staring over Sharpe's head at the tower of the *castillo* and he muttered something so low that Sharpe could not hear the words.

'Pardon, sir?'

Kearsey's eyes flicked to the Rifleman. 'What shall it profit a man, Sharpe, if he gain the whole world and lose his own soul?'

Sharpe sighed. 'I doubt if we're losing our soul, sir. And

anyway, do you think that El Católico planned to give the gold to Cádiz?'

Kearsey slumped on his saddle as if he knew that Sharpe had spoken the truth. 'No.' The Major spoke softly. 'I suppose not. I suppose he wanted to keep it. But he would have used it to fight the French, Sharpe!'

'So will we, sir.'

'Yes. But it's Spanish gold, and we're not Spaniards.' He jerked himself upright and looked somewhat ruefully at the scraps of Sharpe's torn orders. 'We will take the gold to Wellington, Captain. But under my orders. You must release the girl, do you understand? I will not be a party to these threats, to this underhand procedure.'

'No, sir.'

Kearsey looked at him, uncertain whether Sharpe was agreeing with him. 'You do understand, Sharpe?'

'I understand, sir.' Sharpe turned and stared at the *castillo* and then across the Agueda to the far hills where the French patrols were still waiting and where the siege guns would be inching their way to the fortress walls of Almeida.

'I presume the girl has not been harmed?'

'No, sir, she has not.' Sharpe's patience was at an end. If El Católico thought, for one second, that the girl was safe, then his men would fall on the Light Company and Sharpe would face a death more painful than the imagination could invent. He looked up at Kearsey. 'In ten minutes, Major, I am going to cut off one of her ears. Only halfway, so it will mend, but if any of those murderous bastards with El Católico tries to interfere with our crossing of the ford, then the whole ear will be sliced off. And the other ear, and her eyes, and her tongue, and do you understand me, sir? We are leaving, with the gold, and the girl is our passport and I'm not giving her up. Tell her father, tell El Católico, that if they want the gold they can collect it with a toothless, blind, deaf, ugly, and dumb girl. Understand!'

Sharpe's anger battered at the Major, drove him two steps down the slope. 'I am ordering you, Sharpe . . .'

'You're ordering nothing, sir. You tore up my orders! We are going. So tell them, Major! Tell them! You hear the scream in ten minutes!'

He turned away, his anger deafening him to Kearsey's words, and climbed into the stockade of the fort. His men saw his face and said nothing, but turned away and watched as the small, blue-uniformed Major rode his horse back to the Partisans.

Kearsey delivered the message, shaking with rage, and watched, with Cesar Moreno beside him, the high, silent fort. El Católico was with them and swore his vengeance on Sharpe. The Major touched his sleeve.

'He won't do it. Believe me. He won't.'

Kearsey squinted up at the *castillo*, at the silhouettes of the sentries. There was something more on his mind, something that he could not keep in, and he turned to the tall Spaniard. 'Captain Hardy.' He stopped.

El Católico soothed his horse, looked at Kearsey. 'What about him?'

Kearsey was embarrassed. 'Sharpe says you killed him.'

El Católico laughed. 'He would say anything.' He spat on to the ground. 'You are the only officer we can trust, Major. Not people like Sharpe. He has no proof, does he?' He asked the question confidently.

Kearsey shook his head. 'No.'

'He just wants to turn you against us. No, Major, Captain Hardy was captured. Ask Cesar.'

He gestured at Teresa's father, whose face was tortured with worry. The Major shook his head, felt a sense of relief, a feeling that was shattered by the sound that came from the ruined tower of the *castillo*. The scream seemed to linger in the oak grove. It rose to an unbearable pitch and then wavered down to a thin, sobbing desperation that chilled every man. Cesar Moreno spurred forward with a dozen men, his face set with a determination they had forgotten, but a sentry on the ramparts gave a signal to the tower and the scream came again, higher this time, like the sound of the Frenchmen whose lives they had stripped, inch by inch, with their long knives. Teresa's father reined in, knowing he was beaten, swearing that for every blade that was laid to his daughter Sharpe would suffer a hundred.

El Católico had killed northerners before, Frenchmen, and some had taken three moons to die and every second they had known their own pain. Sharpe, El Católico promised himself, would plead for such a death.

After the sobbing, the noise of boots on stone, came shouted orders, and the Company marched out with fixed bayonets on shouldered guns, and in the lead was the Captain holding a rifle sling looped round the neck of Teresa Moreno. The Partisans growled, looked at the father, at El Católico, but dared not move. Teresa was crying, her face half hidden by her hands, but every man could see the white bandage, torn from the bottom of her dress, and they could see the bright blood which stained the cloth. Sharpe was holding a gleaming, saw-backed bayonet at her head and if she stumbled he pulled at the sling round her throat. Kearsey felt a terrible shame as he watched the Rifle Officer shield himself from El Católico's guns with the girl's body, and as the Company, in a silence that seemed as if it could explode at any instant in a dreadful violence, marched past the poised horsemen, Cesar Moreno gazed at the blood-soaked bandage, at the spots of blood on his daughter's dress, and he promised himself the luxury of this English Captain's death. Kearsey touched his arm.

'I'm sorry.'

'It does not matter. I will catch them and kill them.' Cesar Moreno watched the faces of the Company and he thought they looked shocked, as if their Captain had dragged them into new depths of horror. 'I will kill him.'

Kearsey nodded. 'I'm sorry.'

Moreno looked at him. 'It was not your doing, Major.' He nodded at where the Light Company were beginning their crossing, the lightly loaded men forming a human dam to help the gold-carriers to cross. 'Go in peace.'

Sharpe crossed last, holding the girl and feeling the long weeds snatch at his legs and try to drag him under. The water level was low but the current still strong, and it was awkward with one arm round Teresa's neck, but they made it and were pulled on to the far bank by Patrick Harper, who nodded back over the river.

'Felt sorry for her father, sir.'

'He'll find out she wasn't touched.'

'Aye, that's true. The Major's coming.'

'Let him.'

They set off across the grassland, in the heat of the morning, their boots leaving a wide swath through the pale stalks and with the Partisans never far behind. Harper walked with Sharpe and Teresa and he looked over the girl's head at his Captain.

'How's the arm, sir?'

'It's fine.' Sharpe had cut open his left forearm for the blood with which to soak Teresa's bandage.

Harper nodded ahead, to the Company. 'Should have cut open Private Batten. It's all he's good for.'

Sharpe grinned. The thought had occurred to him, but he had rejected it as petty. 'I'll survive. You'd better tell the lads that the girl's not harmed. Quietly.'

'I'll do that.'

Harper went ahead. The men were silent, shocked, because Sharpe had let them believe he was working the great blade on the girl. If they had known the truth they would have marched past El Católico with grinning faces, suppressed glee, and the whole thing would have been lost. Sharpe looked at the Partisans, to the side and behind, and then at Teresa.

'You must keep pretending.'

She nodded, looked up at him. 'You keep your promise?'

'I promise. We have a bargain.'

It was a good one, too, he decided, and he admired Teresa for its terms. At least, now, he knew why she was on his side, and there was only one regret: he knew they would not be together long, that the bargain called for them to be far apart, but the war would be long and, who knew, perhaps he would meet her again.

At midday the Company climbed a steep ridge that ran directly west, towards their goal, and Sharpe led the way up its steep, razor-stoned flank with a sense of relief. The Partisans could not take their horses up the slope and their figures grew smaller and smaller as the Company laboured upwards. The men carrying the gold needed frequent rests, lying and panting beneath the sun, but each hour took them nearer the Coa, and for a time Sharpe dared to hope that they had shaken off El Católico and his men. The spine of the ridge

156

was a bare, rocky place and littered with small bones left by wolves and vultures. Sharpe had the feeling of walking in a place where no man ever trod, a place that was commanded by the beasts, and all round them the hills crouched in the searing, aching sun, and nothing moved except for the Company crawling along the high crest, and Sharpe felt as if the world had ended and they had been forgotten. Ahead he could see the hazed hills that led to the river, to safety, and he forced the Company on. Patrick Harper, carrying two packs of gold, nodded at the western hills to their front.

'Are the French there, sir?'

Sharpe shrugged. 'Probably.'

The Sergeant looked round their high, sun-bleached path. 'I hope they're not watching for us.'

'Better than being down with the Partisans.' But he knew Harper was right. If the French were patrolling the hills, and they must be, then the Company would be visible for miles. Sharpe made his own gold-filled pack more comfortable on his shoulder. 'We'll keep going west in the night.' He looked at his tired men. 'Just this one effort, Sergeant, just this one.'

It was not to be. At dusk, as the westering sun dazzled them, the ridge dropped away and Sharpe saw they had been cheated. The ridge was like an island, separated from the other hills by a wide, convoluted valley, and in its shadows, far below, he could see the tiny dots that were El Católico's men. He stopped the Company, let them rest, and stared down.

'Damn. Damn. Damn.' He spoke quietly. The Partisans had ridden an easy path, either side of the ridge, and the Company had slogged its useless toil over the baking rocks, the edged stones, the scorpion-infested ridge. On the far side of the valley the hills rose again and he looked at the bouldered slope they would have to climb, but he knew that before they could go on they must cross the valley. It was a perfect place for an ambush. Like an indented sea-coast the valley had hidden spurs, deep shadows; even, to the north, some scrubby trees. Once they were on the valley's grassed floor they would be terribly vulnerable, unable to see what lurked behind the spurs of the hill, in the dead folds of ground. Sharpe stared into the shadowed depth and then at his exhausted Company with their battered weapons and heavy packs.

'We cross at dawn.'

'Yes, sir.' Harper looked down. 'The Major's coming, sir.'

Kearsey had abandoned his horse and, his blue uniform melding with the shadows, was climbing the slope towards the Company. Sharpe grunted.

'He can say a prayer for us.' He looked at the valley. A prayer, maybe, would not be a bad thing.

CHAPTER 16

The water in the canteens was brackish, the food down to the last mildewed crumbs, and in the hour before dawn the ground was slippery with dew. It was cold. The Company, foul-mouthed and evil-tempered, slithered and fell as they went down the dark hillside to the black valley. Kearsey, his steel scabbard crashing against rocks, tried to keep up with Sharpe.

'Almeida, Sharpe. It's the only way!'

Sharpe stopped, towered over the Major. 'Damn Almeida, sir.'

'There's no need for cursing, Sharpe.' Kearsey sounded peevish. He had arrived, as night fell, and launched himself into a rehearsed condemnation of Sharpe that had petered out when he saw an undamaged Teresa calmly watching him. She had spoken to him in Spanish, driving down his objections, until the Major, confused by the speed of events that he could not control, had fallen into an unhappy silence. Later, when the wind stirred the night grass, and sentries twitched as the black rocks seemed to move, he had tried to persuade Sharpe to turn south. Now, in the creeping dawn, he had returned to the subject.

'The French, Sharpe. You don't understand. They'll be blocking the Coa. You must go south.'

'And damn the bloody French, sir!'

Sharpe turned away, slipped, and cursed as a boot flew from beneath him and he sat down, painfully, on a stone. He would not go to Almeida. The French were about to start the siege and would be concentrating in force. He would go west, towards the Coa, and take the gold to the General.

The turf on the valley floor was springy, easy to walk, but Sharpe crouched and hissed at his men to be quiet. He could hear nothing, see nothing, and his instinct told him the Partisans had gone. Sergeant Harper crouched beside him.

'Bastards have gone, sir.'

'They're somewhere.'

'Not here.'

And if not, then why had they gone? El Católico would not give up the gold, nor Moreno the chance to punish the man whom he thought had mutilated his daughter, so why was the valley so empty and quiet? Sharpe led the way over the grass, his rifle cocked, and looked at the hill ahead, littered with rocks, and he imagined the muskets ambushing them as they climbed. The hillside could hide a thousand men.

He stopped again, at the foot of the slope, and the eerie feeling came back of being alone in the world, as if, while they were walking on the ridge the day before, the world had ended and the Angel of Death had forgotten the Light Company. Sharpe listened. He could hear his men breathing, but nothing else. Not the scrabble of a lizard on the rocks, the thump of a frightened rabbit, no birds, not even the wind on the stones. He found Kearsey.

'What's over the hill, sir?'

'Summer pasture for sheep. Spring water, two shelters. Cavalry country.'

'North?'

'A village.'

'South, sir?'

'The road to Almeida.'

Sharpe bit his lip, stared up the slope, and pushed away the sensation of being alone. His instinct told him that the enemy was near, but which enemy? Ahead was foraging country, enemy patrols, and Kearsey had claimed that the French would hold the countryside in force so that they could strip it of food. And if the French were not there? He looked behind, at the valley, and was tempted to stay in the low ground, but where was El Católico? Waiting up the valley? Or had his men hidden the horses and climbed the hill? He knew the Company was nervous, frightened both of the stillness and Sharpe's caution, and he stood up.

'Rifles! Skirmish line. Lieutenant! Follow with the Company. Forward!'

This, at least, was a trade they knew, and the Riflemen split into skirmishing pairs and spread out into the thin, elastic screen that sheltered the main battle-line in a fight. The Rifles were trained to this, taught to think independently and to fight on their own initiative without orders from an officer. One man moved as his partner covered him, just as in battle one man reloaded while the other watched to see if any enemy was aiming at his comrade during the vulnerable and clumsy wielding of ramrod and cartridge. Fifty yards behind the Green Jackets, clumsy and noisy, the Redcoats climbed the hill, and Teresa stayed with Knowles and watched the elusive shapes, fleeting glimpses, of the Riflemen. She was wearing Sharpe's greatcoat, covering the white dress, and she could sense the apprehension among the men. The world seemed empty, the dawn rising on grey rocks and limitless grass, but Teresa knew, better even than Sharpe, that only one thing could have driven away the Partisans and that the world was not empty. Somewhere, watching them, were the French.

The sun rose behind them, lancing its light across the ridge they had walked the day before, and Sharpe, ahead of the Riflemen, saw it touch gold on the hill-crest seventy yards ahead. The rock was covered in light and at its base, half hidden by shadowed grass, was a dull red colour and he turned, casually, and waved his men flat as if he wanted to give them a rest. He yawned, massively, stretched his arms, and sauntered across the line to where Harper had stopped the left-hand pairs. He looked down the slope and waved at Knowles, laconically indicating for the heavily laden group to lie down, and then he nodded amicably at the Sergeant.

'Bloody voltigeurs on the crest.'

Voltigeurs, the French skirmishers, the light infantry who fought against the British Light Companies. Sharpe squatted on the ground, his back to the enemy, and talked softly.

'Saw the red epaulette.'

Harper looked over Sharpe's shoulder, flicking his eyes along the crest, and swore quietly. Sharpe plucked a blade of grass and pushed it between his teeth. Another twenty yards and they would have been in range of the French muskets. He swore as well.

Harper squatted. 'And if there are infantry, sir...

'There are bloody cavalry as well.'

Harper jerked his head sideways, down the slope, to the empty, still-shadowed valley. 'There?'

Sharpe nodded. 'They must have seen us yesterday. Walking on a bloody ridge like virgins.' He spat into the grass, scratched irritably through the torn hole in his left sleeve. 'Bloody Spanish.'

Harper yawned for the benefit of the watching enemy. 'Time we had a proper fight, sir.' He spoke mildly.

Sharpe scowled. 'If we could choose where.' He stood up. 'We go left.'

The hillside to the left, to the south, offered more cover, but he knew, with a terrible certainty, that the Light Company was outnumbered by the enemy and almost certainly outflanked as well. He blew his whistle, waved to the south, and the Company moved along the side of the hill while Sharpe and Harper, quietly and slowly, warned the Riflemen of the enemy skirmishers above.

Kearsey climbed up from the Redcoats. 'What are we doing, Sharpe?'

Sharpe told him about the skirmishers above. Kearsey looked triumphant, as if he had been proved right.

'Told you, Sharpe. Pastureland, village. They're locking up the country and the food. So what do you do now?'

'What we do now, sir, is get out of this.'

'How?'

'I have no idea, Major, no idea.'

'Told you, Sharpe! Capturing Eagles is all very well, but out here in enemy country things are different, eh? El Católico didn't get caught! Must have smelt the French and vanished. We're sitting ducks.'

'Yes, sir.'

There was no point in arguing. If El Católico had the gold he would not even have come this far, but as Sharpe worked his way round the hill he knew that at any moment the journey could end, the men with the gold caught between voltigeurs and cavalry, and in a month's time someone at the army headquarters would wonder idly whatever happened to Captain Sharpe and the Light Company that was sent on the impossible job of bringing back Spanish gold. He turned on Kearsey.

'So where is El Católico?'

'I doubt if he'll help you, Sharpe.'

'But he won't give up the gold, will he, Major? I suppose he's happy to let the French ambush us and then he'll ambush them, right?'

Kearsey nodded. 'It's his only hope.'

Rifleman Tongue, educated and argumentative, spun round. 'Sir!'

The shout was his last; the bang of a musket muffled it, the smoke hanging in front of a rock just twenty yards from him, and Tongue went on spinning and falling, and Sharpe ignored Kearsey and ran ahead. Harper was crouching and searching for the man who had fired at Tongue. Sharpe raced past, knelt by the Rifleman, and lifted up the head. 'Isaiah!'

The head was heavy; the eyes were sightless. The musket ball had gone cleanly between two ribs and killed him even as he shouted the warning. Sharpe could hear the ramrod rattle as the enemy skirmisher pushed his next round into the barrel; then the unseen enemy's partner fired, the ball missing Sharpe by inches because the Frenchman had suddenly seen Harper. The Sergeant's rifle bullet lifted the Frenchman up off the ground; he opened his mouth to scream, but only blood came out and he dropped back. Sharpe could still hear the scraping of the iron ramrod; he stood up with Tongue's rifle and ran forward. The voltigeur saw him coming, panicked, and scrambled backwards, and Sharpe shot him in the base of the spine and watched the man drop his musket and fall in agony to the hillside.

Parry Jenkins, Tongue's partner, seemed almost in tears. The Welshman stooped over Tongue's body, unbuckling the ammunition pouch and canteen, and Sharpe threw him the dead man's rifle. 'Here!' A French ball thudded into his pack, pushing him forward, and he knew that the enemy skirmish line had bent down the hill, cutting their southward advance, and he waved his men down and ran back to Jenkins.

'Have you got everything?'

'Yes, sir. I'm sorry, sir. God, I'm sorry, sir.'

Sharpe hit him on the shoulder. 'Come on, Parry. Not your fault. Down!'

They went down the hill, the musket balls over their heads, and found cover in the rocks. Tongue's body would have to stay there, another Rifleman lost in Spain, or was this Portugal? Sharpe did not know, but he thought of the school in the Midlands where Tongue had once taught, appropriately enough, languages, and he wondered if anyone would remember the clever young man with the friendly eyes who took to drink.

'Sir!'

Knowles was pointing behind and Sharpe rolled over and looked back the way they had come. French skirmishers in faded blue jackets with red epaulettes were angling down the hill behind them. He stayed on his back, facing his men.

'Rifles! Bayonets!'

The French would understand that all right, and feel the fear. He had unconsciously counted the bullets that missed him when he went forward to Tongue's body and he knew, though he had not thought about it, that the hillside in front was sparsely held. The French had put a skirmish line there, thin and spaced, thinking it was enough to drive the British back downhill where, still unseen, the cavalry must wait.

'Lieutenant!'

'Sir?'

'You'll follow us.'

We buy ten minutes, he thought, but we might get outside their cordon, and we might find a place to defend. He knew it was hopeless, but it was better than being driven like fat sheep, and he tugged out his sword, felt its edge, and was on his feet.

'Forward!'

One man of each pair watched, the other ran, and Sharpe heard the Bakers cracking the morning apart as the Frenchmen put up their heads to fire at the small, spread band of men in green who screamed at them and had twenty-three inches of steel fixed to their rifles. The few skirmishers in their front ran, or else died from the spinning rifle bullets that could not miss at fifty paces, and the Company kept running. Sharpe was ahead, his sword across his body and his rifle bumping on his back. He saw skirmishers above them on the hillside, and below, but muskets were a terrible instrument for precision work, and he let the enemy fire and knew the odds were in the Company's favour. One man went down, hit in the buttocks, but he was dragged up and they were through the gap and there were just a few panicked French fugitives ahead who had not had the sense to climb the hill. One turned, reached with his musket, and found himself faced with a giant Irishman who split him neatly between the ribs, kicked the blade free, and went on. Sharpe cut at a man with his sword, felt the bone-hammering jar as the Frenchman parried with his musket, and then he ran on and wondered what kind of a dent he had put in the heavy steel edge.

'Come on! Uphill!'

That was not what the French expected, so it was the only way to go. The Company had smashed the cordon, lost only one man, and now they forced their tired legs to go up the slope, towards the western crest, and behind them the French orders rang out, the blue-coated officers realigning their men, and there was no time for anything but to force the legs up the impossible slope, feel the pain as the breath hurt the lungs, and then Sharpe made the crest and, without stopping, turned and kept running. The damned French were there, not expecting the British, but there all the same and lined up in files and ranks waiting for orders. Sharpe had a glimpse of a gently falling slope, well grassed, and the French battalion lined in companies, and the French watched, astonished, as the British ran past their front, only a hundred paces away, and not a musket was fired.

There was no escape to the west, none to the north where the skirmishers chased them, and Sharpe knew they must go south and east where the cavalry expected them. It was the only direction that gave time, and time was the only hope. He turned, waved the Riflemen down, and pushed Knowles and the red-jacketed men down the slope.

'Form up a hundred paces down!'

'Sir!' Knowles acknowledged, leapt over a boulder, and the Company was gone.

'Rifles! Hold them up!'

This was a better way of fighting, letting the enemy come to them, and killing them when they were too far away to reply to the rifle fire. Sharpe fought as a Private, ramming the balls down the rifling, picking his targets and waiting for the victim to rush forward. He aimed low, never waited to see if the man fell, but dragged out another cartridge, bit off the bullet, and started to reload. He could hear the rifles around him, firing as fast as they could, which was not fast enough, and he knew that the French would come to their senses soon and overwhelm them with targets and rush them with bayonets. He heard Harper giving instructions, and wondered which of the Riflemen needed to be told that you wrapped the bullet in the small greased patch so that it gripped the rifling, and he was so curious that he dodged through the lingering smoke and saw Teresa, with Tongue's weapon, her face already blackened with powder smoke, kneeling up to fire at a Frenchman.

Then the enemy disappeared, gone to ground, and Sharpe knew the rush was coming.

'Forget the patches!'

It was faster to load a naked ball, even though the rifle lost its accuracy, and then he whistled at them, pulling them back, keeping low, so that the enemy would charge an empty piece of ground and find itself under fire from new cover.

'Wait for them!'

They waited. There were French shouts, French cheers, and the men in blue and red were criss-crossing towards them, muskets and bayonets catching the light, and still they came and Sharpe knew they were outnumbered horribly, but it was always best to wait.

'Wait! Wait!' He saw a confused enemy officer, looking for the British, and knew the man would lose his nerve in just a second.

'Fire!'

It was a small volley, but the last they would fire with greased patches, and it was murderous. The enemy dived for cover, threw themselves behind rocks or their own dead, and the Riflemen reloaded, spitting the bullets into the guns, tapping them down by hammering the butts on the ground and not even bothering with ramrods.

'Back!'

There were a hundred skirmishers in front of them, pressing forward, lapping them, and the Riflemen went back, tap-loading, firing at their enemies, and always losing ground, going downhill towards the rest of the Company, who were getting closer and closer to the open ground of the valley.

'Back!' It was no place to die, this, not while the cavalry had still not appeared and there was a chance, however slim, that the Company could fall back to the far side of the valley. There was no time to think of that, only to keep the Riflemen out of range of the muskets, to harry the Company down the hill, stopping and firing, running, reloading, and finding new cover. They were doing no damage to the enemy, but the French, terrified of rifles, kept their distance and did not seem to realize that the bullets were no longer spinning; that, bereft of the small leather patch, the rifles were less accurate than the ordinary musket. It was enough for the French that their opponents wore green, the 'grasshoppers' of the British army who could kill at three hundred paces and tear the heart out of an enemy skirmish line.

Pausing to watch the men go back, Sharpe glanced up the hill and saw the crest lined with the French companies. He noticed the uniforms were bright, unfaded by the sun, and he knew this was a fresh regiment, one of the new regiments that had been sent by Bonaparte to finish the Spanish business once and for all. Their Colonel was giving them a grandstand view of the fight and it annoyed Sharpe. No damned French recruit was going to watch his death! He looked at the voltigeurs, trying to find an officer to aim for, and it struck him, as he banged his rifle-butt on the ground, that only twenty minutes ago he had felt as if he were utterly alone on the face of the planet. Now he was outnumbered, ten to one, and the bastards were still coming, bolder now as the British reached the foot of the slope, and a ball smacked into the rock beside him and glanced up to hit Sharpe's left armpit. It hurt like a dog chewing his flesh, and, throwing up the rifle for a quick shot, he suddenly knew the ricochet had done damage. He could hardly hold the rifle, but he squeezed the trigger and went backwards, keeping pace with his men and looking behind him, to see Knowles pausing on the very edge of the valley like a man fearful of pushing away from the shore. God damn it! There was no choice.

'Back! Back!'

He ran to Knowles. 'Come on. Cross the valley!'

Knowles was looking at his shoulder. 'Sir! You're hit!'

'It's nothing! Come on!' He turned to the Riflemen, red eyes peering from blackened faces. 'Form up, lads.'

The girl fell in like another Rifleman and he grinned at her, loving her for fighting like a man, for her eyes that sparkled with the hell of it, and then he waved his right arm.

'March!'

They went away from the rocks, from the voltigeurs, out into the unnatural calmness of the grass. The French infantry did not follow but stopped at the foot of the slope for all the world as if the Light Company were on a boat and they could not follow. Major Kearsey was jigging with the excitement, his sabre drawn, but his smile went as he saw Sharpe.

'You're hit!'

'It's nothing, sir. A ricochet.'

'Nonsense, man.'

Kearsey touched Sharpe's shoulder, and to the Rifleman's surprise the hand came away red and glistening.

'I've had worse, sir. It'll mend.' It was hurting, though, and he hated the thought of peeling away jacket and shirt to find the wound. Kearsey looked back at the motionless French infantry.

'They're not following, Sharpe!'

'I know, sir.' His tone was gloomy and Kearsey glanced sharply at him.

'Cavalry?'

'Bound to be, sir. Waiting for us to get into the centre of the valley.'

'What do we do?' Kearsey seemed to see nothing odd in asking Sharpe the question.

'I don't know, sir. You pray.'

Kearsey took offence, jerking his head back. 'I have prayed, Sharpe! Precious little else for the last few days.'

It had been only a few days, Sharpe thought, and was it all to end like this, between a French battalion and cavalry? Sharpe grinned at the Major, spoke gently.

'Keep praying, sir.'

It was thin pastureland, close-cropped and tough, and Sharpe looked at the grass and thought that in a year's time the sheep would be back as if there had been no skirmish. The sun had reached the valley floor and insects were busy in the grass-stems, oblivious of the battle overhead, and Sharpe looked up and thought the valley was beautiful. It wound south and west, climbing between steep hills, and ahead of him, out of reach, was a streambed that in spring would make the place a small paradise. He looked behind, saw the voltigeurs sitting by the rocks, the other French companies coming slowly down the hill, and somewhere in the tortuous valley, he knew, the cavalry would be waiting. He was sure they would come from behind now; the way ahead seemed to offer no hiding place, and he knew the Company was trapped. He looked at the ground, level and firm, and imagined the horses walking the first hundred yards, trotting the next fifty, into the canter, the swords raised, and the final gallop of twenty yards that would be split by the fire of the small square, but forty infantry could not hold out long. Pipe smoke went up from the sitting French infantry, front seats for the slaughter.

Patrick Harper fell in beside him. 'How bad?' He was looking at the shoulder.

'It'll mend.'

The Sergeant grabbed his elbow and, ignoring Sharpe's protest, pulled the arm up. 'Does it hurt?'

'Jesus!' He could feel a grating in the shoulder, but the huge Irishman's hands were there, squeezing and hurting. Harper let go.

'There's no bone broken, sir. The ball's trapped. Ricochet?'

Sharpe nodded. A full hit would have broken his shoulder and upper arm. It hurt. Harper looked at the girl and back to Sharpe. 'It'll impress the wee girl.'

'Go to hell.'

'Yes, sir.' Harper was worried, trying not to show it.

Trumpets sounded and Sharpe stopped, turned, and as the Company marched on he saw the first horses appear to the north. His heart sank. Lancers again, always bloody lancers, and their green uniforms and pink facings mocked his meagre hopes. The lances were tipped with red and white pennants, held jauntily, and they trotted into formation in the valley and stared at the small group of British infantry. Harper came back to him. 'Two hundred, sir?'

'Yes.'

He had heard men say they would rather die of a lance than a sabre, that a sabre just gave horrific cuts that festered and bled a man dry over weeks of agony, whereas a lance was quick and deep. Sharpe spat into the grass; he cared for neither, and he looked left and right.

'That way.' He pointed to the eastern side of the valley, back the way they had come, away from the French infantry. 'On the double!'

They ran, a lurching, stumbling, hopeless run, because even if the lancers waited a full two minutes before they were ordered forward they would still catch the Light Company and lean their weight into the silver blades. Then it really was all over, the whole thing hopeless, and Sharpe remembered the stories of small bands of soldiers who fought out against hopeless odds. He had been wrong. There was a hiding place further up the valley, a deep fold of dead ground to the south that had been shadowed and hidden but suddenly he saw horsemen were filing from it, men in foreign uniforms, sabres drawn, and they were not waiting like the lancers. Instead they trotted forward, knee to knee, and Sharpe knew it was all over.

'Halt! Company square!' He put the girl in the centre, with Kearsey. 'Bayonets!'

They did it calmly and he was proud of them. His shoulder hurt like the devil and he suddenly remembered the rumour that had gone through the army that the French poisoned their musket balls. He had never believed it, but something was wrong, everything blurred, and he shook his head to clear his vision and gave his rifle to Kearsey.

'I'm sorry, sir. I can't hold it.'

His sword was still drawn, a dent in the foreblade, and he pushed his way through to the front of the tiny square, an almost useless gesture of defiance, and suddenly realized his men were grinning. They looked at him, started to cheer, and he tried to order silence. Perhaps it was a fine way to die, to cheer the enemy on to the bayonets, but it made no sense to Sharpe. They should save their breath for the killing. The sabres were nearer, the men riding like veterans, without excitement or haste, and Sharpe tried to place the French regiment with blue uniforms, a yellow stripe on the overalls, and tall brown busbies. God damn it! Who were they? At least a man should know who he's fighting. Sharpe tried to order the muskets up, for the men to take aim, but nothing happened. His voice faded; his eyes seemed not to see.

Harper caught him, lowered him gently.

'Hold on, sir, for God's sake, hold on.'

Captain Lossow, resplendent in blue and yellow, saw Sharpe fall, cursed that his squadron had been delayed, and then, like a good professional of the King's German Legion, forgot about Sharpe. There was work to be done.

CHAPTER 17

Lossow had two minutes, no more, and he used them well. He saw the Company disappear behind his left shoulder; then the lancers were all that was ahead of him while far off to the left a battalion of infantry scrambled untidily down the hill to add their firepower to the valley. He would not wait for the infantry. He spoke to his trumpeter, listened to the charge, loved every note, and then he put his sabre in the air and let Thor have his head. A good name for a horse, Thor, especially a horse like this one that could bite a man's face off or beat an enemy down with its hooves. It was good ground, comfortable, with no damned rabbits, and Lossow would pray at night for an opportunity like this. Lancers, idiots with long spikes who never knew how to parry, and all you had to do was get inside the point and the life was yours. He could hear his men galloping behind; he twisted in the saddle to see the fine sight, the horses neck and neck, as they should be, clods of turf flung up behind, blades and teeth shining, and was it not good of the German King who sat on the English throne to give him this chance?

The French were slow and he guessed they were new troops, on remounts, and a lancer should always meet the enemy at full speed or he was done. He steered Thor to the right; they had practised this, and the trumpeter gave the call again, ragged this time because of the motion of the horse but enough to make a man's blood run cold, and he touched Thor with his left heel, never a spur in his life, and the huge horse turned like a dancer; the sabre was dropped so it pointed down like a spike from Lossow's outstretched hand, and he galloped, laughing along the face of the enemy, and simply knocked the lances away. It would not last, it never did, and someone was bright enough to face him, but by then the chaos he had created in half a dozen Frenchmen had let his first troop into the gap, and Lossow knew the job was done and he let Thor rear up and deal with the brave fellow who challenged him. The trumpeter was there, of course, because that was his duty.

'Left!' Lossow ordered, and the Germans turned, chewing up the French line, the sabres wicked in their work, and Lossow was satisfied.

'Lieutenant?'

The man saluted, oblivious of the fight. 'Sir?'

'Stirrup the infantry.'

'Sir.'

And his duty was done. He had a minute left and Thor needed exercise so Lossow touched with his heels and the horse went forward, and the sabre turned a galloping lance so neatly that Lossow thought he would remember that moment till the day he died, preferably in Germany, and the Kligenthal steel of the curved blade opened the Frenchman's throat as far as his spine, and he wished that every moment was this good, with a fine horse, a good turf, a blade made by the dwarves themselves, and an enemy for breakfast.

He watched his men work, proud of them. They were disciplined, protecting one another, their sword drill immaculate and thorough, and Lossow knew why the lord Wellington preferred German cavalry. Not as flashy as the English, not as good for a parade, but for killing Frenchmen – they were as good as British infantry at that. Lossow, a happy man, thought in the valley's bottom – as part of his mind watched the enemy infantry, another checked on the fleeing lancers – that this army, Wellington's army, could be as perfect an instrument of war as any in history. With men like these horsemen and with that infantry? It was beautiful!

'Re-call.'

The trumpet sounded, the men pulled back in perfect order, and Lossow waved the sabre. The lancers were done for, utterly beaten, but he had expected no less. Poor devils. They were not to know that Lossow's men had tracked this valley for three days, waiting for a sight of Sharpe, and Lossow was glad it was he and not that pig Schwalbach further south who had found the British infantry. He looked up the valley. The rescued infantry were moving fast, each man holding on to a cavalryman's stirrup, and Lossow brought the other hundred and fifty sabres back slowly, screening the retreat, enjoying the warm sun, and saluting the French infantry who were forming up, too late, their show spoiled.

'Compliments of Hanover!' he shouted, but the garlic-eating slime did not understand German.

An hour later Sharpe opened his eyes, saw Harper leaning over him, pinning him to the ground, and Teresa was holding one hand, and then a German soldier came to him with a piece of iron, glowing hot, and Sharpe knew the dream of the last few minutes, of his shoulder being pinned by an Indian with a lance, was just that: a dream. The Indian, turbaned and smiling, had played with him, and every time Sharpe had tried to jerk free the lance would come back, hoisting him a little higher.

'Still, Captain.' Harper spoke gently, gripped hard.

The cauterizing iron hit him like the devils of hell. His shout was cut off as he fainted, as the flash burned and stank, and it took all Harper's strength to hold him down, but it was done and Lossow's horse-doctor nodded his satisfaction. They splashed water on his face, trickled brandy into his throat, and Sharpe opened his eyes, grimaced as the pain shot through him, and struggled upwards. He looked at Harper.

'You said it would mend.'

'Didn't want to worry you, sir. Almost bled to death.' He propped Sharpe against a rock. 'Food! Bring that food!'

Sharpe looked up to see a German officer with crinkled eyes and a good smile looking down on him. He had met the man before. Where? He remembered. In the village where Batten had been caught by the provosts. He stuck out his good hand.

'Captain –'

'Lossow, sir. At your service!'

Sharpe smiled, a bit wanly. 'You have our thanks, sir.'

The German waved away the formality. 'On the contrary. You have ours. A lovely fight!'

'Did you lose anyone?'

'Lose anyone? They were lancers, Captain! An angry toad

would be more dangerous! Now, if they put lances in the front rank, and sabres behind, they might be dangerous. But just lancers? No problem to us!'

Sharpe nodded, grateful. 'But thank you.'

Lossow took the mug of stew from Harper and put it on Sharpe's lap.

'You got the gold.'

'You know about it?'

'Why do you think I am here? A patrol to the south, me here, and all for you, Captain. The lord Wellington wants the gold badly!'

Kearsey sniffed, said nothing, and Sharpe sipped at the stew. It tasted miraculous after the hard tack of the last week.

'He can have it.'

'*Ja*, but there are problems.'

Sharpe put the mug down, willed the pain in his shoulder to go down. 'Problems?'

'French patrols.' Lossow's hand described an arc to the west. 'Like fleas on a bottom.'

Sharpe laughed and the pain came back, but he forced his left hand round to hold the hot mug and it worked. He spooned the tough beef into his mouth.

'We must get to the army.'

'I know.'

'We must.'

He looked to his right and saw one of Lossow's men sharpening his sword, using a stone and oil to smooth down the dent. It was only this morning that he had cut down on the voltigeur and the man – Sharpe remembered yellow teeth – had pushed his musket up and saved his life. 'We must.'

'We will try.'

Sharpe lifted Lossow's brandy bottle; the Germans were never short of captured brandy, and the spirit flowed like cream into his throat. He coughed.

'The Partisans? Have you seen Partisans?'

Lossow turned and spoke to one of his officers, a short exchange, and turned back to Sharpe. 'Two miles away, Captain, keeping in touch with us. They want the gold?'

Sharpe nodded. 'And me.' He looked at the girl and back to the German.

'Don't worry, Captain.' Lossow stood up and hitched his sword-belt round. 'You're in good hands.'

The girl smiled at Sharpe, stood up and came to him. Her dress was another four inches shorter and Sharpe realized he had been bandaged after the cauterizing iron had driven him in agony back to unconsciousness. She still had the rifle, slung proprietorially on a shoulder, with Tongue's ammunition pouch and bayonet strapped to her waist. Lossow moved to one side to let her sit by Sharpe.

'Any more wounded, Captain, and she will be naked!' The German Captain laughed. 'We should all cut ourselves!'

Teresa looked at Sharpe, spoke softly. 'The Captain's already seen me. Haven't you?'

How did she know? Sharpe thought. He wondered if his telescope was undamaged by the fight and he remembered a French bullet thumping into his pack and throwing him forward. He could not be bothered to check right now, but leaned back, sipped at the brandy, and slept in the sun. The girl sat beside him, watching the Light Company rest, while beyond them, beyond the tethered horses, Lossow's picquets watched French patrols comb the western valleys. The Light Company would move soon, cutting westward, but for now they could sleep and forget the one more river they had to cross.

CHAPTER 18

Dogs barked in the town, horses moved restless feet on the wooden stable-boards, and on the stone front steps the sentries shuffled in the darkness. In the hallway of the house a clock ticked heavily, but in the ground-floor room, lit by candles, the only sound was the rustling of paper until the tall, hooked-nosed man leaned back and tapped a long finger on the table's edge.

'The siege has not begun?'

'No, my lord.'

The General leaned forward and drew a square map towards him, scraping it over the table, and put the long finger on a white space in its centre.

'Here?'

Major Michael Hogan leaned into the candlelight. The map showed the country from Celorico, where they sat, across the border to Ciudad Rodrigo. Crawling up the map, dividing it into three, were the Coa and Agueda rivers, and the long finger was pointing between the rivers, north of Almeida.

'As best we can judge, my lord.'

'And what is there, pray?'

The General's finger relaxed and traced an unconscious line down to the writing on the bottom. Drawn by Maj. Kearsey. Q'Master Gen's Dep't. Hogan wondered idly when Kearsey had drawn the map, but it did not matter. He drew a piece of paper to him.

'Four new French battalions, sir. We know the 118th of the Line are there, probably at strength. A regiment of lancers, one of chasseurs.'

There was a brief silence. Wellington snorted. 'After food, I suppose?'

'Yes, my lord.'

'And round the town?'

Another piece of paper. 'A loose ring, my lord. Mostly to the south where the artillery park is building. We know of just two battalions of foot and, of course, cavalry patrols.'

'They're slow, Hogan, slow!'

'Yes, sir.'

Hogan waited. If the French were slow, all to the good, and the reports that filtered back from Partisans and exploring officers suggested that Masséna was having problems assembling his transport, his siege materials, and, above all, his rations. There was also a rumour that he was with his mistress and reluctant to leave the comfort of her bedroom for the discomforts of the campaign. The General put his hand back on the map.

'Nothing from the KGL?'

'Nothing, sir.'

'Damn, damn, damn.' The words were spoken softly, almost reflectively.

He picked up a letter, postmarked London, and read it aloud, though Hogan suspected the words were known by heart.

'"I write in confidence, trusting to your discretion that however precarious the position of the army it is matched by our own. An opposition rampant, a press malignant, an ailing monarch, and there can be no hopes for a further draft of monies before the autumn. We put our faith in your exertions."' He put down the letter, dismissing the new government's fears, and looked at the map. 'I wonder where he is?'

It was not like the General, Hogan reflected, to articulate his worries. 'If I know him, my lord, and I do, then I suspect he will be avoiding Almeida. Coming the direct way.'

'He'd be better off in Almeida.'

'He would, my lord, but no one could expect that. And in two days...' Hogan shrugged. In two days the enemy would lock up the town as effectively as the countryside.

The General frowned, drummed the table with his fingers. 'Do I warn Cox?'

The question was asked of himself, not Hogan, but the

Irishman knew what was in Wellington's mind. The fewer people who knew of the gold, the better. The Spanish government, in impotent obscurity at Cádiz, would assume the gold to have been captured by the French when the armies collapsed in the north, and if they were to discover that their allies, the British, had purloined it? No. The General's fingers slapped down in finality; he would not burden Almeida's commander with another problem.

'If Sharpe is alive, Hogan, we'll assume he does what you say. Avoid Almeida.' He dismissed the problem, looked up at the Irishman. 'How does the work go?'

'Well, my lord, excellently. But . . .'

'I know. The money. Can it wait a week?'

'Ten days.'

Wellington's eyebrows went up in mock surprise. 'Some good news. Let's hope for more.'

He passed on to other business, to a General Order that limited field officers' leave in Lisbon to just twenty-four hours. If they couldn't find a woman in that time, the General claimed, they might as well not stay on and look. There would be only one exception. The blue eyes looked at Hogan.

'If that damned rogue gets back, give him a month.'

The damned rogue, with a hurting shoulder and a seething sense of frustration, was riding a horse into the intricate defences of Almeida. Lossow rode beside him.

'I'm sorry, Sharpe. We had no choice!'

'I know. I know.'

It was true, too, however grudgingly he admitted it. Every move was headed off by damned Frenchmen who seemed to be everywhere. They had been chased twice, lost a German trooper, and in the end, exhausted and hunted, they turned for the safety of the town. Sharpe had wanted to lay up in the country, travel in darkness, but the French were alerted and he knew that there was no sense in being chased ragged round the east bank of the Coa.

Straw torches, soaked in resin, flamed and smoked in the tunnelled gateway, casting lurid shadows on the Portuguese infantry who had dragged open the huge doors and now watched the tired men ride and walk into the town. The insides of Sharpe's legs were sore; he hated riding horses, but Lossow had insisted. The gold was all on horseback, carried by the Germans, and Sharpe looked at them, all alert, and then at Lossow.

'Why don't we ride straight through? Out the other side?'

Lossow laughed. 'They must be fed! The horses, I mean. One good dinner of corn and they'll go through the French like the pox through a regiment. We go in the morning, *ja*?'

'Dawn?'

'Yes, my friend. Dawn.'

There was still hope. The French had not even surrounded Almeida; they had ridden the last few miles unmolested, and Sharpe guessed that the cavalry patrols were concentrated to the north. In the southern sky, beyond the bulk of the castle, he could see the glow of fires, and assumed that the French had chosen the easier countryside in which to build their artillery park. To the west, where the river was so tantalizingly close, he had seen no fires, except in the distance, and they were British. Success was so close.

Kearsey, on yet another borrowed horse, led the procession into the Plaza. The castle and cathedral were close to the northern gate where they had entered, and the big Plaza seemed to be the only inhabited place in the town. Sharpe looked for Knowles.

'Lieutenant?'

'Sir?'

'Go to the lower town. You'll find billets. Knock a house open.' There were dozens of empty houses. 'Meet me back here. Sergeant?'

Harper came alongside the horse and Sharpe gestured at Teresa. 'She'll need a room. I'll join the Company when I'm finished here.'

Harper grinned. 'Yes, sir.'

Cox's headquarters were dark inside and Kearsey, Sharpe, and Lossow waited in an echoing hallway while a sleepy orderly went upstairs. The German officer grinned.

'In bed! Lucky man!'

'Major!' Cox was at the top of the stairs, his hair ruffled, dressed in a long red gown belted at his waist. 'You're back! A moment! Go into the drawing-room. Candles!'

Sharpe pulled back a heavy velvet curtain and across the Plaza could see the dark shape of the squat cathedral. There was a bustle behind him as Portuguese servants brought in candles and tapers, wine and food, and he let the curtain drop and sat, exhausted, in a deep, comfortable chair. Down the road, he thought, in the morning. One last effort, one last surprise attack, and it was done. He helped himself to the wine, offered some to Lossow, ignored the disapproving look from Kearsey.

The door opened. 'You helped yourself. Good!' Cox had pulled on a shirt and trousers, brushed his hair, and he nodded amicably at Sharpe. 'Captain. Captain Lossow. What can I do for you?'

Sharpe sat up, surprised. Did Cox not know? He exchanged a glance with Lossow; they both looked at Kearsey, expecting him to speak, but the Major sat tight-lipped. Sharpe put down his wine.

'You know about the gold, sir?'

Cox nodded; a shadow on his face hid the expression, but Sharpe thought it was guarded. 'I know, Captain.'

'We have it, sir. We must take it to Celorico. We wanted to feed the horses, rest, and leave at dawn. With your permission, sir, we'd like the western gate opened an hour before first light.'

Cox nodded, leaned over and poured himself a small glass of wine. 'Whose gold is it?'

Sharpe felt an immense burden come back. 'I am under orders from Lord Wellington, sir. Orders that tell me to take the gold to him.'

Cox's eyebrows shot up. 'Good! Let me see the orders, then!'

Sharpe glanced at Kearsey, who reddened. The Major cleared his throat. 'The orders were accidentally destroyed, sir. No blame to Captain Sharpe.'

Cox's hope seemed to diminish. He peered at Kearsey over his wine. 'You saw them? What did they say?'

'That all officers should render assistance to Captain Sharpe.' Kearsey spoke in a neutral voice.

Cox nodded. 'And Sharpe is taking the gold to Lord Wellington, right?'

Sharpe nodded, but Kearsey interrupted. 'The orders did not say, sir.'

'For God's sake, sir!' Sharpe exploded, but Cox banged on the table.

'Did your orders specifically mention the gold?'

'No, sir.'

Sharpe damned Kearsey for his quibbling honesty. Without the Major's last remark the Light Company might be homeward-bound in a few hours. Cox's fingers drummed on the table.

'I have a problem, gentlemen.' He pulled papers towards him, muttered something about tidiness, and held out a thick piece of parchment, sealed with a heavy wax circle, and waved it in the candlelight. 'A request from the Spanish government, our allies, that the gold does not pass through British hands. Damned strange, really.'

Lossow coughed. 'Strange, sir?'

Cox nodded. 'Fellow arrives today, full fig, and tells me about the gold. It was the first I knew about it. He's got an escort for it. Spanish Colonel. He's called Jovellanos.'

Sharpe looked at Kearsey. He knew the answer. 'Jovellanos?'

'El Católico.' Kearsey stretched for the piece of paper and held the seal up to the candle before reading the words. 'It's in order, sir. Genuine.'

'How the hell can it be in order?' Sharpe's right hand was gripped tight into a fist. 'He's a bloody bandit! A crook! He wrote the damned thing himself! We have orders, sir, from the General. From Lord Wellington. That gold goes to Celorico!'

Cox, who had been friendly, scowled at Sharpe. 'I see no need for anger, Captain Sharpe. Colonel Jovellanos is here, my guest.'

'But, sir' – Lossow broke in, glancing at Sharpe sympathetically – 'Captain Sharpe speaks the truth. We were told that the gold was important. It had to go to the lord Wellington.'

Cox took a deep breath, let it out, tapped his toe on the floor. 'God damn it, gentlemen, I am facing a siege which will begin any day now. The enemy's guns are in sight, the placements are being dug, and you bring me this?'

Sharpe repeated doggedly, 'We have orders, sir.'

'So you say.' Cox picked up the paper. 'Is there a Junta for Castile?'

Kearsey nodded. 'Yes, sir.'

'And does Joaquím Jovellanos have authority from it?' Kearsey nodded again. 'And the gold is theirs?' The nod again. The paper dropped on to the table. 'The General gave me no orders!'

Sharpe sighed. An English Brigadier in the Portuguese army faced with a Spanish Colonel, an English Captain, a German cavalryman, Spanish gold, and no orders. He had an idea.

'Sir, is the telegraph working?'

Lossow snapped his fingers. Cox frowned at the German. 'Yes, Captain. There's a relay station over the river, towards Pinhel.'

'When can the first messages be sent?'

Cox shrugged. 'Depends on the weather. Usually an hour after dawn.'

Sharpe nodded impatiently. 'Would you, sir, consider a message to the General requesting orders concerning the gold?'

Cox looked at him, shrugged again. 'Of course. First thing tomorrow?'

'Please, sir.'

Cox stood up. 'Good! Problem solved. I'll tell Colonel Jovellanos tomorrow and you can get a night's sleep. I must say you look as if you need it. Good God.' He was peering at Sharpe's shoulder. 'You're hurt!'

'It will mend, sir.' Sharpe finished his wine; damned if politeness would stop him. And damn Wellington, too, who had held the cards too close to his chest so that Cox, a decent man, was put in this position. 'Sir?'

Cox turned away from the doorway. 'Sharpe?'

'How many men in Colonel Jovellanos's escort?'

'Two hundred, Sharpe. God save me, I wouldn't want to meet them in a dark street.'

Nor I, thought Sharpe. Nor I. He stood up, waited for the Commander of the garrison to leave. Where was El Católico he wondered. Upstairs asleep? Or watching from a darkened window?

Lossow, at least, understood. 'My men will guard tonight.'

Sharpe smiled his thanks. 'And tomorrow?'

The German shrugged, fitted his tall, plumed busby on to his head. 'If we cannot leave at dawn, then at dusk, my friend.'

Cox put his head back round the door. 'I forgot! Remiss of me! You'll stay here, gentlemen? My orderlies can find beds.'

Kearsey accepted, the two Captains pleaded they would rather be with their men, and Cox wished them a good night at the front door as if he were a host bidding a genial farewell to valued dinner guests. 'And sleep well! The message goes first thing!'

Knowles and Harper waited outside and with them two Germans, one of them a barrel of a Sergeant who grinned when he was told that the Partisans were in the town. Lossow looked from his Sergeant to Harper.

'A good match!'

'I'll bet on the Irish.' Sharpe said the words without offence, and Lossow laughed.

'Home. We sleep!'

Knowles had done well, unbarring a huge house that stabled the Germans' horses, housed everyone, and on the second floor, behind a huge, polished door, was a bedroom with a feather mattress, a canopied bed, rugs, and the smell of old wood and fresh sheets. Sharpe closed the door, cutting off the sounds of his men who were sharing wine with the Germans, and looked at the girl.

'El Católico's here.'

She nodded. 'What did you expect?'

He unbuckled his belt, untied the faded red sash, and knew that his shoulder was too stiff, too painful, for him to undress properly. Teresa saw it, pushed back the sheet, and he saw she was already naked. She crossed the floor, helped him, went back to the huge, soft bed with him. Sharpe lay flat and the girl propped herself beside him.

'What does he want?'

'Later,' Sharpe said. 'Later.' His right arm was still good and he pulled the girl on top of him, felt her hair fall either side of his face, her hands explore the scars on his back. Her mouth was beside his ear.

'Can I keep the rifle?'

'It's all yours,' he said. 'All yours.' And it was.

CHAPTER 19

Her finger pressed on the scars of the flogging. 'Who did it?'

'A man called Morris, and a Sergeant. Hakeswill.'

'Why?'

He shrugged. 'They lied.'

'You kill them?'

'Not yet.'

She nodded slowly. 'You will?'

'I will.' It was not yet dawn, but the sky had the grey luminance that came before first light, and Sharpe wanted to be at the telegraph early. He was reluctant to move, to lose the warm body, but others were stirring in the house and a cockerel, exploding into sound in the courtyard, jerked him upright. He lay back again, taking five more minutes, and pulled Teresa close.

'Did Hardy want you?'

She smiled, said something in Spanish, and he assumed she was asking if he was jealous. 'No.'

She wagged her head, seemed to shrug. 'Yes. He wanted me.'

'And did you?'

She laughed. 'No. Joaquím was too close.'

Joaquím, damned Joaquím Jovellanos, El Católico, Colonel and crook. The girl had told him, when they were lying hot and sweaty in the wide bed, of her father, of El Católico, of the business of staying alive in the mountains when the enemy is everywhere and there is no law and no government. Her father, she said, was good, but weak.

'Weak?' Sharpe had winced as he propped himself on an elbow.

'He was strong.' Teresa still had problems with English and she shrugged helplessly.

Sharpe helped her. 'And El Católico?'

She smiled, pushed hair away from her eyes. 'He wants everything. My father's men, land, money, me. He's strong.'

Somewhere a door scraped on old hinges, boots crossed a yard, and Sharpe knew it was time to be up.

'And you?'

Her hand felt his scars. 'We will fight. Ramon, me, Father. Joaquím only thinks of what happens afterwards.'

'Afterwards?'

'When there is peace.'

'And you?' Her hair had the smell of a woman and his hand rested on the long, muscled waist.

'I want to kill Frenchmen.'

'You will.'

'I know.'

Now, looking at the sudden smile, he wished that she was not going. He could, he decided, be happy with this woman, but he laughed inside as he remembered he had thought the same of Josefina.

'What are you smiling for?'

'Nothing.'

He swung his legs out of bed, pulled up his crumpled clothes and put them on the bed. She pulled the jacket towards her, opened the pocket.

'What's this?' A silver locket lay in her hand.

'A locket.'

She hit him. 'I know.' She opened it and, inside, saw the gold-haired girl with the generous mouth. 'Who's that?'

'Jealous?'

She seemed to understand and laughed. 'Who is she?'

'Jane Gibbons.'

She imitated him. 'Jane Gibbons. Who is she? Is she waiting for you?'

'No. I've never met her.'

She looked at the face in the miniature painting. 'She's pretty. Never?'

'Never.'

'Why do you have it?'

'I knew her brother.'

'Ah.' Friendship made sense to her. 'Is he dead?'

'Yes.'

'The French?' She said the word with her customary spite.

'No.'

She looked exasperated at his answers. 'Was he a soldier?'

'Yes.'

'Then how did he die?'

Sharpe pulled on the French overalls. 'I killed him.'

'You?'

Sharpe paused. 'No. The Sergeant killed him. I killed the other one.'

'What other one?' She sat up, flinched as he pulled back the curtain.

Across the street was a church with ornate stonework and a laddered bell-tower. The soldier in Sharpe automatically understood that the church roof must have a platform for the ladder, a possible firing position.

'They were enemies. They hurt a friend.'

She understood the half truth. 'A woman?'

He nodded. 'Not mine.' Another half truth, but by the time the two Lieutenants had died, Josefina had already found Hardy.

She laughed. 'You're a good man, Richard.'

'I know.'

He grinned at her, picked up the locket and pushed it back into his pocket. Why had he kept it? Because Gibbons's sister was so beautiful? Or was it now his talisman, his magic charm against the killing lance and El Católico's rapier? Teresa helped him with the jacket buttons.

'You'll come back?'

'I'll be back. The soldiers are here; you're safe.'

She leaned off the bed, pulled up the rifle. 'I'm safe.'

He left her in the bedroom, feeling his loss, and went down to where the kitchen fire was blazing and Lossow was drinking beer from an earthenware bottle. The German Captain grinned at Sharpe.

'A good night, my friend?'

Knowles winced, Harper looked at the ceiling, but Sharpe growled something approximately polite and crossed to the fire. 'Tea?'

'Here, sir.' Harper pushed a mug over the table. 'Just wet it.'

A dozen men of the Company were in the kitchen, and some Germans, and they were sawing with knives at the new bread and looking surprised because there were pots of butter, fresh butter, on the table. Sharpe scraped his boot on the hearth and his men looked up.

'The girl.' He wondered if he sounded embarrassed, but the men seemed not to mind. 'Look after her till I get back.'

They nodded, grinned at him, and he was suddenly immensely proud of them. She would be safe with them, scoundrels though they were, just as a King's ransom in gold was safe with them. He had never thought of it, not in detail, but it occurred to Sharpe that most officers would never have trusted their men with the gold. They would have feared desertion; that the temptation of so much money would be simply too much, but Sharpe had never been worried. These were his men, his Company, and he trusted his life with their skills, so why not gold, or a girl?

Robert Knowles cleared his throat. 'When will you be back, sir?'

'Three hours.' An hour till the message could be sent, an hour for the reply to come, and then another hour unpicking the details with Cox. 'Keep an eye out for El Católico. He's here. Keep a guard, Robert, all the time, and don't let anyone in, no one.'

The men grinned at him, laughed as they thought what they could do to anyone who interfered with them, and Lossow clapped his hands together.

'We surprise the Spanish, yes? They think they have the gold? But they don't know about the telegraph. Ah! The wonders of modern war.'

It was cold in the street, the sky still dark grey, but as Sharpe, Lossow, and Harper mounted the final steps to the rampart of the castle they could see the eastern sky blazing with the coming sun. The telegraph was unmanned, the sheep bladders tied to the mast, and in the cruel, grey light it reminded Sharpe of a gallows. The wind slapped the ropes in a forlorn tattoo against the mast.

The sun shattered the remnants of night, dazzled over the

eastern hills, and streaked its bleak, early light into the countryside round Almeida. As if in salute there was a blare of bugles, shouts from the walls, and Lossow clapped Sharpe's good shoulder and pointed south.

'Look!'

The bugles had responded to the first formal move of the siege. The waiting was over, and through his undamaged telescope Sharpe saw that the dawn light had revealed a mound of fresh earth that had been thrown up a thousand yards from the fortifications. It was the first French battery and, even as Sharpe watched, he saw the tiny figures of men throwing up more earth and battening great fascines to the crest of the mound. It had been years since he had carried a fascine to war, a great wicker cylinder that was filled with soil and provided an instant battlement to protect men and guns from enemy artillery. The Portuguese gunners had seen the fresh earthworks and were running along the town wall.

Lossow pounded his fist on the ramparts. 'Fire! You bastards!'

A Portuguese gun team on the town defences seemed to hear him, for there was the flat crack of a cannon, and through the glass, Sharpe saw an eruption of earth where the roundshot struck the ground just in front of the French battery. The ball must have bounced right over the top and he knew the Portuguese gunners would be satisfied. After another two firings their gun barrel would be hot and the shot would carry farther and he listened for the next shot, saw it fall a little beyond the first, and watched as the French soldiers hurried to take cover.

'Next one.'

He let the telescope lie where it was and straightened up. Over the roofs of the town he could see the smoke of the cannon drifting in the breeze, saw another smudge as the Portuguese fired again, and then, a second later, heard the crash and watched the fascines blow apart.

'Bravo!' Lossow clapped his hands. 'That's held them up for five minutes!'

Sharpe picked up the telescope and panned it to the south. There were few Frenchmen visible – the new battery, an encampment half a mile beyond that, and a few figures on horseback riding the circuit well beyond the range of the defenders' guns. The close siege had not started yet, the careful digging of the zigzag trenches that would bring the infantry to striking distance of the breach that the French would hope to blast through the walls with battery after battery of huge, iron siege guns. And all the time the howitzers, untouchable in their deep pits, would lob their bombs into the town day after day. He looked westward, to the road that led to the Coa, and beyond one earthen barricade there was no real attempt by the French to seal it off. That would come in a day or two, when the siege proper began, and he handed the glass to Lossow.

'We can do it.'

The German looked at the road, smiled. 'It will be a pleasure.'

There were footsteps on the circular stone stairway and the young midshipman, holding a thick sandwich, emerged on to the ramparts and looked startled to see the waiting men. He put his sandwich in his mouth, saluted, rescued his sandwich.

'Morning, sir.'

He put down the pile of books he was carrying in his other hand.

'Morning.' Sharpe guessed the boy was no older than fifteen. 'When do you start sending?'

'When the messages get here, sir.'

Sharpe pointed to the books. 'What's that?'

'Lessons, sir. Principles of navigation. I've got to pass the exam soon, sir, even though I'm not at sea.'

'You should join the Rifles, lad.' Harper picked up the book. 'We don't stuff your head with mathematics.'

Sharpe looked westwards. 'Where's the relay station?'

The boy pointed north-west. 'Between the two hills, sir. It's over the river, on a church.'

Sharpe pointed the glass, held it steady by jamming it next to the telegraph's mast and, far away, like a speck of dust, he could see the tiny telegraph station. 'How the hell do you read it?'

'With this, sir.' The boy unlocked a trunk that was part of the mast's foundation and dragged out an iron tripod that carried a telescope twice the size of Sharpe's. Lossow laughed.

'Thank you, Captain,' Sharpe said drily. He liked Lossow, but was not sure about the man's sense of humour. Harper seemed to enjoy it.

In the Plaza, in front of the cathedral, Sharpe watched the foreshortened shapes of two officers walking towards the castle.

'Are those your messages?'

The midshipman leaned over. 'Yes, sir. Captain Charles usually brings them.'

As Sharpe watched he saw three men rolling a keg of powder from the cathedral, across the Plaza, and towards the warren of streets. He guessed that the guns on the wall kept very little ready powder, fearing a spark and an explosion that would save the French weeks of work, and the soldiers would be busy taking the black powder from the cathedral and delivering it to the gunners who sweated on the defences. He was glad he would not be here for the siege, for the helpless feeling of watching the earthworks creep closer, the siege guns firing slowly, but with massive, hammering force.

'Good morning! You must be Sharpe!' Captain Charles, a Portuguese officer beside him, sounded cheerful. He looked at the midshipman. 'Morning, Jeremy. Sleep well?'

'Yes, sir.' The midshipman had put up the telescope and trained it on the far mast. 'Hold on, sir.'

He looked through the glass for a second, then leaped to the mast, untied the bladder ropes, and hauled on them one at a time so that the black bags shot up to the pulley at the cross-trees and fell down again.

'What was that?' Sharpe asked.

'Just saying good morning, sir.' The midshipman left three bladders down, the other raised. 'That says we're transmitting, sir,' he added helpfully.

Sharpe looked through the big telescope. The far tower, much closer now, had two black dots level and halfway up the mast, presumably the signal that said they were ready to receive a message.

'Here you are, Jeremy.' Charles handed over the first sheet and the boy leaped to the ropes, tugged and dropped them, sometimes looking at the sheet Captain Charles had given him, but mostly doing it from memory. Cox's Staff Captain jerked a thumb at the midshipman. 'Busy little blighter, eh? Used to be two of them, but the other got the pox. Died on us.'

Sharpe looked over the midshipman's shoulder at the sheet of paper and read 48726, 91858, 38197.

'Code,' Captain Charles boomed at him. 'Jolly clever, yes?'

'What does it say?'

The Staff Captain, gold lace at his cuffs, touched his nose. 'Can't say, dear chap. Top secret. Probably says the Brigadier has run out of rum; please send supply urgent. Something like that.'

'Isn't that the gold message?'

'Gold? Don't know about that. Only three messages this morning. That one tells the General that the 68th Regiment of the Line are outside since yesterday. This one's the daily report on available shot, and the last one's about the French battery.'

'Christ Almighty!' Sharpe started towards the stairs, but Lossow touched his arm.

'I'll go.' The German was serious. 'You stay.'

Harper stood beside Lossow. 'You should stay here, sir. You don't know what the Spanish are up to.'

Lossow smiled. 'You see? Outvoted.'

He ran down the stairs and Sharpe turned back to Captain Charles.

'What the hell's happening at headquarters?'

Charles sniffed, handed the second piece of paper to the midshipman. 'Affairs of state. I don't know. Your Major, the Spanish Colonel, and it's all arm-waving and table-thumping. Not my style, dear boy. Oh, I say! That is clever!' He was staring to the south.

Sharpe turned, picked up the telescope, and trained it on the French battery. Nothing was happening; the fascines still lay splayed apart and split open, and there were not even men attempting to repair the damage.

'What is it?' he asked.

'Over there.' Charles was pointing farther to the right. 'A second battery, hidden. We bang away at a heap of earth and the clever devils sneak the real battery into place. Jolly clever.'

It was clever. Sharpe saw French soldiers dragging away branches that had cloaked the excavation of a battery that, judging from the activity around it, was ready to open fire. He could see how well protected it was, by yards of earth, mounted fascines, and trenches for the gunners to use when under fire. The siege gun, hidden by shadows, could harass the defenders' guns as the French built their works forward until the breaching batteries were in place and the two forces, attackers and defenders, got down to work in earnest. The battery was built on the edge of dead ground and Sharpe knew that there would be infantry there, well protected from the Portuguese batteries, ready to repel an attack on the harassing battery.

Charles rubbed his hands. 'Things will hot up soon. They've been slow.'

Harper looked at the elegant Captain. 'How long can you hold out, sir?'

Captain Charles beamed at him. 'Forever, Sergeant! Or at least as long as the ammunition lasts! Once that's gone we'll just have to throw rocks.' That was evidently a joke, for he laughed. 'But there are tons of powder in the cathedral. And the Portuguese are good! By Jove, they're good!'

Sharpe stared at the new battery, and as he looked he saw a cloud of smoke grow at an incredible speed just in front of the earthwork. The smoke was lanced with red flame and, hardly visible, more of an impression than something he really saw, there was a pencil trace in the sky. He knew what it was, the sight of the shot arcing directly towards them.

'Down!'

'What is it?' Charles looked at him, but as he did the castle literally shook, the stones of the huge keep seemed to waver and crack, and mixed with the reverberating crash of falling masonry came the thunder of the siege gun.

'Good Lord!' Charles was still standing. 'Good Lord above! A ranging shot!'

Sharpe leaned over the ramparts. Some stones had fallen into the moat, dust hung in the air, and frightened birds, nesting in the crevices, flew out into the startled air.

'Bloody good shooting,' Harper growled.

The sound of the replying batteries was thinner than that of the giant gun, but more frequent. It took a long time to re-load a siege gun. Sharpe, through the telescope, watched as the smoke of the discharge cleared and the Portuguese balls crashed into the redoubt, but to no apparent damage. The hard-packed earth soaked up the cannonade, and the aperture, just wide enough for its purpose, was plugged with fascines as the artillerymen sponged out and rammed home the huge missile. He kept watching, saw the fascines pulled back.

'Here it comes.'

This time he kept his eyes in the air above the gun and saw the pencil-line clearly as the huge iron ball rose and fell in its flat trajectory.

'For what we are about to receive,' Charles said, and the tower shook again, less violently, and the crash and the rumble mixed with the dust and the squawking birds. Charles brushed at his immaculate uniform. 'Distinctly unfriendly.'

'Has it occurred to you that they're after the telegraph?' Sharpe said.

'Good Lord. You could be right.' He turned to the midshipman. 'Hurry along, sailor!'

A shout from the stairway and Lossow appeared, covered in dust, grinning and holding a piece of paper. 'The message.'

Sharpe grabbed the boy. 'Stop everything. Send that!'

'But, sir!' The midshipman saw Sharpe's face, decided not to argue.

'Hurry!'

Captain Charles looked annoyed but reluctant to interfere, and watched as the boy clattered the ropes up and down.

'I'm just cancelling the last message, sir. Then I'll send yours.'

Another shot boomed overhead, sounding like a giant barrel being rolled fast across floorboards. It left a wind behind it, hot and violent, and Harper glanced at Sharpe and raised his eyebrows. Lossow looked at the battery, at the rolling cloud of dirty smoke, and pursed his lips.

'They've got the range.'

'The boy's doing his best,' Sharpe said irritably. 'What was the delay?'

'Damned politics.' Lossow spread his hands. 'The Spanish insisted on the message saying that the gold was Spanish. They insisted on protesting that they did not want British help. Cox is angry, Kearsey's saying his prayers, and your Spanish friends are sharpening their swords. Ah! At last.'

The black, tarred sheep bladders leaped up on the ropes, quivered for a second, and fell. The boy danced between the halliards, hauling away number by number, the obscene black bags vibrating in the breeze as they jerked up and down.

'Sir?' Harper was watching the battery. 'Sir!'

'Down!'

The ball, twenty-four pounds of iron, struck only a glancing blow on one of the crosstrees. The telegraph was well made, jointed and bolted, and as the French ball spun off into the unknown it ripped itself completely from its base like a tree torn bodily by a hurricane. The boy, holding on to a rope, was spun into the air, screaming until another halliard whiplashed round his neck and tore his head horribly from his shoulders. His blood sprayed the four men falling backwards, and then the mast, still unbroken, pounded back on to the ramparts, killing Charles instantly, broke itself in a great fracture, bounced like a falling cane, and stopped still.

'Sweet Jesus.' Harper stood up. 'Are you all right, sir?'

'Yes.' Sharpe's shoulder hurt like the devil. 'Where's the boy?'

The Sergeant pointed to the head. 'Rest of him's over the wall, sir. Poor wee thing.'

Lossow swore in German, stood up, flinched as he put his weight on his left leg. Sharpe looked at him. 'Are you hurt?'

'Just a bruise.' Lossow saw the midshipman's head. 'Good God.' He knelt by Charles, felt for a pulse, and opened one of the Captain's eyelids. 'Dead, poor fellow.'

Harper looked over the ramparts, at the drifting smoke. 'Just four shots. That's good shooting.' There was a reluctant respect in his voice.

Lossow stood up, wiped blood from his hands. 'We must get out of here!'

Sharpe turned to him. 'We must persuade Cox to let us out.'

'*Ja*. Not easy, my friend.'

Harper kicked the fallen beam. 'Perhaps they can rig another telegraph, sir?'

Sharpe shrugged. 'And who works it? Maybe, I don't know.' He glanced at the battery, its embrasure plugged, and he knew that the French gunners would be celebrating. They deserved it. He doubted if the gun would fire again, not today; the iron barrels had a limited life and the gun had achieved its purpose. 'Come on. Let's see Cox.'

'You don't sound hopeful, my friend?'

Sharpe turned round, blood flecking his uniform, and his face grim. 'We'll get out. With or without him, we'll get out.'

CHAPTER 20

Light, like carved silver, slashed the cathedral's gloom, slanted across the crouching grey pillars, splintered off brass and paint, drowned the votive candles that burned before the statues, inched its way over the broad, worn flagstones as the sun moved higher, and Sharpe waited. A priest, lost in the depths of the choir, mumbled beyond the window light, and Sharpe saw Harper cross himself.

'What day is it?'

'Sunday, sir.'

'Is that Mass?'

'Yes, sir.'

'You want to go?'

'It'll wait.'

Lossow's heels clicked in the side aisle; he came from behind a pillar, blinked in the sunlight. 'Where is he?' He disappeared again.

Christ, thought Sharpe, Christ and a thousand deaths. Damn the bloody French, damn the bloody gunner, and he might as well have stayed in the warm bed with his arms round the girl. Footsteps sounded in the doorway and he swivelled anxiously, but it was only a squad of bare-headed Portuguese soldiers, muskets slung, who dipped their fingers in the holy water and clattered up the aisle to the priest and his service.

Cox had not been at his headquarters; he was on the ramparts, they were told. So the three had hurried there and Cox had gone. Now he was said to be visiting the magazine, so they waited, and the light shaped the dust into silver bars and the muffled responses got lost somewhere in the high stone ceiling, and still Cox had not arrived. Sharpe slammed his scabbard on the floor, hurting his shoulder, so he cursed again.

'Amen to that, sir.' Harper had infinitely more patience.

Sharpe felt ashamed. This was Harper's religion. 'I'm sorry.'

The Irishman grinned. 'Wouldn't worry, sir. It doesn't offend me and if it offends Him then He's plenty of opportunity to punish you.'

I'm in love with her, Sharpe thought, God damn and blast it. And if they were delayed another night, that would mean another night, and if it were a week, another week, but they had to move, and soon, for within two days the French would tie Almeida in a ring of earthworks and infantry. But leaving Almeida meant leaving her, and he hacked down again with the scabbard so that Lossow reappeared.

'What is it?'

'Nothing.'

Just one more night, he thought, and he lifted his eyes up to the huge rood that hung in the grey shadows. Is that so much to ask? Just one more night, and we can leave at dawn tomorrow. Dawn is the time to say goodbye, not dusk, and just one more night? There was the creak of the cathedral door, the rattle of heels, and Cox came in with a crowd of officers.

Sharpe stood up. 'Sir!'

Cox appeared not to hear him and headed straight over the floor towards the crypt steps, the chatter of his officers smothering the muted drone of the Mass at the far end of the cathedral.

'Lossow!' Sharpe called. 'Come on!'

Portuguese soldiers stopped them at the top of the steps and stood silently as they pulled felt slippers over their boots. Sharpe fumbled with the drawstrings, his left arm stiff, but then the slippers were on and the three men, their heels protected against sparking on stone, went down into the crypt. The light was dim and only a handful of lanterns, their horn panes dulling the candle flames, flickered on block-like tombs. There was no sign of Cox or his officers, but at the far end a leather curtain swayed in a doorway.

'Come on.' Sharpe led them to the curtain, forced its stiff weight aside, and gasped.

'Good God.' Lossow paused at the head of a short flight of steps that dropped into a dark cavern. 'Good God.'

The lower crypt was jammed with barrels, piled to the low, arched ceiling, row after row of them, reaching back into a gloom that was relieved only by an occasional horn lantern, double-shielded, and to right and left were further aisles, and when Sharpe turned, at the foot of the stairs, he saw that the steps came down in the middle of the room and the gigantic quantity of powder in front was mirrored behind. He whistled softly.

'This way.'

Cox had disappeared down the aisle and they hurried after, looking at the rotund barrels above them, awed by the sheer destructive power of the gunpowder that had been stacked in the deep vault. Captain Charles, before he died, had said that Almeida could last as long as its powder, and that could be months, Sharpe thought, and then he tried to imagine a French shell smashing through the stonework and sparking the barrels. It could not happen. The floors were too thick, but all the same he looked up and was glad to see the broad buttresses, hugely strong, that arched beneath a floor that could have resisted a thousand French shells, and then still be strong.

Cox was at the very end of the vault, listening to a Portuguese officer, and the conversation was urgent. It was part in Portuguese, part in English, and Sharpe could hear enough to understand the problem. Water was seeping into the crypt, not much, but enough to have soaked two bales of musket ammunition that were stored there. Cox swung round.

'Who put it here?' There was silence. 'We must move it!' He dropped into Portuguese, then saw Sharpe. 'Captain!'

'Sir?'

'In my headquarters! Wait for me there!'

'Sir...'

Cox whirled angrily. 'I have enough problems, Sharpe! Damned ammunition stored in the wrong place! It shouldn't be here anyway! Put it upstairs!' He went back into Portuguese, waved his arms, pointed upstairs.

Harper touched Sharpe's elbow. 'Come on, sir.'

Sharpe turned, but Cox called him again. 'Captain!'

'Sir?'

'Where is the gold?' The faces of the Portuguese officers seemed to be accusing Sharpe.

'In our quarters, sir.'

'Wrong place, Sharpe, wrong place. I'll send men and it will be put in my headquarters.'

'Sir!' But Lossow grabbed him, took him away, and Cox turned back to the damp walls and the problem of moving thousands of rounds of musket cartridges up to the cathedral floor.

Sharpe resisted the German's pull. 'I will not give up the gold.'

'I know, I know. Listen, my friend. You go to the headquarters and I will go back. I promise you, no one will touch the gold. No one.'

Lossow's face was deep in shadow, but by the tone of his voice Sharpe knew the gold was safe. He turned to Harper. 'Go with him. On my orders no one, but no one, is to go near that gold. You understand?'

'Yes, sir. You'll be careful in the street?'

'They're full of soldiers. I'll be fine. Now go.'

The two went ahead. Sharpe called after them. 'Patrick?'

'Sir?'

'Look after the girl.'

The big Irishman nodded. 'You know I will, sir.'

The cathedral bells reverberated with noon, the sun was almost directly overhead, and Sharpe walked slowly across the main Plaza behind two men pushing a barrel of gunpowder. The big French gun, as he had thought, had done its job and was silent, but out there, beyond the spreading ramparts and beyond the killing-ground, the French would be digging their trenches, making new batteries, and the oxen would be hauling the giant guns towards the siege. Almeida was about to become the war, the point of effort, and when it fell, there was nothing between Masséna and the sea, except the gold, and suddenly Sharpe stopped, utterly still, and stared at the Portuguese soldiers who came and went by the cathedral. The gold, Hogan had said, was more important than men or horses. The General, Sharpe remembered, had spoken of delaying the enemy, bringing him to battle, but none of that effort would save Portugal. Only the gold. He looked at the castle, with its granite masonry and the stump of the telegraph jutting a brief shadow over the battlement, and then at the cathedral with its carved saints, and despite the sun, the blistering heat, he felt cold. Was it more important than this? Than a town and its defenders? Out there, beyond the houses, were all the paraphernalia of a scientific defence. The great grey defences of this town, the star-shape of glacis and covered way, of town ditch and counter-guard, of bastion and battery, and he shivered. He was not afraid of decisions; they were his job and he despised men who feared to make them. But in the sudden moment, in the middle of the great Plaza, he felt the fear.

He waited through the long afternoon, listening to the bells of Sunday, the last peaceful day Almeida would know in a long time, and still Cox did not come. Once, he heard a Portuguese battery open fire, but there was no reply, and the town slumbered again, waiting for its moment. The door opened and Sharpe, half asleep in the big chair, started to his feet. Teresa's father stood there with half a smile. He closed the door silently.

'She was never harmed?'

'No.'

The man laughed. 'You are clever.'

'She was clever.'

Cesar Moreno nodded. 'She is. Like her mother.' He sounded sad, and Sharpe felt sorrow for him. The man looked up. 'Why did she side with you?'

Sharpe shook his head. 'She didn't. She's against the French.'

'Ah, the passion of youth.' He came nearer, walking slowly. 'I hear your men won't release the gold?' Sharpe shrugged and the Spaniard followed the gesture with a smile. 'Do you despise me?'

'No.'

'I'm an old man, given sudden power. I'm not like

Sánchez.' He stopped, thinking about the great Partisan of Castile. 'He's young; he loves it all. I just want peace.' He smiled as if embarrassed by the words.

'Can you buy it?'

'What a foolish question. Of course! We haven't given up, you know.'

'We?'

'El Católico and I.' He shrugged, traced a finger through the dust on the table.

It occurred to Sharpe that El Católico may not have given up, but Cesar Moreno, the widower and father, was making sure he had supporters on both sides.

The old man looked at him. 'Did you sleep with her?'

'Yes.'

He smiled again, a little ruefully, and wiped the dust off his hand. 'Many men would envy you.' Sharpe made no reply and Moreno looked at him fiercely. 'She'll not come to any harm, will she.' It was not a question; he knew.

'Not from me.'

'Ah. Walk carefully, Captain Sharpe. He's better with the sword than you.'

'I will walk carefully.'

The Spaniard turned, looked at the varnished pictures on the wall that told of happier times, plumper days, and said quietly, 'He won't let you take the gold. You know that?'

'He?'

'Brigadier Cox.'

'I didn't know.'

Moreno turned back. 'It is a pleasure to watch you, Captain. We all knew Kearsey was a fool, a pleasant fool, but not what do you say – movement? In the head?'

'I know what you mean.'

'Then you came and we thought the English had sent a strong fool after an intelligent fool. You fooled us!' He laughed. It was difficult to make jokes in a strange language. 'No, he won't let you. Cox is an honourable man, like Kearsey, and they know the gold is ours. How will you beat that, friend?'

'Watch me.' Sharpe smiled.

'I will. And my daughter?'

'She'll come back to you. Very soon.'

'And that makes you sad?'

Sharpe nodded and Moreno gave Sharpe a shrewd look that reminded the Rifleman that once this man had been powerful. Could be again.

Moreno's voice was gentle. 'Perhaps one day?'

'But you hope not.'

Teresa's father nodded and smiled. 'I hope not, but she is headstrong. I watched her, from the day I betrothed her to El Católico, and knew one day she would spit in my face, and his. She waited her moment, like you.'

'And now he waits his?'

'Yes. Go carefully.' He went to the door, waved a hand. 'We will meet again.'

Sharpe sat down, poured a glass of wine, and shook his head. He was tired, to the bone, and his shoulder ached and he wondered if his left arm would ever move free again, and the shadows lengthened on the carpet till he slept, not hearing the evening gun, or the door opening.

'Sharpe!'

God Almighty! He jerked upright. 'Sir?'

Cox strode over the floor, trailing staff officers and paper. 'What the devil's happening, Sharpe?'

'Happening, sir?'

'Your men won't release the gold!'

Kearsey came through the door and with him, magnificently uniformed, a Spanish Colonel. It took Sharpe a few seconds, seconds of focusing on the gold lace, the looping silver, to realize it was El Católico. The face had not changed. The powerful eyes, the slight glint of humour, the face of an enemy.

He turned back to Cox. 'I'm sorry, sir?'

'Are you deaf, Sharpe? The gold! Where is it?'

'Don't know, sir. Waited here, sir. As ordered, sir.'

Cox grunted, picked up a piece of paper, looked at it, and let it drop. 'I've made a decision.'

'Yes, sir. A decision, sir.' Sharpe had adopted his erstwhile sergeant's manner, always useful when faced by senior officers, and especially useful when he wanted to think of other things than the immediate conversation. Cox glanced up suspiciously.

'I'm sorry, Sharpe. I only have your word for it, and Lossow's. The gold is Spanish, obviously Spanish, and Colonel Jovellanos is an accredited representative of the government of Spain.' He gestured at El Católico, who smiled and bowed. Sharpe looked at the Partisan leader in his immaculate finery.

'Yes, sir. Accredited representative, sir!'

The bastard must be handy with a pen, he thought, and it suddenly occurred to him that one of the fat coins would make a superb seal, pressed into the red wax with the ornate coat of arms downwards. He wondered how El Católico had obliterated the writing round the edge of the coin, but then thought how he would do it himself with a file, or by hammering the soft gold flat.

Cox sighed. 'You will deliver the gold to Colonel Jovellanos and his men, and you will do it quickly. Is that understood?'

'Yes, sir. Understood!' He was standing ramrod straight, staring at a point just above Cox's head.

The Brigadier sighed. 'I don't think it is, Captain.' Cox sat down wearily, pulled a sheet of paper towards him, uncapped his ink, and took a fresh goose-quill. 'At ten o'clock tomorrow morning, Captain, twenty-seventh August 1810.' He was writing quickly, paraphrasing the formal order as the quill scratched on the paper. 'A detachment of my troops will take charge of the bullion . . .' He paused; the room listened to the scrape of the pen. '. . . Led by . . .' Cox looked round the room, found one of his officers. '. . . Colonel Barrios.' Barrios nodded, a formal gesture. 'You, Colonel, will deliver the gold to Colonel Jovellanos, who will be ready to leave at the north gate.' El Católico nodded, clicked his heels for attention. Cox looked up. 'Colonel?'

El Católico smiled. His voice was at its silkiest. 'I was hoping to persuade you, sir, to allow myself and some of my men to stay and help in your gallant defence.'

Sharpe could not believe it. The bastard. He had as much intention of staying as Sharpe had of handing over the gold.

Cox smiled, blinked with pleasure. 'That's uncommonly

decent of you, Colonel.' He gestured at the paper. 'Does it change anything?'

'Only that the gold, sir, could be handed to Señor Moreno, or one of my Lieutenants.'

'Of course, of course.' Cox dipped the quill, scratched out some words. 'To the Spanish contingent of Colonel Jovellanos.' He raised an eyebrow to El Católico. 'I think that covers it.'

El Católico bowed. 'Thank you, sir.' He shot a look of triumph at Sharpe. 'And, sir?' El Católico bowed again. 'Could the transfer be tonight?'

Sharpe held his breath, let it out slowly as Cox spoke. The Brigadier was frowning, looking at the paper.

'Ten o'clock will do, Colonel.' Sharpe suspected he did not want to cross out the top lines of the closely written order. Cox smiled at El Católico, gestured at Sharpe. 'After all, Captain Sharpe can hardly leave!'

El Católico smiled politely. 'As you say, sir.'

So what was the bastard playing at? Why the suggestion that he might stay on? Sharpe stared at the tall Spaniard, trying to fathom the motive. Could it be just to curry favour with Cox? Sharpe doubted it; the Spaniard was getting most of what he wanted without trying. Except that El Católico did want one thing more. Sharpe thought of the dark hair on the pillow, the slim body on the stiff, white linen sheets. The Spaniard wanted the girl, and his revenge, and if it could not be tonight, then El Católico would stay on till it was accomplished.

Sharpe was suddenly aware that Cox had spoken his name. 'Sir?'

The Brigadier had pulled another sheet of paper forward. 'At ten o'clock tomorrow morning, Captain, your Company will join my defences on the south wall.' The pen splattered ink on the paper.

'Pardon, sir?'

Cox looked up from the paper, irritated. 'You heard me, Sharpe! You join the garrison. Captain Lossow leaves. I don't need cavalry, but you stay. No infantry can hope to escape now. Understand?'

God in heaven! 'Yes, sir.'

The cathedral clock began chiming. Kearsey put a hand on Sharpe's elbow. 'I'm sorry, Sharpe.'

Sharpe nodded, listening to the bell. He was oblivious of Kearsey's concern, of El Católico's triumph, of Cox's preoccupation. Ten o'clock, and all not well. The decision had been forced on him, but it was still his decision. The last echo of the last note died flatly away, and Sharpe wondered if any bell would ever ring, ever again, in the grey-starred, ill-starred fortress town.

CHAPTER 21

'We're stuck. That's the problem. We're stuck.'

'Pardon, sir?' Sergeant Harper was waiting for Sharpe outside Cox's headquarters.

'Nothing.' Sharpe stood there, conscious of Patrick Harper's worried look. The Sergeant probably thought that his wound was going bad, poisoning the blood and sending insane vapours into his head. 'Are you alone?'

'No, sir. Private Roach, Daniel Hagman, and three Germans.'

Sharpe saw the others waiting in the shadows. The small, squat German Sergeant was there and Harper jerked a thumb at him.

'That's Helmet, sir.'

'You mean Helmut?'

'That's what I said, sir. He's a one-man army. Are you all right, sir?'

'Yes.'

Sharpe still stood on the steps, his escort waiting below, and fingered a piece of his sword's silver-wire hilt-wrapping that had worked itself loose. He made a mental note to have it soldered flat when they were back with the Battalion, and then marvelled that the mind could dwell on such a triviality at a moment like this.

Harper coughed. 'Are you ready, sir?'

'What? Yes.' He still did not move. He stared at the cathedral.

Patrick Harper tried again. 'Home, sir?'

'No. Over there.' He pointed at the cathedral.

'Yes, sir. Anything you say, sir.'

They walked across the Plaza, lit by the moon, and Sharpe pulled his thoughts back to the present.

'Is the girl all right?'

Harper nodded. 'Lovely, sir. She's fought all day.'

'Fought?'

The Irishman grinned. 'Helmet taught her how to use a sabre.'

Sharpe laughed. It sounded like Teresa. He looked at the small German Sergeant and smiled at the man's curious walk: the legs bent apart like a lyre-frame, the stocky, immensely strong body scarcely moving as the legs pushed it forward.

Harper saw Sharpe's change of mood. 'We reckon you could just point Helmet at anything, sir, and he'd chew his way through. Houses, walls, regiments. They'd all have a wee hole, just his shape, straight through them.' Harper laughed. 'Bloody good with a sabre.'

Sharpe thought of the girl, knew that El Católico had another score to settle, more personal than the gold, and was glad of his escort, of Harper with his seven-barrelled gun. 'What happened at the house today?'

Harper laughed. 'Not a lot, sir. They turned up for the gold, so they did, and first we couldn't speak the Portuguese and then Mr Lossow couldn't understand their English, and then Helmet growled a bit, chewed up some furniture, and the lads put on their spikes, and the Portuguese went home.'

'Where's the girl now?'

'Still there, sir.' Harper grinned at him, reassuringly. 'Down in the kitchen with the lads, having her weapons training. She'd make a good recruit.'

'And Mr Knowles?'

'Enjoying himself, sir. All round defence, sir, and keep your eyes open, and Mr Knowles doing the rounds every ten minutes. They won't get in. What's happening to us, sir?'

Sharpe shrugged, looked up at the dark windows of the houses. 'We're supposed to hand the gold over tomorrow. To El Católico.'

'And are we, sir?'

'What do you think?'

Harper grinned, said nothing, and then one of the Germans crouched, sabre held up, and the group stopped. One of the few Portuguese civilians left in the town, hurrying from an alleyway, shrank into the wall and babbled incoherently at the odd group of soldiers who bristled with swords and guns and were looking at him as if sizing him for slaughter.

'All right,' Sharpe said. 'On we go.'

By the cathedral doors Sharpe could see the dark shapes of sentries guarding the ammunition. He crossed to them, his escort's heels echoing over the vast stone square, and the Portuguese guards snapped to attention, saluted, as Sharpe turned to the three Germans.

'Stay here.' Helmut nodded. 'Hagman, Roach. Stay with them. Come on, Sergeant.'

He stared over the Plaza before opening the small door that pierced the huge wooden gate into the cathedral. Was there a dark shape on the far side? Hovering by a corner of an alleyway? He suspected the Partisans were scouting the town, looking for him, but nothing would happen till they reached the dark warren of streets down the hill. He went inside.

The candles had come into their own, throwing small, wavering pools of yellow light on patches of the great stone vault. The tiny red glow of the eternal presence flickered at the far end, and Sharpe waited while Harper dipped a casual finger and crossed himself.

The Irishman stepped alongside Sharpe. 'What are we doing, sir?'

'I don't know.' Sharpe chewed his bottom lip, stared at the small lights, then walked towards the cluster of lanterns that marked the steps to the vault. More sentries stiffened as they approached and Sharpe waved them down. 'Slippers, Sergeant.'

There was a small pile of ammunition by the head of the steps, put there for the soldiers who came to fetch it for the ramparts to save them the bother of pulling on the felt slippers. Sharpe guessed that about twenty men would work the magazine, bringing up the barrels, living their days in the damp, cold air of the cathedral's underworld. Harper saw Sharpe staring at an opened bale of cartridges.

'There's more by that door, sir.'

'More?'

Harper nodded, pointed at a door that flanked the great

processional gates. 'There, sir. Bloody great pile of cartridges. Did you want some?'

Sharpe shook his head, peered into the gloom, and saw that against the door there were a dozen bales of the paper cartridges. He guessed they were placed so that infantry battalions could replenish swiftly without getting in the way of the men who brought up the huge powderkegs. He turned back to the crypt. Planks had been laid down the stairs, two feet apart, so that the barrels could be rolled up easily.

'Come on.'

They went down the stairs, into the intermittent light of the horn lanterns, and Sharpe saw that the rest of the garrison's supply of small arms ammunition was now stacked either side of the vault, forming a corridor to the leather-curtained steps of the deep crypt. He padded down the corridor and knelt by the curtain. Two thicknesses of stiff leather, weighted at the bottom, a precaution in case there was a small explosion in the first vault. The stiff leather could soak up a minor blast, protect the massive dump of gunpowder beneath, and Harper watched, astonished, as Sharpe drew his sword and cut off the weights, clenching his teeth as he sawed through the leather.

'What the hell, sir?'

Sharpe looked up at him. 'Don't ask. Where are the sentries?'

'Upstairs.' The Sergeant knelt beside him. 'Sir?'

Sharpe stopped the desperate cutting, looked at the broad, friendly face. 'Don't you trust me?'

Harper was offended, even hurt, and he bent past Sharpe, took hold of the torn part of the curtain in one hand, the upper leather in the other, and pulled. As a demonstration of strength it was remarkable, the veins standing out in his neck, his whole body rigid with effort as the double-thick leather peeled apart, silently and slowly, and Sharpe helped it with the sword blade until, after thirty seconds, Harper leaned back with a grunt and in his hand was the separated bottom two inches of the curtain with its heavy lead weights sewn into the hem.

'Of course I bloody trust you. Just tell me.' The Irishman's anger was real.

Sharpe shook his head. 'I will. Later. Come on.'

Upstairs, taking off the slippers, Sharpe nodded at the candles.

'Funny keeping them alight.'

Harper shook his head. 'They're a hell of a way from the vault, sir.' His voice showed that he was slightly mollified, still insulted, but ready to be friendly. 'Anyway. It's what they call insurance, isn't it?'

'Insurance?'

'Sure.' The huge head nodded. 'A few prayers never did any army any harm.' He stood up. 'Where now, sir?'

To a bakery. The soldiers, British and German, were mystified as Sharpe traced a gutter away from the cathedral to a building not far from the north gate. He tried the door, but it was well locked, and Harper gestured him to one side.

'Helmet? Door.'

The German Sergeant nodded, moved ponderously at the barrier, grunted as he hit it, and then turned with what passed as a smile as the wood splintered away in front of him.

'Told you, sir,' Harper said. 'Any provosts about?'

'If there are any, kill them,' Sharpe said.

'Sir! You hear that, Helmet? Kill the provosts!'

It was pitch black inside but Sharpe felt his way over the floor, past a table that must once have been the counter for the shop, and found huge brick ovens, cold now, hunched at the back of the bakery. He went back to the street, empty of Portuguese provosts or patrols.

They climbed the shallow ramp to the first wall and stopped by the battlements. Sentries lined the rampart, bunched near the gleaming batteries that had been dug into the wall's heart and, in front of them, crouched like grey fingers, were the outer defences, gently sloping, deceptive, filled with Portuguese troops whose fires cast strange glows on the deep ditches that were unseen by the enemy. Further out, beyond the dark strip of earth that was cleared of cover so that the defenders could tear the heart out of an assault, Sharpe could see French fires, some half hidden, and from the far darkness came the occasional ring of a pickaxe, the thump of earth being pried loose.

He jumped, startled by a sudden report, and realized that

the Portuguese were sending the occasional missile in the hope of disturbing the French engineers. Night was when the batteries were dug, trenches extended, but the time was not yet right for the Portuguese troops to sally out of the defences and raid the French works in the night-time assault of bayonets in enemy trenches. The French were not close enough yet. A siege worked to a timetable, understood by both sides, and this was just the beginning when the besiegers' ring was not yet complete and the fortress town was at the height of its strength and pride.

He led the way on the rampart's top to the north gate, and Harper watched his Captain stare moodily down at the sentries, the vast gate, the companies of infantry who lived between the granite traps to guard the entrance of the town. Harper guessed what was in Sharpe's mind. 'No way out, sir.'

'No.' The last small chance gone. 'No. Back to the house.'

They went down steps and found a street that went towards the lower town and Sharpe stayed away from the dark houses with their blind windows and shut-up doors. Their boots rang cold on the cobbles, as they peered into alleyways, up the cross streets, and once or twice Harper thought he saw a shadow that was too irregular to be part of a building, but he could not be sure. Almeida was quiet, eerie. Sharpe drew his sword.

'Sir?' Harper's voice was worried. 'You wouldn't be planning, would you, to...'

They had forgotten the rooftops, but Helmut, alerted by a sound, had turned, looked up, and the man who dropped on him screamed terribly as the sabre pierced him. Sharpe went right, Harper left, and the street was suddenly full of men with swords, dark clothes, and the dying man's pathetic whimpers. Hagman was using his bayonet, backed against a wall and letting El Católico's men come to him, and Sharpe, by the same wall, twisted desperately to one side as a rapier blade came at him and missed his waist by inches. He parried a second man with the sword, remembered El Católico calling it a butcher's weapon, and, forsaking technique for anger he hacked with it once and felt the edge hit something, bite, and slide free. He turned back to the first attacker, but

Roach was there, massive and ponderous, pounding the life from the man with his rifle-butt, and Sharpe twisted back, flickered his sword out in a blind lunge and felt it parried, pushed aside, and he leaped back, knowing the attack was coming, tripped on the dead man and fell backwards.

The fall saved his life. The seven-barrelled gun, held against the far wall, fizzed as the spark lit the pan and then blasted a channel clear across the street. The sound, magnified by the close walls, rang in Sharpe's head, but he saw three men staggering, one down, and Roach pulled him to his feet and he went forward, into the confusion of the blast, and chopped down on one man, kicked a second, and suddenly the four British were together, across the street, and the Spanish were caught between them and the three men of the King's German Legion.

The Germans had done well. The sabre was their weapon and they fought the swordsmen with their own skills. Sharpe knew he had to learn the art of the sword but this was no time to try. He hacked forward, his left arm hurting but the right chopping diagonally down, left and right, pushing opponents to either side, where Roach and Hagman bayoneted them, and the Partisans, their surprise gone, began to run, to slip past the Germans and escape into the night.

Helmut growled. With these odds there was no point in trying to kill, and he had small chance of beating the long rapiers with their delicate finesse. He used his curved sabre in short, economic strokes, going for the eyes, always the eyes, because a man will run before he loses his sight, and Helmut sent his attackers reeling, one after the other, hands clasped to their faces and blood showing between the fingers. The Spanish had had enough; they ran, but the short Sergeant dropped his sabre, grabbed one by the arm, hugged him like a bear, and then, quickly releasing him, swung him against a wall with all his force. It sounded like a sack of turnips falling from the top of a barn on to a stone floor.

Harper grinned at him, wiped blood from his sword-bayonet. 'Very nice, Helmet.'

There was a shout from down the street, the flare of torches, and the six men whirled round, weapons raised, but Sharpe ordered them to wait. A Portuguese patrol, muskets ready, pounded towards them, and Sharpe saw the officer leading with a drawn sword. The officer stopped, suspicion on his face, and then grinned, spread his arms, and laughed.

'Richard Sharpe! Of all the devils! What are you doing?'

Sharpe laughed, wiped the blood off his blade, and pushed it into the scabbard. He turned to Harper. 'Sergeant, meet Tom Garrard. Once a Sergeant in the Thirty-third, now a Lieutenant in the Portuguese army.' He took Garrard's hand, shook it. 'You bastard. How are you?'

Garrard beamed at him, turned to Harper. 'We were Sergeants together. Christ, Dick, it must be bloody years. I remember you blowing the face off that bloody little heathen! It's good to see you. A bloody Captain! What's the world coming to?' He gave Sharpe a salute and laughed.

'It's years since anyone called me Dick. You well?'

'Chipper. Couldn't be better.' He jerked a thumb at his men. 'Good lads, these. Fight like us. Well, well, well. You remember that girl in Sering? Nancy?'

Sharpe's men looked at Garrard curiously. It was a year since the Portuguese government had asked the British to re-organize their army and one of the changes, started by the Englishman, Marshal Beresford, who now commanded the Portuguese troops, was to offer commissions to experienced British Sergeants so that the raw, untrained Portuguese troops were given officers who knew how to fight. It was good, Garrard said, and working well, and he looked at Harper.

'You should join up, Sergeant.'

Harper grinned, shook his head. 'I'll stay with him.'

'You could do worse.' Garrard looked at Sharpe. 'Trouble?'

'It's over.'

Garrard sheathed his sword. 'Anything I can do?'

'Open a gate for us. Tonight.'

Garrard looked at him shrewdly. 'How many of you?'

'Two hundred and fifty. Cavalry and us.'

'Christ, mate. That's impossible. I thought you meant just you seven only.' He stopped, grinned. 'You with this gold?'

'That's us. You know about it?'

'God Almighty! Bloody orders from everyone to stop

the gold leaving. We didn't even know there was any gold here.' He shook his head. 'I'm sorry, Dick. Can't help.'

Sharpe grinned. 'Doesn't matter. We'll manage.'

'You will.' He grinned again. 'I heard about Talavera. That was bloody well done. It really was.'

Sharpe pointed at Harper. 'He was with me.'

Garrard nodded to the Irishman. 'Proud of you.' He looked at his men. 'We'll do it next time, won't we, lads?' The Portuguese smiled back, nodded shyly to Sharpe.

'We must go, Tom. Work to do.' The farewells were said, promises to look each other up, that might or might not ever be kept, and Sharpe accepted Garrard's offer for the Portuguese soldiers to clear the bodies off the street.

'Go easy, Dick!'

'And you.' Sharpe looked at Harper. 'Did you see El Católico?'

The Sergeant shook his head. 'There were enough of them, sir. But not him. Perhaps he doesn't do his own dirty work?'

Then where? Sharpe looked up at the roofs. The rooftops. He turned to the Sergeant.

'Do we have sentries on the roof?'

'The roof?' Alarm showed on the big face. 'Sweet Jesus!'

'Come on!' They began running. Not again, thought Sharpe. Please, God, not again. He remembered Josefina lying in the blood-stained sheets; he ran faster, the sword in his hand. 'Open up!'

The sentries turned, startled, and pushed open the courtyard gate. There was the smell of horses, torchlight, and he leapt up the steps, banged open the kitchen door, and there was the Company, eating, the firelight, candles, and Teresa, unharmed, at the end of the table. He breathed a sigh of relief, shook his head, and Lossow came over the floor.

'Welcome back! What is it?'

Sharpe pointed to the ceiling. 'Upstairs!' He was trying to catch his breath. 'Upstairs. The bastard's waiting upstairs.'

CHAPTER 22

Lossow shook his head. 'He's not here.'

'He's close.'

The German shrugged. 'We've searched.' They had looked in every room, every cupboard, even up chimneys and on the thick-tiled roof, but there was no sign of El Católico or his men.

Sharpe was not satisfied. 'The other houses?'

'Yes, my friend.' Lossow was patient. The Germans had opened up houses either side, to sleep in glorious space and comfort, and all had been searched. The cavalryman took Sharpe's elbow. 'Come and eat.'

The Company, those not on guard, were in the kitchen, where a pot bubbled on the flames. Parry Jenkins lifted it clear with a pot-hook. 'Real stew, sir.'

The gold was locked in a store-room with a barrel of wine, Sergeant McGovern in grim charge, and Sharpe glanced at the door as he spooned down the meat and vegetables. Behind the padlock and bolts was the dragon's hoard and Sharpe remembered the stories well. If a man stole buried gold, the dragon would take its vengeance; and there would be only one way to avoid that revenge: by killing the dragon. The attack in the street, only half pressed home, was not the end of the matter. Sharpe guessed that El Católico had parties throughout the small town looking for the Riflemen, but the dragon would want to be there at the death, to see the agony.

Lossow watched Sharpe eat.

'You think he'll come tonight?'

Sharpe nodded. 'He offered to stay on tomorrow, to help the defence, but that's just insurance. He wants it over with; he wants to get out before the French seal this place tight.'

'Then he wants to leave tomorrow.'

Knowles shrugged. 'Perhaps he won't come, sir. He's getting the gold, isn't he?'

Sharpe grinned. 'He thinks so.' He glanced at Teresa. 'No, he'll come.' He grinned at the girl. 'Major Kearsey thinks you should go back.'

She raised her eyebrows, said nothing. Before Sharpe had left Cox's headquarters Kearsey had taken him aside, pleaded that Teresa should be returned to her father. Sharpe had nodded. 'Send her father at ten o'clock tomorrow, sir.' Now he watched her. 'What do you want to do?'

She looked at him, almost with a challenge. 'What will you do?'

Sharpe's men, and some of the Germans, were listening to the conversation. Sharpe jerked his head at the door. 'Come into the small room. We'll talk.'

Harper took a jug of wine, Lossow and Knowles their curiosity. The girl followed them. She paused outside the small sitting-room door and put cool fingers on his hand. 'Are you going to win, Richard?'

He smiled. 'Yes.' If he did not, then she was dead. El Católico would want revenge on her.

Inside the small room they pulled off dust-covers and sat in comfortable chairs. Sharpe was tired, bone-tired, and his shoulder was aching with a deep, throbbing pain. He trimmed a candle wick, waited for the flame to grow, and talked softly.

'You all know what's happening. We're ordered to surrender the gold tomorrow. Captain Lossow is ordered to leave; we are ordered to stay.'

He had already told them as they searched the houses, but he wanted to go over it, to look for the flaws, because he still hoped that the decision would prove unnecessary.

Lossow stirred in his chair. 'So it's all over?' He frowned, not believing his own question.

'No. Whether Cox likes it or not, we go.'

'And the gold?' Teresa's voice was steady.

'Goes with us.'

By some strange instinct they all relaxed, as if the statement were enough. 'The question is,' Sharpe went on, 'how?'

There was silence in the room. Harper looked asleep, his

eyes closed, but Sharpe guessed that the Irishman was way ahead of the others. Knowles pummelled his chair-arm in frustration. 'If only we could get a message to the General!'

'We're too late. Time's run out.'

Sharpe did not expect them to provide an answer, but he wanted them to think through the steps, to know the argument, so that when he provided the solution, they would agree.

Lossow leaned forward into the candlelight. 'Cox won't let you go. He thinks we're stealing the gold.'

'He's right.' Teresa shrugged.

Knowles was frowning. 'Do we break out, sir? Make a run for it?'

Sharpe thought of the granite-faced ditches, the rows of cannon, the bent tunnels in the gateways with their portcullises and grim-faced sentries.

'No, Robert.'

Lossow grinned. 'I know. Murder Brigadier Cox.'

Sharpe did not smile. 'His second in command would back up his orders.'

'Good God! I was joking!' Lossow stared at Sharpe, suddenly convinced of the Rifleman's seriousness.

Somewhere a dog barked, perhaps in the French camp, and Sharpe knew that if the British survived this campaign, if he did his duty this night, then it would all have to be done again. Portugal reconquered, the border fortresses retaken, the French beaten not just from Spain but from all Europe. Lossow must have mistaken his expression for despair.

The German spoke softly. 'Have you thought of abandoning the gold?'

'No.' It was not true. He took a deep breath. 'I can't tell you why, I don't know how, but the difference between victory and failure depends on that gold. We have to take it out.' He nodded at Teresa. 'She's right. We are stealing the gold, on Wellington's instructions, and that's why there are no explicit orders. The Spanish' – he shrugged apologetically at the girl – 'God knows they're difficult allies. Think how much worse if they had written proof of this?' He leaned back. 'I can only tell you what I was told. The gold is more important than men, horses, regiments, or guns. If we lose it the war is over; we'll all go home, or more likely end up as French prisoners.'

'And if you do take it?' Teresa was shivering.

'Then the British will stay in Portugal.' He shrugged. 'I can't explain that, but it's true. And if we stay in Portugal, then next year we'll be back in Spain. The gold will go with us.'

Knowles snapped his fingers. 'Kill El Católico!'

Sharpe nodded. 'We'll probably have to. But Cox's orders are still for the gold to go to the Spanish.'

'So...' Knowles was about to ask how. He shrugged instead.

Teresa stood up. 'Is your coat upstairs?'

Sharpe nodded. 'Cold?' She still had only the thin white dress. He stood up as well, thinking of his fear of El Católico. 'I'll come with you.'

Harper and Lossow stood, but Sharpe waved them down. 'We'll be all right, a minute, no more. Think about it, gentlemen.'

He led the way up the stairs, peering into the darkness, and Teresa put a hand out to him. 'You think he's here?'

'I know he is.'

It seemed ridiculous; the house had been searched and re-searched, sentries put on balconies and roof, yet all Sharpe's instincts said that El Católico would come for his revenge this night. Revenge, the Spanish said, was a dish best eaten cold, but for El Católico it was a dish that should be taken quickly before Sharpe was locked up in the siege. And Sharpe had no doubt that El Católico wanted revenge, not for the gold but for the insult to his manhood, and the Rifleman drew his sword as they went into the candlelit room with its canopied bed and wide cupboards.

Teresa found Sharpe's coat, put it round her shoulders. 'See? It's safe.'

'Go downstairs. Tell them I'll be two minutes.'

She raised her eyebrows at him, looked puzzled, but he pushed her through the door and watched as she went back to the small room. Sharpe could feel the hairs rise on his neck, the prickling of the blood beneath the skin, the old signs that the enemy was near, and he sat on the bed and pulled off his heavy boots so he could move silently. He wanted El Católico to be near, to get this thing over, so that he could concentrate on what must be done tomorrow. He thought of the Spaniard's flickering rapier, the careless skill, but it must be faced, be beaten, or else in the morning he would be constantly looking behind him, worrying about the girl, and he padded across the boards and blew out the candles. The sword was monstrously heavy: a butcher's blade, the Spaniard had called it.

He opened the curtains and stood on the balcony. On the next balcony a sentry stirred; above him, between the pitches of the roof, he could hear the mutterings of two Germans. It had to be this night! El Católico would not let the insult go, would not want to be immured in Almeida as the French sapped their way forward. But how? Nothing stirred in the street; the houses and church across the road were dark and shuttered; only the glow of the French campfires lit the southern sky beyond the walls where he was supposed to stand guard tomorrow. The tower of the church was silhouetted by the red glow, its two heavily counterweighted bells sheened by the distant fires. And there was no ladder! There had been that morning, he knew. He tried to be sure, and remembered opening the curtains, turning away from Teresa's nakedness and seeing the bells with the metal ladder that was leaning against the tower. Then he had turned back, but he was sure the ladder had been there.

So why take the ladder? He looked left and right, at the sentries on the balconies. Of course! Knowles, with his sense of decency, had placed no sentry on this balcony, on every balcony in the street except this one, so that no member of the Company should be forced to listen to the unmarried exploits of Captain Sharpe. And El Católico was no fool. It was a hundred to one that the unguarded balcony would be the one to assault, and the ladder would reach from the church roof, with its convenient platform, across the street, and while muskets from the church took care of the sentries, El Católico and his best men would be across the iron rungs, through the curtains, and revenge was sweet.

He paused there, thinking it was fantastic, but why not? At the dead of night, three or four in the morning, when the sentries were struggling to stay awake, and, anyway, there was only one way to find out. He swung his leg over the balcony, hushed the sentry at the next balustrade, and dropped into the street.

The group in the small room would wonder where he was, but it need not take long. Forewarned was forearmed, and he sneaked silently, on his bootless feet, into the alley that angled behind the church. He was out of sight of the sentries, close to the church wall, and he held his huge sword in front of him, its blade a dull sheen in the darkness, and listened for any noise. Nothing, except the far off dog, the sound of the wind. He felt the excitement inside, the imminence of danger, but still there was no sound, no movement, and he peered up at the church roof's edge, innocent in the moonlight. There was a small door in the wall, barred and locked, and beside it the masonry was rough and crudely repaired. It occurred to him that maybe his idea was too fantastic, that all El Católico had to do was pour musket-fire from the church roof into the unguarded room, that the ladder had merely been taken to help the Partisans climb up from the alley; but he knew he would not be satisfied until he had seen over the roof's edge, so he stuck the huge sword behind his back, jammed it into his belt with the handle over his shoulder, and reached up with his right hand for a grip on the masonry blocks.

He moved infinitely slowly, climbing as silently as a lizard, feeling with his toes for each foothold and reaching up with his hands for the convenient gaps between the stones. His left shoulder hurt, made him wince with pain, but he moved up because he could see the top, and it was not far, and he could not rest until this private business was done. Harper would be annoyed at not being invited, but this was Sharpe's business. Teresa was his woman, and he knew, as he inched upwards, that he would miss her terribly. The handholds ran out as he neared the top. A cornice went round the roof, a foot deep and smooth-faced, and he could not reach the top. He needed one more handhold and he saw it, off to his left, where a metal stanchion jutted diagonally downwards to support a lamp-holder over the doorway. He reached for it, found the rusting metal, tugged, and it held. He transferred his weight, brought up his right foot, could feel the burden of his body transferred to his piercing left shoulder, and then the stanchion moved. It was a tiny movement, a grating of metal on stone, but it threw him off balance. His left arm saved him, and it was as if someone had plunged a flesh-hook into his armpit, was gouging and twisting, and he sobbed with agony as fresh blood sprang from the opened wound and soaked his chest. He clenched eyes and teeth, gasped with the pain, and, throwing caution aside, threw up his right arm, found the very top of the cornice and slowly, with exquisite relief, took the weight from his left arm.

He froze, waiting for a blow on his exposed right hand, but nothing moved. Perhaps the roof was deserted. He pushed with his right foot, pulled upwards with his hand, and slowly, inch by inch, his eyes went past the stonework and there, suddenly, was the sky, and he was forced to use his left arm, over the top, endured the pain while his right found a secure purchase, and he could heave himself on to the flat top of the cornice and see what he had feared to see: an empty roof. Except that one thing was wrong: there was a smell of tobacco where there should have been none.

He took his sword from its place behind his back and crouched just within the cornice, his left arm next to the deeply curved tiles that rose above him blocking his view of the house where Harper and Lossow would now be looking for him. Behind him the roof was deserted, deeply shadowed in the moonlight, but in front he could see the bell-tower, the ladder lying at its foot, and the flat space that held the trapdoor. He could see only part of the space, a small part, and he could smell tobacco smoke and it was not from his sentries; the wind was from the south, and he felt a fierce confirmation of his suspicions as he crept forward, each step showing more of the flat roof that was tucked into a corner of the church's cross-like roof shape.

It was empty, mocking him, white stonework in the moonlight, and the ladder had presumably been put there for some repairs and later taken down, though who would repair anything just before the French began their bombardment was a mystery. He padded into the space, a large, square area, and still was hidden from the house by the loom of the transept roof, and now he could hear voices, across the street, calling him. He could hear Harper, alarmed, and Lossow shouting at sentries, and he was about to call back when he heard the creak, and jumped to one side.

The trapdoor opened, an inch or two at first, sending out a plume of cigar smoke. Then it was pushed back until held by a chain and a man appeared, dark-cloaked, who climbed on to the roof and did not see Sharpe in the shadow by the tower, because he did not expect to see anything. The man, heavily moustached, crossed to the transept roof, leaned past it till he could see the street, then softly called back in Spanish. The Partisan must have heard the commotion, Sharpe thought, and sent a sentry to look. The man puffed on his cigar, listened to the shouts, and crouched to stub it out. No one else had appeared; the church interior was in darkness; Sharpe hardly breathed as he pushed himself close to the stonework.

An urgent whisper came from the ladder beneath the trapdoor. The man with the cigar nodded. '*Sí, sí.*' He sounded weary, yawned, and came back to the ladder. At first he was not sure what he saw, just a shadow, and he peered at the shape.

The shape moved, turned into a man with a sword, and the tired sentry jumped back, opened his mouth, but Sharpe was ramming the blade forward, aiming at the throat, and he missed. It grated on a rib, slid, and then went home, but the man had shouted and there were feet on the ladder. The damned sword was stuck. Sharpe let the blade go down with its victim, put his foot on the man's chest, turned, and felt the suction give way and the blade free itself. There was a second man half out the trapdoor, a pistol in his hand, and Sharpe ducked, threw the sword out as the gun exploded and the ball hammered into the roof tiles. Sharpe shouted an inarticulate challenge, flailed the blade down on the man, and heard him fall from the ladder. He grabbed the trapdoor, was about to shut it.

'No!' The voice was from below; the church suddenly lit up. 'Wait!' It was El Católico's voice, deep and silken. 'Who is that?'

'Sharpe.' He was standing behind the trapdoor, invisible from below, unassailable.

El Católico chuckled. 'May I come up?'

'Why?'

'You can't come down. There are too many of us. So I have to come up. Will you let me up?'

There were shouts across the street. 'Captain! Captain!'

He ignored them. 'Just you?'

'Just me.' The voice was amused, tolerant. Sharpe heard the footsteps on the ladder, saw the light coming, and then a hand put an unmasked lantern on the roof and there was El Católico's dark head, turning, smiling, and the other hand brought up his rapier, which he tossed, ringing, on to the far side of the roof. 'There. Now you can kill me. You won't, though, because you are a man of honour.'

'Am I?'

El Católico smiled again, still halfway through the trapdoor. 'Kearsey doesn't think so, but Kearsey equates honour with God. You don't. May I come up? I'm alone.'

Sharpe nodded. He waited till the tall Spaniard was on the roof and then kicked the trapdoor shut. It was heavy, thick enough to stop a bullet, but for added safety Sharpe pulled the iron ladder on top.

El Católico watched. 'You are nervous. They won't come up.' He cocked a friendly eye at Sharpe. 'Why are you here?'

'The ladder was missing.'

The tall Spaniard looked puzzled. The hands spread apart in an uncertain gesture. 'Missing?'

Sharpe kicked it. 'It was up the tower this morning. This evening it was gone.'

'Ah!' He laughed. 'We used it to climb the church wall.' He looked at Sharpe's dishevelled uniform. 'I see you had other methods.' In one of his graceful gestures he opened his cloak. 'You see? No pistol. I have only the sword.' He made no attempt to pick it up.

Above the church roof Sharpe could see the sudden flare of torches. Search parties were starting out. There was sweat on the palm of his sword hand, but he would not give the Spaniard the satisfaction of seeing him wipe it off.

'Why are you here?'

'To pray with you.' El Católico laughed, jerked his head at the street. 'They're making so much noise they won't hear us. No, Captain, I'm here to kill you.'

Sharpe smiled. 'Why? You've got the gold.'

El Católico nodded. 'I don't trust you, Sharpe. As long as you're alive I don't think the gold will be easy to collect, though Brigadier Cox presents you with a problem.' Sharpe acknowledged it with a nod and El Católico looked at him shrewdly. 'How were you going to solve it?'

'The same way that I intend to solve it tomorrow.' He wished he were as confident as he sounded. He had seen El Católico in action, measured swords with him, and he was thinking desperately how he could win the fight that must start soon. The tall Spaniard smiled, gestured at his rapier.

'Do you mind? You can kill me, of course, before I reach it, but I don't think you will.' He had talked as he moved and then he stopped, picked it up, and turned round. 'I was right. You see? You are a man of honour!'

Sharpe could feel the new blood wet on his chest and he rested his sword as the Spaniard, with a studied ease, dropped his cloak and flexed the blade. El Católico took the tip of the rapier in his left hand and bent it, almost double.

'A fine blade, Captain. From Toledo. But then, I forgot, we have already tried each other.' He moved into the swordsman's crouch, right leg bent, left leg extended behind. '*En garde*!'

The rapier flickered towards Sharpe, but the Rifleman did not move. El Católico straightened. 'Captain, do you not want to fight? I assure you it is a better death than the one I had planned.'

'What was that?' Sharpe thought of the ladder, the sudden rush in the dark.

The Spaniard smiled. 'A distraction down the street, a fire, lots of shouts, and you would have come to your balcony. The ever ready Captain, prepared for battle, and then a volley of shots would have stopped you forever.'

Sharpe smiled. It was far simpler than his extraordinary imaginings, and it would have worked. 'And the girl?'

'Teresa?' El Católico's pose slipped a little. He shrugged. 'What could she have done with you dead? She would have been forced back.'

'You would have enjoyed that.'

The Spaniard shrugged. '*En garde*, Captain.'

Sharpe had so little time. He had to unsettle the Spaniard's elegant posture. El Católico knew he would win, could afford to be magnanimous, was anticipating the inevitable display of his superior swordsmanship. Sharpe still kept his blade low and the rapier went down.

'Captain! Are you frightened?' El Católico smiled gently. 'You're afraid I'm the better man.'

'Teresa says not.'

It was not much, but enough. Sharpe saw the fury in El Católico's face, the sudden loss of control, and he brought up the huge blade, rammed it forward, and knew that El Católico would not parry but simply kill him for the insult. The rapier flickered, lightning-fast, but Sharpe turned his body, saw the blade go past, and brought his elbow hard into El Católico's ribs, turned back and hammered down with the brass-guarded hilt of the sword on to the Spaniard's head. El Católico was fast. He twisted away, the blow glanced off his skull, but Sharpe heard the grunt and he followed it with a sweeping killer of a blow, a stroke that would have disembowelled an ox, and the Spaniard leapt backwards, and again, and Sharpe had failed, and he knew, with a fighter's instinct, that El Católico had recovered, survived the devastating attack, and would now fall back on his skill.

There was a hammering from downstairs, the blast of a musket, and El Católico smiled. 'Time to die, Sharpe. *Requiem aeternam dona eis, Domine.*' He came forward like quicksilver, past Sharpe's clumsy parry, and the blade drew blood at Sharpe's waist. '*Et lux perpetua luceat eis.*' The voice was like silk, beautiful and hypnotic, and the blade went to the other side of Sharpe's waist, razored his skin, and was gone. Sharpe knew he was being toyed with, a plaything, while the prayer lasted, and he could do nothing. He remembered Helmut's techniques and went for El Católico's eyes, stabbing the empty air, and the Spaniard laughed. 'Go slow, Sharpe! *Te decet hymnus, Deus, in Sion.*'

Sharpe lunged desperately for the eyes; Helmut had made it look easy, but El Católico just swayed to one side and the rapier came low at the Rifleman, aiming at the thigh for another flesh wound, and Sharpe had only one, desperate, insane idea left. He let the rapier come, kicked his right thigh forward, and pushed the blade painfully into his flesh so that El Católico could not use it. The Spaniard tried to drag it free; Sharpe felt the tearing in his leg, but he had the initiative, was still driving forward, and he hit the Spaniard with the heavy guard of the sword, scraping it up the face, and El Católico abandoned the rapier and went backwards. Sharpe followed, the rapier stuck clean through his thigh, and El Católico grabbed at it, missed, and Sharpe swept his blade down, caught El Católico's forearm; the Spaniard cried out and Sharpe back-swung him with the flat of his blade, a scything crack across the skull, and the Partisan fell.

Sharpe stopped. There were shouts below. 'Captain!'

'Up here! On the church roof!'

He could hear footsteps below, pounding in the alleyway, and he suspected the Partisans were abandoning the unequal conflict. He stopped and took hold of El Católico's rapier. The wound hurt, but Sharpe knew he had been lucky; the blade had gone through the outer muscles and the blood and pain were worse than the damage. He pulled at the sword, clenching his teeth, and it slid free. He held the rapier in his hands, felt its fine balance, and knew he could never have defeated it except for the madness of driving his body on to the inlaid blade and denying El Católico his skill.

The Spaniard moaned, still unconscious, and Sharpe crossed to him, bleeding and limping, and looked down at his enemy. His eyes were closed, the lids flickering slightly, and Sharpe took his own sword, put it at El Católico's throat. 'A butcher's blade, eh?' He stabbed down till the point hit the roof, twisted it, then kicked the neck free of the blade. 'That was for Claud Hardy.' There would be no fiefdom in the mountains, no private kingdom, for El Católico.

There was a thumping on the trapdoor. 'Who's that?'

'Sergeant Harper!'

'Wait!'

He pushed the ladder to one side and the trapdoor was pushed up and Harper appeared, a smoking torch in one hand. The Irishman looked first at Sharpe, then at the body. 'God save Ireland. What were you doing, sir? A competition to see who could bleed the most?'

'He wanted to kill me.'

The eyebrows went up. 'Really?' Harper looked at the dead man. 'He was a fine swordsman, sir. How did you do it?'

Sharpe told him. How he had gone for the eyes, failed, so had impaled himself on the sword. Harper listened, shook his head.

'You're a bloody fool, sir. Let's see the leg.'

Teresa came up, followed by Lossow and Knowles, and the story had to be told again, and Sharpe felt the tension flow out of him. He watched Teresa kneel by the body.

'Does it upset you?'

She shook her head, busy at something, and Sharpe watched as she searched beneath the blood-stained clothes and found, round the dead man's waist, a money-belt thick with coins. She opened one of the pockets.

'Gold.'

'Keep it.'

Sharpe was feeling his leg, tracing the wound, and he knew he had been lucky and that the blade had torn a smaller wound than his stupidity deserved. He looked up at Harper. 'I'll need the maggots.'

Harper grinned. In a tin box he kept fat white maggots that lived only on dead flesh, spurning healthy tissue, and nothing cleaned a simple wound better than a handful dropped into the cut and bound in with a bandage. The Irishman took Sharpe's sash as a temporary dressing, bound it tight. 'It'll mend, sir.'

Lossow looked at the body. 'What now?'

'Now?' Sharpe wanted a glass of wine, another plate of that stew. 'Nothing. They have another leader. We still have to hand the gold over.'

Teresa spoke in Spanish, angry and vehement, and Sharpe smiled.

'What was that, sir?' Knowles was stunned by the blood on the roof.

'I don't think she likes the new leaders.' Sharpe flexed his left arm. 'If El Católico's Lieutenants don't produce the gold, then they may not be leaders much longer. Is that right?'

She nodded.

'Then who will be?' Knowles sat down on the parapet.

'La Aguja.' Sharpe had trouble pronouncing the Spanish 'J.'

Teresa laughed, pleased, and Harper looked up from his own excursion into El Católico's pockets.

'La what?'

'La Aguja. The Needle. Teresa. We have a bargain.'

Knowles looked astonished. 'Teresa? Miss Moréno?'

'Why not? She fights better than most of them.' He had made up the name, saw that it pleased her. 'But to make that happen we must keep the gold from the Spanish, get it out of the city, and finish this job.'

Lossow sighed, scraped his unused sabre back into its curved scabbard. 'Which brings us back to the old question, my friend. How?'

Sharpe had dreaded this moment, wanted to lead them gently towards it, but it had come. 'Who's stopping us?'

Lossow shrugged. 'Cox.'

Sharpe nodded. He spoke patiently. 'And Cox has his authority as Commander of the garrison. If there were no garrison, there would be no authority, no way to stop us.'

'So?' Knowles was frowning.

'So, at dawn tomorrow we destroy the garrison.'

There was a moment's utter silence, broken by Knowles. 'We can't!'

Teresa laughed at the sheer joy of it. 'We can!'

'God in his heaven!' Lossow's face was appalled, fascinated.

Harper did not seem surprised. 'How?'

So Sharpe told them.

CHAPTER 23

Almeida stirred early, that Monday morning; it was well before first light as men stamped their boots on cobbled streets and made the small talk that is the talisman against great events. The war, after all, had come to the border town, and between the defenders' outer glacis and the masked guns of the French, the hopes and fears of Europe were concentrated. In far-off cities men looked at maps. If Almeida could hold, then perhaps Portugal could be saved, but they knew better. Eight weeks at the most, they said, and probably just six, and then Masséna's troops would have Lisbon at their mercy. The British had had their run and now it was over, the last hurdles to be cleared, but in St Petersburg and Vienna, Stockholm and Berlin, they let the maps curl up and wondered where the victorious blue-jacketed troops would be next sent. A pity about the British, but what did anyone expect?

Cox was on the southern ramparts, standing by a brazier, waiting for the first light to show him the new French batteries. Yesterday the French had fired a few shots, destroying the telegraph, but today, Cox knew, things would begin in earnest. He hoped for a great defence, a struggle that would make the history books, that would block the French till the rains of late autumn could save Portugal; but he also imagined the siege guns, the paths blasted through the great walls, and then the screaming, steel-tipped battalions that would come forward in the night to drown his hopes in chaos and defeat. Cox and the French both knew the town was the last obstacle to French victory, and, hope as Cox did, in his heart he did not believe that the town could hold out till the roads were swamped and the rivers made impassable by rain.

High above Cox, by the castle and cathedral that topped

Almeida's hill, Sharpe pushed open the bakery door. The ovens were curved shapes in the blackness, cold to the touch, and Teresa shivered beside him despite being swathed in the Rifleman's long green greatcoat. He ached. His leg, shoulder, the sliced cuts either side of his waist, and a head that throbbed after talking too deep into the early morning.

Knowles had pleaded, 'There must be another way!'

'Tell me.'

Now, in the cold silence, Sharpe still tried to find another way. To talk to Cox? Or Kearsey? But only Sharpe knew how desperately Wellington needed the gold. To Cox and Kearsey it was unimaginable that a few thousand gold coins could save Portugal, and Sharpe could not tell them how, because he had not been told. He damned the secrecy. It would mean death for hundreds; but if the gold did not get through it would mean a lost war.

Teresa would be gone, anyway. In a few hours they would part, he to the army, she back to the hills and her own fight. He held her close, smelling her hair, wanting to be with her, but then they stepped apart as footsteps sounded outside and Patrick Harper pushed open the door and peered into the gloom.

'Sir?'

'We're here. Did you get it?'

'No problem.' Harper sounded happy enough. He gestured past Helmut. 'One barrel of powder, sir, compliments of Tom Garrard.'

'Did he ask what it was for?'

Harper shook his head. 'He said if it was for you, sir, it was all right.' He helped the German bring the great keg through the door. 'Bloody heavy, sir.'

'Will you need help?'

Harper straightened up with a scoffing look. 'An officer carrying a barrel, sir? This is the army! No. We got it here; we'll do the rest.'

'You know what to do?'

The question was unnecessary. Sharpe looked through the dirty window, across the Plaza, and in the thin light saw that the cathedral doors were still shut. Perhaps the pile of cartridges had been moved. Had Wellington sent a messenger on a fast horse with orders for Cox on the half chance that Sharpe was in Almeida? He forced his mind away from the nagging questions.

'Let's get on with it.'

Helmut borrowed Harper's bayonet and chipped at the centre of the barrel, making a hole, widening it till it was the size of a musket muzzle. He grunted his satisfaction. Harper nodded at Sharpe. 'We'll be on our way.' He sounded casual. Sharpe made himself grin.

'Go slowly.'

He wanted to tell the Sergeant that he did not have to do it, it was Sharpe's dirty-work, but he knew what the Irishman would have said. Instead he watched as the two men, one tall and the other short, picked up the barrel by its ends, jiggled it until powder was flowing from the hole, and then started an awkward progress out the door and across the Plaza. They kept to the gutter, Helmut above it and Harper below, which made the task easier, and Sharpe, through the window, watched as the powder trickled into the shadow of the stone trough and went, inexorably, towards the cathedral. He could not believe what he was doing, driven by the General's 'must' and the questions came back. Could Cox be persuaded? Perhaps, even worse, gold had arrived from London and all this was for nothing, and then, in a heart-stopping moment, the cathedral doors opened and two sentries came out, adjusting their shakoes, and Sharpe knew they must see what was happening. He clenched his fists, and Teresa, beside him at the dirty glass pane, was moving her lips in what seemed to be a silent and inappropriate prayer.

'Sharpe!'

He turned, startled, and saw Lossow. 'You frightened me.'

'It's a guilty conscience.' The German stood in the doorway and nodded down the hill, away from the cathedral. 'We have the house open. The cellar door.'

'I'll see you there.'

Sharpe planned to light the fuse and then run back to a house they had chosen, a house with a deep cellar that opened on to the street. Lossow did not move. He looked at the two Sergeants, still ignored by the sentries.

'I don't believe this, my friend. I hope you're right.'

So do I, thought Sharpe, so do I. It was madness, pure madness, and he put his arm round the girl and watched as the two Sergeants threaded the bollards which kept traffic and market-stalls from encroaching on the cathedral's ground. The sentries were watching the two Sergeants, seeing nothing unusual in two men carrying a barrel, not even stirring as they put it down, on one end, hard by the smaller door.

'God.' Lossow whispered the word, watching with them, as Helmut squatted by the barrel and began to work a strake loose so that the fuse could reach the remaining powder in the keg. Harper strolled the twenty yards to the sentries, chatted with them, and Sharpe thought of the men who must die. The sentries would surely see the German splintering the wood! But no, they laughed with Harper, and suddenly Helmut was walking back, yawning, and the Irishman waved at the sentries and followed him.

Sharpe took out the tinder-box, the cigar, and with hands that were shaky he struck flint on steel and blew the charred linen in the box into a flame. He lit the cigar, puffed it, hated the taste until the tip glowed red.

Lossow watched him. 'You're sure?'

A shrug. 'I'm sure.'

The two Sergeants appeared at the doorway and Lossow spoke in German to Helmut, then turned to Sharpe. 'Good luck, my friend. We see you in a minute.'

Sharpe nodded, the two Germans left, and he drew on the cigar again. He looked at the Irishman in the doorway.

'Take Teresa.'

'No.' Harper was stubborn. 'I stay with you.'

'And me.' Teresa smiled at him.

The girl held his arm as he went into the street. The sky was pearl grey over the cathedral with a wisp of cloud that would soon turn white. It promised to be a beautiful day. He drew on the cigar again and through his mind went jumbled images of the men who had built the cathedral, carved the saints that guarded its doors, knelt on its wide flagstones, been married there, seen their children baptized in its granite font, and been carried on their last visit up its pillared chancel. He thought of the dry voice saying 'must', of the priest whitewashing the rood-screen, of the Battalion with its wives and children, the bodies in the cellar, and he leaned down and touched the cigar tip to the powder, and it sparked and fizzed, the flame beginning its journey.

The first French shell, fired from an ugly little howitzer in a deep pit, burst on the Plaza, and flames shot through the smoke as the casing burst into unnumbered fragments that needled outwards. Before Sharpe could move, before the first explosion had ceased, the second howitzer's shell landed, bounced, rolled to the powder trail just yards from the cathedral, hit a bollard, and the sentries dived for shelter as it flamed crashingly apart, and Sharpe knew that there was no time to reach the cellar. He plucked at Teresa and Harper.

'The ovens!'

They ran, through the door and over the counter, and he picked up the girl and thrust her head-first into the great brick cave of the bread oven. Harper was clambering into the second and Sharpe waited till Teresa was at the back and then he heard an explosion. It was small enough, scarcely audible over the crash of French shells and the distant sound of the Portuguese batteries' reply, and he knew, as he climbed in behind the girl, that the barrel had exploded, and he wondered if the cathedral door had held the blast, or if the cartridges had been moved, and then there was a second explosion, louder and more ominous, and Teresa gripped his thigh where it was wounded, and the second explosion seemed to go on, like a muffled volley from a battle in deep fog, and he knew that the cartridges, down in their stacks behind the door, were setting each other off in an unstoppable chain of explosions.

He wondered, crouched foetus-like in the oven, what was happening in the cathedral. He saw, in his mind's eye, the lurid flames, gouting shafts of light, and then there was a bigger explosion and he knew that the chain had reached the powder stacked at the top of the steps, and it was all done now. Nothing could prevent it. The guards in the cathedral were dead; the great rood was looking down on its last seconds; the eternal presence would soon be swatted out.

Another French shell exploded, the fragments clashing on the bakery walls, and it was drowned by a seething roar, growing and terrifying, and in the first crypt, crate by crate, cartridge by cartridge, the ammunition of Almeida was exploding. The stabbing flames were reaching the weakened curtain; the men in the deep crypt would be on their knees, or in panic, the powder for the great guns all round them.

He had thought that the sound could only grow till it was the last sound on earth, but it seemed to die into silence that was merely the crackling of flames, and Sharpe, knowing it was foolish, uncurled his head and looked through the gap between the oven and its iron door, and he could not believe that the leather curtain had held, and then the hill moved. The sound came, not through the air but through the ground itself, like the groaning of rock, and the whole cathedral turned to dust, smoke, and flames that were the colour of blood that scorched through the utter blackness.

The French gunners, pausing with shells in their hands, jumped to the top of their pits and looked past the low grey ramparts and crossed themselves. The centre of the town had gone, turned into one giant flame that rolled up and up, and became a boiling cloud of darkness. Men could see things in the flame: great stones, timbers, carried upwards as if they were feathers, and then the shock hit the gunners like a giant, hot wind that came with the sound. It was like all the thunder of all the world poured into one town for one moment for one glimpse of the world's end.

The cathedral disappeared, turned into flame, and the castle was scythed clean from the ground, the stones tumbling like toy things. Houses were scoured into flaming shards; the blast took the north of the town, unroofed half the southern slope, and the bakery collapsed on to the ovens, and Sharpe, deafened and gasping, choked on the thick dust and heated air, and the girl gripped him, prayed for her soul, and the blast went past like the breath of the Apocalypse.

On the ramparts the Portuguese died as the wind plucked them outwards. The great defences, nearest the cathedral, were smashed down, and debris filled the ditches so that a huge, flat road was hammered into the heart of the fortress, and still the powder caught. New boilings of flame and smoke writhed into the horror over Almeida, shudder after shudder; a convulsive spasm of the hilltop and the monstrous explosions died, leaving only fire and darkness, the stench of hell, a silence where men were deafened by destruction.

A French gunner, old in his trade, who had once taught a young Corsican Lieutenant how to lay a gun, spat on his hand and touched it to the hot muzzle of the barrel that had fired the last shot. The French were silent, unbelieving, and in the killing-ground before them stones, tiles, and burnt flesh dropped like the devil's rain.

Twenty-five miles away, in Celorico, they heard the sound and the General put down his fork and went to the window and knew, with terrible certainty, what it was. There was no gold. And now the fortress that could have bought him six weeks of failing hope had gone. The smoke came later, a huge grey curtain that smeared the eastern sky, turned morning sunlight into dusk, and edged the border hills with crimson like a harbinger of the armies that would follow the cloud to the sea.

Almeida had been destroyed.

CHAPTER 24

Kearsey was dead, killed in an instant as he said his prayers on the town rampart, and five hundred other men snatched into eternity by the flame, but Sharpe did not know that yet. He knew he was dying, of suffocation and heat, and he braced his back against the smooth, curved interior of the massive oven and pushed with his legs at a charred length of timber that blocked the door. It collapsed and he pushed himself out, into a nightmare, and turned to pull Teresa clear. She spoke to him, but he could hear nothing, and he shook his head and went to the other opening and pushed away some rubble as Harper crawled out, his face ashen.

The ovens had saved their lives. They were built like small fortresses, with walls more than three feet thick and a curved roof that had sent the blast harmlessly overhead. Nothing else remained. The cathedral was a flaming pit, the castle gone, the houses so much dust and fire, and down the street Sharpe had to look a hundred yards before he saw a house that had survived the blast, and it was ablaze, the flames licking at the rooms which had been opened to the world, and the heat was grey around them as he took Teresa's arm.

A man staggered into the road, naked and bleeding, shouting for help, but they ignored him, ran to the cellar door that was covered with fallen stone, and dragged it clear. There was a thumping beneath and shouts, and Harper, still dazed, pulled back the stones and the cellar flap was forced open, and Lossow and Helmut came out. They spoke to Sharpe, who could not hear, and ran towards their own house, at the bottom of the hill, away from the horror, through the Portuguese soldiers who stared, open-mouthed, at the inferno that had once been a cathedral.

Sharpe dropped in the kitchen, found a bottle of the

Germans' beer, and knocked the top off, put it to his lips, and let the cool liquid flow into his stomach. He hit his ears, shook his head, and his men stared at him. He shook his head again, willing the sound to come back, and felt tears in his eyes. Damn it, the decision had been made, and he put his head back and stared at the ceiling and thought of the General, and of the blazing pit, and he hated himself.

'You had no choice, sir.' Knowles was speaking to him; the voice sounded far away, but he could hear.

He shook his head. 'There's always a choice.'

'But the war, sir. You said it had to be won.'

Then celebrate it tomorrow, Sharpe thought, or the next day, but dear God, I did not know, and he remembered the flung bodies, stripped of all dignity, wiped out in an instant, draped like streaked fungus on the hot rubble.

'I know.' He turned on his men. 'What are you staring at! Get ready to move!'

He hated Wellington, too, because he knew why the General had picked him: because he wanted a man too proud to fail, and he knew he would do it for the General again. Ruthlessness was good in a soldier, in a General or a Captain, and men admired it, but that was no reason to think that the ruthless man did not feel the bloody pain as well. Sharpe stood up, looked at Lossow.

'We'd better find Cox.'

The town was stunned, bereft of sound except for the crackling of flames and the coughing of vomit as men found comrades' charred and shrunken bodies. The smell of roast flesh hung in the air, like the stench of the burning bodies after Talavera, but that, Sharpe remembered, had been a mistake, an accident of wind and flame, while this chaos, this glimpse of damnation, had been caused by a powderkeg that Sharpe had caused to be pierced and trailed to the cathedral's door. The bodies were naked, the uniforms seared off by the blast, and they seemed to have shrunk into small, black mockeries of human beings. A dead battalion, thought Sharpe, killed for the gold, and he wondered if Wellington himself would have put the cigar on to the powder, and then he thrust the thought away as Lossow led the way up a sloping rampart to where Cox surveyed the damage.

It was all over – anyone could see that, the town indefensible – but Cox still hoped. He had been weeping at the death and destruction, the swath that had gone through his town and his hopes.

'How?'

There were answers offered by the staff officers with Cox, good answers, and they told the Brigadier of the French shells that had landed just before the explosion. The officers looked over the wall at the massing crowd of Frenchmen who had come to stare at the giant breach in the town's defences, and at the pall of smoke, as men might watch a once-proud King on his deathbed.

'A shell,' one of the officers told Cox. 'It must have set off the small ammunition.'

'Oh, God.' Cox was close to tears. 'We should have had a magazine.'

Cox tried to stiffen his will to go on fighting, but they all knew it was done. There was no ammunition left, nothing to fight with, and the French would understand. There would be no unpleasantness; the surrender would be discussed in a civilized way, and Cox tried to stave it off, tried to find hope in the smoke-filled air, but finally agreed.

'Tomorrow, gentlemen, tomorrow. We fly the flag one more night.' He pushed his way through the group and saw Sharpe and Lossow waiting. 'Sharpe. Lossow. Thank God you're alive. So many gone.'

'Yes, sir.'

Cox was biting back tears. 'So many.' Sharpe wondered if Tom Garrard had survived. Cox noticed the blood on the Rifleman's uniform. 'You're wounded?'

'No, sir. I'm all right. Permission to leave, sir?'

Cox nodded, an automatic reaction. The gold was forgotten in the horror of the lost war.

Sharpe plucked Lossow's sleeve. 'Come on.'

At the bottom of the ramp, a puzzled look on his face, Cesar Moreno waited for them. He put a hand out to stop Sharpe.

'Teresa?'

Sharpe smiled, the first smile since the explosion. 'She's safe. We're leaving now.'

'And Joaquím?'

'Joaquím?' For a second Sharpe was not certain whom Teresa's father was talking about, and then he remembered the fight on the rooftop. 'He's dead.'

'And this?' Cesar Moreno's hand was still on Sharpe's sleeve as he looked round the destruction.

'An accident.'

Moreno looked at him and shrugged. 'Half our men are dead.'

There was nothing Sharpe could say. Lossow broke in. 'The horses?'

Moreno looked at him and shrugged. 'They were not in the house that collapsed. They're all right.'

'We'll use them!' The German went ahead and Moreno checked Sharpe with a hand.

'She'll take over, I suppose.'

The Rifleman nodded. 'Probably. She can fight.'

Moreno gave a rueful smile. 'She knows whose side to be on.'

Sharpe looked at the smoke, at the flames on the hilltop, smelt the burning. 'Don't we all?' He shook himself free, turned again to the grey-haired man. 'I'll be back for her, one day.'

'I know.'

The French had left their lines to gape at the smoking ruins at the northern wall. There was nothing to stop the Company leaving, and they took the gold and went west, under the smoke, and back to the army. The war was not lost.

EPILOGUE

'What happened, Richard?'

'Nothing, sir.'

Hogan moved his horse forward to a patch of succulent grass. 'I don't believe you.'

Sharpe stirred in his saddle; he hated riding. 'There was a girl.'

'Is that all?'

'All? She was special.'

The breeze from the sea was cool on his face; the water sparkled with a million flashes of light, like a giant army of lance-tips, and beating northwards towards the Channel a frigate laid its grey sails towards the land and left a streak of white in its path.

Hogan watched the ship. 'Despatches.'

'News of victory?' Sharpe's tone was ironic.

'They won't believe it. It's a funny victory.' Hogan stared at the distant horizon, miles out to sea from the hilltop where their horses stood. 'Do you see the fleet out there? A convoy going home.'

Sharpe grunted, felt the twinge in his healing shoulder. 'More money for the bloody merchants. Why couldn't they have sent it here?'

Hogan smiled. 'There's never enough, Richard. Never.'

'There had better be now. After what we did to get it here.'

'What did you do?'

'I told you, nothing.' He stared a challenge at the gentle Irish Major. 'We were sent to get it, we got it, and we brought it back.'

'The General's pleased.' Hogan said it in a neutral tone.

'He'd bloody better be pleased! For Christ's sake!'

'He thought you were lost.' Hogan's horse moved again,

cropping the grass, and the Major took off his cocked hat and fanned his face. 'Pity about Almeida.'

Sharpe made a face. 'Pity about Almeida.'

Hogan sighed patiently. 'We thought it was done for. We heard the explosion, of course, and there was no gold. Without the gold there was no chance.'

'There was a little chance.' Sharpe almost spat the words at him and Hogan shrugged.

'No, not a chance you'd want, Richard.'

Sharpe let his anger sink; he thought of the girl, watched the frigate flap its sails and bend into its next tack. 'Which would you rather have had, sir?' His voice was very cold, very far away. 'The gold, or Almeida?'

Hogan pulled his horse's head up. 'The gold, Richard. You know that.'

'You're sure?'

Hogan nodded. 'Very sure. Thousands might have died without the gold.'

'But we don't know that.'

Hogan waved his arm at the landscape. 'We do.'

It was a miracle, perhaps one of the greatest feats of military engineering, and it had taken up the gold. The gold had been needed, desperately needed, or the work would never have been finished and the ten thousand labourers, some of whom Sharpe could see, could have packed up their shovels and picks and simply waited for the French. Sharpe watched the giant scrapers, hauled by lines of men and oxen, shaping the hills.

'What do you call it?'

'The Lines of Torres Vedras.'

Three lines barred the Lisbon peninsula, three giant fortifications made with the hills themselves, fortifications that dwarfed the granite-works at Almeida. The first line, on which they rode, was twenty-six miles long, stretching from the Atlantic to the Tagus, and there were two others behind it. The hills had been steepened, crowned with gun batteries, and the lowland flooded. Behind the hillcrests sunken roads meant that the twenty-five thousand garrison troops could move unseen by the French, and the deep valleys, where they could not be filled, were blocked with thorn-trees, thousands of them, so that from the air it must have looked as if a giant's child had shaped the landscape the way a boy played with a few square inches of wet soil by a stream.

Sharpe stared eastwards, at the unending line, and he found it hard to believe. So much work, so many escarpments made by hand, crowned with hundreds of guns encased in stone forts, their embrasures looking to the north, to the plain where Masséna would be checked.

Hogan rode alongside him. 'We can't stop him, Richard, not till he gets here. And here he stays.'

'And we're back there.' Sharpe pointed towards Lisbon, thirty miles to the south.

Hogan nodded. 'It's simple. He'll never break the lines, never; they're too strong. And he can't go round; the Navy's there. So here he stops, and the rains start, and in a couple of months he'll be starving and we come out again to reconquer Portugal.'

'And on into Spain?' Sharpe asked.

'On into Spain.' Hogan sighed, waved again at the huge scar of the unbelievable fortress. 'And we ran out of money. We had to get money.'

'And you got it.'

Hogan bowed to him. 'Thank you. Tell me about the girl?'

Sharpe told him as they rode towards Lisbon, crossing the second and third lines that would never be used. He remembered the parting after they had left the river fortress, unchallenged, and the Light Company, clumsily mounted on the Spanish horses, had bounced after Lossow's Germans. One French patrol had come near them, but the Germans had wheeled to meet it, their sabres drawn in one hissing movement, and the French had sheered away. They had stopped beside the Coa and Sharpe had handed Teresa the one thousand gold coins he had promised.

She had smiled at him. 'This will be enough.'

'Enough?'

'For our needs. We go on fighting.'

The wind had brought the stench of burning and death into the hills and Sharpe had looked at her, at the dark, hawk-like beauty.

'You can stay with us.'

She had smiled. 'No. But you can come back. One day.'

He had nodded at the rifle slung on her shoulder. 'Give it to Ramon. I promised.'

She looked surprised. 'It's mine!'

'No.' He had unslung his own rifle, checked the butt-plate, that all the cleaning equipment was there, and handed it across with his ammunition pouch. 'This is yours. With my love. I'll get another one.'

She had smiled, shaken her head. 'I'm sorry.'

'So am I. We'll meet again.'

'I know.' She turned her horse and waved.

'Kill a lot of French!' he shouted.

'All there are!'

And she was gone, galloping with her father and his men, her men, up to the secret paths that would lead them home, to the war of the knife and ambush, and he missed her, missed her.

He smiled at Hogan. 'You heard about Hardy?'

'Sad. He has a brother. Did you know?'

'No.'

Hogan nodded. 'A Naval Lieutenant. Giles Hardy, and just like his brother. Mad as a coot.'

'And Josefina?'

Hogan smiled, sniffed his snuff, and Sharpe waited for the sneeze. Hogan wiped away the tears. 'She's here. You want to see her?'

'Yes.'

Hogan laughed. 'She's rather celebrated now.' He did not explain.

They rode in the lengthening shadows down the paved highway into Lisbon. It was crowded with carts, carrying building stone, and with the labourers who were making one of the great wonders of the military world, a fortress covering five hundred square miles that would stop the French in the year of 1810 and would never be used again. Sharpe admired Wellington for a clever man, because no one, utterly no one outside Lisbon, seemed to know the lines existed, and the French, their tails up, would come hallooing down the southern road. And stop.

The South Essex, shorn of its Light Company, was up

north and soon, Sharpe knew, they must march to join it. One battle more, Hogan had said, with any luck and a fair wind, and then the army would march south to the safety of its Lines, and Colonel Lawford had greeted him with open arms and waved a despatch at Sharpe.

'Reinforcements, Richard! They're on their way! You can bring them up from Lisbon! Officers, Sergeants, two hundred and seventy men! Good news!'

The ships had still not come, beating down from Plymouth on the journey that could take seven days or seven weeks, and Sharpe was content to wait. He slid, with relief, off the horse and gave Hogan the reins.

'I'll see you tomorrow?'

The Major nodded, scribbled on a piece of paper. 'That's her address.'

Sharpe smiled his thanks, turned, but Hogan called after him.

'Richard!'

'Sir?'

'We needed that gold. Well done.'

Sixteen thousand coins, two hundred and fifty stolen by El Católico, a thousand to Teresa, fourteen thousand to the General, and the rest was being spent by the Light Company and the Germans as if money were issued with the rations. Sharpe had ordered them to get drunk, to find their women, and if any provost asked where the money came from they were referred to Sharpe, and somehow they did not want to argue with the tall, scarred Rifleman who simply told them it was stolen. There was even money in Sharpe's name in London, held by the agents, Messrs Hopkinson and Son of St Alban's Street, Knowles's agents, and Sharpe wondered, as he walked towards the address Hogan had given him, just what a four per cent stock was. The Lisbon office had laughed politely when he told them it was stolen. He had not given them all the coins.

The house looked rich, and he imagined Hardy using the big front door that was answered by Agostino, Josefina's servant, who now wore a fancy powdered wig and a coat that was all buttons and lace.

'Sir?'

Sharpe pushed him out of the way, strode into a marble hall with palms, rugs, and latticed screens. He thought of Teresa, pushed the thought away because he wanted her, and thought how she would have despised the scent that filled the hallway.

He went into a huge room that opened through archways on to a terrace high above the Tagus. Orange trees framed the view, their scent mingling with the smell of perfume.

'Josefina!'

'Richard!'

She was in an archway, the evening light round her body so he could not see her face. 'What are you doing?'

'Visiting you.'

She came forward, plumper than he remembered, and smiled at him. She touched his face with a finger, looked his uniform up and down, and made a face of disapproval.

'You can't stay.'

'Why not.'

She gestured outside. 'He was first.'

He looked at her, remembering her differently, and he would have left if Patrick Harper had not already claimed the dark-haired maid at the American Hotel. Instead, he walked on to the terrace where a languid cavalry Lieutenant sat with a glass of wine.

The Lieutenant looked up. 'Sir.'

'How much did you pay?'

'Richard!' She was behind him, pulling at him. Sharpe laughed.

'Lieutenant?'

'Damn you, sir!' The Lieutenant stood up, the wine quivering in the glass.

'How much did you pay?'

'Damn your eyes, sir! I'll call you out!'

Josefina was laughing now, enjoying herself. Sharpe smiled. 'You can. The name's Sharpe. In the meantime, get out!'

'Sharpe?' The Lieutenant's expression had fallen.

'Out.'

'But, sir . . .'

Sharpe drew the sword, the great steel sword. 'Out!'

'Madame!' The Lieutenant bowed to Josefina, put down his wine, glanced once at Sharpe, and was gone. She hit him, lightly.

'You shouldn't have done that.'

'Why not?' He pushed the sword back into the scabbard. She pouted. 'He was rich and generous.'

He laughed, opened his new ammunition pouch, the black leather still stiff, and threw the thick gold coins on to the patterned tiles.

'Richard! What is it?'

'Gold, you fool.' The convoy could take another month for all he cared. He tossed more coins, thick as butter. 'Josefina's gold, your gold, our gold, my gold.' He laughed again, pulled her towards him. 'Sharpe's gold.'

HISTORICAL NOTE

Almeida's garrison surrendered after the explosion of August 27th, 1810. The event was much as described in *Sharpe's Gold*. The magazine in the cathedral blew up and destroyed, beside the cathedral itself, the castle, five hundred houses, and part of the fortifications. It was estimated that more than five hundred of the garrison died. Brigadier Cox wanted to continue the defence but bowed to the inevitable and surrendered the next day.

It must have been one of the biggest explosions of the pre-nuclear world. (Certainly not the biggest. A year before, in 1809, Sir John Moore deliberately exploded four thousand barrels of powder to keep them from falling into French hands at Corunna.) A year later the French added to the destruction. They, in turn, were besieged in Almeida and abandoned its defence after blowing up part of the walls; their garrison of fourteen hundred men successfully escaped through the much larger British besieging force. Despite its misfortunes the town's defences are still impressive. The main road no longer passes through Almeida; instead it runs a few miles to the south, but the town is just half an hour's drive from the border post at Vilar Formoso. The awesome defences are repaired and intact, surrounding what is now a shrunken village, and on the top of the hill it is easy to see where the explosion occurred. Nothing was rebuilt. A graveyard marks the site of the cathedral; the castle moat is a square, stone-faced ditch; granite blocks still litter the area where they fell, and wild flowers grow where once there were houses and streets.

No one, conveniently for a writer of fiction, knows the precise cause of the catastrophe, but the accepted version, pieced together from the stories of survivors, is that a leaking keg of gunpowder was rolled from the cathedral and an exploding French shell ignited the accidental powder train, which fired back to musket ammunition stored by the main door. This, in turn, flashed down to the main magazine, and so the greatest obstacle between Masséna and his invasion of Portugal was gone. One Portuguese soldier, very close to the cathedral, saved his life by diving into a bread oven, and now his presence of mind has been borrowed by Richard Sharpe. The most unlikely stories often turn out to be the truth.

The Lines of Torres Vedras existed and truly were one of the great military achievements of all time. They can still be seen, decrepit for the most part, grassed over, but with a little imagination Masséna's shock can be realized. He had pursued the British army from the border to within a day's march of Lisbon, had survived Wellington's crushing victory at Busaco on the way, but surely, so close to Portugal's capital, he must have thought his job done. Then he saw the lines. They were the furthest point of retreat for the British in the Peninsula; they were never to be used again, and four years later Wellington's superb army marched over the Pyrenees into France itself.

Sharpe's Gold is, sadly, unfair to the Spanish. Some Partisans were as self-seeking as El Católico, but the large majority were brave men who tied up more French troops than did Wellington's army. The Richard Sharpe books are the chronicles of British soldiers and, with that perspective, the men who fought the 'little war' have suffered an unfair distortion. But at least, by the autumn of 1810, the British army is safe behind its gigantic Lines and the stage is set for the next four years: the advance into Spain, the victories, and the ultimate conquest of France itself.

Richard Sharpe and Patrick Harper will march again.

For a complete list of books available from Penguin in the United States, write to Dept. DG, Penguin Books, 299 Murray Hill Parkway, East Rutherford, New Jersey 07073.